INTEGRATING ART INTO THE INCLUSIVE EARLY CHILDHOOD CURRICULUM

Carol L. Russell, EdD

INTEGRATING ART INTO THE INCLUSIVE EARLY CHILDHOOD CURRICULUM

Carol L. Russell, EdD

COMMON GROUND RESEARCH NETWORKS 2018

First published in 2018
as part of The Learner Book Imprint
doi: 10.18848/978-1-86335-030-3/CGP (Full Book)

Common Ground Research Networks
2001 South First Street, Suite 202
University of Illinois Research Park
Champaign, IL
61820

Library of Congress Cataloging-in-Publication Data

Names: Russell, Carol L., author.
Title: Integrating art into the inclusive early childhood curriculum / Carol
  L. Russell, Ed.D.
Description: Champaign, IL : Common Ground Research Networks, 2018. |
  Includes bibliographical references and index.
Identifiers: LCCN 2018028050 (print) | LCCN 2018028276 (ebook) | ISBN
  9781863350303 (pdf) | ISBN 9781863350280 (hardback : alk. paper) | ISBN
  9781863350297 (pbk. : alk. paper)
Subjects: LCSH: Art--Study and teaching (Primary)
Classification: LCC N350 (ebook) | LCC N350 .R87 2018 (print) | DDC
  707.1--dc23
LC record available at https://lccn.loc.gov/2018028050

Cover Photo Credit: "A Clean Life" by Mikelle, age 8.

Table of Contents

DEDICATION

This labor of love is first and foremost dedicated to Fletch, for his loving support, contributions, and encouragement towards its completion. Our partnership in life, collaboration in our work, and advocacy of creative arts for ALL children and adults, has profoundly impacted me personally and professionally.

This is also dedicated to our lovely, intelligent, expressive daughters, Cassie, Mikelle and Tally, who have lovingly supported and directly demonstrated for me the true meaning and power of creativity. And finally, this book is dedicated to our first grandchild, Aaley Love. We anticipate the delight of observing and nurturing her creative growth and expression.

ACKNOWLEDGEMENTS

I am grateful first and foremost to Fletch, my partner in life and in collaborating and advocating for creative arts as a right for ALL children and adults. His loving support, contributions, collaboration and encouragement have made this project completion possible.

I have truly treasured the creative expressions of our lovely daughters, Cassie, Mikelle and Tally. It has been an honor to directly experience the meaning and power of creativity throughout their childhood and young adulthood. They have greatly increased my awareness of the individuality of creative expression and the importance of making art accessible for all individuals. I am honored they have allowed me to share some creativity from their young lives to demonstrate various aspects of art growth and development.

I greatly appreciate the support from, and collaboration with, my colleague, Dr. Heather Caswell. Her belief in the importance of enhancing creativity and the interdisciplinary nature of creative possibilities has been deeply meaningful.

I am also thankful to my long-time friend and colleague, Dr. Carol F. Marshall, for her belief in and support of the Creative Spirit in children, both young and old. We shared in our philosophy, efforts, and endeavors to promote creativity, and collaborated on many projects for years.

My father-in-law, Tom Russell, artist, professor, and wonderful grandfather, had always been a role model for valuing and advocating for the arts. He was my first college art professor. His artwork, teaching, and overall attitude impacted and helped to form my awareness of authentic creativity.

I am grateful to my dear mother, Gladys Hahs Deye, who allowed me to observe that amidst a busy schedule as spouse of a clergyman and life of constantly taking care of and giving to others, she could make time for her own creations. Even after having three strokes, she continued painting with the assistance of art therapy. I treasure each of her creations. They remind me of the importance of creative expression for young and old, regardless of differing abilities.

Much appreciation is extended to many young artists for sharing their creativity, and to their parents for giving permission to reproduce images of their work. Thanks to the photographers for documenting the creative process and products and for their permission to reprint their photos for publication. Support from Emporia State University, and in particular, The Teachers College, and Department of Elementary Education/Early Childhood/Special Education for many projects to enhance the creativity of young children has been more than appreciated.

Preface

Children draw what they know; however, their manipulative skills are developing at an individual rate. Children may know what they want to draw, however getting their perceptual motor skills to represent their thoughts and feelings can be challenging, particularly if making their own mark is difficult.

Art is a right for all children. Authentic creative art experiences should be available to every child. Integrating Art into the Inclusive Early Childhood Curriculum recognizes that children who have differing abilities desire to create and make their own, individual mark through their artwork. As a book on art in early childhood education that focuses on inclusion, this desire is respected and facilitated through content that stresses appropriate accommodations, art tools, and materials. This also requires sensitivity to the personal nature of art, as it is created and based on what a child has seen, heard, touched, tasted, or smelled. To expect what something should look like when completed ignores the nature of individual differences and personal experience. As we consider this in relation to all children, we must remember that some children have not seen, heard, touched, smelled, or moved the same as their peers or teachers.

Children need creative freedom with opportunities to problem solve and build independence. Creative freedom and a "non-stifling" promotion of divergent and creative thinking is needed more now than ever in education. With increased standards, requirements for more testing and documentation, meeting Individualized Family Service Plans (IFSP) and Individualized Education Program (IEP) goals and outcomes, and less fun and play in education, we have reached a crisis in education of our children. Creativity does not have to end in kindergarten. Creativity and art can be integrated into the curriculum throughout every child's education and at home, and yes, you can still meet the standards with the documentation you need, and even integrate IFSP outcomes and IEP goals and objectives!

Integrating Art into the Inclusive Early Childhood Curriculum offers clarity about authentic creative art experiences, with resources to make these experiences available to ALL children, birth to age eight, regardless of ability level, culture, or native language. Contemporary theories regarding creativity and enhancement of artistic creativity are reviewed. Topics also include brain development and the creative process, evaluating creative and artistic growth, culturally diverse opportunities through art, inclusion of children with special needs and children with culturally diverse backgrounds, art as communication, integrating art throughout the curriculum and advocating for the arts. Special features that emphasize techniques for implementing diversity and inclusion of all children are the "Window into a Classroom: Best Practices for Inclusion" boxes. These boxes occur throughout the book and offer some practical applications and ideas for teachers working with a diverse population of early childhood art students. Emphasis on art appreciation, aesthetic and creative risk-taking environments, experiences / interaction to promote divergent thinking, and many authentic art experiences, with accommodations for individual needs, to "try out on Monday" are provided.

Integrating Art into the Inclusive Early Childhood Curriculum also encourages the adult reader to explore their own creativity and reflect upon their childhood art experiences. Each chapter includes, suggestions for Creativity Experience and Reflective Journal Entry for both a teacher/pre-teacher or parent/family member, and for the child (with four levels of age and development: Infants, Toddlers, Pre-schoolers, and School-agers).

CHAPTER 1

Early Childhood Art: The Process of Exploring, Expressing, and Creating

"Every child is an artist. The problem is how to remain an artist once he grows up."

- Pablo Picasso

CHAPTER OVERVIEW

Young children are all about Doing! They are naturally inquisitive. Many exploratory questions come to mind to children as they are presented with art materials, such as: What can I do with these materials? How do they work? How does it feel, smell, taste? How do I feel today? What colors can I mix? Can I show what I know and how I feel today? Am I safe to explore? Do I feel safe to express? Is there time to finish what I want? These questions may race through a child's mind when approaching an art area, or having art materials available at home. This chapter focuses on early childhood art as a process: exploration of art materials, expression of knowledge, feelings, relationships, and sensorimotor experiences. Children draw what they know. The end result of the art work, or product, becomes more important as the child grows older. That being the case, it is important to maintain a balance between the process and the end result of the art work.

This chapter also focuses on the importance of this philosophy for children with special needs, as the process of creating art may take more time if it is to be truly their own. A child with physical or developmental delays may need more accommodations, assistive technology, or may need to see a breakdown of the steps within a process; however, respect for the child and his or her creative process should be the same as it is for any other child. A child who speaks English as a second language or has a different cultural background deserves the same respect and accommodations (language interpretation, for example) in order to preserve his or her creative process and spirit. This chapter also includes ideas for sharing this philosophy and these methods with families to help them recognize the importance of, and ensure respect for, the creative process.

In addition, an extensive list of the developmental and academic/pre-academic benefits of authentic creative art experiences will be presented. Specific examples of each type of benefit will be detailed with an emphasis on best practices for inclusion.

Art in Early Childhood

Art is an important aspect of quality early childhood programs. According to Friedrich Froebel, the "Father of Kindergarten," making art and enjoying other people's art and cultures are important to the development of the whole child (Froebel, 1826). Froebel stated that art activities and appreciation were important because they help educators recognize children who demonstrate creative talent and foster each child's "full and all-sided development" (Fox & Berry, 2008).

Children should feel free to express themselves, particularly through their art, in 2D or 3D form. Children should be able to express themselves freely, safely, respectfully, and from their own perspective, without feeling their expression is right or wrong or the need to meet the adult's expectation of a specific outcome or product. Children should have daily access to a variety of materials that are developmentally appropriate along with an adult reinforcing and fostering creative problem solving and ample time for the creative process. Children also have the right to accommodations, modifications, and assistive technology as needed for self-expression.

According to Susan Striker (1986), author of Please Touch and The Anti Coloring Books, there are three major gifts we can give to our children:

1) Foster a confident feeling of being thoroughly loved, liked, and respected

2) Freedom to satisfy curiosity and safety in knowing accomplishment is valued, despite messes and inconveniences

3) License to perform as many tasks as expressed interest in without feeling the need to live up to preconceived expectation of right or wrong. This applies to all children and may require a bit more thought, planning and understanding to be truly inclusive. (Striker, 1986, p. 16)

As Pablo Picasso states, "Every child is an artist. It is our responsibility, as teachers and parents of young children, to be facilitators of that creative process, so that children can become artists of some form, and creative problem solvers when they grow up." Children are creative by nature. Teachers and parents can foster or stifle their creative spirit and need to be aware of the environments and interactions that can enhance creativity, as well as those that can inhibit the creative process. Care should be taken to also foster children's individuality to allow the freedom and time needed to create. Just as each child has his or her own developmental timetable and pace, every child also has individual interests that should be encouraged.

Window into a Classroom: Best Practices for Inclusion

This freedom to explore and create applies to all children, and may require a bit more thought, understanding, and planning to be truly inclusive. For example, some children may need assistive technology such as an adapted device to fully participate. Others might need their own materials and designated work space to be successful. Additional work time is an accommodation that is relatively simple to provide and can have a significant impact. Alex, a three-year-old preschooler with autism, is able to complete his finger-paint creation to his satisfaction because he is given the extra time to use all of the colors that are available. Alex is only content about his work if he is given the access and time to include all of the finger-paint colors. Whatever the accommodation, the work should be the authentically created by the child.

Art from a Child's Perspective: Children Draw What They Know

Children draw what they know; however, their manipulative skills and other abilities are developing at an individual rate. To experience this perspective, consider taking a moment to grab a pen, pencil or marker between your teeth or put the utensil between your toes. Take some paper and try drawing a geometric shape. Now try a realistic looking nose, ear, lips, or face. Take a look at your drawings. This is similar to the manipulative limitation a young child might have, or an older child who has weak hand muscles. The child may know what he or she wants to draw, but may experience difficulty getting his or her perceptual motor skills to represent his or her thoughts, particularly if the child experiences challenges in making his or her own mark. In addition, the type of materials used can impact the success of the child's mark on paper. For example, try this exercise again, contrasting the use of a pencil, a pen, and then a marker. Doing this might give an adult a similar feeling of what a child might feel when trying to manipulate utensils with still developing motor abilities.

Children create what they know from their various sensorimotor experiences, relationships, and feelings. Miller (1996) advises that teachers should be sensitive to the personal nature of art, as it is created and based on what a child has seen, heard, touched, tasted, or smelled. Expecting what something should look like when completed ignores the nature of individual differences and personal experience. As we consider this in relation to ALL children, we must remember that some children have not seen, heard, touched, smelled, or moved as their peers or teachers have.

Let's try another avenue to better understand the child's perspective. Take yourself back to your own early childhood. Try to remember your earliest art experiences. Close your eyes and think about:

- What were the art project and the materials?

- How old were you?

- What motivated you? Was this project a school assignment or something you did on your own?

- Where were you?

- Was the project in 2-D or 3-D?

- What colors did you use?

- How did you feel about both the process and the product? Did you enjoy or dislike what you created? Why?

- Where were you and who were you with at the time? At home? At school?

- Can you remember how your parents and/or teachers responded? Can you remember their verbal comments or nonverbal communication?

- Was your work displayed on the refrigerator, the wall, or framed? How did you feel about this?

- Did the product look like other children's work (if at school), or was it your own creation?

- What, if anything, has happened since childhood to influence your abilities or feelings about art?

We, as parents and professionals, may not only lack understanding of our children's artwork, we may not have had authentic artistic experiences ourselves. How often do you hear someone say (or perhaps you, yourself say), "I can't draw"? According to Capacchione (1989),

> "These learned beliefs usually stem from criticism or early attempts at self-expression. Fear of further ridicule and failure easily leads to the conclusion that you lack talent. The truth is that people can't draw because they think they can't and because they never do it. It's as simple as that. They were educated with little or no encouragement, training, or opportunity in art." (Capacchione, 1989, p. 4)

The problem is that we try to make our drawings look like something, rather than expressing the way we may look at something or how we feel about it. Children express what they know and what they feel through this process. That makes art authentic. By authentic, we mean individually creative, true and free, with a focus on process, not just the product (or end result).

Focus More on the Creative Process than the End Result

Remembering that experiencing the creative process is essential for young children will help the early childhood teacher in guiding students as they work. Mary Ann Kohl, in Preschool Art: It's the Process, not the Product (1994), also author of the all-time favorite art for young children resource, MUDWORKS, refers to this focus on the process rather than the end result of the art work:

> "Process not product' means that you can explore art materials and enjoy what happens. You don't have to copy what an adult makes or even try to make something a friend has made. There is no right or wrong way for these art ideas to turn out; there is only YOUR way. YOU are the artist. It's perfectly all right if you don't want to save whatever art experience you just finished. You can throw it away or take it home or cut it up into little pieces and glue them on something else! Simply enjoy creating." (Kohl, 1994, p. 5)

ACTIVITIES MASQUERADING AS CREATIVE ART

Many of us, as well as our children, have experienced activities masquerading as creative art. Some are confused about what creative art should be for children, as they may have only experienced activities labeled as "art" that were teacher directed and highly structured with a specific product as the outcome.

Activities that masquerade as creative art include:

- Xeroxed worksheets or coloring sheets

- Cut and paste according to specific directions

- Coloring book pages

- Dot-to-dot

- Craft kits

- Holiday gifts (patterned, pre-designed)

- Activities in which the products look the same as every other child's

- Art that looks like an adult did it

- Projects that are beyond the developmental level of the child

- Molds for clay and play dough

- Activities that require following models or step-by-step instructions

These activities often have an emphasis on teacher input and direction, a high degree of structure, and a specific product as the outcome (Schirrmacher, 1988). Although these activities may have some merit for developing fine motor skills or eye-hand coordination, they lack artistic and creative merit and should not take the place of authentic creative art experiences! They should not be labeled as "art" in the curriculum. See Figure 1.1 for an example of children creating an "art" activity that masquerades as art. This activity featured a model to follow of the final project provided by the teacher (in the middle of the table). The children were instructed to follow this model. Children were given pink paper with a pre-drawn Easter basket and outlines of eggs in the basket. Directions were to glue the basket shape and paper eggs that were provided within the pre-drawn lines. Next, they were instructed to draw a line with a marker over the pre-drawn line of the handle to the basket.

Figure 1.1: A high-structured, product-oriented "art" activity
that MASQUARADES as creative art.
Source: Russell, 1981

An authentic creative art activity could make use of the similar materials (paper, markers, and glue), but allow freedom of expression from the child rather than the adult. A steady diet of high-structured, product-oriented, adult-directed "art" experiences may frustrate some children and can be detrimental to the creative spirit. These experiences often reflect someone else's artwork rather than the child's, and can lead children to question their own creative abilities. These projects often require adult intervention, assistance or completion for many children, particularly those who may have some manipulative or processing challenges. In addition, these types of activities do not allow children to practice making personally meaningful art. This may result in older children and adults who think that they cannot create for themselves, have less self-confidence in their creative abilities, and respond to artistic requests with something like, "I can't draw" or "Will you draw one for me?"

The impact of coloring books has been debated for many years. According to Irene Russell, what children learn from coloring books is, "that adults draw better, by adult standards, then they do. At this point, most children spurn their own refreshing and expressive drawings" (in Striker,1986, p. 108). Russell offers a classic example that supports this research by demonstrating how children imitate the drawings in coloring books once they are exposed to them. Her results supported that coloring books can stifle independent thinking and self-expression through art. Figure 1.2 shows examples from Russell's research on children's imitation of coloring book drawings.

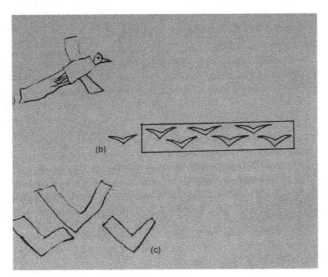

Figure 1.2: Irene Russell's research on impact of coloring books on children's self-expression
Source: Striker, 1986

a) shows the child's depiction of a bird before being exposed to coloring books

b) the depiction of a bird in the coloring book, of which the child was asked to copy

      c)   after copying the coloring book illustration, the child repeated the following drawings of birds, demonstrating originality lost in subsequent drawings.

(Striker, 1986, p. 108)

Russell observed a few behaviors, including the child's hesitancy to draw and tendency to continue to copy existing images from coloring books rather than drawing own unique design and drawing. Russell's research indicated that coloring books and other pre-drawn color inside the lines activities could result in children feeling that adults drew better than them. Russell cautions that these activities can bring about children losing expressiveness, uniqueness, and spontaneity in their artwork.

The risk of the impact of copying images relates to both two-dimensional (2D) and three-dimensional (3D) artwork. Children need both 2D and 3D experiences, however, 3D experiences must also be evaluated for offering authentic creative opportunities. Experiences that include molds of figures, cookie cutters, and patterns to follow are all examples of masquerading art. A quick search online for "children's creative art sculptures" or "children's 3D art ideas" results in a majority of kits that include popular animated characters sculpture kits, step-by-step directions for a specific product outcome (like one often pictured on front of the box), and much holiday art. Even the kits that offer some genuine materials that could result in a truly creative process and product have patterns to follow or examples with step-by-step directions. Again, this is not to say that crafts or following a pattern might have some value for fine motor and eye hand coordination skills, however it is not authentic creative art. The difference must be clearly understood to foster and enhance creative art growth in young children.

Striker also states, "Too many parents and preschool teachers offer these activities (such as those whose products look like robots, turkeys, Easter baskets, bunnies, Christmas trees, etc.) because of their own insecure feelings about their art expertise" (Striker, 1986, p. 331). It is also possible that teachers and parents have only had such experiences and not considered the creative process.

Model Techniques Only

Please remember to model only techniques rather than the end result of the art work. Even as children get older, this idea still holds true. Children can come up with their own art work product if they are given the tools, techniques, methods, and materials to do so. Illustrating experiences, problems to solve, and demonstrating knowledge are all motivators for both young and older children. The product does become more important as the child grows older; however, the process is still important and should be balanced with the end result. This is particularly important for children who have challenges. For children with developmental delays or sensory integration issues, the process may continue to be the focus. When one is truly creative, the product will never overpower the process. Creative problem solving can occur throughout the process for all developmental levels. The product may not even be the end solution—

it may be a part of an ongoing, imaginative, and innovative process. This process can be integrated into all areas of the curriculum. Problem-solving in the areas of math, science, language arts/communication/literacy, social studies, and expressive arts can be illustrated through art.

Alternately, the problem-solving could originate with the art process, which can stimulate learning in various curriculum areas, as well. For example, a child might illustrate what he or she may understand about shapes (math), details of seasonal changes (science), or how she/he felt about a new baby in the family (expressing emotions/language arts/communication). On the other hand, by starting with the creative art process, children might be working with art materials and discover how colors can be mixed (science), or they could be painting flowers and decide to count them (math), or after a walk to the park, they could decide to create a map of their home and neighborhood park (social studies).

Authentic creative art experiences should be a right for ALL children. Accommodations, modifications, and assistive technology, as needed, can assure all children can participate in these experiences. Appropriate accommodations and modifications may take some problem solving and creative solutions on the part of the teacher, parent, adult, but it can be done. It is a matter of "how", not "if." This may take a team effort by consultation with physical or occupational therapists, art therapists, psychologists, or other professionals. The art experiences offered should foster the child's personal creative expressions rather than that of the teacher, therapist, paraprofessional, or educator.

Para-educators or other assistants in the classroom need to have a clear understanding of authentic creative art experiences and how to respect children's expression and abilities. This might take more time, patience, modifications, assistive technology, and a constant self-reminder to not overtake the project.

Window into a Classroom: Best Practices for Inclusion

Offering support or assistance in holding clay sturdy as a child with special needs adds more clay is fostering their independence and self-expression. However, putting the structure together for the child when she/he is having trouble connecting the parts results in the adult's work, not the child's. Demonstrating a sequence of painting with watercolors (from water to paint to paper) with additional verbal cues, allows the child to create with the medium, while using the technique that was demonstrated. However, if the adult takes the child's hand-over-hand, not only to complete the water, paint, paper sequence, but continues to make a model to follow, it then becomes the adult's artwork rather than the child's.

We must assist families and other professionals in understanding this essential aspect of authenticity of children's art. The child will take pride in her/his own work and be motivated to create more. More detailed examples and suggestions will be offered in Chapter 4 Strategies for Using Art as a Learning and Intervention Tool in Early Childhood.

The child has the right to make her or his own unique mark and have control over the process. Whether the child is illustrating what she knows or discovering knowledge while involved in a creative process, the child still has the right to direct the process. Even if a child expresses artistically through use of assistive technology or modified materials the process and unique expression is still the child's right. For example, when a child who has physical challenges needs larger grips or handles on art tools, must use his mouth to paint, or requires a non-skid surface so the paper does not slide, the child can still, and has the right, to make his own unique mark and have control over the process. Authentic creative art experiences should offer free and accessible exploration and expression, the opportunity for problem solving, and joy for the child in having produced her own product inspired by her own imagination and ideas. The process and product should be based on what the child desires and is able to express. Chapters 5 and 6 will feature many activities, accommodations, modifications, assistive technology, and assessment of activity goals.

WHAT IS THE VALUE OF AUTHENTIC CREATIVE ART EXPERIENCES FOR ALL CHILDREN?

Table 1.1: Developmental Benefits of Authentic Creative Art Experiences

Developmental benefits of authentic creative art experiences
a) Sensory experiences (cognitive, physical, emotional)
b) Opportunities to experiment (Cognitive: science, physics, cause/effect, invention, discovery; Physical: fine motor, manipulating objects to experiment; Emotional: satisfying a sense of curiosity and wonder; Social: sharing problem solving and discoveries with peers and adults)
c) Spatial relations (Physical: fine and large motor, manipulating materials and objects in space provided or maneuver more space, visual spatial skills; Cognitive: math, problem solving, balance, physics; Emotional: use of space to express emotions)
d) Planning, sequencing (Cognitive: math, patterning, ordering sequence; Physical: fine and large motor, visual spatial skills)
e) Problem solving (Cognitive: trial and error; Social/emotional: satisfying sense of curiosity and wonder, problem solving with peers or adult)
f) Motor skills (Physical: large and fine motor, hand-eye coordination, perceptual motor skills)
g) Pride, sense of accomplishment (Emotional/social: self-esteem, feeling of success, as authentic creative art experiences are success oriented, with no wrong way of completing)

Early childhood art activities should: promote personal expression; balance artistic process and product; enhance creativity; invite experimentation, discovery, and messes; allow hands-on opportunities through assistive technology and accommodations as needed, promote continued involvement; be motivating and success-oriented; be developmentally appropriate (both age and individually); include quality materials with accommodations/modifications as needed; and be available to each and every child.

Developmental and Academic Benefits

The developmental benefits of authentic creative art experiences reach across all domains and curricular areas. Table 1.1 lists the developmental benefits of authentic creative art experiences. These will be reviewed below with examples illustrating each benefit and suggestions for how to maximize such creative art experiences for young children. The list illustrates the benefits to the child across developmental domains and curricular areas, which can be easily linked to various standards. Academic and pre-academic benefits are also highlighted. In addition, the connection between potential goals/objectives/outcomes of a child's Individualized Education Program (IEP), Individual Family Service Plan (IFSP), or Rehabilitation 504 Plan, and consultation with the family and professional therapists equate to more successful experiences for children with differing abilities. More specifics of the latter will be included in Chapter 4: Strategies for Using Art as a Learning and Intervention Tool in Early Childhood.

Sensory Experiences (Cognitive, Physical, Emotional, and Social Benefits)

Sensory experiences lead to building perceptions and concepts. For example, the tactile sense is perceived through touch, which results in a pleasant or unpleasant feeling. Those feelings cause one to think and analyze the experience, which builds concepts of texture. We learn about and build concepts of roughness in the surfaces of bumpy rocks, rough gravel, or sandpaper. Concepts of smoothness are built with experiences such as touching a pet's fur, leather, glass, or a smooth plastic surface. These can relate to most any art process and project. Social and cognitive skills develop with adult interaction noting and labeling sensory concepts. Questioning the child about her feelings regarding textures facilitates concept building and conveys value of the child's individual preference. Expressing feelings about sensory experiences can also enhance social interactions. Art experiences such as fingerprinting, painting with sand, nature collages or sculptures, painting rocks, and painting to music are all examples of sensory art experiences.

Although sensory experiences through art are beneficial, we must be aware of and sensitive to the need for individualization. For some children, sensory experiences can be overwhelming, particularly if they have a neurological or sensory integration issue that makes this difficult. Be sure to follow preferences of each child and avoid forcing or trying to convince the child to experience textures they do not want to. Too much auditory, busy visuals, heavy smells, or some tactile experiences might be disturbing and difficult to handle. It can make all the difference in the child's participation and behavior. Break down the activity to the sensory aspects that the child can do, and slowly, if ever, introduce more. Doing this with family input and in consultation with an occupational therapist or neuropsychologist can contribute to the success of sensory experiences in art. If the child has this area as a goal or outcome on an IEP, IFSP, or Rehab 504 Plan, the goal/outcome can easily be integrated into the art lesson plan and progress can be noted from creative art experiences to record for this process and document.

Opportunities to Experiment and Problem Solve (Cognitive, Physical, Emotional, and Social Benefits)

Creative art leads to experimenting, discovering cause/effect, using trial and error. These experiences can be filled with opportunities to invent and discover in the cognitive domain and the curricular areas of math, science, and physics. Physically, fine motor skills are enhanced with manipulating objects and materials with which to experiment and problem solve while involved in art activities. It can be emotionally satisfying for children to experiment with art materials, and this process can increase sense of curiosity and wonder. Socially, children are sharing ideas, hypotheses, problem-solving outcomes, and observing each other's art process and products. Mixing colors, adding textures, and balancing sculptural materials all demonstrate the opportunities to experiment and problem solve within the creative art process.

The experimentation and problem-solving aspects of creative art experiences benefit all children. However, individualization is essential to a positive experience. Children with cognitive challenges, differing physical abilities, or emotional/behavioral issues might need the activity broken down to meet them on their cognitive or physical level. Doing this with suggestions from the family and consultation of an occupational or physical therapist, neuropsychologist or psychologist, and/or speech language pathologist can impact the success of experimentation and problem-solving in creative art experiences. If experimentation or problem solving is a goal or outcome on the child's IEP, IFSP, or Rehab 504 Plan, this can easily be integrated in the art lesson plan. Progress in these areas should be documented from these creative art experiences.

Spatial Relations (Physical and Cognitive Benefits)

Children deal with spatial relations each time they decide where to place marks on their paper, how much of the page to use, or drawing what they know to fill the space. When a child decides where to place or layer collage materials on paper or how and where to place several balls or rolls of clay, he or she is dealing with spatial relations. Physically, they are using fine and gross motor skills. Cognitively, they are utilizing their math and visual spatial abilities. When sharing with others their ideas and solutions of working with the space in their 2-D or 3-D artwork, children are using social skills and when taking pride in their special relations outcome of their work, they are growing emotionally, increasing self-esteem.

Children with physical and/or neurological challenges might need some accommodations and individualized approaches in this area. Spatial relations can be especially challenging for children with neurological issues. We must motivate children and approach them with the philosophy of "how can we do this" rather than "if we can do this." The concept of "can't" should not be used or considered. Teacher/parent/therapist guidance, along with assistive technology and a verbal description of the space, can enable children with these challenges to benefit from the spatial relations features of creative art endeavors. Children with physical and/or cognitive or neurological delays may have spatial relations difficulties and would have this as a goal or outcome on their IEP, IFSP, or Rehab 504 Plan. Again, this can easily be integrated in the art lesson plan and progress should be documented on their IEP, IFSP, or Rehab 504 Plan from these creative art activities.

Planning, Sequencing (Cognitive, Social, and Physical benefits)

As children approach their creative art experiences they are learning more about the planning process and technique of using the materials. As fine motor skills increase, children are able to physically take on more detailed planning and meticulous features in their artwork. Some children may need more discussion with planning and techniques. Posing thoughts and questions as children work through this process enhances planning, problem solving, sequence, and social interaction. Be certain to honor a child's need for pause to contemplate, or a need for less interaction or interruptions during this process.

Planning and sequencing aspects of creative art experience benefits all children. However, just as with problem-solving and experimentation, individualization is vital for a positive process and outcome. Children who have cognitive challenges, differing physical abilities, neurological challenges, or emotional/behavioral issues often require accommodations and assistive technology to the meet the child's needs. Consulting with the family and collaborating with professional team members, such as occupational or physical therapist, Neuropsychologist or Psychologist, Speech Language Pathologist, can make the difference for building the child's planning and sequencing skills through creative art activities. The child's IEP, IFSP, or Rehab 504 Plan that includes work on planning and sequencing skills could be integrated into the activity and progress toward the goal be documented.

Motor Skills (Physical Benefits)

Benefits to the child's motor skills are obvious within the process of any art experience for young children. Creative art experiences benefit both fine and gross motor skills, as well as promote eye-hand coordination and perceptual motor skills. For authentic art activities to benefit all children, physical accommodations and essential assistive technology is necessary for children with physical challenges. This along with consultation with the child's family and IEP/IFSP team of professionals will ensure the child's participation and physical progress. This area of motor skills would be included in the IEP, IFSP, or Rehab 504 Plan of a child with physical challenges and art would be a fitting area to include such a goal, objective, or outcome. Skills observed and progress toward this goal, objective, or outcome should be documented.

Verbal and Written Expression (cognitive, language benefits).

As children mature to a representational level of their artwork, they draw what they know, what is important to them, what or how things are in their lives, be it positive or negative, or how they would like them to be. With this representational stage comes words, stories, and verbal expressions. Telling and writing stories about creations is a very natural event for children. Even before children can write, they dictate their stories about their art to an adult to put them in print. Through art, children gain more fine motor strength and dexterity, as well as increased eye-hand coordination, all of which are pre-writing skills.

Again, this is an area requiring accommodations and assistive technology for some children. IEP, IFSP, or Rehab 504 goals/objective/outcomes in this area can clearly be integrated into creative art experiences. Skills observed and progress toward this goal, objective, or outcome should be documented on the IEP, IFSP, or Rehab 504 Plan.

Pride, Sense of Accomplishment (Emotional and Social Benefits).

As children create, they enjoy the process and take pride in and feel a sense of accomplishment in their work. When adults give positive feedback, display children's creations, and help them reflect on their artwork, children are reinforced in their efforts and accomplishments. Children also enjoy the attention and positive feedback from adults.

Many children with differing abilities work hard in therapies, trying to meet goals and pleasing others. For some tasks their exertion level is multiplied many times over while in effort to meet the same level or accomplish as their peers. Small steps and bits of progress are worth celebrating for children with such challenges. This sense of pride and accomplishment also motivates children to try more, accomplish more, and create more.

Success-oriented (Emotional and Social Benefits).

In authentic creative art, there is no wrong way to do it, rather it supports individuality. As noted in the process focus of creative art experiences, it is the child's right to have free expression with her/his art. It is okay to paint a hole through the paper, cut it into pieces, or throw it away without an adult's halting. It is also okay to start a project all over again without being told one has failed. In authentic art, there are no mistakes, just minor accidents that can lead to new discoveries. A success-oriented approach is a major component of authentic creative art for young children and should be the foundation of every art experience.

Children with differing abilities face challenges and have an increased possibility of experiencing repeated failures in various areas, more so than their peers who are typically developing. As stated earlier, children with special needs learn at an early age what and how others can do things that they have great difficulty doing, or can only do with assistance of technology or assistance from others. "Success" and "normal" have different meanings for children with differing abilities and their families. Individualized authentic creative art experiences offer many ways of completing the activity. Adults must respect the child and foster her or his individual pathway within the process and refrain from any taking over of the project in order to finish it up in the time allowed. More time for completion is a valid accommodation. When adults, as well meaning as they may be, complete a child's art project for him or her, it only gives the illusion of the child's success or completion. It robs the child of her or his authentic process and work. As adults, we must motivate children and their families with the philosophy of "how can we do this" rather than "if." This will

15

lead to success and enthuse and motivate children's independence and creative process.

Early childhood art activities should:

- promote personal expression

- balance artistic process and product

- enhance creativity

- invite experimentation, discovery, and messes

- allow children hands on with assistive technology as needed for individual needs, continued involvement

- be motivating and success oriented

- be developmentally appropriate (both age and individually)

- include quality materials with accommodations/modifications as needed

- be available to each and every child.

More detail and examples of developmental benefits of authentic creative art experiences will be included in Chapter 6.

PARTNERING WITH FAMILIES

We must partner with families in our efforts to make authentic creative art experiences available for all children. Understanding the philosophy and importance of valuing the creative process over product (or end result of the art work), activities that masquerade as creative art, and the values of authentic creative art experiences for ALL children are important aspects of quality art experiences to share with families. Helping families understand that children draw or sculpt what they know is essential. Children's artwork can be a window into their minds and offer insight on how they understand their world. Once they have the cognitive and motor skills to express, they draw or sculpt various sensorimotor experiences, including their relationships and feelings from their perspective.

According to Fox and Berry (2008), "Sharing with families the role of art in the curriculum and the activities in which their children are participating will encourage their support of the program and of their children's learning (Fox & Berry, 2008). This can be done in a number of ways, including inviting families to art museum field trips, involving parents in classroom art activities, assigning at-home art projects to extend classroom learning, or linking art projects with book themes that can be extended to home activities. Fox and Berry (2008) also suggest "artists' knapsacks" in order to foster the same use of creative materials at home as at school. These knapsacks would each feature one art medium (e.g. paint/paper, clay, collage) and would be available for the children and families to check out.

Figure 1.3 is a sample letter that can be shared with families so that they may attain a better understanding of authentic creative art experiences. This letter also includes ways for families to foster and enhance the creative spirit of their children.

Sample Letter to Families

Dear Families,

Children love to do artwork, and we can work together to support truly creative experiences. Children draw what they know; however their manipulative skills are developing at an individual rate. There are many developmental benefits of creative art experiences for your child.

Benefits include:
- Sensory experiences (cognitive, physical, emotional)
- Opportunities to experiment (e.g. science, physics, cause/effect, invent, discover, cognitive)
- Spatial relations (physical, cognitive)
- Planning, sequencing (math, cognitive)
- Problem solving (cognitive)
- Motor skills (physical)
- Eye-hand coordination, perceptual motor skills (physical)
- Pride, sense of accomplishment (emotional/social)

Here are some examples of questions/comments that can encourage creativity and the discovery process when talking with your child about her/his work:
- Can you tell me about your painting/sculpture
- What part did you like best?
- You've used many colors.
- Did you enjoy making this?
- How did the paint feel?
- The yellow looks so bright next to purple!
- How did you make such a big design?

We can also say, "I like the way you....
- are working so hard."
- are coming up with your very own idea."
- trying new ways."

We can invite children to tell us about their work. Rather than "What is it?", simply "Would you tell me about your picture" offers, without pushing, the opportunity to share if they wish. The choice should be theirs. In addition, it may not be "something" – it may be just a design. Expecting your child to label her/his products may convey that it is not good to tell what it is, or it may not be something specific.

Ideas for what you can do at home:

- Have a designated art shelf, drawer, or easy to access caddy for storing art materials that are developmentally appropriate for your child's age and individual development. Crayons, markers (thick and thin), pencils, chalk, large paper, colored paper, paints (watercolors and tempera), oil pastels, scissors, shaped hole punchers, glue stick, etc. Have your child help "stock" the storage area, this way he/she will know all the items available.
- Have a separate storage section for materials for 3-D projects, with items that are developmentally appropriate for your child's age and individual development. For preschoolers: pipe cleaners, tissue paper, cotton balls, yarn, pom poms, colored masking tape, air dry clay, clay tools, play dough, glue, popsicle sticks, wire, beads, wire tools, etc.
- Show your child the areas (table, floor, outside) where they can work on projects, being free to make messes. Use a drop cloth or be sure the areas are easy to clean.
- Sit with your child and participate with the materials, making scribbles, doodles, and demonstrating technique rather than the product. Try the comments and questions suggested earlier to extend and foster their creative expression. Do your best to tolerate the mess by preventing with plastic tablecloth or paper. Creating outdoors makes for less clean up.
- Reinforce when your child initiates taking the materials out independently. Be sure to provide blocks of time for them to create, without rush and hurry.
- Have a source of music and vary the music: classical, jazz, marches, country, rock and roll, and musical soundtracks.
- Display your child's art. Besides the refrigerator, set up locations for displaying your child's 2-D and 3-D art projects. You can hang frames in hallways, bedrooms, living room, rec room, and change out the artwork from time to time. Let your child choose which project to hang or frame or display. Be sure to hang frames low enough for both you and your child to enjoy. Designate a shelf to change out 3-D projects. Again, let you child be the "curator" of the works, and help setting up the display. Displaying your child's work builds their self-esteem, offers them pride and a sense of accomplishment.

Enjoy and celebrate your child's creativity!

Figure 1.3: Sample of letter to families about creative arts and its benefits

Chapter Summary and Looking Ahead

In this chapter, we looked at what early childhood art should be and the importance of free expression through the arts, how to explore art from a child's perspective and how children draw or sculpt what they know (based on individual differences and personal experience), and the significance of the process over product for every young child. We identified activities masquerading as creative art, and although beneficial in some developmental areas, cautioned against offering as art activities or interpreting them as creative experiences. We noted how authentic creative art experiences should be a right for ALL children, as well as the developmental importance of creative art experiences. We also noted the benefits of and methods for partnering and keeping families involved in their child's creative expressions.

In order to provide "Art for ALL," we must also address the following questions throughout the book:

- What role does creativity and brain development play in children's art experiences?

- What is artistic creativity? What is not?

- What are some of the developmental stages children go through in relation to creative art, and how do we recognize these stages?

- What is the value of authentic creative art experiences for children?

- How do we provide equal access to the arts in inclusive settings and promote art growth for ALL children? How do we best respond to children's artistic creativity?

- What kinds of authentic creative art experiences can we provide at school (throughout the curriculum), home, in therapies, and in community settings?

You will find answers to these questions, and more, as you explore the chapters ahead.

Suggestions for Additional Reflection and Review

Creativity Experience and Reflective Journal suggestions for adults and for children will be presented at the end of each chapter. The creativity journal exercises for children are offered for four age groups: infant, toddler, preschooler, early school aged. The Creative Journal for both the adult and child allows the safety of expressing one's self openly, honesty and also has the benefit of promoting relaxation in sharing thoughts and feelings without judgments or edits, and can offer a place to gather ideas and be creative.

- For the teacher or pre-teacher, parent/family member or any adult: This Personal Creativity Journal will help the reader explore the chapter contents through drawings and reflections.

- For the child: This Personal Creativity Journal will help the teacher or parent motivate children to keep their own journals with entries of drawings and reflections. This could easily be a partnership activity between home and school.

INITIATING CREATIVITY JOURNALS FOR ALL AGES: INTRODUCTION OF ADULT'S PERSONAL CREATIVITY JOURNAL

A major component of this text is using a "hands on" approach and will include suggestions for a "visual arts journal." You will need a sketchbook or spiral drawing pad without lines. Try to keep this journal with you at all times to record thoughts, visions, drawings, etc. The Adult Journal Activities for each chapter will be provided with more specific directions on what to include, when, and how. The adult could also work on another piece of paper and staple or tape it in your journal. This can include even items such as napkins, scratch paper, post-its, etc. (which is sometimes all you can find if you need to draw or write down an idea quickly). Space is also provided within this book for jotting down ideas or sketches as you work on lesson planning and other class preparations. There is no right or wrong way of doing this. This is your personal reflection. Hopefully this reflection will help you to grow creatively, in addition to reflecting and progressing in your role as a facilitator of the creative spirits in young children.

Adult Journal Activity #1

An activity noted earlier in this chapter will be the first adult journal activity. In your journal, record your drawings and responses to the following prompts: Drawing: From a Child's Perspective and Try to Remember Your Earliest Art Experiences activities.

Drawing: From a Child's Perspective

- Take your writing utensil (pencil, crayon, felt tip pen, markers) in your mouth or between your toes.

- In your journal, draw two geometric shapes, a circle or square or triangle, or any you choose.

- Now, draw a realistic ear (still using your mouth or toes)

- Next, label each of your drawings.

Address the following questions in your journal:

- How did you feel?

- Add blank lines for educator to record reflection.

- Did you feel you had control over the utensil?

- Add blank lines for educator to record reflection.

- Did you know what you wanted to draw, but getting it on paper was "a different story"?

- Add blank lines for educator to record reflection.

This is not unlike a child, knowing what he or she wants to draw (not always), and trying to get his or her perceptual motor skills to allow him or her to represent his or her thoughts. Also, using the materials that work (e.g. markers versus pencil or crayons) that can easily/successfully make a mark will make the difference. Children who may have some motor problems would also benefit from utensils that make an easy mark.

Try to remember your earliest art experiences

This activity was also noted earlier in this chapter and is suggested for an introductory journal activity. Close your eyes and think about the following, then note your responses in your journal:

- Take a slow deep breath. Think back. Try to remember your earliest art experience(s). What were the art project and the materials?

- How old were you?

- What motivated you?

- Was this an assignment in school or something you did on your own?

- Did it involve any of the following?

    Xeroxed worksheets or coloring sheets

    Cut and paste according to presubscribed directions

Coloring book pages

Dot-to-dot

Craft kits

Holiday gifts (patterned, pre-designed)

Looks the same as every other child's

Looks like an adult did it

Beyond the developmental level of the child

Molds for clay and play dough

Activities that require following models or step-by-step instructions

- Where were you?

- Was it 2-D or 3-D?

- What colors did you use?

- How did you feel about it? Did you enjoy or dislike what you did? Why?

- Where were you and who were you with at the time? At home? At school?

- Can you remember how your parents and/or teachers responded? Can you remember their verbal comments or nonverbal communication?

- Was your work displayed, on the refrigerator, the wall, or framed? How did you feel about this?

- Did it look like other children's work (if at school), or was it your own creation?

- Do you still have the art project?

- What, if anything, has happened since childhood to influence you're feeling about or abilities in art?

INTRODUCTION OF CHILD'S PERSONAL CREATIVITY JOURNAL

This Personal Creativity Journal for a child will help the teacher or parent suggest and motivate children to keep their own journals with entries of drawings and reflections. This could easily be a partnership activity between home and school.

Since children draw what they know, this could be an avenue to observe the child's knowledge about various aspects of life, relationships, various sensorimotor experiences, feelings, and perspectives of his or her world. In addition, as the adult, you can observe progression in a child's fine motor skills and understanding of various concepts. It is truly an opportunity to see through the child's eyes!

Child's Personal Creativity Journal Activity #1

Activity #1 for Infants

Infants (Birth to walking, or 16 months) take in everything through their senses: feeling (with fingers and orally), tasting, smelling, hearing, and seeing. Since this essentially becomes documentation of the infant's sensory experiences, you can take photos of infants exploring various foods, for example, whipped cream, Jell-O, or birthday cake, with taste, touch, smell and vision, or infant's reaction to texture in the environment, even touching the family pet's fur. Attach these photos in the journal. Artwork such as finger-painting, first scribbles, or first marks with marker or crayon can be attached or completed right in the journal. This journal should include only the infant's work or photos of the sensory experiences. In other words, the items included in the infant's journal should only be the child's work or photos of her or his work, rather than decorative boarders and other scrapbooking features. More specific infant journaling suggestions will be included with each chapter.

Activity #1 for Toddlers

As with infants, toddlers (walking or 16 months to 3-years-old)_too take in everything through their senses: feeling, tasting, smelling, hearing, and seeing. In addition to their newfound skills of mobility (for those who are able) and more control of their world, toddlers also experience more control of objects, environment, and social relationships. Along with documentation of the toddler's sensory experiences, specific artwork such as finger-painting, first scribbles, or first marks with marker or crayon can be attached or completed right in the journal. As noted under the infant creativity journal, the items included in the toddler's journal should only be the child's work or photos of her or his work, rather than decorative boarders and other scrapbooking features.

Music Dancing Scribbles. For the toddler's first journal entries, focus on trying various art supplies for 2D work. If the child has not yet experienced markers (non-toxic, of course), try putting on some classical music and letting the child enjoy "his or her marks." Markers make it easier to make marks without having to use pressure. Use words to describe the child's movements, the music, and reflect on his or her marks, colors, lines, etc. Try changing the music to jazz, marches, and musical soundtracks. Observe if the rhythm or marks change. Try offering different colors of markers and crayons (large or easy grip crayons are best for small hands). Take photos of the process. Attach photos of the process and one of the scribble drawings in the journal. Bigger paper is better for toddlers, so if the scribble drawing is too large for the journal, take a photo of the final product or try having the child draw directly in the journal.

Activity #1 for Preschoolers (ages 3 – 5)

This is me! self-portrait: Using pencils, crayons, or markers, first encourage the child to draw a picture of themselves in their journal. Next add a mirror, and ask him/her to draw another self-portrait on the next journal page, using a mirror. Reflect with the child, comparing the two. Then offer paints, chalk, or other materials not already utilized, and encourage the child to add color and details, but only if they wish to elaborate. Take photos of the process. Attach photos of the process and one of the child's self-portrait drawings in the journal.

Activity #1 for Young School-agers

All about me self-portrait: Explore a variety of self-portraits online, in art books, or in an art gallery or museum. Using a large mirror, ask the child to observe her/his reflection, and encourage a self-portrait as the first entry in his or her journal. Help the child notice details about him or herself in the mirror and add those details to the self-portrait. If the child would like to write about him or herself, what he/she likes, the child's family, or whatever is on his or her mind, promote continuance of ideas, words, and illustrations. Give the child the time, space, materials, and positive feedback and reinforcement to create! Take photos of the process. Attach photos of the process and one of the child's self-portrait drawings in the journal.

Chapter 2

Linking Creativity and Child Development

"Imagination gives wings to the intellect."

-   Frank & Teresa Caplan

Chapter Overview

This chapter clarifies the role creativity and brain development play in children's art experiences, including those for children who have developmental delays or special needs (cognitive, physical delay or social/emotional delays). In addition, creativity related to child development theories and practices is discussed, including the influences of Reggio Emilia, The Project Approach, art growth developmental stages and evaluation (e.g. Kellogg's Art Growth Stages and Lowenfeld's Art Growth Stages); and the need for understanding and incorporating developmentally appropriate inclusive theories and practices into early childhood art.

All children are creative—some more creative in one area more than others. The environment plays a major role in how each child's creative spirit is fostered to develop, or how the creative potential is stifled. Within the environment, how adults respond to children's creative expressions can have a major impact on their creative development. "Educators have an important role in the development of creativity. They can actively support creativity or squelch it by concentrating only on the product that emerges. And they can enhance the experience by having children think more about the process, as it will impact the product" (Deiner, 2005, p. R-130). How we define creativity and learning more about creativity research and theories impacts our educational philosophies and practices.

Defining Creativity

How do we define creativity? It means different things to different people, and the meaning varies with various disciplines and cultures. Creativity brings to mind words such as: novel, original, imaginative, innovative, or unique. Perhaps your first thoughts are of creative works in visual arts, music, literature, and movement. Or, maybe you first think of individuals who are known for their creative works, perhaps: painters Vincent van Gogh, Claude Monet, or Paul Cezanne; or sculptors Henry Moore or Michelangelo; or architect, Frank Lloyd Wright.

Several psychologists and educators have attempted to define creativity. According to Fox and Schirrmacher (2015),

Generally Accepted Definitions of Creativity

- Ability to see things in new ways

- Boundary breaking going beyond information given

- Thinking unconventionally

- Making something unique or original

- Combining unrelated things into something new

(Fox & Schirrmacher, 2015, p. 7)

In order to foster creativity in our children, several questions come to mind: What behaviors should we nurture? What are characteristics of creative adults that we could cultivate in children? According to Fox and Schirrmacher (2015), Gardner sees, "the creative individual as a person who regularly solves problems, fashions products, or defines new questions in ways that are initially considered novel but that ultimately become accepted in the particular cultural setting" (Fox & Schirrmacher, 2015, p. 5). Healy (2004) lists characteristics of creative people in Your Child's Growing Mind: (a) Intense absorption in activities; (b) Seeing patterns and relationships; (c) Combining things or ideas in new ways; (d) Challenging assumptions because of a reasoned-out difference of opinion; (e) Coming to a decision independently and taking action based on it; (f) The ability to shift from one idea to another; (g) Having a strong intuition—"seeing" the answer to a problem; (h) The ability to take a risk; (i) Asking "what if " questions and making insightful observations; (j) The tendency to create and test hypotheses; (k) Tolerating ambiguity while exploring alternatives; (l) Finding enjoyment in thinking and working alone.

Howard Gardner's Theory of Multiple Intelligences had an impact on education for the last decade, proposing "seven kinds of smart" with the purpose of maximizing the potential of each child. Gardner's (1983) definition of creativity has four aspects:

1. One can be creative in one developmental domain, not necessarily across all domains

2. Those who are creative demonstrate ongoing creativity, rather than a onetime surge of creativity

3. The definition of creativity includes not only devising products, but includes problem solving and formulating new questions, thus no tangible product as an outcome

4. Creativity is defined and depends on culture and its judgment

Fox and Schirrmacher (2015) stated, "Although there is no single definition of creativity, there are different ways to explain it. Creativity can be explained as: an attitude, not an aptitude; a process; a product; a skill; a set of personality traits (e.g. curiosity, flexibility, sensitivity to problems, originality, insightful); a set of environmental conditions (e.g., people, places, objects, and experiences" (p. 7). E. Paul Torrance (1974), known as the Father of Modern Creativity and creator of the Torrance Tests of Creative Thinking (TTCT), described creativity as a natural human process which involves and fulfills strong human needs. Torrance (1992) artistically defined creativity in the following verse:

Creativity is digging deeper.

Creativity is looking twice.

Creativity is crossing out mistakes.

Creativity is talking/listening to a cat.

Creativity is getting in deep water.

Creativity is getting out from behind locked doors.

Creativity is plugging in the sun.

Creativity is wanting to know.

Creativity is having a ball.

Creativity is building sand castles.

Creativity is singing in your own way.

Creativity is shaking hands with the future.

E. Paul Torrance

Creativity, related to young children, has been defined as, "the capacity of the child to sense gaps and produce something new, novel and previously unknown to the child to fill those gaps. Creativity (of young children) is regarded as a process and could (but did not always) lead to a product" (Russell, 1981). With this definition of something new or novel to the individual child describes creativity as very personal and distinct to each young child. Therefore, is creativity a process or should it result in a product? As discussed in Chapter 1, "When one is truly creative, the product will never overpower the process. Creative problem solving can occur throughout the process, for all developmental levels. The product may not even be the end solution it may be a part of an ongoing, imaginative, and innovative process" (Russell, 1981, p. 8).

Creativity and the Brain

Creativity is an inherent and natural function of the brain that has the capacity to be fostered or stifled. Changes in the central nervous system and various organs underlie many emerging abilities. Most importantly is brain growth and maturation. For example, brain weight at two years is 75% of adult weight; at five years the brain is 90% of adult weight. The ongoing process of myelination in the brain provides nerves with insulating substance on nerve cells and neurons, thus speeding up transmission of neural impulses of the brain. For instance, the area of the brain associated with eye-hand coordination is fully myelinated at age four years. The brain area for maintaining full attention is myelinated by the end of childhood; and language and intelligence is fully myelinated at age 15 years. These are important implications for education and expectations.

The left hemisphere controls the right side of the body while the right hemisphere governs the left side. Hemispheres are joined by the corpus callosum, which serves as communication between them. Although both hemispheres work together, we refer to "left-brain" as controlling speech, reasoning, math, and factual kinds of activities and "right-brain" as the spatial skills, visual imagery, nonverbal, sensory, and creative side.

For example, five-year-old Marwa is standing at the easel trying to paint a picture of her family. How might her brain approach this task? Her left-brain reacts logically, telling her she needs 4 figures—2 males and 2 females. If her left side dominates, her father would be painted with his beard and depicted taller than her mother. Marwa would plan to paint herself smaller than her older brother. If the right brain predominates, she might react emotionally rather than logically. She could become focused on missing colors and making designs to highlight clothing, or her mother could be painted larger than life and wearing a crown and earrings, while her older brother might be in the background or bottom of the page, lacking facial features.

Dominance is not established at birth, so it is important to have experiences that integrate functioning of both sides. Schools typically teach to the left-brain, and may offer limited authentic creative experiences. Early childhood/early elementary educators are in a key position to provide experiences that engage both hemispheres.

Creativity Research and Theories

As mentioned earlier in this chapter, Howard Gardner's theory of multiple intelligences had a significant impact on education, proposing "seven kinds of smart" or "multiple intelligences" with the purpose of maximizing the potential of each child. Rather than a single general ability to define intelligence, there are eight intelligences, according to Gardner (1983):

1. Verbal-Linguistic: Excels in words and language (reading, writing, speaking and listening)

2. Logical-Mathematical: Excels in reasoning, logical thinking, problem solving and numbers.

3. Musical: Excels in musical expression, learning through songs, sensitivity to rhythms and beats.

4. Visual-Spatial: Excels in shapes and designs, learning visually, able to organize ideas and represent images visual-spatially.

5. Bodily-Kinesthetic: Excels in sports, learning through physical movement and awareness of body and environment; able use body to convey ideas/emotions and problem solve.

6. Interpersonal: Ability to work effectively with others, organize people, work cooperatively and collaboratively.

7. Intrapersonal: Ability to understand inner feelings, learning through feelings and attitudes, involving self-reflection and metacognition; understanding one's own emotions and goals.

8. Naturalistic: Loves and understands the natural world, plants, animals, nature.

Gardner's Theory of Multiple Intelligences lends itself to the arts in early childhood programs and school systems. Sensitivity to different strengths and ways of knowing and expressing allows children to demonstrate their knowledge in a variety of ways. Music, movement, drawing or sculpture, collaborative projects to demonstrate knowledge and understanding can all draw on individual strengths of each child. Curriculum and environment that is presented only one way, or teaches to one intelligence type, will result in some, but not all children absorbing the material or concepts. Matching the child's strengths with appropriate approaches to teaching and learning motivates children and makes learning fun. It increases the potential for positive educational experiences and educational success.

The developmental domains of a holistic model of children's development include the young child's physical, social, emotional, and cognitive development. Fox and Schirrmacher (2015) include creativity as its own domain within child development. These domains do not develop in isolation of each other, nor do they develop evenly. Each child has an individual rate and area of growth as influenced by their genetics (nature) and their environment (nurturance, or lack of it). Examples of these domains include:

- Physical This includes gross motor skills involving large muscles; fine motor or small muscle skills; eye-hand coordination and visual perceptual skills; self-care; sensory development; and physical health.

- Social relations with others, as well as development of self

- Emotional Personality, self-concept, temperament, expressions of feelings

- Cognitive Problem solving, language, reasoning, discovery, thinking and learning

- Creative imagination, original thinking, verbal and non-verbal expression

(Fox & Schirrmacher, 2015, p. 69)

Psychologists and educators have long recognized the importance of creativity for individuals and to society. According to Hurlock, the creative act is valuable to the young child because it makes play pleasurable and successful, and therefore the child is happy and contented, which leads to personal and social adjustment (Hurlock, 1972). If creativity is natural and joyful for young children, in addition to being valuable for social and emotional development, how can we design environments that foster and nurture creativity? What can we do to support the creative spirit when children are young, how can we maintain it throughout our lives? What are we doing to stifle creative growth in many children and adults?

Creativity Research and Assessing Creativity

Creativity studies with young children have not been considered worthwhile by some in the past (Torrance, 1974), as they felt that children identified as creative may not have developed into creative adults. Yet, Torrance (1998) wrote that although this could be true, he was studying children to see what elements might lead to the abandonment of creativity. The Torrance Tests of Creative Thinking (TTCT) is one of the most common tests used to assess creativity in both children and adults. The TTCT provides measuring tools through a series of exercises in two areas: Figural (Thinking Creatively with Pictures/Drawings) and Verbal (Thinking Creatively with Words). Through these exercises, children or adults demonstrate their creative abilities.

The following are modified examples (Russell, 1981) of the Incomplete Figures Test and the Circles Task from the TTCT (Torrance, 1998).

Incomplete Figures Test is a nonverbal test. Responses are evaluated on originality, closure, complexity and productivity. Figure 2.1 is an example of a modified incomplete figures test. The following instructions are given to the person taking this test: "By adding lines to the figures below, make something that no one else will think of. Try to make as many different things as you can. Keep working until you are finished, and then make up a name for each one."

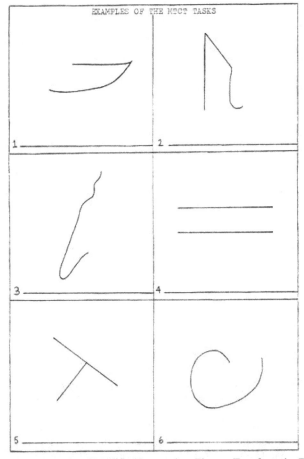

Figure 2.1: Example of Modified Incomplete Figures Test from the TTCT
Source: Russell, C., 1981, modified from Torrance, 1998.

The modified Circles Task (the original had nine circles rather than six) is a nonverbal test. Responses are evaluated on originality, closure, complexity, and productivity. Figure 2.2 is an example of a modified circles task. The following instructions are given to the person taking the test: "See how many things you can make from the circles below. The circle should be the main part, and you may draw inside and outside of the circle. Try to think of things that no one else will. Them make up a name for each and tell me what it is."

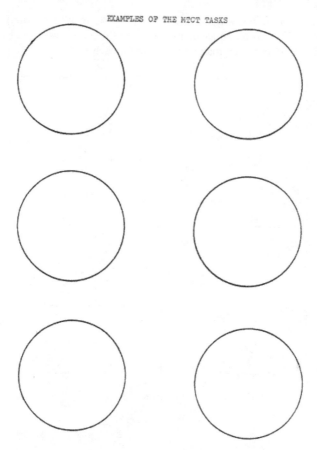

Figure 2.2: Example of Modified Circles Task from the TTCT
Source: Russell, C., 1981, modified from Torrance, 1998.

The TTCT was first developed in 1966 and re-normed five times: in 1974, 1984, 1990, 1998, and 2008. A decline in creativity scores of the TTCT has been observed and occurs at approximately ages 5, 9, 12, and 17 (Torrance, 1962). Torrance suggests this decline might be due to a change in authority or other transitions in school and the child's life (e.g. transition from preschool to kindergarten).

Kim (2011) identified a decrease in creative thinking scores since the 1990s. Kim studied TTCT scores from a sample including 272,599 kindergartens through 12th grade students and adults. Results indicated that since 1990, although IQ scores rose, creative thinking scores have significantly decreased. The decrease for kindergartners through third graders was the most significant (Kim, 2011). Kim stated, "The decline begins in young children, which is especially concerning as it stunts abilities which are supposed to mature over a lifetime. Efforts to encourage creativity should begin in preschool or before" (Kim, 2011, p. 1).

For many years, several psychologists have studied children's drawing as ways of measuring creativity (Goodenough, 1928; Grippen, 1933; Torrance, 1959; Urban, 2004). However, Lewis (1972) stated that most research and literature has focused on justifying art as a means to dexterity, and fine motor and coordination development; then on artistic skills and creativity abilities. Research by Reichenber-Hackett (1964) utilizing children's drawings as a measure incorporated both the children's drawings and the adult's teaching style. Reichenber-Hackett (1964) evaluated 120 preschool children's drawings, investigating influences of the preschool curriculum on potential creativity and artistic abilities. He evaluated drawings on the basis of: utilization of space, size of figure, placement of figure, scattering and jumbling of parts, use of utensils, peculiarity of drawing, clarity of lines, and scribbling. Analysis indicated a relationship between supportive, yet non-dictative teaching style and higher creative artistic abilities.

As stated earlier, Torrance (1974) described creativity as a natural human process which involves and fulfills strong human needs. Factors in the environment or within the children can interfere with this human process. These factors need to be identified and efforts to design environments that foster, and nurture creativity need to be put into practice. One such interference of creativity is conformity. Hurlock (1972) stated a major factor that interferes with the development of creativity is conformity in educational methods.

Education and Conformity

Educational practices have been evaluated for their contribution to creativity for many years. Some writers claim that conformity caused by a highly-structured curriculum (e.g. authoritarian treatment with only one correct way, one correct answer), stifles creativity. Other research supports that some educational practices, such as directive teaching, are incompatible with the needs, interests and behaviors of creative students, and suppress the development of creative abilities. Wodtke and Wallen (1965) found that higher controlling 4th grade teachers allowed less self-initiated talk in the classroom than the lower controlling teachers.

> "Our schools no longer serve our children," says creativity expert, Sir Ken Robinson. He goes on to state, "Our current system is based on the conformity principle, but the human life thrives on diversity" (Robinson, 2014). Sir Ken Robinson is an author and advisor on educational reform in the United Kingdom; he has served in this capacity since the 1980s. He notes how we are born inherently diverse, yet our educational systems have become preoccupied with conformity. "Our school system's industrial roots are the reason that schools are more interested in conformity than creativity. Compliance—another industrial virtue—is also prized by schools. Kids don't come in standard shapes and their minds don't either. Our real resource is the creative capacity of its people. Life is not linear, it's organic" (Robinson, 2014).

Conformity in the classroom has also been caused by a structured and precise time schedule, according to some researchers (Lark, Lewis & Luca, 1967). These authors state that time boundaries limit children's freedom to work at their own pace. Similarly, other researchers warn that time limits could inhibit novel and unconstrained thinking in children. Prescribed patterns and copying also contribute to conformity in the classroom. Lowenfeld stresses that one should not impose images or forms of expression on the child, because the child has had her/his own experiences and needs to individually express those events. Hildegrand (1974) guards against emphasis on the product, which results in hindering the process of the child's creative expression.

Studies also support the concept that the authoritarian treatment of intelligent adolescents causes lack of originality, as well as conformity of thought and expression, but results in "good behavior." These authors felt that many educations set curriculums caused repression of independence and constructive play, and resulted in environmental limitations on mental and creative development. Rogers (1975) stated that education was turning out conformists, stereotypes, and individuals whose education was completed rather than freely creative and original thinking individuals.

OTHER BARRIERS AND OBSTACLES TO CREATIVITY

According to The Creative Spirit, a book based on a PBS series on creativity, authors Daniel Goleman, Paul Kaufman, and Michael Ray point out these common ways adults discourage creativity in children:

1. Surveillance—Hovering over children, making them feel that they are constantly being watched while they are working, under constant observation, discourages the risk-taking, and the creative urge goes underground and hides.

2. Evaluation—When we constantly evaluate and judge, we make children worry about how they are doing, and they ignore satisfaction with their accomplishments.

3. Rewards—The excessive use of prizes deprives a child of the intrinsic pleasure of creative activity.

4. Competition—Putting children in a win-lose situation, where only one person can come out on top, negates the process that children progress at their own, individual rates.

5. Over-control—Constantly telling children how to do things often leaves children feeling like their originality is a mistake and any exploration is a waste of time.

6. Restricting choice—Telling children which activities they should engage in instead of letting them follow where their curiosity and passion lead restricts active exploration and experimentation that might lead to creative discovery and production.

7. Pressure—Establishing grandiose expectations for a child's performance often ends up instilling aversion for a subject or activity. Unreasonably high expectations often pressure children to perform and conform within strictly prescribed guidelines can deter experimentation, exploration, and innovation. Grandiose expectations are often beyond children's developmental capabilities.

(Plume, 1993, pp. 61-62)

Unfortunately, these practices are all too common in many educational settings. Besides squelching creativity and discouraging problem solving, these practices can cause anxiety, frustration, and stress. This negative impact has potential to be greater for children with differing abilities. For example, using these practices with children with motor challenges, rather than promoting choice and free creative expression, could affect future creative efforts and negatively impact self-esteem. These methods could also cause increased inappropriate behavior and frustration in children with behavioral challenges. A child on the autism spectrum, for example, could become so distracted by the thought of earning a reward that he or she is not able to complete the art project. If a child with tactile defensiveness (e.g. child with Autism, Sensory Processing Disorder, Nonverbal Learning Disorder, etc.) has difficulties with textures is allowed enough time to desensitize to the material, or allowed to use gloves to finger paint, this child might feel encouraged and motivated to try other art experiences. Respecting the child's pace without rushing is important. We must do our best to use methods to motivate and foster creativity for every child, and approaches need to be sensitive to individuality.

Individuality in Education

Some researchers and authors have emphasized the need for individuality in schools (e.g. non-authoritarian, offering a variety of solutions and encouraging self-expression), to nurture creativity. Years ago, Hildebrand (1974) stated that adding a non-structured curriculum would be adding creativity to the curriculum, stating that divergent thinking was still in the "embryo state" and must be nurtured. Goodale (1970) also stated that the emphasis should be on the personal and individual development of the learner, rather than the types of materials used in the classroom. Patterns and use of models tend to hinder the creative process and not offer individual freedom. Recent research (Boat, Dinnebeil, & Bae, 2010; Russo, 2013; Bongiorno, 2014) also supports individualizing the curriculum and process art based on the individual learner. Social learning theory has indicated that the quality and quantity of creative responses were greatly affected by the model she or he observed (Truman, 2011).

MacKinnion (1962) found that adults in various occupations who scored highly on creativity assessments, recalled as children, they were allowed to develop individuality and work at their own unique pace. These individuals also felt that their skills and creativity were not pushed, but allowed to develop.

Harms (1972) wrote that a teacher could guide the child's creative growth by arranging an appropriate learning environment where the child could function with minimum assistance from an adult. This physical setting of materials should be functional for the individual child. Shelves should be open and easily accessible so that children are able to experience a sense of relaxed boundaries that help to facilitate the creative process. Torrance (1965) reported creative thinking abilities revealed individual preferences for ways of learning. For example, creative persons preferred to learn through experimentation, manipulation, inquiry, and spontaneity.

Individuality in educational approaches also directly relates to working with children with varying abilities. Children with special needs can successfully learn and participate with individual accommodations and modifications based on their needs. For example, having a physically accessible environment with enough space to move and materials that are easy to access, promotes participation for a child who uses a wheelchair or walker. The accessible environment also allows the child to work and play alongside of her or his peers. Russell (1996) found that young children with special needs participated significantly more in creative movement activities when they were in inclusive versus non-inclusive groups of children.

In summary, these authors encouraged individuality in the classroom through a low structured or less teacher directed curriculum. This is described as an environment offering a variety of materials for function rather than structure, and offers independence and freedom for self-expression and creative growth.

CHARACTERISTICS OF DIVERGENT THINKING AND STRATEGIES TO PROMOTE CREATIVE THOUGHT

Divergent thinkers tend to have certain characteristics in common. According to Schirrmacher (2012) and Torrance (1969) characteristics of divergent or creative thinking include:

- Fluency - many ideas or solutions; emphasis on number of ideas produced

- Flexibility - different ideas which cross categories or break boundaries; ability to think in another way or change direction

- Originality - unique or original ideas; one-of-a-kind idea

- Elaboration - add details to the ideas; expanding to make it more complex

We can include creative thinking activities in our daily curriculum, offering divergent thinking opportunities that stretch the imagination and promote creative thinking and problem solving. Integrating divergent thinking, creative problem solving, and open-ended questions into the daily routine and curriculum will value and promote creative thinking. Schirrmacher (2006) offers some wonderful activities to facilitate children's creative thinking. Examples of these activities include:

> What Would Happen If? Ask children to answer (could tape record or print answers), what would happen if: refrigerators ate food; dreams came true; you never had birthdays, etc.?

> Unusual Uses: Present items such as: as shoe, cork, golf tee, and shoebox for children to inspect. Have them think of different ways they could use these items.

> Your Own Book Ending: Have children make up their own ending to a story, stopping just before the end when you are reading it to children.

> Just Suppose: Have children finish the "Just Suppose" with an ending. For example: Just suppose: You found $1 million dollars, how would you spend it? You could be someone else, who would you be? You could be invisible for a day, where would you go and what would you do?

> How Many Ways: With a small group of children, ask: How many ways can you: celebrate a birthday? make a new friend? spend a Saturday? be happy?

> Finish my Picture: Provide the child with paper on which a few angled markings or partial lines of a shape with straight or curved lines have been placed. Ask the child to complete the picture, and have them share with you or peers. Challenge children to come up with their own ideas, not looking at others. Finish my picture (Figure 2.3) is a great one-on-one activity.

(Schirrmacher, 2006, p. 29 – 34)

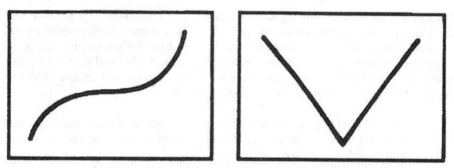

Figure 2.3: Example of Finish my Picture Activity

Picture Possibilities: Show children the lines or patterns below, or draw them on the board or paper. Allow time to think about possible meanings. Ask what it could be what else. Encourage more ideas. Then turn the paper to look at the lines or patterns from another angle, and ask again. An example of picture possibilities is shown in Figure 2.4.

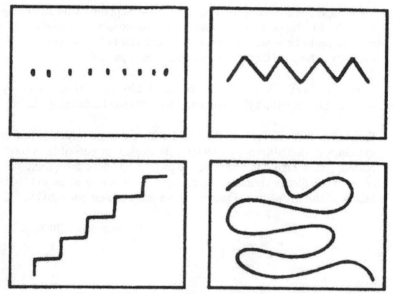

Figure 2.4: Example of Picture Possibilities Activity

"Imagination is more important than knowledge."

-    Albert Einstein

Meaningful Interactions to Promote Creativity

Appropriate, meaningful, and individualized interactions can foster and promote creative thinking and processes in young children. These interactions need to be exchanges, with communication in both directions. Listening is an essential part of this exchange. In order for these meaningful interactions to be successful both listening, and the wait time sometimes required for children to respond (especially for children with special needs) are crucial. Kim stated, "Also lost in the rush to provide ever more stimuli and opportunities to children is time for adults to listen to their children. Parents and teachers must personally provide receptive, accepting, and engaged psychological support to encourage creativity" (Kim, 2011, p, 10). Each child needs meaningful and positive interactions to enhance their creative expressions.

Meaningful interactions include appropriate feedback to a child's creative process, which is individualized and accommodated as needed. Being a "mirror" for the child's efforts and reflecting verbally what the child is doing provides opportunity to describe this process using art vocabulary. These interactions also provide reinforcement for children on an individual basis. Using the elements of art (e.g. commenting on: color, line, mass or volume, pattern, shape or form, space, and texture) as a framework for our verbal response, can offer both information and concept formation. These comments invite further discussion and encourage the child's discovery and process. During this dialogue, it is important to note nonverbal communication, both yours and the child's. Keep the dialogue going IF the child wishes, yet respect the children's need to work without disruptions. Expanded discussion and suggestions for appropriate, meaningful, and individualized feedback are included in Chapter 4.

Creativity and Time

In discussion of methods to promote artistic creativity in young children, the element of time—or lack of it—can greatly impact the creative process. Russell (2012) emphasizes the significance of time in relation to the creative process of children with the following statement, "I cannot over emphasize the importance of what we do and how we do it! It is amazing how children can be engaged and focused when you foster creativity with the right environment, materials, interactions, and TIME! We tend to structure so much of their young lives and hurry them through processes; rather than slowing down for learning through play, giving them TIME to show us how much they know, and allowing TIME for problem solving opportunities, and TIME to create" (Russell, 2012, p. 2).

The Hurried Child by David Elkind (1981) is a classic that has helped shape our early childhood profession. Elkind describes the harmful effect of hurrying our children through life. According to Elkind, we confuse the boundaries of what is age or developmentally appropriate by expecting and imposing too much too soon. We pressure them to grow up too soon, and expect them to take on the content, haste, and pace of adults, while they hunger for play and the innocence of their childhood. Elkind explains that young children are treated like miniature adults, needing to adjust, cope and survive the stresses of life (Elkind, 1981, p.42). Children need more than to simply survive childhood; they need time to learn, to process, to play, to create, to be a child!

Artistic Creative Experiences Related to Theory-Based Best Practices

Creative activities have great developmental and academic/pre-academic benefits, as noted in Chapter 1, Table 1.1. The last benefit notes, "success-oriented with no wrong way of completing a project" makes creative activities particularly beneficial to children who have special needs. Karns (n.d.) stated, "The value of art activities for children with special needs can't be overemphasized! They provide all young children, and especially children with special needs, with an outlet for expression and creativity that enhances learning." With a success-oriented philosophy of creative arts, the focus becomes "how", to accommodate rather than "if." Keeping a "can do" attitude will promote full participation and involvement of a child with differing abilities. Karns also adds, "Art activities are good ways to foster self-esteem. Because no work of art is ever 'wrong,' children with special needs don't need to worry that their art won't be 'as good as' others!" (retrieved from: http://www.scholastic.com/browse/subarticle.jsp?id=4082) Authentically creative experiences can indeed offer success when a child with differing abilities might be facing many challenges. This is also an opportunity for children with special needs to experience success and satisfaction. Being able to create independently, making one's own choices, working without time restrictions or a right or wrong way, can enhance the creative process for all children, particularly children who have special needs. Children with differing abilities often experience less control, depend on others for many aspects of their lives, and have fewer choices. Authentic creative experiences include many choices and options, locus of control, and respects individual expression. Creative experiences can also provide an outlet for many emotions, from stress, sadness, and frustration to excitement, joy, and enthusiasm. A child experiencing anger or depression might benefit from covering the entire paper with some darker color or smashing the clay as a sensory outlet. He or she may need this before focusing on a subject or topic for the artwork. A child might draw what it feels like to have his parents divorcing, a grandparent's death, or a new sibling. A sibling of a child with who has physical challenges and uses a wheelchair might depict herself and her sister on a mountain top. More specific examples of developmental benefits of creative activities for all children are further discussed and illustrated in chapters 4, 5 and 8.

EARLY CHILDHOOD PLAY-BASED LEARNING AND CREATIVITY

Some early childhood educational practices take the directly teach skills approach, feeling this is the only way to really teach children. Young children learn best through play. Play-based activities and environments give children the opportunity to learn about new concepts and ideas through play.

Educators Friedrich Froebel and Maria Montessori strongly supported the importance of play. Froebel, who developed the first kindergarten, viewed play as the most important path to learning. Montessori's curriculum also focused on learning through play, with children choosing what to play with and how. Observing children at play is at the heart of both of these methods. Through observation, teachers can identify what children are interested in, and can facilitate and develop the curriculum around those interests. (Downey & Garzoli, 2007, p. 1)

The importance of play and prioritizing the interests and needs of young children was strongly supported by John Dewey. "Dewey advocated an education for young children that was embedded in their current experience in the world that surrounded them. He thought play could be used to help children reconstruct their experience and to gain meaning from it" (Saracho & Spodek, 1995, p. 133). At that time in history, play was clearly categorized as different from work, such as chores. However, today we continue to value learning through play in early childhood education. Different program models view play uniquely to their philosophy.

Clear recommendations about learning through play have been collaboratively noted within the Developmentally Appropriate Practice in Early Childhood Programs Serving Children from Birth through Age 8, Third Edition published by NAEYC. They emphasized the importance of learning and development through play, as well as the complexity of play. "Rather than diminishing children's learning by reducing the time devoted to academic activities, play promotes key abilities that enable children to learn successfully. In high-level dramatic play, for example, the collaborative planning of roles and scenarios and the impulse control required to stay within the play's constraints develop children's self-regulation, symbolic thinking, memory, and language—capacities critical to later learning, social competence, and school success." The statement further noted, "Because of how they spend their time outside of school, many young children now lack the ability to play at the high level of complexity and engagement that affords so many cognitive, social, and emotional benefits. As a result, it is vital for early childhood settings to provide opportunities for sustained high-level play and for teachers to actively support children's progress toward such play. (NAEYC Position statement on DAP)

Reggio Emilia schools of northern Italy have been committed to quality early childhood education and support for families for over 60 years. Many theorists including Rousseau, Pestalozzi, Froebel, Dewey, Piaget, and Vygotsky influenced founder of Reggio Emilia schools, Loris Malaguzzi.

> Learning is viewed within an interactive-constructivist framework. It is something that children do, not something done to them. Based on Dewey's concept of progressive education, schools should promote children's natural curiosity and creativity as well as active interaction with their community. Children are actively learning - exploring, inquiring, problem solving, and representing their experience in a number of ways.
>
> Fox & Schirrmacher, 2015, p. 150

"It is something that children do" as a key phrase. This emphasizes that children are motivated, inspired, and enthused about their learning. More so, they have some control over the content, and individuality is honored and fostered.

The Reggio philosophy emphasizes that "children learn better in a child-led environment which allows for the curriculum to be developed based on their interests: Classrooms have dramatic play, dress-up areas, but early reading and math skills are not specifically taught" (Fox & Schirrmacher, 2015, p. 150). Rather, the teacher uses the children's own interests as the focus for the curriculum. These individual interests and ideas are guided via multiple approaches, such as visual arts, print, drama, puppetry, music and dance. Reggio supports children as the teachers, and learning through what Reggio describes as, 100 Languages of Learning. "Children proceed in an investigation of generating and testing their hypotheses. They are encouraged to depict their understanding through one of many symbolic languages, including drawing, sculpture, dramatic play, and writing. This is a way that children are active learners and are 'learning with all senses or from action to thought" (Samuelsson & Williams, 2007, p. 19).

Documentation of the creative process and product is a major component of the Reggio approach, and used to illustrate and reflect on the process and inspire thinking. Through use of various types of media (photographs, videos, iPads, etc.) as well as children's creations, the teacher listens closely and carefully observes children. Documentation of words, photographs, videos of experiences, drawings, or other creations offers insight to what is understood and important to children. This documentation also provides feedback for the adult to reflect upon regarding her or his work with children. In addition, the documentation content offers the foundation for any changes to methods or curriculum based on the information. Documentation also serves as an affective and illustrative tool for sharing experiences with families about their children's learning experiences, for parent/teacher conferences, as well as archiving classroom/school activities.

In addition, Reggio Emilia regarded the environment as the third teacher. "The environment incorporates multiple different uses for the development of learning. Stars in the sky can be used to discover what gas is (science) and introduce an interest in Space and the sky. It can provide language development through learning new vocabulary and reading books all about stars and the planets. Children can learn fine motor skills through painting, drawing, and cutting out their own stars. Counting the stars can develop math skills and children telling their own stories about stars can create magical moments of social development, while children practice cognition and understanding of their world around them" (Downey & Garzoli, 2007). This example also illustrated a major component of the Reggio philosophy and practices, where the use of long term projects and cooperative learning are valued "long term projects are common, and cooperative learning is encouraged" (Jacobson, 2007). Projects can be incorporated over days, weeks or months, depending on the continued or shifted interest of the child.

Stemming from the Reggio Emilia philosophy, is the use of the Project Approach to education. The Project Approach is powerful. It uniquely and authentically follows the interests of the child or children, fostering exploration and discovery. According to The Project Approach website (http://projectapproach.org/), "Children have a strong disposition to explore and discover. The Project Approach builds on natural curiosity, enabling children to interact, question, connect, problem-solve, communicate, reflect, and more. This kind of authentic learning extends beyond the classroom to each student's home, community, nation, and the world. It essentially makes learning the stuff of real life and children active participants in and shapers of their worlds" (http://projectapproach.org/).

The Project Approach highly values the child's individuality and self-esteem. Self-esteem should be fostered and cultivated in the classroom. Regarding self-esteem, the Project Approach website noted, "The climate of a classroom is important for appropriate self-esteem to grow in relation to learning. Students can best develop self-esteem in a climate where individual differences are appreciated. They are helped by the setting of clear expectations in terms of classroom work, behavior, and relationships. They are also helped when teachers and other students appreciate and acknowledge their positive contributions to classroom life and learning" (http://projectapproach.org/special-topics/self-esteem/). Regarding competition and educational standards focus, this approach warns that competition with peers can be discouraging for children and might not promote their learning. Central to the Project Approach is fostering creative and original thinking, seeking alternative outcomes without barriers, and observing growth based on one's own earlier performance—thus building on self-esteem and pride in one's own accomplishments.

The Project Approach encourages children to explore divergent or alternative outcomes. It allows different responses at various levels, which also fosters children's contributions in original and creative ways, as well as individual responses at many levels. Additionally, the Project Approach encourages children to evaluate their own achievement with their earlier performance, thus providing a healthy sense of competition.

An excellent, detailed example of the Project Approach is A Study of Bones as elaborated on the following website: http://ecrp.uiuc.edu/v5n1/kogan.html. The project originated and was implemented with 5-year-old students at Eton school in Mexico City. The program utilized local professionals to allow the children to directly experience various technological medical tools to learn about bones and the human body. They began the project with the children's personal stories and objects from home, then moved on and included local medical professionals. This project illustrated wonderful examples of integrating the arts, math, science, and language arts. (Early Childhood Research and Practice, 2003).

Sylvia Chard and Lillian Katz have written extensively about the Project Approach, which originated partially from the work of American educator and philosopher John Dewey (1859-1952). Chard has helped teachers implement the Project Approach, while integrating the curriculum and demonstrating the power of children's drawings. Chard designed and maintains a website on the Project Approach, as well as a blog where she discusses topics of interests to teachers. She offers a free download of a guide to the Project Approach at: http://project approach.org/wp-content/uploads/2014/10/Project-Approach-Study-Guide.pdf. This guide could be helpful for getting started with the Project Approach. It offers many helpful tools, suggestions, and methods for fostering creativity and authentic projects.

A balance of both child-guided and teacher-guided experiences is recommended by NAEYC's DAP position statement. "Both child-guided and teacher-guided experiences are vital to children's development and learning. Developmentally appropriate programs provide substantial periods of time when children may select activities to pursue from among the rich choices teachers have prepared in various centers in the room. In addition to these activities, children ages 3–8 benefit from planned, teacher-guided, interactive small group and large-group experiences" (Copple, C., & Bredekamp, S. Eds., 2009). Therefore, early childhood educators and other professionals working with young children and families must strive for a balance, whatever the theoretical foundation of a program or services. This balance and curriculum must constantly be reviewed and reevaluated to ensure children's creativity is being fostered, not stifled.

In summary, practices in education have been evaluated concerning their contribution to creativity. Some research and theorists felt that too much conformity in education was a problem and hindered the process of creativity. This conformity has been caused by highly structured curriculum, including authoritarian and directive teaching using standard instructions and practices driven solely by standards. The need for individuality and approaches that foster individual freedom and development has been expressed to nurture creativity. The physical environment should be functional, allowing for different ways of learning. Individuality and approaches that foster individual freedom also makes inclusive learning and environments possible.

Studying elements of creativity in young children helps identify reasons why creativity is lost or declines. Artistic creativity is a favorite area for young children's expressions and demonstration of what they know. As noted earlier, elements in children's drawings have been studied to measure artistic growth and creativity. Understanding the elements and principles of art to observe in any level of artwork gives a framework from which to measure growth of children, as well as observe and appreciate other artwork. In addition, the developmental stages of children's art growth will assist in noting and measuring an individual child's art growth progress.

Developmental Stages of Creative Art

First, a brief look at the Elements and Principles of Visual Arts will be helpful to relate to children's art growth stages. Although a more extensive discussion can be found in Chapter 4 Understanding the Elements and Principles of Art and the Importance of Art Appreciation for Effective Teaching, the following descriptions will provide some background.

- Line is a visible mark between two points, with width, direction, and length in 2D artwork. In 3D, we see outlines of the form.

- Color is produced when light is on an object and reflects back to the eye.

- Shape/form Shape is use of area in 2D space or outside form; Form is the volume of 3D.

- Texture describes what 3D work actually feels like to the touch; in 2D there can be a visual feel of texture.

- Space the area the artist uses, as determined by the size of the paper, canvas, wood, stone, etc. There is positive (space taken up by created things) and negative space (space surrounding or between things).

- Value is the lightness and darkness used.

- Mass or volume relates to the height, width, and length of 3D artwork.

- Pattern demonstrates repetition or reoccurring sequence or alternating of shapes, colors, textures, lines, etc.

- Design or Composition involves the overall success of arrangement and artwork, relating more to the adult artist.

- Balance is demonstrated how an artist incorporates positive and negative space. This involves two ways: symmetrical (evenly or equally balanced) and asymmetrical (not evenly or equally balanced).

These elements can be seen in two-dimensional (2D) and three-dimensional (3D) works of art at any level of artistic creation. Not every artwork has all of these elements and principles contained in them. The most salient elements in children's artwork, as well as developmentally appropriate elements and terminology with which to start are: lines, color and shape. Even in infancy it is possible to notice and talk with babies about these elements when looking at paintings, drawings, sculptures, and another artwork.

Developmental Stages of Artistic Growth

Several authors have written about artistic development (Kellogg, 1970; Lowenfeld, 1957; Goodenough, 1928). The stages of artistic growth are universal and have even been linked with the first marks of the human race. Kellogg, in Analyzing Children's Art (1970), found 20 basic types of scribbles alone, which are also universal. How many of us have looked at our infant's and toddler's scribbles as JUST scribbles? Kellogg presents children's artistic development in 5 universal stages:

a) Scribble with 20 basic scribbles, under age 2 years. Figure 2.5 is a sample of 20 basic scribbles.

THE BASIC SCRIBBLES

Scribble 1		Dot
Scribble 2		Single Vertical Line
Scribble 3		Single Horizontal Line
Scribble 4		Single Diagonal Line
Scribble 5		Single Circular Line
Scribble 6		Multiple Vertical Line
Scribble 7		Multiple Horizontal Line
Scribble 8		Multiple Diagonal Line
Scribble 9		Multiple Circular Line
Scribble 10		Roving Open Line
Scribble 11		Roving Enclosing Line
Scribble 12		Zigzag or Waving Line
Scribble 13		Single Loop Line
Scribble 14		Multiple Loop Line
Scribble 15		Spiral Line
Scribble 16		Multiple Line Overlaid Circle
Scribble 17		Multiple Line Circumference Circle
Scribble 18		Circular Spread Out
Scribble 19		Single Crossed Circle
Scribble 20		Imperfect Circle

Figure 2.5: Sample of 20 basic scribbles (adapted from Kellogg, 1970)

b) Placement as scribbles become more controlled, placement becomes important, two to three-years-old. Figure 2.6 is an example of Kellogg's placement stage.

Placement Stage (2 – 3 years)
As children's scribbles become more controlled, they pay attention to placement. Some examples of placement are below:

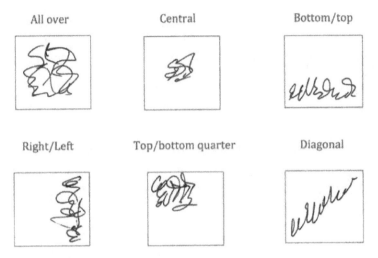

Figure 2.6: Sample of Kellogg's Placement Stage

c) Shapes starts with scribbles emerging into shapes, then progress to single outlines, three-years-old. Figure 2.7 shows Kellogg's shapes stage.

Shape Stage (3 years)

Shapes emerge from Scribble Stage:

Figure 2.7: Sample of Kellogg's Shapes Stage

Diagrams using shapes, including: circle (and oval); cross; X, square (and rectangle); triangle, and odd or organic form, three-years-old. Figure 2.8 is a sample of Kellogg's diagrams stage.

The Six Diagrams (3 years)

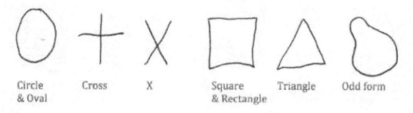

| Circle & Oval | Cross | X | Square & Rectangle | Triangle | Odd form |

Figure 2.8: Sample of Kellogg's Diagrams Stage

d) Design

The designs stage has two components: combines and aggregates.

Combines two united diagrams form a combine. This is typically demonstrated by three to four-year-old children.

Aggregates three or more united diagrams form an aggregate. This is also typically demonstrated by three to four-years-old. Figure 2.9 shows an example of Kellogg's designs stage.

Design Stage (3 – 4 years)

Two diagrams unite to form a combine, such as:

Examples:

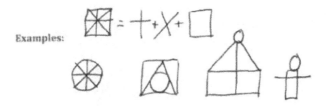

Three or more diagrams unite for form an aggregate, such as:

Examples:

Figure 2.9: Sample of Kellogg's Designs Stage

e) Pictorial (with early and later substages) structured designs start to look like recognizable objects, four to five-years-old. Figure 2.10 is a sample of Kellogg's pictorial stage.

Figure 2.10: Sample of Kellogg's Pictorial Stage

Remember, these are not just age related, but are developmentally related. Individual children might or might not reach all of these stages, depending on their developmental abilities.

Lowenfeld and Brittain (1987) teamed together to present stages of artistic development, listing substages in great detail, noted by Schirrmacher (2006, p. 118–120).

Stage I: Scribbling

a) Random Scribbling (1 ½ - 2 ½ years) Infants/toddlers first marks are random and uncontrolled. They make marks on any surface, with or without tools (e.g. in sand, dust on a table, paper or walls). Fine motor is still developing, so marks are large, and big surfaces are needed for movement. The focus is process with little concern about a product. Figure 2.11 is a sample of random scribbling (1 ½ - 2 ½ years).

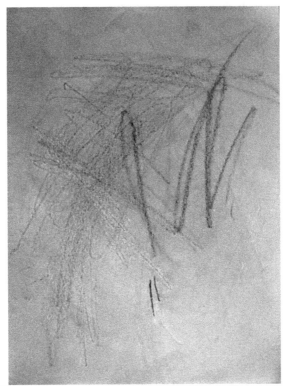

Figure 2.11: Sample of Lowenfeld's Random Scribbling Stage

b) Controlled Scribbling (2, 2 ½ - 3 years) Toddlers gain more motor control, as well as cognitive development, and make the cause effect connection of their actions and the marks they are creating. They experiment with their lines and control of their scribbles to create lines that zigzag, emerge into shapes, and fill the space.

Figure 2.12: Sample of Kellogg's Controlled Scribbling Stage

c) Named Scribbling (3, 3 ½ - 4 years) As toddlers develop, they gain
    more control over their fine motor movements, resulting in more
    refined shapes, combining shapes and design, using a variety of
    materials, and naming their forms. This was later termed the Basic
    Forms Stage.

Figure 2.13: Sample of Lowenfeld's Named Scribbling Stage

Stage II: Preschematic (4–7 years)

Figure 2.14: Sample of Lowenfeld's Preschematic Stage

Stage III: Schematic (7–9 years)

Figure 2.15: Sample of Lowenfeld's Schematic Stage. Mixed media by Tally, age 9.

There are additional stages that go through 17 years. According to Kellogg (1970), children prefer to draw humans, as is evident from observing most any child draw. Children often draw themselves and those closes to them. They know their family members and what they do. They may draw how life is, how they would like it to be, what they imagine, or even what they fear. Regardless, humans are a major subject of children's art. Kellogg states that it would take more than an entire book to display and discuss children's depictions of human. Figure 2.16. shows Kellogg's stages of drawing a human (adapted from Kellogg, 1970). Starting from the bottom to top, one can see the evolution of children's drawings of humans from the Basic Scribbles to: Diagram and Combines; Aggregates; Sun faces and figures; Humans with arms attached to head; Humans with varied torsos and arms attached to torsos; to Humans relatively complete (adapted from Kellogg, 1970). This evolution and depictions of humans is evident in other 2D mediums and 3D art, as well.

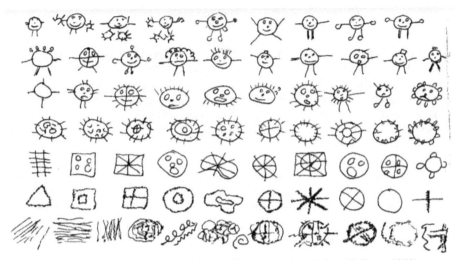

Figure 2.16: Kellogg's stages of drawing a human (adapted from Kellogg, 1970).

These stages are a great source to share with parents to watch the individual growth and development of their children. Consider including this information during parent / teacher conferences. Assist parents in noting the art growth stages in their children's drawings and sculptures.

As with all stages, children develop at their own rate, and individual development may vary. It is vital not to rush children or do their work for them, simply because they are not at the next stage, or because we cannot recognize what their drawing, painting, or sculpture represents. Paraeducators assisting children with special needs should have in-service training or specific instructions regarding how to support children so that they are able to make their own mark and complete their own artwork.

Window into a Classroom: Best Practices for Inclusion

Ms. Patricia, a paraeducator working with Rashmi, offers support by facilitating his independent completion of his painting by allowing him extra time while other children are finishing their projects and cleaning up. He is given the option of putting his unfinished painting on a storage shelf to finish the next day, or allowed to work a bit longer and start the next activity later than other children. Rashmi has fine motor challenges due to Cerebral Palsy. He is focused on his project, but takes longer to apply the paint with his adapted paintbrush (with a thicker handle for grasping ease). Ms. Patricia also arranges the paints closer to Rashmi in non-spill containers for easy access and to prevent spilling paint. These accommodations of allowing extra time and scheduling modifications, along with easier access to materials offer Rashmi a potentially successful experience without lowering expectations of his independent work.

Example of Assessment of Scribbles: Using the chart below, circle each type of mark the child makes. Record how long the child attends to marking with utensils, before switching colors or utensils, and before switching activities.

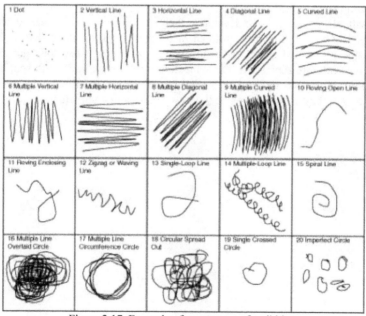

Figure 2.17: Example of assessment of scribbles.

Art Growth Stages Exercise

Practice discussing the art growth stages with various children's drawings. For the following children's drawings, identify the stages observed in each. Art growth stages and discussion about each will be noted following the figures below.

Figure 2.18: Children's Drawing Example #1   Figure 2.19: Children's Drawing Example #2

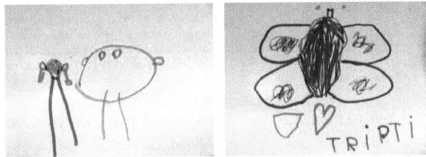

Figure 2.20: Children's Drawing Example #3   Figure 2.21: Children's Drawing Example #4

Discussion of Art Growth Stages Exercise

Art growth stages for each drawing illustrated earlier in this chapter are noted below:

> Children's drawing example #1. According to Kellogg (1970), this child would be in the Scribble Stage, typically observed in children 2 years of age and under. Sometimes older children take pleasure in the sensory act of scribbling, as well. The Placement Stage is also observed. The placement on this drawing is all over the page. Scribbles become more controlled and placement becomes important for two to three-years-old. Lowenfeld and Brittain (1987) would say this child is in Stage I: Scribbling, and either in the substage of Random Scribbling (1 ½ - 2 ½ years) to Controlled Scribbling (2, 2 ½ - 3 years). It appears more controlled, as the child seems to be purposeful in colors chosen and marks placed at different areas of the paper.

Children's drawing example #2. Kellogg (1970) would place this child in the stage of Pictorial (with early and later substages), as the designs are structured, the flowers, sun and grass are recognizable objects, characteristic of children four to five years of age. There is also definitive Placement of this drawing, with purposeful central location of the sun and flower. Placement of the grass across the bottom of the page appears to also be purposely placed. Lowenfeld and Brittain (1987) would say this child is in the Preschematic Stage (4–7 years).

Children's drawing example #3. The child who produced this drawing is in the early substage of the Pictorial stage, according to Kellogg's stages (1970), as the designs are structured, the early drawings of humans are recognizable, with details of eyes and ears. There is also definitive Placement of this drawing, with purposeful locations of both figures. Lowenfeld and Brittain (1987) would say this child is in the Preschematic Stage (4–7 years).

Children's drawing example #4. According to Kellogg's stages, the child who produced this drawing is in the later substage of the Pictorial stage. The design is structured; the butterfly is recognizable, with symmetry and details antenna, eyes, and balanced decorative wings. There is also definitive Placement of this drawing, with purposeful central and balanced location. Lowenfeld and Brittain (1987) would say this child is in the Preschematic Stage (4–7 years).

CREATIVE ARTISTIC ABILITIES, AGE AND INDIVIDUAL DEVELOPMENT

Several artistic growth scales have been developed (Goodenough, 1928; Lowenfeld, 1957; Lee & Lee, 1960; Arnheim, 1974). Research has shown little precise relationship between age and development of artistic creativity in children or their state of drawing. Just as children of the same age chronologically would vary in their mental age, so children's drawings vary individually in their rate of artistic growth (Arnheim, 1974). In addition, the need for understanding individual development and needs of children with differing abilities must be incorporated into quality early childhood art programs. Linking developmentally appropriate inclusive theories and practices into early childhood art educational methods programs make art for all children possible. Educators must provide all children with daily creative opportunities, and advocate nurturing the creative spirit in young children in an effort to assure creative growth throughout their lives.

Chapter Summary and Looking Ahead

This chapter clarified the role creativity and brain development play in children's art experiences, including children with differing abilities. Creativity theories were blended with early childhood theories. The influences of Reggio Emilia, The Project Approach, and art growth developmental stages were provided so that the reader could have a better understanding of children's art growth and learn about strategies for fostering such growth. Likewise, the need for understanding and incorporating developmentally appropriate inclusive theories and best practices into early childhood art was emphasized.

No matter how creativity is defined or understood, all should agree that it is a precious element of human life that should be preserved and nourished. To create conditions that offer free self-expressions and foster individual creative growth is a challenge for all who guide children, and it is a right to live in such an environment. There is no choice regarding differing abilities that some children may have, nor of the environment or culture in which they may be living, however, every effort should be made to preserve their creativity. Art programs and authentic, inclusive art integrated into the curriculum offers a special opportunity for creative growth, as well as growth in all developmental domains. Art thrives in the same atmosphere that offers creative growth. In such an environment, there is a strong message that there is not just one right answer that makes all other answers wrong. There are many ways of accomplishing things and problem solving through the creative process. It is this philosophy that is at the heart of creative art experiences, and it is the responsibility of all who guide children to provide this freedom to each and every child.

Chapter 3 will provide an overview of the Elements and Principles of Art and the importance of aesthetics and art appreciation in early childhood programs. Activities illustrating art elements and principles for parents, teachers and children will be included, as well as discussion of how early learning standards and IFSP/IEP outcomes/goals could be integrated with Elements and Principles of Art and art appreciation.

Suggestions for Additional Reflection and Review

Additional resources on play based learning. Many teachers feel that you must directly teach skills, when young children learn best through play. For example, you do not have to teach during center-time or circle-time only, to create "play-based activities." Young children learn through play, so it is a matter of setting up the activities for children to learn about new concepts and ideas through play. The Reggio Emilia methodology is centered on play-based curriculum and activities. Their website is:

http://www.teachplaybasedlearning.com/first.html

Below are some great web-based article links that define play-based curriculum and provide more information about how to achieve this in early childhood:

http://teachplaybasedlearning.com/8.html

http://www.earlychildhoodnews.com/earlychildhood/article_view.aspx?ArticleID=453

http://www.earlychildhoodnews.com/earlychildhood/article_view.aspx?Artic leID=362

http://wps.prenhall.com/chet_childhood_cluster_1/0,6413,497843-,00.html

View YouTube on Creativity:

http://www.youtube.com/watch?v=iG9CE55wbtY

TED Talks by Sir Ken Robinson: Do schools kill creativity?

http://www.ted.com/talks/ken_robinson_says_schools_kill_creativity/transcri pt?language=en

CREATIVITY JOURNALS FOR ALL AGES

Adult Journal Activity #2

Try to locate any of your childhood artwork. Is it 2D or 3D? How old were you at the time? Analyze the Art Growth Stage you were in by comparing your work to Kellogg's Universal Stages of Art Growth Development. If representational, what else do you remember that was happening in your life at that time that might have influenced the content? For example, was it a representation of your family, your house, your pet, your school, friends, or did it illustrate you going somewhere? Did you have siblings and were they included in the picture? What was the focus of the picture? Was it reality or fantasy? Did it depict emotions? Does it still? If so, were the emotions positive or negative? Take photos of your work and place them in your journal along with your reflections and responses to the questions.

Now take a look at several samples of artwork from the children in your classroom, and/or your own children. Analyze the children's Art Growth Stage by comparing their work to Kellogg's Universal Stages of Art Growth Development. If representational, ask the same questions from above when you looked at your own childhood artwork. Does this give you more information about the child, what she/he understands and how she/he is feeling about themselves, others, or a situation? Take photos of the children's work and place them in your journal along with your reflections and responses to the questions about the children's artwork and their art growth stage, and what you learned about the children.

Child's Personal Creativity Journal Activity #2

Activity #2 for Infants (Birth to walking, or 16 months)

Magical paint bag: Fill a heavy-duty plastic bag that has a zipper closure, three tablespoons of tempera paint. Liquid starch and food coloring could also be used. Securely tape the closure to prevent leakage. Place paint filled plastic bag over white paper or a white surface. Tape down the edges. Briefly demonstrate "drawing" lines, dots, and designs on the bag. Then erase like a magic slate by wiping your hand across the plastic surface. Whatever marks the infant makes, the paint is displaced, and the white surface underneath shows through. The cause and effect can be delightful. Encourage the infant with verbal and non-verbal reinforcement.

This activity can be particularly successful if the infant is hesitant about the tactile aspects of paint. It is also fun for all ages, particularly helpful with children who have sensory integration challenges or tactile defensiveness.

Remember that infants take in everything through their senses, and the infant's journal becomes a documentation of the infant's sensory experiences. Again, please attempt to approach this as a journal, and not a scrapbook. It should include only the infant's work or photos of the sensory experiences.

Activity #2 for Toddlers (walking or 16 months to 3-years-old)

Foil squeezing sculptures: Aluminum foil can be scrunched, bent, squeezed, folded, twisted, or curled, while making fun tinny and crunching sounds. Tear off a piece of foil and place on table, tray, or in the hand of the child. Encourage exploration, and reinforce movements by labeling the action, such as: squeezing, folding, twisting, rolling, pressing, scrunching, stomping, etc. This is a very different feel than clay or play dough. Give the child the time, the space, the materials, and the positive feedback and reinforcement to create! Take photos of the process. Attach photos of the process and one of the child's creations in the journal.

Activity #2 for Preschoolers (ages 3 – 5)

What would happen if? Try the What Would Happen If? activity noted earlier in this chapter (see p. 16). Have children finish the What Would Happen If? with an ending. Ask children to answer (could tape record and print answers), what would happen if: refrigerators ate food; dreams came true; you never had birthdays, etc.? Have the children choose one of these (or others you make up), and think of all of the possibilities. Encourage them to illustrate their ideas in a drawing, painting, or sculpture. Give the child the time, the space, the materials, and the positive feedback and reinforcement to create! Take photos of the process. Attach photos of the process and one of the child's artwork in the journal to accompany their writing.

Activity #2 for Young School-agers

Just suppose. Try the Just Suppose activity noted earlier in this chapter (see p. 39). Have children finish the "Just Suppose" with an ending. For example: Just suppose: You found $1 million dollars, how would you spend it? If could be someone else, who would you be? If you could be invisible for a day, where would you go and what would you do? Have the children choose one of these (or others you create), and think of all of the possibilities. Encourage them to illustrate their ideas in a drawing, painting, or sculpture. Give the child the time, the space, the materials, and the positive feedback and reinforcement to create! Take photos of the process. Attach photos of the process and one of the child's artwork in the journal to accompany their writing.

CHAPTER 3

Understanding the Elements and Principles of Art and the Importance of Art Appreciation for Effective Teaching

Carol L. Russell and Fletcher L. Russell

"I found I could say things with color and shapes that I couldn't say any other way things I had no words for."

- Georgia O'Keeffe

CHAPTER OVERVIEW

This chapter will provide an overview of the Elements and Principles of Art and the Observable Properties of Matter including line, shape and form, space, texture, value (lights and darks), color, and time. The importance of aesthetics and art appreciation in early childhood programs will be discussed. To further the understanding of the Elements and Principles of Art and Art Appreciation, this chapter will include specific activities illustrating these elements and principles for parents and teachers who work with young children. Also included are activities for children that focus on each of these art elements. This chapter will conclude with a general discussion about how early learning standards and IFSP/IEP outcomes/goals can be integrated with Elements and Principles of Art and art appreciation.

What is Art?

Art happens when someone takes any type of material and transforms it into a purposeful statement. Art is taking an idea or feeling and giving it form. Art can be two-dimensional (2D), developed on a flat plane or surface, such as drawing, painting, printmaking, or photography. Art can also be in three-dimensional (3D) form, with spatial depth as well as height and weight. Examples of 3D artwork include sculpture, crafts (glass, wood, metal, fiber, clay), and architecture. Art is everywhere. More discussion on this topic related to aesthetics will be included in Chapter 7 Fostering Children's Understanding and Appreciation of Art.

Visual Art Elements and Principles

Individual taste and preference can determine what art we enjoy or dislike. However, regardless of preference, visual art elements and principles offer criterion by which we can describe, dialogue, give feedback, and critique works of visual arts. Adults can model and familiarize children with this terminology and assist them in understanding how their work, as well as those of famous artists, illustrates these elements and principles.

Elements and principles of art are the observable properties of matter that are briefly defined below:

- Line is a visible mark between two points, with width, direction, and length in 2D artwork. In 3D, we see outlines or edges of the form.

- Color is produced when light is on an object and reflects back to the eye.

- Shape/form Shape is use of area in 2D space or outside form, bending lines into geometric or organic shapes; Form is the volume of 3D.

- Texture describes what 3D work actually feels like to the touch; in 2D there can be a visual feel of texture.

- Space the area the artist uses, as determined by the size of the paper, canvas, wood, stone, etc. There is positive (space taken up by created things) and negative space (space surrounding or between things).

- Value is the lightness and darkness used.

- Mass or volume relates to the height, width, weight and length of 3D artwork.

- Pattern demonstrates repetition or reoccurring sequence or alternating of shapes, colors, textures, lines, etc.

- Balance is demonstrated how an artist incorporates positive and negative space. This involves two ways: symmetrical (evenly or equally balanced) and asymmetrical (not evenly or equally balanced).

- Design or Composition involves the overall success of arrangement of the space in order to achieve unity in artwork.

These elements can be seen in 2D and 3D works of art of any level of artistic creations. Not every artwork contains all of the elements and principles, however, most have several. The most salient elements in children's artwork—as well as the most developmentally appropriate elements and terminology with which to start—are lines, color, and shape. Adults working with young children can self-talk using these elements when looking at paintings, drawings, sculptures, and other artwork starting as early as infancy.

The components of any artwork include subject, form, and content. Simply stated, these are the What, the How, and the Why of the artwork. These are generally defined below:

- Subject or the What: The Subject is the central focus of the artwork: the person, thing, ideas, intension of the work.

- Form or the How: Form refers to how the artwork is organized or arranged. The Form gives the artwork unity.

- Content or the Why: The Content offers the essential meaning or significance of work of art. It gives more to the story, the details, and the elaboration of the meaning.

These components combine to give the artwork Unity. Figure 3.1 displays the components of art.

Figure 3.1: Components of Art: Subject, Form, & Content Creates Unity

Visual Exercise Illustrating Elements and Principles of Art

The following visual illustration exercise is provided to clarify the art elements and principles for better understanding. With it, you should be able to observe and discuss these art elements and principles of organization in any artworks and creative processes. This can be implemented as an activity for yourself or for a child of at least 4 years of age, who is already representational in her/his artwork. A child will dive right into such an activity, unknowingly applying the elements and principles. This natural process is amazing and innate for children who are typically developing. It illustrates creative spirit and is at the heart of creative growth and process. Young children know what a line is, and they naturally create lines. Most young children in the representational stage of art (around the age of 4) know colors and work on organizing principles of balance and emphasis intuitively.

When you look at the examples and illustrations below, little auditory explanation is needed. The lines, shapes, colors, textures, values, space, emphasis, proportion, rhythm, and unity all work within their drawing. When the child starts with the contour line, the line is the most basic element that they are going to express. This does not have to be a black mark; it can be any color with any utensil or even with their finger or toes. When they use the color along with the lines, they are already using two elements. They may use natural colors that match what they are depicting, or they might not choose to do the sky blue or grass green. The sky can be any color they choose. Realistically, multiple colors can be observed in a sunrise or sunset. The child might choose bright colors when remembering a sunset, particularly if someone has talked with him or her about the many colors.

Please note that the following directions for this activity are not totally free expression. It is a lesson to illustrate the art elements and principles. Although there are parts of this exercise that one can freely express details, the steps are important to clearly define and illustrate these elements and principles. The first two steps are sequentially important for the rest of exercise. We do not recommend such a step-by-step approach for authentic creative art.

1. Present the child or adult with the paper of a framing line, creating an edge. Ask the individual to trace her/his hand. This first illustration is a contour of the individual's hand. This is not really copying the hand, rather it is tracing around the hand. The lines depict that individual's hand and it gives the viewer not only an approximate age of the child who is doing this, but it is also the child's distinct mark and hand doing it. If color is used with this first illustration, we already see three art elements of line, color, and shape. Step 1 of illustrating art elements and principles is shown is Figure 3.2.

LINE, COLOR, SHAPE,

Figure 3.2: Illustrating Art Elements and Principles Step 1 (Not in files)

2. Next, we look at giving depth and beginning to fill the space provided. In doing so, we begin to unify the space used. Ask the child or individual to draw a line behind the hand. In doing this we begin to create the space of the ground. This becomes the implied line or horizon line, which indicates depth. In looking at figures and ground, the hand outline becomes the figure because the outline represents something and is recognizable. Step 2 of illustrating art elements and principles is shown is Figure 3.3.

Figure 3.3: Illustrating Art Elements and Principles Step 2

3. Next, ask the child or individual to add whatever details they desire to the drawing, allowing time to include as many ideas as she/he may want. Encourage the child or adult to continue to fill the space provided adding more details and elaboration in this drawing. For example, you might see rings or nail polish or even a red streak on one's depiction of a hand to show where a cat scratched it that morning. As children grow, they notice more details in their environment and they reflect this with elaborations in their artwork. More detailed features appear (e.g. eye lashes, beards, eyebrows, earrings, rings, and other jewelry, nail polish, types of clothing, shoes, etc.).

Texture comes into play when the child fills in the negative space with a mark. It can be deep and heavy with broad strokes of a marker or light and delicate with a fine point of a pencil or pen. Much of this depiction will be with contour lines.

It is interesting to note how children depict the sun. Children will most likely include the sun in outdoor portrayals. The sun is quite abstract to depict, not quite as direct as the moon. We cannot look directly at the sun, but we know what it does and know its size and power. We use words like "rays of sunlight" which can be somewhat abstract to represent. Children usually represent the sun up in the corner, most often not showing the entire shape. Additionally, they will find spaces for birds, trees, even apples on trees, animals, flowers, grass, etc. Step 3 of illustrating art elements and principles is shown is Figure 3.4.

LINE, COLOR, SHAPE
CONTOUR LINE, IMPLIED LINE, GESTURE LINE
TEXTURE, VALUE, SPACE
EMPHASIS, REPETITION (PATTERN), BALANCE,
RYTHEM, VARIETY AND UNITY

Figure 3.4: Illustrating Art Elements and Principles Step 3

Once the hand is done and more details emerge, one can see both descriptive and textured type of lines. In this illustration one can see texture with dots. The skill level and details will vary depending on the child's physical development, general experiences, exposure to using various art materials and mediums, and opportunities to create.

With representational art, children are not just painting abstract forms. They are working on their fine motor skills to control the pencil, crayon, marker, or other drawing utensil. Children are cognitively thinking of the shapes or things they are trying to reproduce while simultaneously putting the marks on paper. They are not referencing shapes or things while they are drawing them. Children draw what they know, feel, remember, and have experienced. They draw what have seen in the environment and nature, which can include themselves, their families, house, pets, trees, flowers, the sun, rainbows, and more. In general, children are representing their world and surroundings.

Depth in space is created when the line behind the hand tracing is drawn. Children do this intuitively, even though they might attempt to erase an overlapping line. This line has given the space more depth. By doing so, the child or adult unified that space with a different type of line. While you or the child continues to draw she/he is also getting the form and the content. Most children will work as long as they need to in order to get the subject down to their liking. Children can demonstrate very complex content, which tells us much about what they know, what is happening in their lives, and how they feel. Remember and note the components of art Subject (the What), Form (the How), and Content (the Why), which combine to give the artwork Unity.

Looking back at the whole content of this exercise, we see first the contour line of the hand followed by the implied line of the horizon and ground behind the contour line which indicates space through overlapping lines and depth. We observe the texture of the ground and the value of the different depth of texture with darkness and lightness. We notice emphasis with the hand tracing being right in the center of the page of the composition and the repetition with fingers and birds (whenever you have two to three different shapes, repetition is built). The composition is balanced, and it moves your eyes around the page, noticing the rhythm and variety of the various lines, colors, textures; which gives the composition unity.

Window into a Classroom: Best Practices for Inclusion

The individual child's mark is like no other. It is hers or his, it is unique, and it is designed and developed only by them. Although you might guide a group of young children to complete this activity, you are not going to get the same drawing from each child. This is the magic of the individual mark, and it is universal. The diversity and individuality of each child's experiences, cultures and abilities add to the distinctiveness of her or his mark. This activity provides a superb visual demonstration of inclusion and diversity that the educator could point out to the students once they have completed their drawings.

Understanding Art Elements and Principles

To assist children in understanding art elements and principles, start with line, color and shape/form and define each at the child's level. Then note these elements and principles in the child's as well as famous artists' artwork. Gradually facilitate children identifying these art elements and principles on their own.

Line: We can ask children, "What is a line?" and record their responses. Then offer your own definitions, such as, a line: a) is a continuation of a dot; b) helps the artist define shape; c) can be big or small; d) can move in different directions, e) be different lengths, heights, thickness, or size; f) can make letters, words, numbers, etc.

Activities to illustrate line: To help children understand line, we can offer activities that focus on lines, such as:

- Painting with or gluing spaghetti (some cooked, some not) on large paper

- Collage comprised of gluing different lengths of yarn, string, thread, toothpicks, pipe cleaners, and other material that clearly defines lines

- Painting or drawing to music and different sounds. Vary the music, noting the different rhythms and how the music can affect how one paints. Add other recorded sounds, such as thunder, water flowing, water dripping, hammering, phone ringing, door squeaking, cat meowing, tiger roaring, etc. The children could even help record the sounds, then play them back, noting the difference and how their lines might change with the sound variation.

- Using glue to make lines and sprinkle with glitter, colored salt, or sand.

- A 3D experience to illustrate lines would be to demonstrate the technique (not the product) of rolling clay in thick or thin rolls (or snake like form). Encourage children to use these rolls to create a sculpture, noting and counting the lines, describing what the lines are doing, and how they vary in thickness, length, and size.

- Another 3-D material is "wiki sticks" or "bendable sticks" that can clearly demonstrate the versatility of lines. These are wax-covered strings that can easily be bent, twisted, and formed in various shapes or representations. This experience illustrates how lines can be formed in different directions to represent something or simply for the pleasure of assembling lines, shapes, and forms. Figure 3.5 shows the chalk string project, blending line and color, resulting in geometric shapes.

Figure 3.5: Chalk String Project Blending Line and Color, Resulting in Geometric Shapes

Color: Color is produced when light shines on an object that reflects back to the eye. This explanation is a bit abstract for young children. Asking children, "What is color" might lead to responses like, "It's everywhere it's a rainbow it's the sun and sky it's what I'm wearing" Studies have shown that children and adults have different reactions to color. Children associate colors with experiences, even with product logos, as young as the age of 2. The classroom environment and activities should offer a plethora of experiences with richness in colors to illustrate the variety, the difference, the blends of primary and secondary colors, the tones, shades, and values. Color mixing is natural for children. Guiding them to recognize how colors can be mixed to make new ones, color identification, and ways to experiment with color and various materials provides experiences to build upon for greater understanding of color. Dialogue noting the element of color in the child's art and observed artwork facilitates this comprehension.

Activities to illustrate color: Experiences to enhance color awareness might include:

- Sorting objects by colors.

- Finger painting with primary colors to observe creation of secondary colors.

Window into a Classroom: Best Practices for Inclusion

For children who have tactile defensiveness or sensory aversion, put the paint in zip lock bags, taping the ends and taping to a tabletop. Taping on a window gives additional brightness to the colors and the mixing process.

- Using two primary colors, drop colors in clear water bottles or clear bowls. Observe colors blending when stirred in a bowl or shaken in the bottle to note secondary colors forming.

- Using gunk (corn starch and water) on a flat pan or sensory table, place a few drops of primary colors (start with two) at opposite ends of the pan or sensory table. Observe and note the mixing of new colors when the primaries are blended. Again, for children who have tactile defensiveness this process can be done using zip lock bags, taping the ends, and taping to a table top or window.

- 3-D experiences include using two primary colors of soft clay or play dough, encouraging squishing and blending of the primary colors to make secondary.

- Read books about color:

  o My Very First Book of Colors by Eric Carle

  o Andy Warhol's Colors Board Book by Susan Goldman Rubin

  o Let's Paint a Rainbow by Eric Carle Figures 3.6, 3.7., and 3.8 show some examples of working with color.

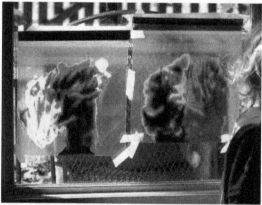

Figure 3.6: Example of mixing primary colors with paint in zip lock bags, taped on the window.

Figure 3.7: The colors in zip lock bags are brilliant when taped on a window.

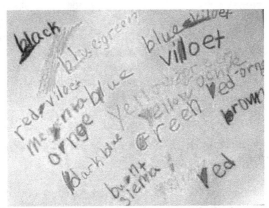

Figure 3.8: As children learn to write, playing with names of color becomes more meaningful and fun!

Shape/Form: Shape is use of area in 2D space or outside form, connecting and bending lines into geometric or organic shapes. Form is the volume of 3D. This outcome of connecting of lines can be large or small, symmetrical or asymmetrical, and abstract or realistic. We tend to be more comfortable with, and discuss the geometric shapes with young children. Often neglected is the appreciation for organic shapes. Geometric shapes are overall concrete, absolute, identifiable, and easily related to mathematics. Organic shapes are abstract, nonfigurative, not easily recognizable, and unpredictable. Some of us must "self-nudge" to reach out of our comfort zone to discover the joy and aesthetics of nonrepresentational and abstract art. More extensive discussion on this issue will be included in Chapter 7 Fostering Children's Understanding and Appreciation of Art.

Activities to illustrate shape/form: To encourage shape and form awareness (both geometric and organic in 2D and 3D forms) try some of the following activities:

- Make large cardboard colored shapes, at least two of each, creating both geometric and organic shapes. During group time, pass out the shapes. Have each child match up with the other child who has the same shape, identifying the shape and color.

- Take these same shapes and have some of the children help you hide one of the shapes on the playground, retaining the matching shape in their hand. The other group of children must find a shape and locate the child who has the matching shape. Ask them to identify the shape and color. Take the easels outside and encourage painting and combining shapes into any creation they wish. Be sure to adapt for children with differing motor or visual abilities.

- Tape large geometric and organic shapes to tabletops. Using primary colors of tempera paint, place two blobs of primary colored paint in zip lock bags. Tape the ends and then tape to the tabletop over each of the geometric shapes. Encourage children to mix the colors, and locate, outline, and identify the shape underneath. This can also be done on trays or flat boxes to retain and repeat the activity. Also try this one on a window, which gives additional brightness to the colors and the mixing process, and more clarity to the bold shape under the bag.

- Assist children in observing shapes in nature, home, and other environments.

- Cut shapes (both geometric and organic) out of sandpaper. Glue them on sturdy pieces of cardboard or poster board. Place them in a small basket or connect them by hole-punching the corners of the shapes and linking them with a spiral ring. Encourage children to feel the shapes and run their fingers along the edges. You can also cut a thick outline of the shapes for the same effect, particularly for older children.

Window into a Classroom: Best Practices for Inclusion

Be sensitive to children who may have tactile defensiveness and offer non-latex gloves or alternative experiences that do not require toughing materials that might be uncomfortable or irritating. Activities such as: finger painting without touching the paint by using large zip-lock bags (strongly sealed with tape) filled with different colored paints; using play dough or play dough recipes that are not gooey or sticky for 3D projects (polymer clay works well); activities that gradually introduce texture, allowing the child to choose whether to observe or participate, what materials to touch or how long to continue an activity.

- Encourage children to dance to music. When the music stops, ask them to make a shape with their bodies. Start with calling out specific shapes for them to represent when they freeze (including both geometric and organic), then have them make their own and identify what shape they have created. Figures 3.9 and 3.10 show examples of how lines, color, and shape combine.

Figure 3.9: Bendable sticks art combines lines, color, and shape for rich art dialogue.

Figure 3.10: Four-year-old child's drawing demonstrating lines, color, and shape for rich art dialogue.

Aesthetics: There are four areas of aesthetics regarding children's art programs.

1. Sensory Experiences: Children come to know their world through their senses. For example, they pay attention to detail, such as ladybugs, leaves, rocks, etc.

2. Beautiful and Creative Experiences: Children need to take time and perceive the beauty in their everyday environments. Encourage time to observe beauty during nature walks, or gazing at rainbows, snowflakes, or the moon, and stars.

3. Time, Space and Materials for Making Art: Encouragement, facilitation, materials, inviting environment, an atmosphere that welcomes creativity, and messes are okay. Plenty of time is allowed for extending the creative process and product.

4. Introduction to the Art World: Children are provided prints of the works of masters and modern artists, Google images, calendars (e.g. Impressionists paintings), and given access to other technology providing images of art. Artwork and prints should be displayed at a child-friendly level for ease of viewing.

According to Striker (1986) in Please Touch: How to Stimulate Your Child's Creative Development Through Movement, Music, Art and Play, people often think of art museums as, "something sophisticated and for adults only" (Striker, 1986, p. 61). She suggests taking infants to museums and encourages adults to point out things that relate to the infant, such as, "Look, there is a baby, just like you" or "See that big house. It's bigger than Grandma's house." Striker (1986) further suggests, "Your comments about paintings in museums or art galleries do not have to be insightful or crammed full of knowledge of art history. Just focus on one aspect of the picture that might interest the child and try to personalize the experience for him or her. If it's an abstract painting, simply focus on one of its characteristics, for example: 'Look at all of those squares, some are big, and some are little.' Or, 'That picture has a lot of yellow in it, just like your room at home does" (p. 62-63).

Introducing children to the foundations of good art and our artistic heritage is important and should be presented at their level. Suggestions for art critique and art discussions with children should be at their developmental level, and include:

- What type of artwork is it? Is it a painting, drawing, weaving, print, sculpture?

- What are the physical properties (e.g. round, square, solid, moving, framed, hard, soft, large, small, etc.?)?

- What is it made out of? Did the artist use clay, wood, paper, paint, yarn, metal, and items from nature/outside?

- What do you see when you look at this artwork? Look at the art elements (line, color, shape, form, design, pattern, space, balance, texture).

- What do you think the artist is trying to say? Try to put the picture into words. What is the message? Pretend the artwork is a book with pictures. What words might go with the artwork? Discuss what you see: people, buildings, animals, events, actions, nature, etc.

- How does it make you feel? Do you feel funny, sad, mad, happy, scared? What did the artist do to make you feel this way?

- Do you like it? Why or why not? What about it makes you like or dislike it? If you could, how might you change it?

More detail about introducing children to the foundations of art and ways to foster art appreciation are included in Chapter 7 Fostering Children's Understanding and Appreciation of Art. Suggestions for art gallery visits with young children and recommendations for art dialogue using Art Elements and Principles will also be provided in Chapter 7.

HOW CAN EARLY LEARNING STANDARDS AND IFSP/IEP OUTCOMES/GOALS BE INTEGRATED WITH ELEMENTS AND PRINCIPLES OF ART AND ART APPRECIATION?

Art and art therapy can address children's IEP goals in all six areas of performance, as noted on the IEP:

- Academic/Cognitive

- Communicative Status

- Motor and Perceptual Skills

- Prevocational/Vocational Skills

- Self-Help Skills

- Social/Emotional Status

Some examples of IEP or IFSP goal or outcomes that could be addressed through art are noted under each of these areas below:

- IEP or IFSP Goal or Outcomes related to Academic/Cognitive areas can be met through art. Examples include:

  o Problem solving, language, reasoning, discovery, thinking and learning through art

  o Art integrated throughout the curriculum (Math/Pre-Math; Science/Sensory; Language Arts, Communication, and Literacy/Pre-Literacy; Social Studies/ Pre-Social Studies; and Expressive Arts Music, Movement, and Theater) offers many possibilities for cognitive and academic growth and progress

- Communicative Status: Children who have challenges in the area of communication can benefit from art activities that include:

  o Expressive language and articulation through art dialogue, telling stories about artwork, sharing and talking about artwork with others

  o Receptive Language through dialogues and listening to others, following techniques

- Written language: Through use of a journal, drawing then adding writing about experiences, feelings, etc.

- Motor and Perceptual Skills: The individual child's challenges in fine and gross motor, and perceptional areas can be addressed through art. For example:

  - Fine motor challenges with grasping and in manipulating objects can be addressed with clay, cutting, and pasting, drawing, collages, sorting and stringing beads, and using various utensils in drawing, painting, collaging, and sculpting.

  - Gross motor challenges such as a lack of coordination or balance can improve with art activities such as making murals, using large paper and large paintbrushes, body tracing, and filling in detail.

  - Sensory motor integration challenges could be addressed through art with the numerous art activities in drawing and manipulating utensils and objects in both 2D and 3D artwork because such activities offer eye/hand coordination practice and visual spatial skills.

  - Visual perception can be strengthened with drawing, collages, clay, noting special relations, directional language, and practice, etc.

- Self-Help Skills can easily be addressed through art by encouraging the child to do more for her/himself, such as getting out materials, accessing or asking for any assistance needed, or cleaning up area when finished with art project.

- Social/Emotional Status: Self-concept, personality, temperament, body image, appropriate expression of feelings, and how one gets along with others can all be areas addressed through art. For example, the following activities could address social/emotional challenges of children:

  - Self-portraits

  - Collaborative projects

  - Making puppets and role playing

○ Offering authentic creative activities that have freedom of expression with reinforcement for self-expression in a safe environment

Chapter Summary and Looking Ahead

This chapter offered an overview of the Elements and Principles of Art. Specific activities for children and adults illustrating Elements and Principles of Art and Art Appreciation were offered. Aesthetics and art appreciation in early childhood programs were noted. This chapter concluded with a general discussion about how early learning standards and IFSP/IEP outcomes/goals can be met and integrated with Elements and Principles of Art.

Looking ahead to Chapter 4 Strategies for Using Art as a Learning and Intervention Tool in Early Childhood, more detail is offered about providing equal access to the arts, and the focus shifts to promoting creative art growth for ALL children. More specifics will be illustrated of how art experiences can meet early learning standards and be integrated into IEPs and IFSPs. Strategies for valuing individual differences, working with young children from culturally diverse backgrounds, and guidelines for accommodating young children with various special needs will also be incorporated. Chapter 4 concludes noting the importance of feedback and how to best respond to children's artistic creativity.

Looking further ahead, and related to the content of this chapter is Chapter 7 Fostering Children's Understanding and Appreciation of Art, which offers more specifics regarding introducing children to the foundations of art, art heritage, and talking with children about art while integrating basic art elements and principles.

Suggestions for Additional Reflection and Review

Take a look at the following children's books related to art. A more comprehensive list can be found in Appendix C.

Aigner-Clark, J. (2002). *Baby Einstein: The ABC's of Art*. New York: Hyperion Books for Children. ISBN: 078680882-9.

Every letter of the alphabet has a masterpiece to provide an example of its sound.

Aigner-Clark, J. (2001). *Baby Einstein: Van Gogh's World of Color*. New York: Hyperion Books for Children. ISBN: 078680805-5.

Children are shown color through the famous paintings of masterpiece artist Vincent van Gogh.

Auch, M. J. (1996). *Eggs Mark the Spot*. New York: Holiday House. ISBN: 0-8234-1305-5 Reading Level: Preschool-Grade 2.

A chicken named Pauline can lay magical eggs. She can copy anything she sees. Her eggs will help solve a mystery at the art gallery.

Black, H. (2000). *A Magic Color Book*. New York: Sterling Publishing. ISBN: 0-8069-0600-6.

Alice likes to paint, but when she discovers colors, everything takes on a new life. This book includes pull-tabs to change the colors on Alice's paintings.

Carle, E. (1992). *Let's Paint a Rainbow*. New York: Scholastic. ISBN: 0-590-32844-1.

This board book teaches children about the colors of the rainbow, as well as the order of these colors.

CREATIVITY JOURNALS FOR ALL AGES

Adult Journal Activity #3

Visit a gallery and complete Art Gallery Visit for Adults in Chapter 7. Try to view and complete the form for both 2D and 3D pieces.

Child's Personal Creativity Journal Activity #3.

Activity #3 for Infants (Birth to walking, or 16 months)

Self-talk the elements: With daily interactions, self-talk about lines, colors, and shapes in the various environments, in nature, home, at the grocery store, everywhere. Continuing to remember that infants take in everything through their senses, and the infant's journal becomes a documentation of the infant's sensory experiences. Again, please attempt to approach this as a journal, and not a scrapbook. It should include only the infant's work or photos of the sensory experiences.

Activity #3 for Toddlers (walking or 16 months to 3-years-old)

Color Mixing: Provide toddlers with material to finger paint with primary colors to observe creation of secondary colors. For children who have tactile defensiveness or sensory aversion, put the paint in zip lock bags, taping the ends and taping to a tabletop. Taping on a window gives additional brightness to the colors and the mixing process. Give the child the time, the space, the materials, and the positive feedback and reinforcement to create! Take photos of the process. Attach photos of the process and final product (if there is one) in the toddler's journal.

Activity #3 for Preschoolers (ages 3 – 5)

Dancing Lines: Painting or drawing to music and different sounds helps children to become more auditory aware, and respond creatively. Vary the music, noting the different rhythms and how the music can affect how one paints. Add other recorded sounds, such as thunder, water flowing, water dripping, hammering, phone ringing, door squeaking, cat meowing, tiger roaring, etc. The children could even help record the sounds, then play them back, noting the difference and how their lines might change with the sound variation. Give the child the time, the space, the materials, and the positive feedback and reinforcement to create! Take photos of the process and note the types of music of which they listened. Assist the child in attaching photos of the process in the journal.

Activity #3 for Young School-agers

Visual exercise illustrating elements and principles of art: Complete the Visual Exercise Illustrating Elements and Principles of Art noted earlier in this chapter. If the child wishes to use more than four pages of their journal to repeat some steps, or the entire activity, encourage it. Give the child the time, the space, the materials, and the positive feedback and reinforcement to create! Take photos of the process. Assist the child in attaching photos of the process, as well as their reflection of the entire experience in their journal.

CHAPTER 4

Strategies for Using Art as a Learning and Intervention Tool in Early Childhood

"Art is as natural as sunshine and as vital as nourishment."

- Mary Ann Kohl

CHAPTER OVERVIEW

How best to provide equal access to the arts in inclusive settings, and to promote creative art growth for ALL children is an ongoing question in education and the arts. Every child needs many opportunities for creative thinking and expression. The possibilities are endless. This chapter begins with a plethora of examples of authentically creative art experiences for children of various ages and developmental levels. Specific illustrations of how these experiences can meet early learning standards are shared, as well as ways of integrating sample IFSP/IEP goals for children. This chapter continues with specific strategies for valuing individual differences, implementing person first philosophy, and providing accommodations for individual differences. The developmental importance of making creative art experiences accessible for all children is emphasized. General guidelines for working with young children with special needs are provided, in addition to specific strategies and ideas to accommodate young children with various special needs (physical; motor, visual, hearing; social, emotional, behavioral; and/or cognitive, language, communication). Suggestions for working with children with advanced cognitive development are also included. Accommodations in response to infants, toddlers, preschoolers, and primary school-age children with special needs will be provided.

Guidelines for working with young children from culturally diverse backgrounds and those learning English as a second language are also included, in addition to guidelines for working with young children from varied economic groups. Wonderful culturally diverse opportunities through arts are also illustrated, with strategies to embed them throughout the early childhood environment.

How do we best respond to children's artistic creativity? Guidelines for interactions with ALL children are be provided, such as: effective interactions with children about their art; keeping the dialogue going IF the child wishes, yet respecting the children's need to work without disruptions; mirrored feedback (reflecting verbally what the child is doing regarding their art process and project); responding to "I can't draw" statements; watching for nonverbal messages, and troubleshooting. Strategies and suggestions for effective dialogue with children to promote the creative process will be offered in the following sections.

PROVIDING EQUAL ACCESS TO THE ARTS FOR ALL CHILDREN IN AN INCLUSIVE SETTING

How do we provide equal access to the arts in inclusive settings while promoting creative art growth and expression for all children?

Inclusive Settings

Our society is one of increasing diversity. Learning to work, learn, and live together, while attempting to understand and learn from each other makes a truly inclusive setting. Inclusion has been a major focus and goal of educational efforts and legislation regarding the education of children with special needs, the most recent legislation being the Individuals with Disabilities Education Improvement Act (IDEA) of 2004. This law requires that children with disabilities be educated in the least restrictive environment (LRE), and have the same opportunities and access to programs as their peers without disabilities. Although there are federal mandates outlining inclusion practices, implementing inclusion is a process.

Inclusion is defined as the current educational practices of providing experiences for children with special needs within their natural environment alongside children without similar challenges. A joint position statement by the Division of Early Childhood (DEC) and National Association for the Education of Young Children (NAEYC) (2015) stated that early childhood inclusion, "embodies the values, policies, and practices that support the right of every infant and young child and his or her family, regardless of ability, to participate in a broad range of activities and contexts as full members of families, communities, and society" (DEC 2015).

The DEC and NAEYC's description of inclusion as a value and philosophy supports the right of all children to be educated and to participate in their natural setting (one in which the child would spend time if she did not have a disability). This position statement continued with the hopeful outcome of inclusion in education, "The desired results of inclusive experiences for children with and without disabilities and their families include as sense of belonging and membership, positive social relationships and friendships, and development and learning to reach their full potential. The defining features of inclusion that can be used to identify high quality early childhood programs and services are access, participation and supports" (DEC 2015). Access, participation, and supports are the key components and goals for inclusive settings. Although implementing inclusion is often a challenge, these are guiding principles.

Turnbull and Turbiville (1995) and Turnbull (2008) noted the challenges of applying these principles of inclusion and how educators often struggle to transfer recommendations based on research findings to everyday classroom practice. Educators appear to know what to do, but often fail to focus on the process of doing it. Of great importance when implementing inclusionary practices are knowledge, experience, and observation of inclusive practices. Many service providers have limited experience and observation of inclusive practices. This is especially true if inclusion was not part of their own childhood education or if they have had limited experience in their adult professional careers. However, an increasing number of programs are based on inclusive practices with an overall focus on abilities rather than disabilities of children. This seems to be a key component for successful inclusion. (Turnbull & Turbiville, 1995).

Inclusion and the Benefits of Role Models for Creative Experiences

In my own research, I have found increased participation for the children with special needs in inclusive versus non-inclusive groups, within the context of creative movement experiences Russell (1996). This research also supports the importance of role models and suggests additional benefits for all children in the inclusive setting. Justification for inclusive arts is demonstrated by Chandler's (1994) rationales for including children with special needs in programs (which go beyond legal requirements). Her points include the following:

1) Children with special needs will have better role models if they are with children who are typically developing. If they are only with other children with special needs, children with differing abilities may have no one from whom to learn developmentally appropriate behaviors. I also found this to be relevant in creative movement settings (Russell, 1996).

2) More realistic expectations will be placed on children with special needs who attend the same programs as children with typical behaviors and abilities. Expectations often determine how people behave and are therefore very important. Perhaps expectations are also influenced by not only teachers, but peers.

3) Children with special needs will be perceived as less "different" if they are part of the same environment as other children; as a result, they will be more readily accepted by others—their families, their peers, and the community. Inclusive programs that focus on children being more similar than different promotes a sense of belonging and acceptance which can enhance participation.

4) Including children with special needs in regular early childhood programs can positively affect the development of attitudes in all children toward persons who are "different" in some way. Inclusion, or integration of children with special needs in typical early childhood programs has value for all children. It has potential for many positive outcomes. (Chandler, 1994, pp. 7-8).

The following examples of authentically creative art experiences for children of various age and developmental levels are designed to be implemented in inclusive settings. However, they could also be used for individual children within therapy sessions or at home. Developmentally appropriate creative activity suggestions are also included in Table 4.1. Full and comprehensive lesson plans are for various age and developmental levels are provided in Chapter 5.

ART EXPERIENCES BASED ON DEVELOPMENTAL APPROPRIATENESS

We learn from our earliest experiences using all of our senses, including what we see, hear, touch, smell and taste. We experience through our visual, auditory, olfactory, and tactile environment. When observing an infant, he or she can be seen taking in the world with all the senses. One can observe the movement of his or her eyes, arms, legs, and mouths when the child is in an alert state. The excitement of discovering hands and feet, exploring objects with his or her mouth, or beginning movement of a journey towards an interesting destination is how an infant learns about him or herself and the world. Experiences are what form our aesthetic understanding of the world. As educators and parents, we must promote and make the time to allow for and foster this sensory-filled aesthetic world for our children.

First, we need to go back and explore our own understanding and use of our senses to better promote the full use and understanding of these senses and explorations for the child. Can you remember first being in awe of a rainbow? Did you see the ocean as a child? Can you remember the smells and sights and sounds of the water? Can you remember tasting a lemon or pickle? Can you remember hearing thunder, seeing the lightning, and how you felt? Did you ever help Grandma make bread or cookies? How did the dough feel, the smell of the baking bread or cookies? These experiences can be enhanced or stifled, as we grow older. The goal is to foster these sensual and aesthetic experiences, while being sensitive to individual abilities and cultural heritage.

The following activity examples range from those appropriate for infants through school-age children. The sensory experiences for infants should be continued for older children. Why stop finger painting at 2 years old? The following guidelines and ideas are provided for various developmental ages.

Infants: Sensorimotor Experiences

According to Piaget, infants learn through sensorimotor experiences, or through senses and movement. Art experiences for infants should include experimentation, manipulation, and discussion about what the child is doing. For example, how the child's arm is moving, how materials feel, how space is being used, etc. Most activities include edible materials. Finger painting with various materials, such as pudding, whipped cream, or yogurt are especially fun. Note that cleanup will be easy if this is done in the bathtub!

Since the very young child demonstrates movement from the shoulder and hand control is immature, it is important to have large utensils and large paper available.

Crayons should be offered one at a time, beginning with black (as it is very easy to be successful with the contrast of black on white). Tearing paper off the crayon allows the child to experience all characteristics of the crayon. Manufacturers now offer "easy grip" crayons for the young hand, in a teardrop shape. This can also be used for older children who may have physical needs that make smaller utensils more difficult to manipulate. A triangular, easy to grasp crayon for very small hands or for children with fine motor delay is shown in Figure 4.1. Figure 4.2 shows washable marker, designed for little hands. The longer triangular design promotes a more advanced grasp of the utensil.

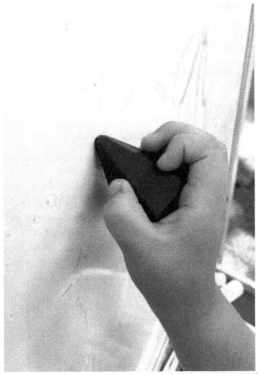

Figure 4.1: Crayons designed for easy grasp provide drawing accommodations for smaller hands or for children with fine motor challenges.

Figure 4.2: Marker designed to promote a more advanced grasp of the utensil.

Edible play dough is fun, fosters sensory exploration, and can also be nutritious. The following recipes are examples of edible play dough. The adult is encouraged to self-talk while mixing ingredients, verbalizing, and labeling every ingredient and action. This could enhance the infant's language development and exploration as they observe and listen. Offering each ingredient for the infant to touch before and after mixing could increase sensory development.

Peanut Butter Play Dough

- 1 cup peanut butter

- ½ cup honey

- 2 cups powdered sugar

Peanut Butter Play Dough Variation (less sugar)

- 1 cup creamy peanut butter

- 3 tablespoons honey

- 1 cup non-fat dry milk

> - 1/4 cups powdered sugar
>
> For an older infant, you could add raisins, peanut butter chips, etc. for texture. Be sure to check with the infant's parents or guardians regarding any allergies the child may have to these ingredients prior to the activity.

Be certain to follow guidelines or policy when it comes to using food for art projects. Some programs (e.g. Head Start) prohibit use of food with art, as many children do not get enough food to eat. For example, using noodles or peanut butter in an art project seems illogical to a child who is hungry every day or does not have the luxury of eating three meals a day.

Table 4.1 lists general suggestions for activities with infants that can foster creative play. Please remember that experiences typically designed for infants and toddlers could also be beneficial and relaxing for older children and even adults. Finger painting or edible play dough can be soothing and fun for most any age.

This table includes general suggestions for developmentally appropriate creative activities for infants. Full and comprehensive lesson plans are provided in Chapter 5.

Table 4.1: Ideas for Early Childhood Art Activities by Age Range

Ideas for Infants	Ideas for Toddlers	Ideas for Preschoolers	Ideas for Young School–age Children
Verbally label movements, sounds, tastes, smells, and textures to enhance the sensory motor experience	Finger painting with various materials and textures (nontoxic, of course)	representational drawings and sculptures; give opportunities to integrate their stories (naming objects or characters)	Sock puppets
Experimentation, manipulation, and discussion about WHAT the child is DOING	Various doughs, (play dough, bread dough, doughs in zip lock bags)	include 3D as often as 2D experiences	Object painting
Edible materials	Paints in secure zip lock bags taped to table or window	small utensils with large paper plus a variety of sizes and types of utensils (variety will allow for those children with a developmental need for larger or adaptive utensils.	Clay and play dough sculptures
Finger painting with yogurt, oatmeal, Jell-O, whipped cream (discuss texture, temperature, smells,	Use large utensils and surfaces such as chalk, large paintbrushes, large paper, boxes, etc.	Variety of chalks, crayons, paints, clays, various objects to paint with, various surfaces and textures,	Nature rubbings of tree bark, leaves, and other nature items

tastes, and marks they make with fingers and hands)		encourage experimentation.	
Body painting	First rubbings	Plan for long range and cooperative projects. Gently assist children who may have social or developmental needs	Origami
Try the bathtub for painting activities for easy cleanup	Collages, contact paper collages	Body tracing and fill in features	Different ways of applying paint: spray, dropping, feathers, sponge, bubble wrap, rollers
Large utensils, large paper	Edible play dough (for the less oral toddler, clay with pipe cleaners, foil, etc. can be introduced)	Eggshell mosaic	Crayon resist
Offer crayons one at a time, beginning with black (for contrast)	Painting: with feet, body painting, finger painting with mud, with bubble wrap, painting with water	Marble painting	Rock painting
"Easy grip" crayons for the young hand, in a teardrop shape	Paper tearing (crumbling and folding); note the sounds and feeling with the tearing and crumpling	Toy car painting	Mosaic
Tear paper off of crayon to allow child to experience all characteristics of crayon	Large boxes for painting, drawing on, playing in	Include activities from earlier age ranges. The preschooler is not as oral, so danger of choking on small items should not be feared for the typically developing child.	Self-portrait
Edible play dough (Watch out for allergies.)	Creative shadows	refer to list of Enjoyable Junk & Terrific Trash Suitable for Art in Appendix B.	Plaster sculptures
Nature walks noting the sights, sounds, smells, movements, using all senses	Sidewalk chalk	More variety is welcomed, but continue to offer the sensory experiences	Foil creatures

		from the infant and toddler columns.	
Bring in a pan of snow for playing (offer mittens if infant is hesitant)	Activity suggestions from the infant column should still be offered, but with a broadened choice of utensils, surfaces, and 3-D materials	Add more 3-D variety (pipe cleaners, bendy sticks, foil, tissues, beads, collage materials, wood, string, rope, etc.)	Wooden pieces, foam, pipe cleaners, wire, etc. for sculptures

Toddlers: Scribbling and Exploring

The toddler has a strong need for scribbling and exploring everything. Trying out every utensil, whether or not it makes a mark, demonstrates discovery and learning through play for the toddler. The toddler will scribble even if there is no access to art materials. We see toddlers (as well as older children and even adults) scribbling on foggy windows, dust on tables, in sand, and in leftovers on their plates. The toddler should still be offered the activities from the infant stage, but with a broadened choice of utensils, surfaces, and 3-D materials. We need to continue to foster sensual and aesthetic experiences, while being sensitive to individual abilities and cultural heritage. A section later in this chapter, "Working with Young Children with Diverse Backgrounds" will address sensitivity to individual abilities and in more detail. Figure 4.3 shows a toddler learning through play as she tries out various utensils.

Figure 4.3: Trying out every utensil, whether or not it makes a mark, demonstrates discovery, trial and error, and learning through play for the toddler.

Developmentally appropriate creative activity suggestions for toddlers are also included in Table 4.1. Full and comprehensive lesson plans are provided in Chapter 5.

Preschoolers: Representational Drawings and Sculptures

The preschooler is moving from scribbling to naming a picture, or from unplanned to representational drawings and sculptures. Please be sure not to write on the child's drawing. You can write any narrative on a separate piece of paper. One can observe a wide range of development from children ages 3 to 5 years, in addition to individual development. Note the range of development displayed in Figures 4.4 and 4.5 of 3-year-old students compared to 5-year-olds creating a mural on canvas.

Figure 4.4: Three-year-olds working on a mural, emerging from Kellogg's Scribble Stage to Emerging Shapes.

Figure 4.5: Five-year-olds working on a mural, clearly in Kellogg's Pictorial Stage, more purposeful and representative in their artwork.

The 3-to-5-year-old is ready for more variety, but the basics should always be offered. Utensils can be smaller if the child's fine motor development warrants, however, large paper should still be available. Long-range projects or cooperative and group projects have more meaning and demonstrate cognitive and social skills growth. Process is still more important than product. Figure 4.6 shows a preschool child who is more precise and purposeful with her artwork as a result of her increased fine motor skills and concept development.

Figure 4.6: With increased fine motor skills and concept development, the preschooler is more precise and purposeful with her/his artwork.

Developmentally appropriate creative activity suggestions for preschoolers are also included in Table 4.1. Full and comprehensive lesson plans are provided in Chapter 5. Be sure to refer to the list of Enjoyable Junk & Terrific Trash Suitable for Art in Appendix B.

Young School-age Children: Exploring Art Media

The young school-age child needs more opportunities to perceptualize, but they are still exploring art media. Projects are more purposeful and intentional with more detail. With increased cognitive, physical, emotional, and social skills, the child's work should have more elaboration, originality, fluency, and flexibility of ideas. The child's attention span is longer, and the desire to portray all areas of the curriculum through art media is greater. More intricate long-range projects are possible, and cooperative/group projects have more depth, meaning, and demonstrate cognitive and social skills growth. It's important to ask open-ended questions, to allow children to problem solve and discover. Try to refrain from interfering while the child is working. Timing of encouragement and interactions is important. Process is still important, yet the product becomes increasingly important to the child. Continue to ask "how" something was done, and highlight that process. We need to continue to be sensitive to individual abilities and cultural heritage.

Developmentally appropriate creative activity suggestions for school agers are also included in Table 4.1. Full and comprehensive lesson plans are provided in Chapter 5. Be sure to refer to the list of Enjoyable Junk & Terrific Trash Suitable for Art in Appendix B.

Specific illustrations of full lesson plans, which illustrate how these experiences can meet early learning standards, as well as integrating sample IFSP/IEP goals for children are offered in Chapter 5. The following comprehensive format is used for these detailed plans. It is important to understand the aspects of each component of the lesson plan format with explanations (e.g. adaptations, assessment, linking to standards, and best practice).

Lesson plan format:

- Title of activity

- Curricular area(s) (e.g. science, math, language)

- Goals/objectives these directly align with the assessment

- Age levels

- Materials: equipment, resources, space etc.

- Instructions or teacher's role: What is the role of the teacher/ special things to watch out for, etc. Included will be any special instructions crucial to this activity.

- Linking to IEP or IFSP goals or outcomes: (Examples of IEP (ages 3 to 8 years) or IFSP (birth to age 3) goals or outcomes related to the activity will be included here, depending on age of child)

- Adaptations: Included in this section will be: How to accommodate for children who need a different approach, special equipment, etc. Importance of checking if accommodations or modifications are needed for the goals/objectives, materials, procedure, or evaluation for a child based on their special needs. Collaborating with other specialists on the child's IEP or IFSP team (e.g. physical therapist, occupational therapist, speech therapist, nurse, etc.) is also noted under this section. Noted here are essential instructions to related specifically to goals/objectives, including specific directions for Para educator or teacher's aide.

- Assessment: This section is about accountability. How will you know what the children learned? This relates directly to the objectives, and demonstrates how the data will be record or documented. The documentation or tool for documentation is essential. A chart, checklist or specific manner you will collect this data. Also, evaluation of one's teaching should be included here.

- Linking activity to Standards and Best Practices: This section links the activity to Early Learning Standards, Best Practices from: NAEYC and DEC, and/or NEA standards. The may depend on the age range of the activity, as NEA standards are elementary level. Appendix A includes a summary of these standards for reference.

In Chapter 5, these activities are presented first by developmental levels (infants, toddlers, preschoolers, and young school-age children), then several suggested thematic units, demonstrating how art can be integrated throughout the curriculum. These units are "ready to go" and set to implement in your classroom, home, therapy, art center, or other program promoting learning through art. Figure 4.7 is a sample lesson plan from Chapter 5; it follows the lesson plan format noted above. More on integrating art throughout the curriculum is offered in Chapter 6: Integrating the Arts across the Early Childhood Curriculum.

Sample Lesson Plan
Curricular Area: Expressive Arts (Music, Movement, Theatre & Visual Arts)
Activity: Dancing Markers
Age: Preschooler (3–5 years)
Goals/Objectives:
The preschooler will:
- draw to different styles and tempos of music.
- use words to describe how different music makes her feel.

Materials:
- Large white pieces of paper
- Large washable markers in a variety of colors
- CD music (or music played via smartphone) of varying tempos and styles (Presto vs. Largo; Classical vs. Rock n' Roll; Jazz vs. Celtic)

Instructions or teacher's/adult's role:
- Offer the markers and paper to the children.
- Tell them to let the markers dance to the music. Encourage the children to listen carefully to the rhythm and tempo of the music, feel the music, and let their markers follow along. Tell them to stop when the music stops, then start again, while changing the types and tempo of music every couple of minutes. Tell them to change colors as often as they like.
- Keep the activity going as long as children are enjoying.

Linking to IEP or IFSP goals or outcomes:
- Developmental areas of IFSP Outcomes that could be linked to this activity:
  o Fine motor, Communication, Cognitive, Social-emotional
- Examples of IFSP Outcomes that could be linked to this activity:
  Social-emotional & Communication:
  o _____ (child's name) will express feelings through words and creative arts.
  Cognitive:
  o _____ (child's name) will increase use of educational materials to _____ (grade or ability level) to complete classroom art projects as measured by _____(evaluation tool).
  o _____ (child's name) will increase ability to rhythmically move to various tempos as measured by _____.
Adaptations:
- Larger grip on marker could be offered if needed.
- Marker could be taped to a glove for children who cannot grip.
- If child has a hearing impairment, have him or her work close to the CD player (or smartphone) and (if needed) place him or her hand on it. Make sure that the bass is turned up and allow the child to feel the vibrations that the music is making. Then allow more time and arrangements for drawing with other hand.
- Use Sign Language or child's native language for vocabulary words.

Assessment:
Using the checklist below will assist in taking notes during the activity. Writing an X within the checklist will show that the goal or objective within the activity has been observed and completed.

Goals/Objectives	Toddler	Comments
Child drew to different styles and tempos of music	Name: Yes/no	
Child used words to describe how different music makes he or she feel	Name: Yes/no	

Linking activity to Standards and Best Practices:
- ELS: ALT(a,c), PHD(b), SED(c,d), CL(a,f), CA(a,b,d)
- NAEYC Early Childhood Program Standards: #1, 2, 3, 4, & 9
- NAEYC Guidelines for developmentally appropriate practice: #1, 2, 3, 4
- DEC Recommended Practices in Early Intervention/ Early Childhood Special Education: #2 (A8, A9, A10), 3 (E1, E3), 5 (INS3, INS4, INS5, INS6, INS7, INS11, INS12) & 6 (INT1, INT2, INT3, INT4, INT5)

Figure 4.7: Sample lesson plan following the lesson plan format.

STRATEGIES FOR VALUING INDIVIDUAL DIFFERENCES

Person First Philosophy

You may have heard of person-first philosophy, but how are your person-first skills? When you see someone in a wheelchair, what do you honestly see first: the wheelchair, the physical disability, or the person? Do you find yourself still using phrases like "wheelchair bound," "confined to a wheelchair," "handicapped," or even "blind as a bat" or "crippled"? If so, you may need to review and make a conscious effort to use person-first philosophy and language.

What is person first? Person first is the foundation of inclusion and underlies our practices of valuing differences while making environments and experiences accessible for all. Person First is a philosophy of seeing the person first, the disability second. This does not deny the disability; it simply views the person first. The person is not the disability (e.g., don't refer to the person as "the disabled" or "the handicapped"); rather, the person has a disability.

Person first means:

- Referring to the person first, and then the disability (e.g. a child with an autism spectrum disorder rather than autistic child or a child with spina bifida rather than spina bifida kid)

- When referring to a group, not labeling people as part of a disability group, such as

- "the disabled," rather, say "people with disabilities")

- Emphasizing abilities, not disabilities or limitations

- Not patronizing or giving excessive praise or attention to a person with a disability (e.g. "You are such an inspiration!" or "You are so brave!"

- Giving the person with a disability a choice and independence. For example, letting the person do or speak for himself/herself as much as possible and as his or her ability permits.

- A disability is a functional limitation that interferes with the person's ability to walk, hear, talk, learn, etc. We no longer use the term "handicap" or "handicapped" when referring to people who have such challenges.

- Use the word handicap to describe a situation or barrier that society and the environment impose by not making environments accessible (for example, not making curb cuts, not placing Braille signage in needed locations, not building ramps or elevators for accessibility for people who need it). Table 4.2 lists some examples of person-first and non-person-first language.

Table 4.2: Examples of Person-First and Non-Person-First Language

Examples of Person-First and Non-Person-First Language

Say ...	Instead of ...
Child with a disability	Disabled or handicapped child
Person who is hard of hearing	Deaf or deaf and dumb person
Person has a cognitive disability/diagnosis	Retarded
Person who uses a wheelchair	Confined to a wheelchair or wheelchair-bound
Person of short stature	Dwarf or midget
Has paraplegia/quadriplegia	Paraplegic/quadriplegic
Accessible parking	Handicapped parking
Accessible bathroom	Handicapped bathroom
Person with a Brain Injury	Brain damaged

How would you introduce someone (e.g., Jane Smith, who doesn't have a disability)? You would most likely introduce her by giving her name, where she lives, what she does or what she is interested in, such as that she likes to swim, ride horses, eat Mexican food, and cook. Why say it differently for a person who has a disability?

We all have many characteristics that make us who we are, mental as well as physical, and not many of us want to be identified only by our ability, for example, to play tennis, or how much we love onion rings, or the freckles or mole on our face. People with disabilities are like everyone else; they just happen to have a disability or differing abilities and may need some accommodations. We are all more alike than we are different. Person-first philosophy and language is a matter of respect for a person with special needs—respect for who he or she is: a person first. Attitudes are reflected in what we do and say. An attitude of respect is reflected in person-first philosophy and practice.

Person first has been around for a long time. In 1990, Federal Laws reworded special education and civil rights laws—Individuals with Disabilities Education Act (IDEA) and Americans with Disabilities Act (ADA))—in person-first language. For several years, special-education journals have required that person-first language be used in articles, and some text publishers require it. A Google search of person-first language resulted in 25,300,000 sites listed a few years ago. Today, searching person-first language on a Google search resulted in 58,300,000 results, over doubling in a couple of years. Still, many people are not even aware of person first, are struggling with its use, or some even ignore the use of person–first terminology. Please "think before you speak" and choose words that demonstrate your respect for seeing the person first!

For more on Person First Philosophy and Language, see:

http://www.familytofamilynetwork.org/parent-resources/people-first-language

http://www.inclusionproject.org/nip_userfiles/file/People%20First%20Chart.pdf

The following sections include general guidelines for working with young children with special needs, in addition to specific strategies and ideas to accommodate young children with various special needs (physical; motor, visual, hearing; social, emotional, behavioral; and/or cognitive, language, communication).

How do we provide equal access to the arts in inclusive settings and promote art growth for ALL children? We must allow for equal access to the arts and art programs. Valuing individual differences means we see the child first. However, providing for individual differences means making adaptations in planning, preparing the physical environment, and assessing children's participation for additional adaptations or modifications. Planning inclusive environments includes both physical and interactive aspects.

The Americans with Disabilities Act (ADA) passed in 1990. In 1998, the Architectural and Transportation Barriers Compliance Board issued ADA Accessibility Guidelines for Building Elements Designed for Children's Use, "establishing alternate specifications for building elements designed for use by children. These specifications are based on children's dimensions and anthropometrics and apply to building elements designed specifically for use by children ages 12 and younger" (Architectural and Transportation Barriers Compliance Board, 1998).

Early childhood environments should be designed to be both adult and child friendly, and the same goes for accessibility features. For example, newly constructed facilities or portions of facilities for use by ages 2 through 12 now must meet requirements that address reach ranges, protruding objects, handrails at ramps and stairs, drinking fountains and water coolers, bathrooms, mirrors, storage, seating, and tables. Included are considerations concerning clear floor space, knee clearance, accessible routes, door hardware, sinks, and signage.

Art for ALL children means setting up an inviting and enticing art area that all children can access. This includes appropriate space and materials. Available to all children should be opportunities for: mixed media, using a variety of tools, both 2-D and 3-D experiences, and choosing from plenty of developmentally appropriate materials. Fox and Schirrmacher (2015) recommend having at least six categories of basic art materials available. Although budgetary constraints could be a barrier, this would be a list to work towards and use when submitting requests for funding or materials. Stores will often give discounts or donations to schools. ENJOYABLE

JUNK & TERRIFIC TRASH SUITABLE FOR ART in Appendix B also offers low or no cost items that fit under some of these categories.

1. Tools for mark making, such as crayons, pencils, markers, chalk, pastels (with larger tools or grippers for children with fine motor challenges), etc.

2. Paper in a variety of colors, shapes, sizes, thickness, and textures (including magazines, cardboard, newsprint, tissue paper, crepe paper, sand paper, white drawing paper, colored construction paper (both traditional and various skin tones), etc.

3. Items for cutting, fastening, and attaching, such as: scissors (some double-handed ambidextrous scissors or with accommodations), glue, glue sticks, paste, tape, hole punches, staplers, string, pipe cleaners, etc.

4. Items for painting and making prints, such as: paint, brushes, sponges and other items with textures, etc.

5. Collage items: nature items, fabric, old jewelry, wall paper, wrapping paper, yarn

6. Material for sculptures, such as: clay, polymer clay, playdough, recipes for various 3-D doughs (Kohl's MUDWORKS is a wonderful resource), aluminum foil, cardboard boxes, bubble wrap, cotton balls, pipe cleaners, beads, pom-poms, etc. (adapted Fox and Schirrmacher, 2015 p. 260)

Window into a Classroom: Best Practices for Inclusion

The teacher arranges materials and options for students with special needs for easy access. Easels are available on a daily basis, and are accommodated for children who use equipment due to physical challenges. Tabletop easels work well as a modification. Tables should be at an accessible level, and plenty of space allowed for mobility around tables and access to art supplies. The art area is near a sink and has good lighting. (Near outdoor light is best, as one can see the colors better.) Good lighting is essential for children with visual impairments. Taking art projects outdoors guarantees good lighting. The teacher provides art outdoors on a daily basis, weather permitting. Easels work well outside, and can easily be transported. Figure 4.8 is an example of a well-organized art shelf with easy access to materials.

Figure 4.8: Example of art shelf with easy access.

Also note that Figure 9.1 in Chapter 9 illustrates offers a diagram and explanation of an inclusive classroom that integrates art throughout the classroom environment. Accommodations of space and access to materials are included in the description accompanying Figure 9.1.

The teacher also assuring that art experiences and materials are sensitive to ethnic and cultural diversity by including multicultural markers, paper, paints, and clays. His classroom materials include fabric pieces that represent cultural diversity, with patterns from different countries. (See additional suggestions noted later in this chapter, including resources for art supplies reflecting cultural diversity.)

As noted in Chapter 1, the child creates what she or he knows, from various sensorimotor experiences, from their relationships, from their feelings. Teachers need to be sensitive to the personal nature of art, since it is created and based on what children have seen, heard, touched, tasted, or smelled in their young lives. This is based on the individual child's environment, culture, experiences, interactions, relationships, and abilities. For example, a child with motor challenges may not have access to certain experiences or materials; a child with severe vision challenges may not have any reference to colors, basing all concepts on sounds, touch, or taste; a child with a sensory integration disorder may have a severe reaction to certain tastes and textures and may respond intensively or with aggression to an attempt to introduce activities involving certain textures. The educator should be informed regarding the realities of sensory integration challenges, while being sensitive to these individual differences. Taking small steps forward while slowly desensitizing the child if possible, and using alternative materials or activities when needed offers a responsible and respectful approach. Figure 4.9 demonstrates the personal nature of art based on this child's experience.

Figure 4.9: Please be sensitive to the personal nature of art, as it is created and based on what a child has seen, heard, touched, tasted, or smelled.

Some children with differing abilities, such as ADHD or ASD have social, emotional, behavioral, and learning challenges, so suggestions for accommodations are located under multiple sections. Children with spina bifida and nonverbal learning disorders have both learning and physical needs, in addition to possible social, emotional, and behavioral challenges, and would also benefit from the accommodations described in several of the following sections. Please keep the individual child and their unique needs in mind when considering accommodations.

Window into a Classroom: Best Practices for Inclusion

When working with a child with special needs, make sure you consult with the child's IEP or IFSP team for support, strategies, assistive technology, and other resources. Utilize this team's expertise by having questions ready for them. You may have to be assertive with your requests, but know this is the child's right to participate in a meaningful way, without barriers. Be certain to also consult with the child's family, as they know the child best and have most likely tried many modifications already. Remember that siblings might also have some great accommodations and ideas. Many siblings are very attuned to the abilities of their sibling who may have special needs, and have often never been asked about their ideas or any informal modifications they have found successful. Figure 4.10 is an example of a sibling implementing an accommodation for her younger sister who has special needs.

Figure 4.10: Remember that siblings might also have some great accommodations and ideas.

Some general guidelines for working with young children with varying abilities include:

- Accept the child unconditionally

- Build on strengths; use strengths to work on challenges.

- Focus on what the child CAN do

- Adapt the physical environment: Get in a wheelchair yourself and see! Try art projects yourself with fingers taped together to simulate fine motor challenges; or with wax paper goggles to simulate a visual impairment, etc. The awareness will help you to understand what adaptations are needed.

- Encourage independence please assist, but do not complete the work for them! Instruct paraeducators to assist without taking over a project. Mouth painting or painting with toes can be amazing.

- Try to wean overdependence, which can become a pattern of our children who have received early intervention, and have been pleasing therapists, teachers, and parents their entire young lives. There must be a balance of supports, which sometimes differs from day to day.

- Offer equal opportunities (not the same as "treating equally"). Equal opportunities mean individual consideration and accommodations.

- Be informed and educate yourself about the child's disability. Do your homework.

- With permission, and perhaps with the parent's participation, share general information about a child's special needs with other children. Demonstrate what works, what helps.

- Sensory integration visual, hearing, touching, tasting, smelling Build on sensory strengths; provide multisensory stimulation

- Allow ample time, practice, and repetition for learning.

- Provide for success and mastery.

- Break down tasks into smaller steps.

- Foster positive self-concept feeling good about self. Foster viewing self as unique (adapted from Fox and Schirrmacher, 2015)

Window into a Classroom: Best Practices for Inclusion

Disability Awareness

Include disability awareness activities for all children. Be open to group problem solving and encourage children to help find solutions to making environments more accessible to all. Some ways to this includes:

- Discuss with children the many ways we are the same and different. Just as we each have different hair color, skin color, eye color, etc.; we also have different abilities that make us unique. Note how we are more alike than different.

- Include awareness activities for all children, such as:

   o Secure a paintbrush on a helmet to simulate how it might feel to paint without arms or hands

   o Tape fingers together on each hand to simulate fine motor challenges and then paint or draw

   o Paint or draw while wearing wax paper goggles to simulate a visual challenge

   o Create in art area while using a wheelchair for accommodating space and access to materials

   o Use cotton or earplugs in ears to simulate a hearing challenge. Teach children some beginning sign language, so they can try communicating with each other while simulating being hard of hearing.

- Use of volunteers or a buddy system would be helpful to serve as aides for children simulating a disability and needing assistance. Remind children that you cannot just take off a disability because you are uncomfortable, or you are not able to do a desired activity.

- Be open to ideas from various resources: Peers sometimes have great adaptation ideas. This can offer some brilliant problem-solving possibilities about accommodations.

- It is important for adults, as role models, to also participate in these awareness activities.

- Resources such as books, videotapes, examples of Braille, using sign language to learn new songs, poems or just to communicate.

- Displays could include books, adaptive toys, standing frame, adaptive seating, and tray (with large dolls in them), braille and signing examples, computers, etc.

- General classroom should exhibit an appreciation for diversity on a daily basis. For example:

  o dolls with broken limbs should be bandaged, braced, or make a prosthesis for the doll.

  o Wheelchairs, walkers, and guide cane/guide dogs for various dolls and other play equipment are now available from various manufacturers.

  o Anti-bias classrooms should have various equipment and materials (books, posters, videos) that depict individuals with special needs, as well as multicultural and non-gender bias materials.

- Special guests (both children and adults) who are visible in the community who have disabilities could come and talk about what they do and participate in discussion and questions. The questions and discussions from these visits can be most beneficial and enlightening to teachers. An artist who also has a disability would be beneficial to demonstrate to children how anyone, regardless of differing abilities, can express themselves through the arts.

Additional information about specific needs and adaptations for physical considerations (motor, visual, hearing); social, emotional, behavioral disorders; and cognitive, language, communication disorders include the following (adapted from Miller, 1996):

Physical Considerations: Motor

Children with physical challenges (large or fine motor) need positive creative experiences, which most likely require adaptations in order to fully participate. Even children who are left-handed need accommodations (e.g. ambidextrous scissors, utensils, rulers, pencil sharpeners, journals, etc.). Although hand preference begins to emerge between ages of 2 and 4, most children at the age of 5 have established definite hand dominance. Physical accommodations for full participation are essential. If not, the experience can be disappointing and could cause the child to avoid trying the accommodation again. Creative arts must be inclusive, which may mean problem solving and creative solutions on the part of the adults, peers, family, and the child him/herself. Some wonderful accommodations have occurred as the result of sibling or peer input. As noted earlier, consult with the child's family, as they know the child best and have most likely tried many modifications already. Siblings are very attuned to the abilities of their sibling who may have special needs, and might come up with successful accommodations and ideas.

Some suggestions for accommodating children with physical challenges include:

- If the child cannot reach the easel, modify the easel first, not the child. Lower it, raise it, use a stander, secure a paintbrush on headgear (this can also provide an experimental / awareness opportunity for other children).

- A child who uses a wheelchair might benefit from having a wedge to support elbows to reach the easel.

- Use the child's wheelchair tray as a last option, so as not to isolate child from others.

- Do not isolate children needing modifications from peers. Let all children try the modifications.

- Secure paper for success. For tabletop work, tape down paper or use dycem or plastic non-skid shelf liner, adjustable tables, enough space to access art shelf (remember to check this with chair from table pulled out, not pushed in).

- Be sure child has access to sinks.

- May need to use materials in different ways, e.g. lying on the floor over a bolster.

- For children with hand strength challenges use lighter brushes, Velcro (on glove or mitten), put paint brush in small foam ball (place in child's closed fist, with gentle support at the elbow, or insert brush through foam rollers or tennis ball.

- Use double handed ambidextrous or loop scissors that work with a squeeze motion.

- Glue sticks are less frustrating.

- Materials and activities that do not require fine motor accuracy can foster success for children with a variety of special needs, such as paper tearing or crumpling, gluing, larger paper and utensils, foil art, etc.

- Use no-spill cups for painting, or sponges cut to fit in easel tray around juice can paint holders for stability. Sponge will secure paint containers and catch paint drips.

- Offer larger collage materials; use larger markers, crayons, pencils, and paint brushes for ease of grip.

- Activities that require two hands give more opportunities to build strength bilaterally.

- Be sure to offer both 2-D and 3-D experiences. Vary the moisture in clay or play dough for ease of use for children whose motor skills and strength differ. Kohl's MUDWORKS is an excellent source for mixing a variety of materials, and more moisture can be added to most of the play dough variations.

- Offer as little assistance as possible, but as much as needed; minimum assistance for maximum growth. Remember to model only techniques, not the product. As Deiner (2005) emphasized, "Support their attempts to control the medium, not the final product" (Deiner, 2005, p. 406).

Figure 4.11 shows some adaptations that can be made to accommodate children who have motor challenges.

Figure 4.11: For children with physical disabilities, make certain surface is easy to access, secure paper for success, and use larger markers or crayons for smaller hands.

Physical Considerations: Visual

Creative art experiences can offer successful and safe discovery opportunities for children with visual challenges. Texture and high contrast can be used in various ways for accommodations. The individual child and the severity of their visual needs will vary, and consultation with vision specialists, as well as the family, is encouraged.

Children with mild to moderate visual challenges need few modifications:

- Use surface to bring art materials closer (doing the same activities as others).

- Work on white or black to contrast with materials used.

- Mark the boundary of paper or working surface with a thick black line or texture. Paper taped to tray helps define work surface and prevent shifting of paper. Figure 4.12 is an example of these accommodations.

Figure 4.12: Example of a drawing surface with paper taped to the tray to define the work space, using a darker contrasting tape around the sides to mark the boundaries.

- Be sure there is good lighting.

- Use larger tools and surface.

For children with severe visual impairments:

- Verbally describe materials in detail if needed, keeping in mind there are no visual cues (e.g. the finger paint will be cool, the paint has sand in it).

- Go slowly; encourage manipulation of items as you talk.

- Use a tray or textured tape to define work surface. (See Figure 4.12)

- Keep tools close by, labeling with Braille or textures.

- Label art shelf items (and other areas in your classroom) in Braille.

- Focus on tactile experiences, use various textured 2-D and 3-D materials, describing each verbally.

- Offer contrasting textures for collages or placing in clay or play dough.

- Include other senses besides tactile: smell, taste, hearing in art experiences, but be sure to follow preferences of child. Too much auditory might be disturbing, even nauseating for some.

Physical Considerations: Hearing

Since visual arts focus on visual creativity, the child who has hearing challenges is not in need of many accommodations. As long as directions, techniques, and any safety issues are clearly communicated, the educator would need to make few adaptations.

1. Model the process, not the product.

2. Use sign, lip reading or any other method the child understands for directions, communication, labeling, etc.

3. Encourage children to paint or sculpt their feelings.

4. Provide motivation, reinforcement, and a positive social atmosphere through sharing materials, commenting on work, etc.

5. Foster positive interactions with peers. Teach peers sign language. Use words and visual sign language labels to identify materials in the art area and your classroom, in general. Figures 4.13 to 4.15 are examples of ASL Sign Language labels that could be used to label areas of the room. Figure 4.13 illustrates the sign for "book"; Figure 4.14 illustrates the sign for "bathroom"; and Figure 4.15 illustrates the sign for the spelled version of "art."

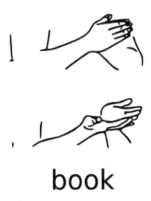

book

Figure 4.13: Example of Sign Language label to use in the Literacy areas which illustrates the sign for "book"

bathroom

Figure 4.14: Example of Sign Language to use as a label for the "bathroom."

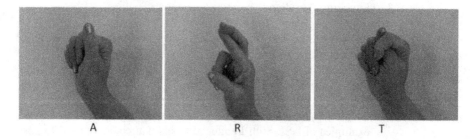

A   R   T

Figure 4.15: Illustrates the signed letters for the spelled version of "art."

There are numerous Public Domain websites as resources for labeling areas of the classroom with sign language or Braille. See:

http://www.wpclipart.com/sign_language/ASL_words/index.html

https://www.wpclipart.com/sign_language/American_ABC_Photos/index.ht ml

http://www.pdclipart.org/thumbnails.php?album=36

Be sure to work with the child's family, Hearing Specialist, Vision Specialist, OT, and PT. You are NOT ALONE! Simulating hearing, vision, or motor challenges for your self-awareness, as well as helping peers be sensitive to differing abilities increases understanding and sensitivity. Try simulating activities for help both peers and teachers to have a "taste" of what it might be like to have a disability while trying to complete small motor tasks.

Social, Emotional, Behavioral

Creative art experiences allow children who have social, emotional, or behavioral challenges to have freedom of expression in a safe environment that offers success oriented opportunities. They have permission and support to explore and take risks. There is little possibility of failure, as long as the experiences are truly authentic creative art and not masquerading as art (with only one right way of completing). Some children with emotional/behavioral challenges may have times they are aggressive and are in need of self-soothing adaptations or other calming interventions. Work with your team on devising individualized strategies to keep a safe environment for all.

Children with autism spectrum disorders (ASDs) or pervasive developmental disorder (PDD) have some unique challenges, which necessitate understanding and accommodations on the part of the adults working with them. Children with ASDs may have tactile defensiveness, which may result in them not wanting to touch paint, clay or other materials. Perseveration of some children with ASD or PDD may cause them to get stuck in only drawing one thing, such as horses or tractors. They may have difficulty with pretend play which can interfere with puppet or dramatic play. As Martin explains, "Addressing and overcoming these challenges is not a difficulty of the work, it is the work" (Martin, 2009, p. 99). According to Martin, quality art experiences for children with ASDs involves a three-part relationship, "Relevant, useful art projects; A caring, supporting relationship with an adult; Individualized adaptations to help ensure success" (Martin, 2009, p. 101).

Chapter 8 includes more detail about how art has been an effective method for therapy, healing, and assisting children with communicating feelings and emotions, particularly during difficult times. Children with social/emotional challenges, facing serious illness or surgery, homeless, dealing with loss, or who have been abused all may have trauma and terribly frightening memories in their young lives. Art and art therapy has also been used to address children's responses to various traumas that some children face regularly, such as domestic violence or drug-related shootings. Art can help children with social and emotional challenges communicate about their world, the good and the bad parts. Art can also facilitate better understanding, processing, and sharing emotions in a safe environment.

Some suggestions for working with children who experience social, emotional, or behavioral challenges are listed below:

- Child may hesitate or not want to participate in new activity, be unsure of what to do, or not understand the open-endedness of the art activities.

- May need more opportunities to watch others. Could set up an area adjacent to the art activity so the child can observe comfortably from a safe distance. The child may need more time and space to do this.

- Start with what the child is interested in, with what they are familiar, and then slowly add variations.

- Change and transitions can be difficult, so start with small steps and prepare for transitions. May need a paraeducator or other assistance to work one-on-one, particularly during transition times.

- Be flexible and allow child to work a bit longer if she/he is very involved in the process. Adequate time is important for the full creative experience, and some children just need more.

- If the child needs to work on improving social skills, art can provide motivation, reinforcement, and a positive social atmosphere through sharing materials, commenting on work, etc. Foster positive interactions with peers.

- A child who has behavior challenges may need support in the area of impulse control. Initially, there may be many messes before moving toward the child gaining more self-regulation.

- Encourage children to paint or sculpt their feelings.

- Expect the mess, but try to prevent with table coverings, space, sleeves up, mats below easel, etc. and have materials for children to use to clean up.

- If a child does not want to wear a smock or if it becomes a strong deterrent to the child's participation, do not insist that they wear it and try not to get into a power struggle.

- Using visual labels (pictures and words) can facilitate independence as well as word recognition. Labeling centers or color-coding different parts of the room assist with order and organization.

- Visual boundaries (e.g. bordering the paper, masking tape on child's work area, or dividing the paper into smaller spaces) can make the space or project more manageable. See Figure 4.12 for example.

- Visual schedules assist with organization of time, space, predictability, and transitions. See Figure 4.16.

Window into a Classroom: Best Practices for Inclusion

Use of Visual Schedules

The use of visualizations for schedules or positive behavior can offer great support to children who need assistance with focus, attention, and predictability. The visuals accompany verbal expectations and encouragement for understanding. Visual schedules cue children, assist them with transitions, and help them understand and predict what is next. These visuals can also support communication, memory, and lessen stress and anxiety. Visual schedules can teach routines, build confidence, and offer positive behavioral supports. They can be individualized and can result in success for young child with behavioral challenges, and conditions such as ADHD, Autism, and Nonverbal Learning Disability. Figure 4.16 is an example of a visual daily schedule? Creating the schedule where items can be attached and moved about (such as with Velcro or magnetic labels) allows for change, flexibility, or individualization.

Figure 4.16: Example of a visual schedule.

- Break down the tasks into smaller steps or parts can help make the project more approachable and not as overwhelming.

- Physical accommodations such as: adapted tools, slant board, options of various places to work (table, floor, wall, easel).

- May combine verbal communication with visual schedules and cues, and simple Sign Language, whatever works best for the individual child.

- A child with social, emotional, or behavioral challenges may need more opportunities and guidance with group activities. Assist them in easing into social activities, whatever their comfort level. Small steps may be needed. (See Creative Group Activities at the end of this chapter).

- Be sure to include both 2-D and 3-D experiences. 3-D materials, such as clay and various play doughs can be beneficial in releasing tension and stress. It is OK to punch, roll or tear the clay, and it is not hurting anyone or anything. It can be a wonderful redirection tool and can be available as needed. Children can learn to go to the clay or play dough when they feel the need during the day. This is an excellent self-calming skill to foster for frustrating times. Try it yourself!

- Talk about art and how artists express their feelings through their artwork.

Some appropriate and creativity focused art games and programs can be found online or downloaded on the class computer, as well as on iPads or tablets. This can allow children to express in a less messy technique. This is particularly helpful for children who many have sensory integration disorders or experience tactile defensiveness. Be sure to print the children's creations and treat it as any other artwork produced. A few of these creativity focused art games are listed in Suggestions for Additional Reflection and Review (see p. 00). Fox and Schirrmacher (2015) stated that some teachers report that art is used as a reward when work is completed. "Good students" get go to the art center or participate in art. Others may be denied art. Even though misbehavior or incomplete homework should not be tolerated, the punishment does not fit the crime. The children in question may be the ones who need art the most! When children have academic or behavior problems, they often have fewer successes. Successful experiences in art may lead to success in academics. For example, a child who has trouble reading may draw hot rods in elaborate detail. We could use his drawings as a way to help him talk, write and read about his passions.

Be sure to consult with the child's family, psychologist, or other professionals on the child's team. You are not alone!

Cognitive, Language, Communication

Children with cognitive challenges/learning disabilities, or language and communication challenges have most likely encountered numerous negative experiences. Creative art experiences can counter these negative experiences by offering successful and positive opportunities, without a right or wrong way of completing it just their own individual expression. Visual arts can provide an avenue for release of emotions and feelings in a safe non-judgmental environment. Free expressions of happy as well as sad or angry feelings should be fostered. Our goal should not be to depict only the positive or joyful feelings. Life is not all happiness. Art offers an opportunity to validate both happy and not-so-happy feelings and experiences. At the same time, assisting children in working through those negative events and feelings, and learning from them, is also the goal. The benefits of art as communications, along with other developmental and academic/pre-academic benefits of authentic creative art experiences (e.g. sensory, experimentations, sense of pride and accomplishment, telling and writing stories) can assist with building important skills that are particularly difficult for children with these challenges. The emphasis needs to be on the process, not necessarily the product.

Suggestions for Working with Children who have Cognitive Challenges/Learning Disabilities, or Language and Communication Challenges:

- Offer extra attention and close supervision as needed.

- As always, provide safe, success-oriented materials for creative process rather than product, not teacher directed. Many steps invite failure.

- Using large paintbrushes and colored markers require less eye-hand coordination and less pressure to make a mark as shown in Figure 4.17.

Figure 4.17: Large paint brushes and bright paint require less eye-hand coordination and less pressure to make a mark.

- Materials and activities that do not require fine motor accuracy can foster success for children with a variety of special needs, such as paper tearing or crumpling, gluing, larger paper and utensils, foil art, etc.

- If cutting, use loop scissors.

- Using a variety of material welcomes more vocabulary and process talk. Remember the art dialogue for building concepts and vocabulary. Include words describing lines, colors, shapes, textures, etc.

- State instructions and procedures in a very simple manner, assuring freedom of expression and insuring safety for all.

- Demonstrate techniques, NOT the product.

- Foster experimentation without pressure to produce a product.

- Promote child to develop their own style, take risks, and take their time.

- Be sure to use Mirrored Feedback about the child's work. Formulate feedback statements using the art elements and principles.

- Observe their nonverbal communication, and be aware of your own. Keep the dialogue going IF the child wishes and respect the children's need to work without interrupting.

- Children with ADD / ADHD need their own materials and space to ensure success, and allow them to make multiple products. Fox and Schirrmacher (2015) say art offers children with ADD / ADHD opportunities to sustain their attention, allow expression of feelings, and artistic competence enhances self-esteem.

- For children with language challenges, art offers a great means for nonverbal expression, and an avenue for initiating communication with peers and adults.

- The art area offers hearing and observing role models (peers and adults) offering materials, asking, and responding to questions.

- Miller (1996) states that by being a part of a group in a safe physical sense, such as in the art area, children with language or communication needs will be encouraged to speak.

- If children have assistive technology (AT) needed in art, peers and adults should know how to interact with the child, and adults should learn how the AT works and how to assist the child if needed.

- Encourage group activities and interaction. For example, creating puppets for a puppet show in dramatic play offers more opportunity for interaction. Sometimes children will vocalize more with activities such as this, rather than direct conversation. See the Creative Group Activities at the end of this chapter for ideas.

- Simulating what it might be like to have differing abilities could assist with awareness and problem-solving accommodations. Try simulating activities for helping both peers and teachers to have a "taste" of what it might be like to have a disability while trying to complete small motor tasks.

- Be sure to consult with child's family, SLP, OT or other specialists. You are NOT ALONE!

CHILDREN WITH ADVANCED COGNITIVE DEVELOPMENT

Keep in mind that children with advanced cognitive ability may also need some modifications in order to realize their maximum capacity. Deiner (2005) noted that children with unique gifts and talents may be advanced cognitively, yet could have motor skills closer to their chronological age. She stated, "Their ability to plan what they want to do may exceed their ability to do it. Small motor skills may be an area of frustration for children whose fine motor skills have not kept in pace with their

121

cognitive abilities" (Deiner 2005, p. 353–354). She also emphasizes that the visual arts allow children with advanced cognitive skills the opportunity to have some control of their world and decision-making. While experimenting, defining problems, and seeking solutions, they are growing creatively.

A few suggestions for working with children with advanced cognitive development include:

- Allow plenty of space for projects, allowing independent or group work, as the child chooses.

- When setting up similar creative activities (e.g. easel, collages, clay, drawing), vary the materials in size, shape, types of paper, various colors and textures). Encouraging children to try similar methods with a variety of materials welcomes problem solving and comparisons.

- Encourage experimentation! Foster the child's discovery about what works, what doesn't with materials and processes (e.g. crayon resist, painting on different surfaces, predictions with mixing colors). Kohl's MUDWORKS is an excellent source for mixing a variety of materials (even dryer lint!), with delightfully creative possibilities, predictions, and outcomes.

- Origami or paper folding can foster children's understanding of moving from 2-D to 3-D, in addition to practice with shapes, sizes, and mathematical problem solving.

- Creativity focused art games and programs can be found online or downloaded on the class computer, as well as on iPads or tablets (as noted earlier under suggestions for children with social, emotional, or behavioral challenges). Be sure to print the children's creations and treat it as any other artwork produced.

- Children with advanced cognitive abilities may not be as advanced emotionally or socially. Group activities that welcome interaction (such as those suggested at the end of this chapter), as well as assisting children with communicating feelings and emotions through their art can be beneficial.

- Visit art galleries/museums. Have famous artwork prints on the walls in your classroom or home. Encourage children to view this artwork and reflect upon why they created it and the feelings or experiences an artist may have had.

WORKING WITH YOUNG CHILDREN WITH DIVERSE BACKGROUNDS

Children's racial, ethnic, and cultural differences make them unique, and can enrich the early childhood classroom and environment, as well as society as a whole. According to Fox and Schirrmacher (2009), there are two reason for this, "First, it is important that each child recognize that he or she is a valued member of the classroom community; cultural influences on learning must be recognized and honored. Second, early childhood teachers are miles for their students" (p. 83).

Fox and Schirrmacher (2009, p. 83) offer the following guidelines for teachers of young children when developing activities as well interactions with families:

1. Accept the child as is, unconditionally, including culture. Treat all children equally. Guidelines, rules, and rewards should apply equally to all children.

2. Except, respect, and encourage the child's native language and culture as strengths and expressions of unique individual difference.

3. Help the child feel comfortable in school. Sights, sounds, and surroundings may be unfamiliar and overwhelming two some children who have nothing to compare.

4. Discuss and study similarities and differences among people. It is important for children to focus on humanist similarities as a framework for individual differences resulting from culture and ethnicity.

(Fox & Schirrmacher, 2009, p. 83)

These guidelines apply to all area of the curriculum, and can be easily aligned with art goals and activities. For example, we all need food, water, shelter, clothing, communication, and someone to care for us. As much as these might vary, depending on culture and values, all of these basic needs can be depicted in artwork.

Art can be a key area for culturally diverse opportunities. Double check to assure that the activity ideas are open-ended and offer an authentic creative experience. Welcome family members to visit and share their native language, culture, artifacts, art, music, and dance. Be certain children who are learning English as a second language have appropriate means to communicate.

Below are seven aspects of the preschool environment (physical and interactive) that can reflect diversity. These suggested features can be easily embedded throughout the early childhood environment and curriculum.

1. Images: Images can be displayed throughout the environment including in the classroom, hallways, and outdoor environment. Be sure that images of people from other cultures are not just pictured

in their native-wear. Posters, puzzles, bulletin boards, and photographs can be easily displayed through the early childhood environment. Encourage families from various cultures to share photographs to display if they are comfortable.

2.   Artifacts: Special things that depict authentic items used in various cultures can be at the "Artifacts Area or Table," or "Cultural Exploration Center" such as: drums and other musical instruments, artwork, table clothes, pottery, figurines, etc. Discussion about the items (with caution for children to handle them with care) allows children to explore artifacts and artwork from other cultures. Encourage families from various cultures to share artifacts to display if they wish.

3.   Music & Movement: According to Fox & Schirrmacher, "Multicultural songs and dances extend children's social horizons and help them see the universality among people – all people everywhere sing and dance. An acceptance of how children sing and move fosters their self-acceptance and promotes positive self-esteem" (Fox & Schirrmacher, 2009. p. 47). Developmental benefits are plentiful. Expressions of feelings and calming effects that music offers has emotional benefits. Voice tone and movements can demonstrate feelings. Children can learn language and cognitive concepts of fast-slow, high-low, animals, colors, numbers, the alphabet, rhythm and patterns. Many social interactions and sharing can occur through music and movement.

As with visual arts, there is no right or wrong way to sing and dance, there is just your individual way. "Adults who accept children's attempts at singing and dancing send a message if there's no right or wrong way. In turn this nurtures children's creative development" (Fox & Schirrmacher, 2009). Accepting and fostering how a child moves and sings, while embracing their culture offers a strong message of accepting the child unconditionally, including and her/his culture.

A variety of music from various cultures brings enthusiasm and welcomes creative movement. Rap (but censor first), classical, jazz, rhythm & blues, rock ballads, Celtic (Irish), Latin, mid-eastern and Greek music all offer diversity reflecting cultures. Invite families from other cultures to share their favorite native music, language and even dance, if they would like.

4.   Books: As with images, check to be certain that people from other cultures are not just pictured in their native-wear in books. A

wonderful checklist of anti-bias books can be found in Derman-Sparks and Edwards book (2010, p.161), Anti-Bias Education for Young Children and Ourselves. Also, be sure to check for Person First Language and images.

5.   Art Materials: Fox & Schirrmacher (2009), suggest including culturally responsive materials in the art area. Their suggestions include:

   * Avoid only black and white art materials for people making

   * Including multicultural art products, help children mix paints that matches their skin colors, keep a mirror handy for the child's reference, mix Play-Doh in shades of light, medium, and dark brown as well as beige, tan, pink, and black.

   * Include fabric scraps that represent various cultures

   * Provide yarn in thick and thin lengths of yellow, red, orange, brown, black, and gray for making hair

   * Provide culturally diverse magazines for collages and murals

   * Include artifacts such as garlic or tortilla press with Clay and Plato tools

   * Focus on how we are alike, look for similarities and common themes that crossed cultures, such as play, family, shelter, etc.

Adapted from Fox & Schirrmacher, 2009, p. 245

There are wonderful multicultural art materials available that were not around 15–20 years ago. Art suppliers now have a separate section of supplies labeled something like "Multiculturalism and Art Education." One can easily find multicultural paper, markers, pencils, paints, finger paints, crayons, etc. that allow a child to find a skin color that matches their own. One manufacturer even offers multicultural lesson plans:

http://www.dickblick.com/multicultural/lessonplans/

http://www.kinderart.com/multic/

Of course, Pinterest has a plethora of ideas, however, do screen the activities to assure authentic creative experiences are being offered:

https://www.pinterest.com/jvanders/multicultural-art-lessons/

6. Teacher's attitudes and beliefs: It is not only materials that enriches and embraces cultural awareness. Attitudes, beliefs, and interactions that impact cultural knowledge and form attitudes in the minds of children. Children learn from the way we handle conflicts, bullying, discriminatory acts, our own biases/stereotypes, etc. They learn from our verbal interactions and nonverbal communication. These attitudes and beliefs can also be reflected in appreciating and sharing artwork that is culturally related.

7. Helping children resist stereotyping and discriminatory behavior: This can be accomplished through everyday practices, even reflected through the child's artwork and artistic expressions. Anti-bias and anti-bullying can effectively be expressed through art. More on this topic can be found in Chapter 8 Children's Art as Communication.

Again, families are your best resource. Learn from families, embrace their cultures, and work towards fostering understanding and incorporating cultures/diversity into your program on a daily basis.

A unique program called SUAVE, which stands for Socios Unidos para Artes via Educacion, Or United Community for Arts and Education, a volunteer professional development program in Southern California, was developed in 1993 by Meryl Goldberg, in collaboration with local arts educators, art center staff, and elementary teachers and principals. "The Philosophy underlying the program is that teaching *through* the arts (in contrast to more traditional teaching *about* the arts) can be a powerful pedagogical tool for teachers to help students both further their subject–matter understanding and be introduced to the arts themselves" (Goldberg, 2004, p. 14). The purpose of SUAVE is to meet the needs of multilingual and multicultural learning communities in southern California. However, the model and philosophy certainly applies to second language learners anywhere. The SUAVE philosophy is effectively illustrated by an elementary teacher in the program, who talks about the way drawing can foster the building a vocabulary:

In this class, a lot of the kids that are very artistic are sort of limited in vocabulary. They can draw a picture that is much more complex but they can't talk about it. Then, (they) use the picture as a basis for using more vocabulary. Since vocabulary is such a part of how we judge and evaluate people, if you come from a situation where there is not extensive vocabulary or a different language used, then a really important part of school is vocabulary. I believe that if you integrate art in any subject, then there is a better chance that the subject will be retained and used by the child. (Goldberg, 2004, p.9)

Other art teachers from the SUAVE project stated, "In many ways it goes beyond language, which can be challenging for many students. Those students whose native language is not English, or English communication is verbally or written difficult for them, it levels the plane and everybody can bring something creative to the game, and I like how it does that" (Goldberg, 2004, p.4). Other teachers stated, "I feel it has offered (the students) a variety of ways to show me their understanding of concepts," and "As we do more art in the classroom, I begin to see children differently, because I see them do well, but other areas they did not seem to do so well. I see them more as valuable individuals, because I am in contact with the *whole* person," and another stated, "I like giving more options for more students to *shine*, especially those not very verbal or academic in the traditional sense" (Goldberg, 2004, p.4).

Examples of how teachers involved in the SUAVE program incorporate the arts in language arts, math, social studies, and science with all children, and particularly for English language learners include:

- Have children perform and draw concepts.

- Sing it, act it out, using full body movements.

- When children are not singled out and can do activities together, it can bring down the fear factor. They might participate on the same level as other children, and more so, than having them do something independently.

- Put everything to music.

- Write a story and have them act out.

- Put concepts in simple tunes.

- Scaffold

- Always remember the importance of the hands-on learning in all curricular areas.

- Take some risks you haven't tried before.

- Encourage participation and make it safe to make mistakes.

- Role model learning from trying new things or from making mistakes.

- Be flexible, don't do too much in one lesson

- Encourage cooperative learning

- Try to develop and incorporate nonverbal activities

- Incorporate storytelling and puppetry for communication and acting out concepts

- Make use of all senses

- Partner some writing with every art project

A wonderful resource, *Anti-Bias Education for Young Children and Ourselves* by Derman-Sparks and Edwards (2010) includes four overall goals for anti-bias education, all of which could be expressed through the arts:

1. Each child will demonstrate self-awareness, confidence, family pride, and positive social identities.

2. Each child will express comfort and joy with human diversity; accurate language for human differences; and deep, caring human connections.

3. Each child will increasingly recognize unfairness, have language to describe unfairness, and understand that unfairness hurts.

4. Each child will demonstrate empowerment and the skills to act, with others or alone, against prejudice and/or discriminatory actions.

Review, discussion, and reflection of these goals, guidelines, strategies, and program aspects are important to include all children. We must question ourselves, how is culture embraced in our early childhood art programs on a daily basis, not just a special day now and then. It should be a constant process that is included in our daily practices.

GUIDELINES FOR SAFE AND APPROPRIATE USE OF ART MATERIALS

The art area needs to be welcoming, inspiring, and accessible to all children. It also needs to be safe and developmentally appropriate. To be so, some guidelines and reasonable limits are necessary for all to work together. A few suggestions for guidelines are offered by Fox and Schirrmacher (2015):

- Be certain that materials are developmentally appropriate for age range (e.g. no chokable items for children under the age of 3 years, or older if they are inclined to be more oral)

- Limit the number of children in the area at any one time

- Use smocks or old shirts to protect clothing

- Use art tools appropriately

- Use only the material you need for your project

- Share the supplies

- Respect other children and their creations

- Return items where they belong (this works best when all materials and tools are organized and clearly labeled using picture, words in English and any other native language of children in the class, and even photo of Sign Language)

- Finish your art activity

- Clean up when finished (directional cards illustrating steps or sequence in use of materials and clean up can be helpful)

(adapted from Fox and Schirrmacher, 2015, pp. 257 - 264)

Feedback

How do we best respond to children's artistic creativity? As noted in Chapter 2, Deiner (2005) states, "As children feel the impact of the environment, the response they get to their creative efforts plays a large part in their creative development. Educators have an important role in the development of creativity. They can actively support creativity or squelch it by concentrating only on the product that emerges. And they can enhance the experience by having children think more about the process, as it will impact the product" (Deiner, 2005, p. R-130). Feedback is an essential part of art programs. This feedback needs to be specific to the individuality of the child, and the process of their creative expression.

Children learn the value of scribbling from adults. Children also learn to please teachers and parents. Many parents tend to prefer product oriented, recognizable artwork that they can easily relate to as an object, rather than process-oriented scribbles or paintings and sculptures that are unrecognizable as objects. Comments like "What is it?" or "That looks like a _____," suggests that the project is not good enough for you to recognize it, or it forces the child to label when there was no intention in that direction. Children do now attempt to render real objects until about age 4. "Very pretty" or "Nice picture" are vague comments and become hollow. Rather, be a mirror for your child's efforts; reflect verbally what your child is doing. DOING is the key word here, as, especially for the preschool child, process is more important than the product. Describing this process provides vocabulary and includes praise on an individual basis. We can use the elements of art as a framework for our verbal response, commenting on: color, line, mass or volume, pattern, shape or form, space, and texture. Commenting on these elements offers both information and concept formation in addition to inviting a discussion. Encourage discovery and process when talking with a child about her/his work:

- Can you tell me about your painting/sculpture?

- What part did you like best?

- You've used many colors.

- Did you enjoy making this?

- How did the paint feel?

- The yellow looks so bright next to purple!

- How did you make such a big design?

We can also say, "I noticed the way you…

- are working so hard."

- are coming up with your very own idea."

- trying new ways."

We can invite children to tell us about their work. Rather than "What is it?", simply "Would you tell me about your picture" offers, without pushing, the opportunity to share if they wish. The choice should be theirs. In addition, it may not be "something" it may be just a design. Again, forcing children to label their products may convey that it is not good to tell what it is, or it may not be something specific.

Watch nonverbal (yours and theirs). Keep the dialogue going IF the child wishes, yet respect the children's need to work without disruptions. Remember to offer "Mirrored Feedback" about the child's work as shown in Figure 4.18. Formulate feedback statements using the elements and suggestions above.

Figure 4.18: Mirrored Feedback reflects back to the child about their work. Feedback statements can easily include the art elements and principles.

Troubleshooting

"I can't draw" "Could you draw it for me?" "I want my picture to look just like Jennie's" "Your sculpture looks stupid" "What can I make, I don't know" "Ewwwww, that's too messy" "This is dumb," followed by tearing up their artwork and throwing it in the trash; are what we sometimes hear or see in an early childhood classroom. Sometimes children get frustrated, doubt their own abilities, and get creatively or artistically blocked or stalled. When children convey these messages, verbally or non-verbally, we need to be ready to respond with guidance and positive supports. They may need encouragement, verbally or nonverbally. Dodge and Carter (1996) suggest the following when a child:

- needs encouragement:

  o Try saying, "What do you think you could do with a different colored clay" or "What would happen if we taped three markers together to make three lines at a time?"

- ends an activity abruptly:

131

- o Try saying, "Is there anything else you would like to add to the collage?" or "What else did you do on your family vacation that would might want to add in your drawing?"

- is unsure about the next step:

  - o Try saying and offering, "Here is some colored chalk. What do you think would happen if we dipped it in water?" or "What if you used some toothpicks, beads, or feathers to add to your clay sculpture?"

- wants you to make a drawing for her/him:

  - o Try saying, "Let's talk about what you want to make. What is your favorite animal?" or "Do you have a pet?" or "What is your favorite thing to do outside?" or "You told me you went to your grandma's last weekend. What did you do?" and encourage the child to draw about or sculpt what they like or experiences they have had.

- avoids the art area:

  - o Try taking art to the area the child prefers to play. For example, if the child only chooses to go to the block area, bring large paper, markers, and cardboard to explore with the blocks, cars, and trucks. Suggest making a road for the cars, or building a bridge or garage for the cars and trucks, etc. Before you know it, the child is using art materials creatively with in the center of their choice.

- criticizes another child's art:

  - o A strong message should be conveyed to children that they cannot criticize another child's ideas or artwork. First defend the child who has heard the criticism by noting how hard they are working and giving them positive feedback about her/his work. Then note to the child who verbalized the criticism, "Abby has worked very hard on her painting. Look at all the colors she used, and she filled the whole page. Abby can make anything she wants; it is her painting."

- does not like their own art:

- When a child is self-critical or gets frustrated, they may be experiencing frustration due to other things happening in their lives, or unrealistically high expectations placed on the child from other sources. We should always try to "look behind the child" to see what other things are happening when as child gets continually frustrated or upset, and find ways to support the child and family. Try saying, "Antonio, I really enjoy all the colors in your painting and would like to keep it for my art collection, would you let me have it?" or in response to the child stating his/her artwork is dumb, try replying, "I don't think your picture is dumb at all! I see all the animals and people you drew. You used so many colors and filled the paper. Look at the detail on the people's faces. You worked so hard on it."

- does not want to get messy:

  - Some children may want to stay neat and clean, and have been reinforced to stay that way. They may have had negative feedback for playing in the mud or making a mess, and encouraged to stay clean. The reason could also be cultural. Children may not have been allowed to play with, collage or finger paint with food items. Other children may have a neurological reason for tactile defensiveness, and have difficulty touching finger paint or textures. Whatever the reason, we do have smocks to prevent clothes from getting messy, zip lock bags (taped securely shut) to place paint or other materials to explore without touching the substance, even gloves can be worn to protect from the texture. Hands can be washed, and that reassurance may be needed. Start with small steps and go slowly. Even one finger in the paint may be a milestone for some children. Be sure to collaborate with families on this and other suggestions above. Include in your letter to parents about messes, to expect them, and to dress their children appropriately for them.

(adapted from Dodge & Carter (1996) as noted in Fox & Schirrrmacher, 2015, p. 300)

CREATIVE GROUP ACTIVITIES FOR ALL CHILDREN, PARTICULARLY
BENEFITTING CHILDREN WITH DIFFERING ABILITIES WHO MAY NEED
ASSISTANCE AND GUIDANCE WITH SOCIAL EXPERIENCES

The following ideas are activities adapted from Art as an Early Intervention Tool for Children with Autism (Martin, 2009). These activities are specific to making connections for children who have more challenges with social interaction. Children with ASD (the Autism Spectrum Disorder) need specific and carefully planned activities in order for social interaction to occur and be successful. Therefore, these activities are noted here, and are not included in Chapter 5.

Group Mural Shadow Tracing

Goals/objectives: Body awareness, posing, reading body language, and figure drawing

Age levels: Preschool to School Age

Materials: Large piece of paper taped to the wall and markers or other drawing materials

Instructions or teacher's role: Shadow tracing is a body-tracing activity but with less physical connection. This is a good way to begin to help the children become more comfortable with close contact. Turn off the lights and invite one child to hold a flashlight while another peer stands in front of the paper, casting a shadow. Invite another child to trace this shadow, or do it yourself. The child can then fill in details of their body and clothing. Continue until all children are represented on the mural. Group murals of the children's bodies are a great way for the children to pay attention to and get to know each other; be sure to have a conversation after you finish about each person in the mural.

Adaptations: If the child does not want to fill in the details, ask if another child could assist. This shadow method works well for children who may use equipment for mobility, as tracing their shadow does not require altering their position (such as laying on the floor).

Assessment: Make a chart to record which children participated, who interacted or assisted with whom, and what was said about each child.

Friendship Boxes

Goals/objectives: Creative decoration, social interaction, memory recall, gift-giving skills

Age levels: Preschool to School Age

Materials: Small boxes (wood or cardboard), paper and markers, paint (tempera or acrylic) and paintbrushes.

Instructions or teacher's role: Allow each child to paint a box and decorate it with personal touches, such as photos from group, favorite topics to draw, etc. Then pass around the boxes one at a time and invite each child to make a drawing especially for each person's box. The drawing should be of or about the person who owns the box. Once finished, each child should have a box filled with drawings from their peers. Friendship boxes are a great project for the end of the year or before a break, as it allows the children to reflect on their knowledge about each other and provides a tangible collection of memories.

Adaptations: If a child does not want to make a drawing for another, make suggestions to prompt their memory and of positive thoughts to draw about that person.

Assessment: Make a chart to record which children participated, who wrote notes to whom, and what was said about each child. Take photographs of the children with their boxes and with their friends.

Portrait Drawing

Goals/objectives: Selecting and working with a partner, attention to faces, attention to detail, and close interaction.

Age levels: Preschool to School Age

Materials: Paper of any size and markers, other drawing materials, watercolor or tempera paint and paintbrushes.

Instructions or teacher's role: For interactive portraits, tape one piece of paper to the wall for each child. Have the children draw each peer in succession, taking turns for each body part (i.e., one child draws the eyes, then passes the marker to the next child who draws a nose, etc.). The result will be a "gallery" of creative portraits, each one containing input from every child.

Adaptations: If a child does not want to participate, encourage small steps of participation, even adding one facial feature.

Assessment: Make a chart to record which children participated. Take videos or photographs of the children with their portrait and friends who drew their portrait.

Chapter Summary and Looking Ahead

The content of this chapter is at the heart of Art for ALL children. Suggestions, recommendations, and guidelines for providing equal access to the arts and promoting creative art growth for ALL children were provided; regardless of ability level, culture, economic level, or other diversity factors. Looking ahead to Chapter 5, numerous creative art experiences for children of various age and developmental levels, with illustrations of how these experiences can meet early learning standards, as well as integrating sample IFSP/IEP goals for children, will be offered.

Suggestions for Additional Reflection and Review

Fun with Messy Play:
Ideas and Activities for Children with Special Needs
by Tracey Beckerleg
ISBN 978 1 84310 641 8

Playing, Laughing and Learning with Children on the Autism Spectrum:
A Practical Resource of Play Ideas for Parents and Careers, 2nd edition
by Christy Gast and Jane Krug; Illustrated by Julia Moor
ISBN 978 1 84310 608 1

The Hidden World of Autism
Writing and Art by Children with High-functioning Autism
by Rebecca Chilvers
Foreword by Uttom Chowdhury
ISBN 978 1 84310 451 3

The Girl Who Spoke with Pictures
Autism through Art
Eileen Miller
Illustrated by Kim Miller
Foreword by Robert Nickel MD
ISBN 978 1 84310 889 4

Nelson, R. (2015). Art therapy may help kids with behavior problems
Retrieved March 12, 2015 from:
http://www.reuters.com/article/2015/01/16/us-child-psychology-art-therapy-idUSKBN0KP22S20150116

Moorer, A. (2015). New Data Shows the Power of Expressive Arts for Children

Retrieved March 12, 2015 from: http://artwithheart.org/new-data-shows-power
-of-expressive-arts-for-children/

- http://www2.crayola.com/coloring_application/index.cfm:
This site offers a palate of virtual colors and tools to draw
on a virtual blank page. It has an option to print the
finished creation.

- Kid Pix Deluxe 4 Fun art tools for big imaginations by:
Broderbund

- http://www.educational-freeware.com/category-Art.aspx:
This site offers software downloads and websites to draw,
paint and doodle. It also includes reviews of the software
downloads and websites.

- Disney's Magic Artist 3D by Disney Interactive

CREATIVITY JOURNALS FOR ALL AGES

Adult Journal Activity #4

Draw what you know. Have your journal ready with a blank page. Read the following
paragraph, then immediately close your eyes. Try to put yourself in this situation and
environment. Then open your eyes and draw it in your journal, use the whole space of
the paper.

It's a beautiful, sunny summer day. You are laying under a tree on a cool, green,
grassy hill. You can see a few billowing, puffy clouds passing by. You view shapes in
the clouds. Now close your eyes and envision the above. Take a few minutes, breath
slowly and deeply. See the images. Then, open your eyes and immediately draw this
image in your journal, using any utensil you wish (pencil, crayon, markers, etc.) You
can put as much, or as little detail as you wish. Just record the image on paper.

Add ¾ or perhaps full page of a journal-type boxed page (maybe use a design
element to designate the space for drawing.

**Please do not continue beyond this point until you have completed the above
activity**.

Look at your drawing. Did you draw the sun? If so, was it a circle with lines
radiating? Or was it a quarter-circle in the corner? Did your tree look similar to a
broccoli crown? How far did you go with your imagery? Did you elaborate with a
squirrel in a hole in the tree, flowers in the grass or bunnies hopping on the hill? (You
did not need to elaborate, but only draw what you saw in your mind, based on the
information that was given.) Is your drawing a line drawing using basic contour
shapes? Write a reflection looking back at this experience.

Child's Personal Creativity Journal Activity #4

Activity #4 for Infants (Birth to walking, or 16 months)

Winter exploration: In winter, bring in a pan of snow for infant play. If hesitant, offer mittens with which to play. If you have no snow, crush ice in snow cone maker. Talk about the cold, make shapes with your hands or small cups, add a little diluted food-coloring if desired. Self-talk while playing, and encourage the child to explore. Take photos of the child exploring. Note verbal and nonverbal reaction and record in the infant's journal.

Continuing to remember that infants take in everything through their senses, and the infant's journal becomes a documentation of the infant's sensory experiences. Again, please attempt to approach this as a journal, and not a scrapbook. It should include only the infant's work or photos of the sensory experiences.

Activity #4 for Toddlers (walking or 16 months to 3-years-old)

Peanut butter play dough: Assist children in making homemade play dough: peanut butter, powdered sugar, honey. It probably best to have the ingredients pre-measured due to the age you are working with. Using hands and larger clay tools encourage their exploration and sculpting. Children can explore the dough with by touching and tasting as desired.

Give the child the time, the space, the materials, and the positive feedback and reinforcement to create! Take photos of the process. Attach photos of the process and of the product (if there is one, as it may be all about the process) in the child's journal.

Activity #4 for Preschoolers (ages 3 – 5)

Rock painting: Find large rocks, or have children hunt for them when on a nature walk. You might want to take a wagon or bucket in order to carry a number of them (as children have a natural love for rocks, and each child will mostly likely want to bring several back). Put out the paints and paintbrushes, and let them go to it. Give the child the time, the space, the materials, and the positive feedback and reinforcement to create! Take photos of the process. Assist the child in attaching photos of the process, including the "rock hunt" and the finished painted rock in their journal.

Activity #4 for Young School-agers

Found Objects Sculpture: Facilitate children to create sculptures from wooden pieces, foam, pipe cleaners, wire, etc. for sculptures. Try using a foam or clay base, wire would work too. Perhaps a nature walk to the park prior to the experience will result in more "found objects." See Appendix B ENJOYABLE JUNK & TERRIFIC TRASH SUITABLE FOR ART for more sculpture assembling ideas.

Give the child the time, the space, the materials, and the positive feedback and reinforcement to create! Assist including the "rock hunt" and the finished painted rock in their journal. the child in attaching photos of the process, take photos of the process, including the "objects hunt" and the finished Found Objects Sculpture for their journal.

CHAPTER 5

Lesson Plans: Implementing Inclusive Art in the Early Childhood Classroom

> "The world is but a canvas to the imagination."
>
> - Henry David Thoreau

CHAPTER OVERVIEW

Specific examples of full lesson plans, which illustrate how these experiences can meet early learning standards, as well as integrating sample IFSP/IEP goals for children, are included in this chapter. Some of the plans that will be introduced are thematic in nature and offer opportunities for integrating creativity throughout the early childhood curriculum.

These lesson plans offer ideas for authentic and creative art projects for the early childhood educator to use in the classroom. The examples outlined here are designed to foster and reinforce a child's sense of exploration. Ideas for making adaptations with respect to cultural or individual differences and abilities are included so that the lessons are truly inclusive.

Lesson plan format for art experiences by developmental level

The following comprehensive format is used for these detailed lesson plans. It is important to understand the aspects of each component of the lesson plan format with explanations (e.g. adaptations, assessment, linking to standards, and best practice).

Lesson plan format:

- Title of activity

- Curricular area(s) (e.g. science, math, language)

- Goals/objectives these directly align with the assessment

- Age levels

- Materials: equipment, resources, space etc.

- Instructions or teacher's role: What is the role of the teacher/ special things to watch out for, etc. Included will be any special instructions crucial to this activity.

- Linking to IEP or IFSP goals or outcomes: (Examples of IEP (ages 3 to 8 years) or IFSP (birth to age 3) goals or outcomes related to the activity will be included here, depending on age of child)

- Adaptations: Included in this section will be: How to accommodate for children who need a different approach, special equipment, etc. Importance of checking if accommodations or modifications are needed for the goals/objectives, materials, procedure, or evaluation for a child based on their special needs. Collaborating with other specialists on the child's IEP or IFSP team (e.g. physical therapist, occupational therapist, speech therapist, nurse, etc.) is also noted under this section. Noted here are essential instructions to related specifically to goals/objectives, including specific directions for Para educator or teacher's aide.

- Assessment: This section is about accountability. How will you know what the children learned? This relates directly to the objectives, and demonstrates how the data will be record or documented. The documentation or tool for documentation is essential. A chart, checklist, or specific manner you will collect this data. Also, evaluation of one's teaching should be included here.

- Linking activity to Standards and Best Practices: This section links the activity to Early Learning Standards, Best Practices from: NAEYC and DEC, and/or NEA standards. The may depend on the age range of the activity, as NEA standards are elementary level. Appendix A includes a summary of these standards for reference.

AUTHENTIC CREATIVE ART EXPERIENCES FOR VARIOUS DEVELOPMENTAL LEVELS: ACROSS DISCIPLINES; EXAMPLE IEP/IFSP GOALS/OUTCOMES ADDRESSED AND ADAPTATIONS; LINKING ACTIVITY TO STANDARDS

These activities are presented first by developmental levels (infants, toddlers, preschoolers, and young school-age children), and then several suggested thematic units, demonstrating how art can be integrated throughout the curriculum. These units are "ready to go" and set to implement in your classroom, home, therapy, art center, or other program promoting learning through art. More on integrating art throughout the curriculum is offered in Chapter 6: Integrating the Arts across the Early Childhood Curriculum.

Infant Plans

Lesson Plan
Curricular Area: Math/Pre-Math
Activity: Big & Little
Age: Infant
Goals/Objectives: The infant will - observe objects that are big and little while hearing words to describe them. - scribble on big and little shapes. - observe big and little square and circle shapes, and hear words to label.
Materials: - Various items in natural environment that are big and little - Large and small white construction paper cut in shapes (squares and circles) - Large washable markers or easy grip crayons

Instructions or teacher's/adult's role:

- Carry infant around environment, noting big and little items. Use low tone of voice for "big" and higher for "little."

- Present large and small white construction paper cut in shapes (squares and circles), labeling each by shape and size.

- Have infant choose which size or shape he or she would like to use, or choose for the child if they do not indicate preference.

- Present easy grip crayons or large washable markers and facilitate the creative scribbles, giving mirrored feedback about infant's marks.

Linking to IEP or IFSP goals or outcomes:

- Developmental areas of IFSP Outcomes that could be linked to this activity:

    o Fine motor, Communication, Cognitive, Social-emotional

- Examples of IFSP Outcomes that could be linked to this activity:

    Communication & Social-emotional

    o _____ (infant's name) will pay attention to adult when talking.

    Fine motor:

    o _____ (infant's name) will grasp and use a large drawing utensil to make marks on paper.

    o _____ (infant's name) will reach out to touch objects.

Adaptations:

Use Sign Language or infant's native language for vocabulary words.

Assessment:

Using the checklist below will assist in taking notes during the activity. Writing an X within the checklist will show that the goal or objective within the activity has been observed and completed. Notes will also be taken to look back at progress in understanding concept.

Child's Name:

Goals/Objectives	Infant Reactions	Comments
Infant reacted to adult's verbalizing "big" and "little" in high and low tones of voice	Yes/no	
Infant indicated choice of paper (large or small, circle or square)	Yes/no	
Infant participated in scribble drawing	Yes/no	

Linking activity to Standards and Best Practices:

- ELS: ALT (a, b, c), PHD(b), SED (c, d), CL (a, f), M (c, d), CA(d)

- NAEYC Early Childhood Program Standards: #1, 2, 3, 4, & 9

- NAEYC Guidelines for developmentally appropriate practice: #1, 2, 3, 4

- DEC Recommended Practices in Early Intervention/ Early Childhood Special Education: #2 (A8, A9), 3 (E1, E3), 5 (INS3, INS4, INS5, INS6, INS7, INS11, INS12) & 6 (INT1, INT2, INT3, INT4, INT5)

Lesson Plan
Curricular Area: Science/Sensory
Activity: Homemade Snow
Age: Infant
Goals/Objectives: The infant will: • Experience what "snow" feels like. • Be exposed to simple vocabulary words by the caregiver that describes the snow, such as "cold," "white," "frozen," "hard," etc. • Practice social skills as they play, interact, and explore the snow
Materials: water, baking soda, bowl, dish tub or bathtub, freezer
Instructions or teacher's/adult's role: • To make the snow by slowly adding water to the desired amount of baking soda in a bowl until it is mold-able and damp but not too wet. If you accidentally add too much water, just add more baking soda. • Place the snow in the freezer for half an hour or longer before it's time to play. This makes the snow cold and crunchy just like real snow! • Facilitate the child's play with the snow outside in a dish tub. At home, this is a great activity in the bathtub. The

baking soda in the snow dissolves in water so no clogging in the drains.

- Use works to describe the snow, such as "cold," "white," "frozen," "hard," etc.

- Caution: best to not eat the snow since it is made out of baking soda.

Linking to IEP or IFSP goals or outcomes:

- Developmental areas of IFSP Outcomes that could be linked to this activity:

  o Fine motor, Communication, Cognitive, Social-emotional

- Examples of IFSP Outcomes that could be linked to this activity:

  Communication & Social-emotional:

  o _____ (infant's name) will verbally and nonverbally react to new experiences in environment.

  Fine motor:

  o _____ (infant's name) will reach out to touch objects.

Adaptations:

- If the child's native language is not English, learn and use descriptive words in child's native language. Use Sign Language plus verbal words if infant has a hearing impairment.

- Add food coloring for all to enjoy, particularly for a child who may have visual impairment.

Assessment:

Note reactions to the "snow" from infant's facial expressions and other non-verbal signs. Also observe how the infant manipulates and what she/he does with the snow. A video or photos would document this experience.

Child's name:

Goals/Objectives	Infant Reactions	Comments
The infant's verbal and nonverbal reactions to the "snow".		
Descriptive vocabulary words used by the caregiver, such as "cold, snow, white, frozen," "hard," etc.		
The infant demonstrated social skills during play, interacted, and explored the snow with caregiver.		

Linking activity to Standards and Best Practices:

- ELS: ALT(a), PHD(b), SED(d), CL(f), S (b, c)

- NAEYC Early Childhood Program Standards: #2 & 4

- NAEYC Guidelines for developmentally appropriate practice: #1, 2, 3, 4

- DEC Recommended Practices in Early Intervention/ Early Childhood Special Education: #2 (A3, A4, A5, A9, A10), #3 (E1, E3), #5 (INS3, ISNS4, INS6, INS7, INS10, INS11, INS12) & #6 (INT1, INT2, INT3, INT4, INT5)

Lesson Plan
Curricular Area: Science/Sensory, Fine Motor, & Language
Activity: Various Textures, Colors, Temperatures, and Tastes of Food
Age: Older Infant
Goals/Objectives: The older infant will: • Use the palmer, pincer grasp or both, while experiencing the parts of the pumpkin. • Hear words describing textures, colors, temperatures, and tastes. • Experience different textures, colors, temperatures, and tastes.
Materials: cut bananas, cold strawberries, raisins, cold soft cream cheese spread on round and square crackers, child-sized chair and table, a camera and/or video camera
Instructions or teacher/adult's role: • Prepared plate with various foods and place in front of infant • As the infant explores and eats pieces of food, use terms to describe what the child is doing and eating. Use specific words describing textures, colors, temperatures and tastes. Note verbal and nonverbal responses. Take photos to review later, repeating the descriptive words

used earlier.

Linking to IEP or IFSP goals or outcomes:

- Developmental areas of IFSP

  - Fine motor, Communication, Cognitive

- Examples of IFSP Outcomes that could be linked to this activity:

  Fine motor:

  - _____ (infant's name) will participate in feeling different textures

  - _____ (infant's name) will taste at least two different foods

  - _____ (infant's name) will reach and successfully pick up at least two different foods and place in his/her mouth

Adaptations:

- If the child's native language is not English, use the interpretation of descriptive words in child's native language. Use Sign Language plus verbal words if infant has a hearing impairment.

- Depending on age and ability of infant, cut the pieces smaller, smash the fruit or make the pieces bigger.

- If the infant is unable to pick up the fruit, the teacher can place the food in their hands or mouth. A plate with a suction cup could be used for children with gross motor challenges.

Assessment:

Using the checklist, note words used during activity and check when used (sweet, smooth, rough, soft, crunchy, blue, white, red and cold). Also note grasp used, sensitivity to, and verbal/nonverbal responses to touch, temperature, texture, or taste.

Checklist for Lesson Plan, "The Different Textures, Colors, Temperatures and Tastes of Food"

Child's name: Yes/No – Comments / Other Notes

Pincer Grasp	
Palmer Grasp	
Both (Pincer and Palmer)	
Sensitive to touching food	
Sensitive to temperature of food	
Sensitive to texture of food	
Sensitive to taste of food	

Words to use describing eating experience, (please check off as the word is used)

- ☐ Sweet:

- ☐ Smooth:

- ☐ Rough:

- ☐ Soft:

- ☐ Crunchy:

- ☐ Blue:

- ☐ White:

- ☐ Red:

- ☐ Cold:

Additional Comments:

Linking activity to Standards and Best Practices:

- ELS: ALT(a), PHD (b, d), SED (d), CL (a & f), S (c, d)

- NAEYC (Early Childhood Program Standards: #2 & 4

- NAEYC Guidelines for developmentally appropriate practice: #1, 2, 3, 4

- DEC Recommended Practices in Early Intervention/ Early Childhood Special Education: #2 (A3, A4, A9, A10), 3 (E1, E3), 5 (INS3, INS6, INS7, INS10, INS11) & 6 (INT1, INT2, INT3, INT4, INT5, INT6)

Lesson Plan
Curricular Area: Language Arts, Communication, and Literacy/Pre-Literacy
Activity: Tummy Time with Musical Toys
Age: Infant
Goals/Objectives: The younger infant will: • Hold up head for at least 5 seconds at a time • Tolerate being on tummy for at least for 2 minutes during activity • Engage with their caregiver/adult and turn head in direction of noise of toy
Materials: 2-3 musical toys (maracas, drum, xylophone, cup, spoon, tray, keys, wind chime, etc.), blanket, open space
Instructions or teacher's/adult's role: When the infant is comfortable (alert, dry, not hungry), place infant on tummy on a blanket in a calm area. Lie on the floor, facing the infant, with 2-3 musical instruments nearby. First engage infant by talking/singing at face level, and encourage hold up head. Next, make noise with an instrument over to the infant's left or right, moving the instrument from side to side, noting infant's tracking with eyes and turning of head. If working with the family, point out signs of engagement to the parent or caregiver, and also discuss the benefits of tummy time, and how to keep the infant entertained while on their tummy.

Linking to IEP or IFSP goals or outcomes:

- Developmental areas of IFSP Outcomes that could be linked to this activity:

    o Gross motor, Communication, Cognitive, Social-emotional

- Examples of IFSP Outcomes that could be linked to this activity:

    Communication & Social-emotional:

    o _____ (infant's name) will turn head towards sounds or voice of adult.

    Gross motor:

    o _____ (infant's name) will hold up head and tolerate being on tummy.

Adaptations:

Consult an OT and/or PT to determine the appropriate time length that the infant could be expected to do and how often per day/week would be recommended.

Assessment:

Using a timer on a phone or other device, measure how long the infant tolerates being on her/his tummy and note tracking with eyes and turning toward sounds. Also note if/when the infant engages with adult, verbally or nonverbally.

Child's name:

Goals/Objectives	Infant Reactions	Comments
The infant holds up head for at least 5 seconds at a time	Yes/No #of sec.:	
Tolerates being on tummy for 2 minutes or more during activity	Yes/No #of min.:	
Responds to caregiver/adult and turns head in direction of noise of toy	Yes/No #of sec.:	

Words to use describing sounds, instruments, and body movements, (check off as the word is used)

☐ maracas:

☐ drum:

☐ xylophone:

☐ cup:

☐ spoon:

☐ tray:

☐ keys:

☐ wind chime:

☐ blanket:

☐ head:

☐ eyes:

☐ ears:

☐ tummy:

☐ other words:

Linking activity to Standards and Best Practices:

- ELS: ALT(a), PHD (a, b, c), SED (d), CL (f), S (d)

- NAEYC Early Childhood Program Standards: #1, 2, 3, 4, & 9

- NAEYC Guidelines for developmentally appropriate practice: #1, 2, 3, 4

- DEC Recommended Practices in Early Intervention/ Early Childhood Special Education: #2 (A3, A4, A7, A8, A9, A10), 3 (E1), 5 (INS3, INS6, INS7, INS10,) & 6 (INT1, INT2, INT3, INT4)

Lesson Plan

Curricular Area: Language & Science/Sensory

Activity: Pumpkin Exploration

Age: Infant, 8-10 months

Goals/Objectives:

The infant will:

- Explore the pumpkins size, color, and shape, strengthening overall sensory and cognitive ability.

- Reinforce his/her language and cognitive abilities by being exposed to simple vocabulary words that describes the pumpkins, such as "big," "round," "orange," "hard," etc.

- Practice social skills as during play, interact, and explore the pumpkins together with parent/caregiver/teacher.

Materials: One large pumpkin, one small pumpkin

Instructions or teacher's/adult's role: The parent/caregiver/teacher will provide one large and one small pumpkin. With the pumpkin on a blanket next to the infant, adult with facilitate exploration, touching and patting both pumpkins. Using one-word descriptors, adult with discuss size, color, shape of pumpkins, encouraging interaction.

Linking to IEP or IFSP goals or outcomes:

- Developmental areas of IFSP Outcomes that could be linked to this activity:

o Fine motor, Communication, Cognitive, Social-emotional

- Examples of IFSP Outcomes that could be linked to this activity:

Communication & Social-emotional:

o _____ (infant's name) will repeat words used by adult to label items.

Fine motor:

o _____ (infant's name) will reach out to touch objects and textures.

Adaptations:

- If needed, assist exploration of pumpkin by modeling and using hand-over-hand assistance when patting and feeling the pumpkins overall texture.

- Be sensitive to individual tactile hesitancy. Some infants may have more tactile defensiveness.

- Use Sign Language or child's native language for vocabulary words.

Assessment:

The adult will use observation and a simple checklist to keep track on the child's performance during the activity. Writing an X within the checklist will show that the goal or objective within the activity has been observed and completed. Notes will also be taken to look back at: if the activity is recurring or if the infant takes part in other activities comparable to this one.

Child's Name:

Goals/Objectives	Infant	Comments
The infant randomly explored the pumpkins size, color, and shape, strengthening his overall sensory and cognitive ability.		
Vocabulary words used by the caregiver that describes the pumpkins such as "big," "round," "orange," "hard," etc.		
The infant demonstrated social skills during play, interacted, and explored pumpkins with caregiver.		

Linking activity to Standards and Best Practices:

- ELS: ALT(a), PHD(b), SED(d), CL (a, f), M (c), S (c, d)

- NAEYC Early Childhood Program Standards: #1, 2, 3, 4, & 9

- NAEYC Guidelines for developmentally appropriate practice: #1, 2, 3, 4

- DEC Recommended Practices in Early Intervention/ Early Childhood Special Education: #2 (A3, A4, A5, A7, A8, A9, A10), 3 (E1, E3), 5 (INS1, INS3, INS6, INS7, INS11, INS12) & 6 (INT1, INT2, INT3, INT4, INT5)

Lesson Plan
Curricular Area: Social Studies/ Pre-Social Studies & Literacy
Activity: Look at Me!
Age: Infant (birth to 18 months)
Goals/Objectives: • Infant will participate to benefit through self-awareness, social awareness, language and communications skills, and sensory motor skills
Materials: Unbreakable mirror, at least 12 inches or larger or mirror mounted on wall
Instructions or teacher's/adult's role: • Place mirror or hold infant so they are in front of it and can see him or herself. Use words to engage the child in viewing self. For example, "Look at you! See your big brown (or blue or green) eyes? Look, there is your nose." Point to other facial parts, using words to label or describe what they are doing. Touch child's face and tap on mirror to direct the reflection of facial parts. • Adult should note his or her own facial parts in comparison to the infant's. This will increase social awareness of others. For example, "Look at your nose. See, I have a nose too. Look at your pretty blue eyes, one, two. I have two eyes too. Mine are brown." • Add music to observe infant's reaction. Model movement. Could try various culturally different types of music.

- Using a mirror mounted close to the floor on the wall allows the infant to view themselves from various positions on stomach, back, or side. The full view allows labeling feet, hands, etc. Encourage infants who are starting to stand to view reflection.

Linking to IEP or IFSP goals or outcomes:

- Developmental areas of IFSP Outcomes that could be linked to this activity:

  o Gross motor skills, Communication, Cognitive, Social-emotional,

- Examples of IFSP Outcomes that could be linked to this activity:

  Gross motor & Cognitive:

  o _____ (infant's name) will participate and engage in sensorimotor activity

  Communication & Social-emotional:

  o _____ (infant's name) will pay attention to adult when talking.

Adaptations:

- The amount of language used could be increased or decreased depending on the developmental level of the child.

- The adult could just repeat one word if the child has little verbal language skills such as "nose, nose, nose" or add Sign Language or child's native language.

- Accommodations should be made for infants who have limited mobility or using assistive technology equipment (e.g. standing frame).

Assessment:

Using a timer on a phone or other device, measure how long the infant gazes at him or herself. Also note if/when the infant engages with adult, verbally or nonverbally.

Child's Name:

Goals/Objectives	Infant Reactions	Comments
The infant gazes at self-reflection at least 5 seconds at a time	Yes/No #of sec.:	
The infant reacts verbally or nonverbally while looking at self-reflection	Yes/No #of times.:	
Responds to caregiver/adult by pointing to body parts or interactions	Yes/No #of times.: _____	Words used or responded to:

Linking activity to Standards and Best Practices:

- ELS: ALT(a), PHD (a, b), SED (a, c, d), CL (a, f), M (a), S (d), SS (d), CA(a)

- NAEYC Early Childhood Program Standards: #1, 2, 3, 4, & 9

- NAEYC Guidelines for developmentally appropriate practice: #1, 2, 3, 4

- DEC Recommended Practices in Early Intervention/ Early Childhood Special Education: #2 (A3, A4, A5, A8, A9, A10), 3 (E1, E2, E3, E4, E5), 5 (INS3, INS4, INS5, INS6, INS7, INS10, INS11, INS12) & 6 (INT1, INT2, INT3, INT4, INT5)

Lesson Plan

Curricular Area: Expressive Arts (Music, Movement, Theater & Visual Arts)

Activity: Pat-a-cake

Age: Infant, birth–12 months

Goals/Objectives:

- When singing the rhyme pat-a-cake, the infant will participate by moving to the words with assistance, as needed, from adult.

Materials: None needed

Instructions or teacher's/adult's role:

Let the child sit up or lay down depending on the child's preference. Sing pat-a-cake with the child, clapping, rolling, patting, and throwing arms up in the air as the rhyme notes.

Pat-a-cake, pat-a-cake, baker's man (clap infant's hands together)

Bake me a cake as fast as you can. (clap infant's hands together)

First you pat it (pat their belly), roll it (roll their arms) and mark it with a B (draw a B on their tummy with your finger or use child's hands to sky write a B)

And throw it (raise their arms in the air gently) in the oven for baby (touch the baby with their hands and your hands together) and me (touch your head with the baby's hands). Pat-a-cake, pat-a-cake, baker's man, bake me a cake, as fast as you can; Pat it, prick it, and mark it with B, Try a variation with the child's first initial instead of the "B", and then "put it in the oven for _____ (infant's name) and me.

Linking to IEP or IFSP goals or outcomes:

- Developmental areas of IFSP Outcomes that could be linked to this activity:

  o Fine motor, Communication, Cognitive, Social-emotional

- Examples of IFSP Outcomes that could be linked to this activity:

  Gross motor & Cognitive:

  o _____ (infant's name) will participate and engage in sensorimotor activity

  Communication & Social-emotional:

  o _____ (infant's name) will interact verbally and nonverbally with adult when talking.

Adaptations:

- Do pat-a-cake with the child's feet instead of hands.

- Use Sign Language or child's native language for vocabulary words.

Assessment:

Observation of the child's reaction to the rhyme. Could video the process to closely observe verbal and non-verbal reactions, in addition to motor development.

Linking activity to Standards and Best Practices:

- ELS: ALT (a, b), PHD (a, b), SED (d), CL (a, d, f), M

(a), CA (b)

- NAEYC Early Childhood Program Standards: #1, 2, 3, 4, 9

- NAEYC Guidelines for developmentally appropriate practice: #1, 2, 3, 4

- DEC Recommended Practices in Early Intervention/ Early Childhood Special Education: #2 (A3, A4, A5, A7, A8, A9, A10), 3 (E1, E3), 5 (INS1, INS3, INS6, INS7, INS11, INS12) & 6 (INT1, INT2, INT3, INT4, INT5)

Toddler Plans

Lesson Plan

Curricular Area: Math/Pre-Math & Science/Sensory & Language

Activity: Goop & Following Recipe

Age: Toddler

Goals/Objectives:

The toddler will:

- explore the physical properties of several materials.

- observe and explore the mixture between the materials.

- repeat words and names of colors.

- observe and assist adult in following recipe, labeling, and measuring ingredients

Materials:

- Cornstarch (1/2 cup)

- Water (1/4 cup)

- Measuring cups

- Food coloring

- Large spoon

- Tray, sensory table, or flat plastic container

- Large recipe with pictures of ingredients and steps

- Smocks, aprons, or oversized shirts

Instructions or teacher's/adult's role:

- Tell the toddler, "We're going to make goop!"

- Refer to the large recipe with pictures of ingredients and steps. Read over steps with child.

- Have the toddler assist adult with gathering ingredients and measuring materials. When all is ready, adult should state, "We have everything gathered and we are ready to start making our goop."

- Start by measuring cornstarch and placing in container. Use words to label items, measuring tools, etc. and refer back to the printed picture recipe. Pause for the toddler to touch and feel the cornstarch. Talk about the next ingredient, and have toddler help pour water into the container.

- Encourage the toddler to mix it up with their hands and see how it feels. Together adult and toddler can discuss how it feels. More water or cornstarch can be added to thin or thicken. Discuss the difference.

- Ask the toddler about colors, identifying each of the colors of food coloring. Have the toddler choose which color he or she would like to use. Assist the toddler by adding a few drops to the mixture. Pause to observe how the color absorbs, then have toddler mix in the color with a spoon. Depending on the age of the toddler, suggest combining colors and predict what new colors could be made.

Linking to IEP or IFSP goals or outcomes:

- Developmental areas of IFSP Outcomes that could be linked to this activity:

  o Fine motor, Communication, Cognitive, Social-emotional, Adaptive self-help skills

- Examples of IFSP Outcomes that could be linked to this activity:

  Communication, Cognitive & Social-emotional:

  o _____ (toddler's name) will repeat words and names of items.

  Fine motor & Cognitive

  o _____ (toddler's name) will explore textures and objects safely.

  Adaptive self-help skills

  o _____ (toddler's name) successfully participate in routines

Adaptations:

- Offer use of a spoon to mix with if toddler is not comfortable putting hands in. The adult could also adapt by feeling the materials with the toddler or physically offering a handful of the mixture. The role model of the adult touching something unfamiliar sometimes gives the child more confidence to try it.

- Be sensitive to individual tactile hesitancy. Some toddler may have more tactile defensiveness particularly with Sensory Processing Disorders.

- Use Sign Language or child's native language for key vocabulary words.

Assessment:

Using a simple checklist will assist in taking notes during the activity. Writing an X within the checklist will show that the goal or objective within the activity has been observed and completed.

Child's Name:

Goals/Objectives	Toddler's Reaction	Comments
The toddler explored the physical properties of various materials.		
The toddler observed and explored the mixing of materials.		
The toddler repeated words and names of materials and colors.		
The toddler demonstrated social skills during activity, interacted, noted the recipe, and explored materials with adult.		

Linking activity to Standards and Best Practices:

- ELS: ALT (a, b), PHD (b), SED (b, d), CL (c, f), M (a, c), S (a, b)

- NAEYC Early Childhood Program Standards: #1, 2, 3, 4, & 9

- NAEYC Guidelines for developmentally appropriate practice: #1, 2, 3, 4

- DEC Recommended Practices in Early Intervention/

Early Childhood Special Education: #2 (A3, A4, A5, A8, A9), 3 (E1, E3), 5 (INS1, INS3, INS4, INS6, INS7, INS11, INS12) & 6 (INT1, INT2, INT3, INT4, INT5)

Lesson Plan
Curricular Area: Language Arts, Communication, and Literacy/Pre-Literacy
Activity: Stuffed Animals/Pretend Play
Age: Toddler (24-36 months)
Goals/Objectives: The toddler will act out familiar routines with stuffed animals or dolls and use 2-3 phrases during play.
Materials: Materials will be provided within the home or natural environment, such as and may include stuffed animals, dolls, action figures, or other characters. Other props or items from around the home or natural environment may be used during pretend play.
Instructions or teacher's/adult's role: The adult will initiate the idea of playing with the stuffed animal or doll. For example, the adult might say that the baby doll is hungry. The adult could model cooking a pretend meal for the baby, and model language. "Hi baby! Are you hungry? Here are some peaches. Yum, yum, yum, peaches!" The adult should interact and facilitate the play as long at the child is engaged. Bring in other dolls or stuffed animals for additional roleplaying and interaction.
Linking to IEP or IFSP goals or outcomes: • Developmental areas of IFSP Outcomes that could be linked to this activity: ○ Fine motor, Communication, Cognitive   • Examples of IFSP Outcomes that could be linked to this

activity:

Communication & Social-emotional:

   o   _____ (toddler's name) will interact and participate in daily routines

Adaptations:

- The amount of language used could be increased or decreased depending on the developmental level of the child.

- The adult could just repeat one word if the child has little verbal language skills such as "drink, drink, drink," or the adult could even add sign language for "cup" or "drink" or "eat."

- The adult needs to assess the situation to determine how much support the child might need to be successful with this activity. Some children might gather props independently, while others may need to have the activity modeled. Some children might need assistance throughout the activity.

Assessment:

Observe and take notes about the child's language, role-playing, and length of time engaged in play. Note routines that are role-played. Include examples of 2-3-word phrases used by the child play. Share these observations with family and encourage them to include this play in child's home routines.

Linking activity to Standards and Best Practices:

- ELS: ALT (a, b, c), PHD (a, b), SED (a, b, c, d), CL (a, f), CA (c)

- NAEYC Early Childhood Program Standards: #1, 2, 3, 4, 9

- NAEYC Guidelines for developmentally appropriate practice: #1, 2, 3, 4

- DEC Recommended Practices in Early Intervention/ Early Childhood Special Education: #2 (A7), 3 (E1), 4 (F3), 5 (INS1, INS2, INS3, INS4, INS5, INS6, INS7, INS11, INS12) & 6 (INT1, INT2, INT3, INT4, INT5)

Lesson Plan
Curricular Area: Social Studies/ Pre-Social Studies
Activity: Me, My family, & Other Important People
Age: Toddler
Goals/Objectives: The toddler will: - increase self-awareness and self-concept - identify photos of self, family members, and others in their lives - broaden concept of family - increase awareness of the roles people play in their world
Materials: Take or locate photographs of the toddler, family members (start with immediate family members, then move to extended family members), and other people in the child's environment (friends, neighbors, doctor, caregiver, therapists, teachers, etc.). Include photos of these people doing things that represent their roles. Put photos in page protectors to keep photo from being damaged. Build upon this collection of photos, placing them in photo album or journal to view whenever the child wishes. Be sure to include non-traditional roles and avoid gender bias (e.g. show Dad cooking or Mom mowing the lawn).
Instructions or teacher's/adult's role:

- Start with photos of the toddler, with family in various routines and activities. Encourage toddler to identify each person in photos and note what they are doing.

- Add photos of other people in the child's environment (friends, neighbors, doctor, caregiver, therapists, teachers, etc.). Include photos of these people doing things that represent their roles. Again, ask toddler to identify each person and what they are doing.

- Have a routine of building upon this collection of photos. Be sure the album or journal is placed in a location where the child could view whenever he or she wishes.

- Video the child identifying the individuals and what they are doing. Videoing the child viewing and discussing the photos on a monthly basis offers wonderful documentation of development in progress (language, concept building, self-awareness, etc.)

Linking to IEP or IFSP goals or outcomes:

- Developmental areas of IFSP Outcomes that could be linked to this activity:

  o Fine motor, Communication, Cognitive, Social-emotional

- Examples of IFSP Outcomes that could be linked to this activity:

Social-emotional:

  o _____ (toddler's name) will participate in activities to increase self-awareness and self-concept

Cognitive, Social-emotional:

  o _____ (toddler's name) will be aware of people around him/her.

Adaptations:

- The amount of language used could be increased or decreased depending on the developmental level of the child.

- The adult could just repeat one word if the child has little verbal language skills such as "grandma, grandma, grandma," or the adult could even add sign language for "mommy," "daddy," etc.

- The adult needs to assess the situation to determine how much support the child might need to be successful with this activity. Some toddlers might need assistance with page turning or verbalizing what the adult is doing. Some might need assistance throughout the activity.

- Enlarge photos or vary contrast if needed for child with visual challenges.

Assessment:

The assessment of the identification of people in toddler's life and verbalizing their roles can be done verbally and recorded.

Checklist for "Me, My family, & Other Important People"

Child's name: Yes/No - Comments

Identified self in photos? • Verbalized or pointed to or both?	
Used words to describe what he/she was doing?	
Identified immediate family members in photos? • Verbalized or pointed to or both?	
Used words to describe what family member was doing?	
Identified extended family members in photos? • Verbalized or pointed to or both?	
Used words to describe what extended family member was doing?	
Identified other people in child's life in photos? • Verbalized or pointed to or both?	
Used words to describe what these people were doing?	

Videoing the child identifying the individuals and what they are doing offers wonderful documentation of development in progress (language, concept building, self-awareness, etc.). The toddler can even view him or herself in the video to review the people in photos and their roles.

Linking activity to Standards and Best Practices:

- ELS: ALT (a), PHD (b), SED (a, c, d), CL (a, f), SS (d)

- NAEYC Early Childhood Program Standards: #1, 2, 3, 4, & 9

- NAEYC Guidelines for developmentally appropriate practice: #1, 2, 3, 4

- DEC Recommended Practices in Early Intervention/ Early Childhood Special Education: #2 (A1, A2, A3, A7, A9), 3 (E3, E4, E5), 4 (F3), 5 (INS1, INS3, INS4, INS5, INS6, INS7, INS10, INS11, INS12) & 6 (INT1, INT2, INT3, INT4, INT5)

Lesson Plan

Curricular Area: Expressive Arts (Music, Movement, Theater & Visual Arts)

Activity: Crayon Resist

Age: Toddler

Goals/Objectives:

The toddler will:

- Grasp and manipulate the crayon and paint brush
- Successfully make marks on paper
- Make use of the space on the paper

Materials:

crayons, watercolor, water, large thick handled brush, white paper, masking tape, child-sized table, smocks, aprons, or oversized shirts

Instructions or teacher's/adult's role:

Prepare supplies, tape paper down and observe. Remove the crayons when the child is no longer engaged with them. Add the watercolor and water to the activity.

Linking to IEP or IFSP goals or outcomes:

- Developmental areas of IFSP Outcomes that could be linked to this activity:

o   Fine motor, Communication, Cognitive

- Examples of IFSP Outcomes that could be linked to this activity:

Fine motor:

o   _____ (toddler's name) will pick up, position, and successfully use writing or art tools.

Adaptations:

- Larger brush could be offered if needed.

- The crayon could be taped to a glove for children who cannot grip.

- The paper could be taped to a drawing board for better positioning for children who are not able to stand or sit easily.

- The paintbrush could have a Velcro strap for children who cannot grasp.

Assessment:

The assessment will be a checklist with these questions:

- How do they grasp the crayon and paintbrush (palmar grasp or pincer grasp)? What type of lines do they produce (dot, single, multiple, curved, zigzag, loops, or spiral)? What part of the page do they use (all over, central, bottom/top, diagonal, right/left or top/bottom quarter)?

Checklist for Crayon Resist

Child's Name:

How do they grasp the crayon/paint brush?

Palmer -	Palmer -
Pincer -	Pincer -

What type of lines do they produce?

Dot	Single	Multiple	Curved	Zigzag	Loops	Spiral

What part of the paper do they use?

All over	Central	Bottom/Top	Diagonal	Right/	Top/

Linking activity to Standards and Best Practices:

- ELS: ALT (a, b, c), PHD (b), SED (d), CL (a, d, e, f), CA (d)

- NAEYC Early Childhood Program Standards: #1, 2, 3, 4, 9

- NAEYC Guidelines for developmentally appropriate practice: #1, 2, 3, 4

- DEC Recommended Practices in Early Intervention/ Early Childhood Special Education: #2 (A3, A4, A5, A7, A8, A9, A10), 3 (E1, E3), 5 (INS1, INS3, INS6, INS7, INS11, INS12) & 6 (INT1, INT2, INT3, INT4, INT5)

Preschool plans

Lesson Plan
Curricular Area: Math/Pre-Math & Literacy/Pre-literacy
Activity: Shapes & Names
Age: Preschooler (3–5 years)
Goals/Objectives: The preschooler will: • review names of basic shapes (square, rectangle, triangle, circle, oval) and colors. • review the letters in each his or her name. • write letters of name, placing one letter on each shape. • use shapes to create.
Materials: • Small precut shapes (squares, rectangles, triangles, circles, ovals) in a variety of colors • Construction paper in a variety of colors • Various collage materials • Markers, colored pencils, or crayons • Glue

Instructions or teacher's/adult's role:

Each child will select a sheet of construction paper, with choice of color. Children will be asked to count the letters of their names, then select that number of shapes. The adult will ask the children to write the letters of their names, placing one letter on each shape and gluing them in order on the paper to make their names. The adult and child will discuss the colors, shapes chosen, and letters on shapes. The child will be encouraged to use the shapes, markers, and various collage materials to create.

Linking to IEP or IFSP goals or outcomes:

- Developmental areas of IEP Goals that could be linked to this activity:

    o Fine motor, Communication, Cognitive, Social-emotional

- Examples of IEP Goals that could be linked to this activity:

    Fine motor:

    o _____ (child's name) will pick up, position and use writing and art tools.

    Cognitive:

    o _____ (child's name) will increase the ability to reason about geometric figures and properties to solve problems as measured by completion of 2D and 3D artwork.

    o _____ (child's name) will increase use of educational materials to _____ (grade or ability level) to complete classroom art projects as measured by _____ (evaluation tool).

Adaptations:

- Encourage child to write name in native language if

needed.

- If needed, provide a strip of paper with child's name printed on it for a guide.

- Assist child if assistance is needed in forming a particular letter.

- Larger shapes should be provided or larger shape with child's entire name printed on it if child has severe fine motor delays.

- Use Braille for labeling letters for child who is blind and learning Braille.

- Use Sign Language when labeling letters, colors, and shapes.

Assessment:

The assessment of the identification of shapes, colors, and letters of name can be done verbally and recorded. This can easily be part of the child's IEP progress.

Checklist for "Shapes & Names"

Child's name: Yes/No - Comments

Named shapes? • Which shapes? • Verbalized or pointed to?	
Named colors? • Which shapes? • Verbalized or pointed to?	
Verbally spelled name? • All letters?	
Wrote name? • All letters?	
Used shapes to create?	

Linking activity to Standards and Best Practices:

- ELS: ALT (a, c), PHD (b), SED (a, b, c, d), CL (a, e, f, g), M (a, d), CA (d)

- NAEYC Early Childhood Program Standards: #1, 2, 3, 4, & 9

- NAEYC Guidelines for developmentally appropriate practice: #1, 2, 3, 4

- DEC Recommended Practices in Early Intervention/ Early Childhood Special Education: #2 (A3, A4, A5, A8, A9), 3 (E1, E2, E3, E4, E5), 5 (INS1, INS3, INS4, INS6, INS7, INS11, INS12) & 6 (INT1, INT2, INT3, INT4, INT5)

Lesson Plan
Curricular Area: Science/Sensory
Activity: Painting with Ice
Age: Preschooler (3–5 years)
Goals/Objectives: The preschooler will: • explore the properties of frozen water. • enjoy the sensory and color exploration. • label primary and secondary colors. • use creativity to paint with colored ice.
Materials: • Ice cube trays • Water • Liquid water color or food coloring • Craft sticks • Freezer • White construction paper • Smocks, aprons, or oversized shirts

Instructions or teacher's/adult's role:

- Days or several hours prior, freeze plenty of ice in trays along with a craft stick. Drop food coloring in each using only primary colors (red, blue, yellow). This will allow discovery of secondary colors (green, purple, orange).

- Provide the children with large white paper, telling them that we are ice painting today.

- Have children identify the colors. As children create new colors by rubbing the ice cubes and blending the marks on paper, the adult can introduce properties of frozen water, facilitate observation of melting ice, and discuss primary and secondary colors that unfold. Depending on the age of the child, the adult could discuss the three states of matter and the properties of each.

- Provide mirrored feedback while the child works, stepping back to pause as child discovers.

Linking to IEP or IFSP goals or outcomes:

- Developmental areas of IEP Goals that could be linked to this activity:

  o Fine motor, Communication, Cognitive, Social-emotional

- Examples of IEP Goals that could be linked to this activity:

  Fine motor:

  o _____ (child's name) will pick up, position and use writing and art tools.

  Cognitive:

○ _____ (child's name) will increase use of educational materials to _____ (grade or ability level) to complete classroom art projects as measured by _____ (evaluation tool).

Adaptations:

- Use larger sheet of paper if child has fine motor challenges.

- Tape paper to table to prevent movement if needed.

- Use Sign Language when labeling colors and properties.

- If a child does not want to participate, try partnering up with another child to observe and discover, perhaps motivating the child to participate.

Assessment:

An information assessment based on efforts of exploration. Note color identification and comments about property change. The dialogue between the child and adult is the assessment.

Linking activity to Standards and Best Practices:

- ELS: ALT (a, c), PHD (b), SED (b, d), CL (a, e, f), S (b, d), CA (d)

- NAEYC Early Childhood Program Standards: #1, 2, 3, 4, & 9

- NAEYC Guidelines for developmentally appropriate practice: #1, 2, 3, 4

- DEC Recommended Practices in Early Intervention/ Early Childhood Special Education: #2 (A3, A4, A5, A8, A9), 3 (E1, E3), 5 (INS1, INS3, INS4, INS6, INS7, INS11, INS12) & 6 (INT1, INT2, INT3, INT4, INT5)

Lesson Plan
Curricular Area: Language Arts, Communication, and Literacy/Pre-Literacy
Activity: Play Dough Letters & Sounds
Age: Preschooler (3–5 years)
Goals/Objectives: The preschooler will: • demonstrate understanding that letters have sounds that make words • identify the letters in his or her name. • create play dough letters of name. • use shapes to create.
Materials: • Play dough in various colors. • Clay tools • Large table and work space for each child • Pans for baking finished letters and creations • Smocks, aprons, or oversized shirts

Instructions or teacher's/adult's role:

- Adult will demonstrate coiling technique, demonstrating how the coil can form shapes and letters. Ask children to try.

- Request children to form the first letter of their name. Make the phonic sound with them. Encourage them to continue making letters for their entire name.

- Review the sounds and letter names with each child.

- Encourage child to create something with the clay that starts with the same sound and letter of the first letter in his or her name.

Linking to IEP or IFSP goals or outcomes:

- Developmental areas of IEP goals that could be linked to this activity:

  o Fine motor, Communication, Cognitive, Adaptive self-help skills

- Examples of IEP goals that could be linked to this activity:

Fine motor:

  o _____ (child's name) will pick up, position, and use writing and art tools.

Cognitive:

  o _____ (child's name) will increase use of educational materials to _____ (grade or ability level) to complete classroom art projects as measured by _____ (evaluation tool).

Adaptations:

- Use Sign Language when labeling letters and colors.

- If a child has fine motor challenges, assist in rolling the dough or forming the letters as needed. However, make sure the child is doing most of the work and participating. This is great therapy for fine motor practice.

- If a child has a visual impairment, add texture or contrasting colors to the dough for better viewing. Use of a light box underneath the dough can increase the visual connection.

- If a child is sensitive to textures, try polymer clay (less sticky) or pipe cleaners.

Assessment:

Note if children can recognize and reproduce letters in their name, both upper and lower case, if they can make their sounds, manipulate the play dough using coil technique, and if they create a sculpture of something starting with the same letter/sound as the first letter in their name.

Child's name:

Recognizes letters in own name	Uppercase: 0-1 2-3 3-4 All	Lowercase: 0-1 2-3 3-4 all		
Verbalizes sounds of letters in name	Yes	Sounds:		
Makes coil with the dough to form letters	Yes independently	Yes with assistance	Uppercase: 0-1 2-3 3-4 All	Lowercase: 0-1 2-3 3-4 all
Creates sculpture starting with same letter/sound as their name.				

Linking activity to Standards and Best Practices:

- ELS: ALT (a, c), PHD (b), SED (a, b, c, d), CL (a, d, e, f, g), CA (d)

- NAEYC Early Childhood Program Standards: #1, 2, 3, 4, & 9

- NAEYC Guidelines for developmentally appropriate practice: #1, 2, 3, 4

- DEC Recommended Practices in Early Intervention/ Early Childhood Special Education: #2 (A3, A4, A5, A8, A9), 3 (E1, E2, E3, E4, E5), 5 (INS1, INS3, INS4, INS6, INS7, INS11, INS12) & 6 (INT1, INT2, INT3, INT4, INT5)

Lesson Plan
Curricular Area: Social Studies/ Pre-Social Studies & Literacy
Activity: Map Painting
Age: Preschooler (3–5 years)

Goals/Objectives:
 	
The preschooler will:
 	
    • define directions of: here, there, down, up, and in painting
 	
    • identify and describe familiar place they go with their families
 	
    • discuss own creation and creations of others

Materials:
 	
    • Tempera paints in primary and neutral colors
 	
    • Paint brushes and sponges in various sizes
 	
    • Large paper on table and at easels
 	
    • Smocks, aprons, or oversized shirts
 	
    • Large area of personal space for each child, respecting each child's need to sit or stand
 	
    • Tape recorder or video recorder to note details of child's description

• Additional paper for child to dictate details to adult

Instructions or teacher's/adult's role:

- Encourage children to think of a place they enjoy going with their family. Have children discuss this individually, or in small or large group. Write down some of their ideas on marker board, chalkboard, or large paper.

- Ask the children to close their eyes to visualize this place and space. Where is it in relation to their house (here, there, down, up)? Do they have to get there in a car or by walking (or rolling if the child uses a wheelchair)? Have them share the place and how they get there.

- Tell the children they are going to make a map and directions. Have children paint this favorite place. Have them dictate how to get there. Adult can write this on a separate piece of paper to partner with the painting.

Linking to IEP or IFSP goals or outcomes:

- Developmental areas of IFSP Outcomes that could be linked to this activity:

   o Communication, Cognitive, Social-emotional, Adaptive self-help skills

- Examples of IFSP Outcomes that could be linked to this activity:

   Fine motor:

   o _____ (child's name) will pick up, position, and use writing and art tools.

   Cognitive:

   o _____ (child's name) will demonstrate understanding of directional concepts _____ (level of accuracy) as measured by

_____ (language sample, conversation sample, probes)

- ○ _____ (child's name) will increase use of educational materials to _____ (grade or ability level) to complete classroom art projects as measured by _____ (evaluation tool).

Social-emotional:

- ○ _____ (child's name) will demonstrate appropriate play skills, peer relations, cooperative learning and assertiveness with _____ (frequency) as measured by_____.

Adaptations:

- Offer larger brushes for children with fine motor challenges, or the brush could be attached to the child's arm using a wristband and tape. A paintbrush on headgear could also be adapted.

- For a child with a visual impairment could use textures to signal the different colors glued onto the paint containers. Use verbal detail to explain directions and location of paint.

- Children with sensory integration challenges could wear the headphones if sounds bother, and could wear gloves if the paint or brush textures interferes.

- Adapt using Sign Language, Braille, or child's native language, as needed.

Assessment:

Use the following checklist to note if the child created a map or familiar place and described directions. Note if the child shared place, directions, or creation with peers.

Child's name:

Created map/ familiar place	Yes/No	Name of place		
Gave details of map/ familiar place	Yes/No	Details (dictated or recorded)		
Able to use directions of (here, there, down, up).	Used all directions	Used 3	Used 2	Used 1 or 0
Discussed creation with peers	Yes/No	Number of peers		

Linking activity to Standards and Best Practices:

- ELS: ALT (a, c), PHD (a, b), SED (a, c, d), CL (a, e, f), M (c), SS (c), CA (d)

- NAEYC Early Childhood Program Standards: #1, 2, 3, 4, & 9

- NAEYC Guidelines for developmentally appropriate practice: #1, 2, 3, 4

- DEC Recommended Practices in Early Intervention/ Early Childhood Special Education: #2 (A3, A4, A5, A8, A9, A10), 3 (E1, E2, E3, E4, E5), 5 (INS3, INS4, INS5, INS6, INS7, INS10, INS11, INS12) & 6 (INT1, INT2, INT3, INT4, INT5)

Lesson Plan
Curricular Area: Expressive Arts (Music, Movement, Theater & Visual Arts)
Activity: Dancing Markers
Age: Preschooler (3–5 years)
Goals/Objectives: The preschooler will: • draw to different styles and tempos of music. • use words to describe how different music makes her feel.
Materials: • Large white pieces of paper • Large washable markers in a variety of colors • CD music (or music played via smartphone) of varying tempos and styles (Presto vs. Largo; Classical vs. Rock n' Roll; Jazz vs. Celtic)
Instructions or teacher's/adult's role: • Offer the markers and paper to the children. • Tell them to let the markers dance to the music. Encourage the children to listen carefully to the rhythm and tempo of the music, feel the music, and let their markers follow along. Tell them to stop when the music

stops, then start again, while changing the types and tempo of music every couple of minutes. Tell them to change colors as often as they like.

- Keep the activity going as long as children are enjoying.

Linking to IEP or IFSP goals or outcomes:

- Developmental areas of IFSP Outcomes that could be linked to this activity:

  o Fine motor, Communication, Cognitive, Social-emotional

- Examples of IFSP Outcomes that could be linked to this activity:

  Social-emotional & Communication:

  o _____ (child's name) will express feelings through words and creative arts.

  Cognitive:

  o _____ (child's name) will increase use of educational materials to _____ (grade or ability level) to complete classroom art projects as measured by _____ (evaluation tool).

  o _____ (child's name) will increase ability to rhythmically move to various tempos as measured by _____.

Adaptations:

- Larger grip on marker could be offered if needed.

- Marker could be taped to a glove for children who cannot grip.

- If child has a hearing impairment, have him or her work

close to the CD player (or smartphone) and (if needed) place him or her hand on it. Make sure that the bass is turned up and allow the child to feel the vibrations that the music is making. Then allow more time and arrangements for drawing with other hand.

- Use Sign Language or child's native language for vocabulary words.

Assessment:

Using the checklist below will assist in taking notes during the activity. Writing an X within the checklist will show that the goal or objective within the activity has been observed and completed.

Goals/Objectives	Toddler	Comments
Child drew to different styles and tempos of music	Name: Yes/no	
Child used words to describe how different music makes he or she feel	Name: Yes/no	

Linking activity to Standards and Best Practices:

- ELS: ALT (a, c), PHD (b), SED (c, d), CL (a, f), CA (a, b, d)

- NAEYC Early Childhood Program Standards: #1, 2, 3, 4, & 9

- NAEYC Guidelines for developmentally appropriate practice: #1, 2, 3, 4

- DEC Recommended Practices in Early Intervention/ Early Childhood Special Education: #2 (A8, A9, A10), 3 (E1, E3), 5 (INS3, INS4, INS5, INS6, INS7, INS11, INS12) & 6 (INT1, INT2, INT3, INT4, INT5)

School Age Plans

<table>
<tr><td colspan="1">Lesson Plan</td></tr>
<tr><td>Curricular Area: Math/Pre-Math</td></tr>
<tr><td>Activity: Symmetry</td></tr>
<tr><td>Age: Primary School Age (Kindergarten to 3rd Grade)</td></tr>
<tr><td>

Goals/Objectives:

The children will:

- understand the concept of symmetry

- create a design the demonstrates symmetry

- explain how their design illustrates symmetry

- give their design a name if they wish

- share their symmetry design with peers

- identify colors used

- create more designs if they are motivated

</td></tr>
<tr><td>

Materials:

- Paper

- Paints of different colors

</td></tr>
</table>

- Paint brushes

- Pictures of symmetrical objects

- Smocks, aprons, or oversized shirts

Instructions or teacher's/adult's role:

The adult will:

- explain what symmetry means.

- show examples of things that have symmetry such as hearts, leaves, and other things in the environment.

- create a design by painting on one side of a paper, then have them fold and gently rub the paper. When children unfold the paper, they will observe the same pattern on both sides of the paper.

- explain what makes their picture symmetrical.

- share their design with peers.

- give their design a name if they wish.

- create more designs if they are motivated.

Linking to IEP or IFSP goals or outcomes:

- Developmental areas of IEP Goals that could be linked to this activity:

    o Fine motor, Communication, Cognitive, Social-emotional

- Examples of IEP goals that could be linked to this activity:

Fine motor:

- ○ _____ (child's name) will pick up, position and use writing and art tools.

Communication:

- ○ _____ (child's name) will correctly produce _____ (target sounds) to _____ (level of accuracy) as measured by _____ (language sample, conversation sample, probes)

Social-emotional:

- ○ _____ (child's name) will demonstrate appropriate play skills, peer relations, cooperative learning and assertiveness with _____ (frequency) as measured by_____.

Adaptations:

- Provide extra time as needed.

- Assist child as necessary in folding or unfolding paper.

- Larger or thick-handed brush could be offered.

- Use larger sheet of paper if child has fine motor challenges.

- Tape paper to table to prevent movement.

- The paintbrush could have a Velcro strap or taped to a glove for children who cannot grasp.

- Use Sign Language or child's native language when labeling colors, symmetry, and other words.

- If a child chooses not to participate, try partnering him or her up with another child to observe and discover, and perhaps motivate the child to participate.

Assessment:

The assessment of the identification of colors, and letters of name can be done verbally and recorded. This can easily be part of the child's IEP progress.

Checklist for "Symmetry"

Child's name: Yes/No - Comments

Created design that illustrated symmetry?	
Explained what makes their picture symmetrical?	
Gave their design a name?	
Named colors? • Which? • Verbalized or pointed to?	
Shared their design with peers?	
Created more designs?	

Linking activity to Standards and Best Practices:

- NEA: 1(a, b, c, d), 2 (b& c), 5(c), 6(a, b)

- Common Core Standards:

  Math: Kindergarten to Grade 3

  ○ K: Geometry, Mathematical Practices (1,5,6,8)

  ○ Gr 1: Geometry, Mathematical Practices (1,4,5,6,8)

  ○ Gr 2: Geometry, Mathematical Practices (1,4,5,6,8)

  ○ Gr 3: Geometry, Mathematical Practices (1,4,5,6,8)

English Language Arts: Kindergarten to Grade 3

- o Reading: Speaking and Listening, Kindergarten through Grade 3

- o Language, Kindergarten through Grade 3

- ELS: ALT (a, b, c), PHD (b), SED (b, c, d), CL (a, f), M (c, d), CA (d)

- NAEYC Early Childhood Program Standards: #1, 2, 3, 4, & 9

- NAEYC Guidelines for developmentally appropriate practice: #1, 2, 3, 4

- DEC Recommended Practices in Early Intervention/ Early Childhood Special Education: #2 (A3, A4, A5, A8, A9), 3 (E1, E2, E3, E4, E5), 5 (INS1, INS3, INS4, INS6, INS7, INS11, INS12) & 6 (INT1, INT2, INT3, INT4, INT5)

Lesson Plan

Curricular Area: Science, Language Arts, Communication, and Literacy/Pre-Literacy & Math

Activity: Spiders & Insects Dig & Drawings

Age: Primary School Age (Kindergarten to 3rd Grade)

Goals/Objectives:

The children will:

- utilize math skills by measuring out ingredients for "goop."

- manipulate materials using fingers and tools.

- identify differences between insects and spiders by using plastic bugs.

- use drawing materials to illustrate understanding the difference between insects and bugs.

- write stories about their insects and spiders, if they wish.

Materials:

- Measuring cups and spoons

- Glitter, Corn starch, Water, Large bowl

- Plastic insects and spiders

- Paper

- Washable markers of different colors

- Pictures of insects and bugs

- Smocks, aprons, or oversized shirts

Instructions or teacher's/adult's role:

- Present the goop recipe and clearly explain to children. Allow them to make the goop with guidance.

- Use visual pictures and discuss differences between insects and spiders, noting number of legs and other differences.

- Bury the plastic spiders and insects in the goop. Could have some children bury them while other find them. Facilitate children identifying differences between insects and spiders by using plastic bugs and referring to the pictures of insects and bugs.

- Have paper and markers easily available and encourage children to draw their own insects and spiders, noting the difference. Suggest giving their insects and spiders names, and/or writing a story about them.

- Encourage sharing drawings and stories with peers.

Linking to IEP or IFSP goals or outcomes:

- Developmental areas of IEP Goals that could be linked to this activity:

  o Fine motor, Communication, Cognitive

- Examples of IEP goals that could be linked to this activity:

  Fine motor:

  o _____ (child's name) will participate _____ will increase ability to manipulate classroom objects, grasp pencil and hold scissors and pencil _____ % of time as measured by _____ (evaluation tool)

Cognitive:

○ _____ (child's name) will count, recognize numerals, and find appropriate quantities at _____ level with _____ percent/frequency as measured by _____

○ _____ (child's name) will increase organization of written work so that it is legible _____% of time as measured by _____ (evaluation tool)

Adaptations:

- Provide extra time, as needed.

- Assist child if needing assistance with measurements, finding insects/spiders, or counting legs of insects/spiders.

- Larger or thick-handed markers could be offered if needed.

- Marker could have a Velcro strap or taped to a glove for children who cannot grasp.

- Use larger sheet of paper if child has fine motor challenges.

- Tape paper to table to prevent movement if needed.

- Use Sign Language or child's native language when labeling insects, spiders, colors, and other words.

- Use visuals for a child with limited speech, have them point to the picture or differences.

- If a child chooses not to participate, try partnering him or her up with another child to observe and discover, and perhaps motivate the child to participate.

- Have child dictate part or all of story to adult if handwriting is

difficult.

Assessment:

The assessment of the identification of insects and spiders, as well as other goals can be done verbally and recorded. This can also be part of the child's IEP progress.

Checklist for "Spiders & Insects Dig & Drawings"

Child's name: Yes/No - Comments

Utilized math skills by measuring out ingredients for "goop"?	
Manipulated materials using fingers and tools?	
Identified differences between insects and spiders?	
Drew, illustrating difference between insects and bugs?	
Named insects/spiders or wrote stories about them?	
Shared their drawing or story with peers?	

Linking activity to Standards and Best Practices:

- NEA: 1(a, b, c, d), 2 (a, b, c), 5(a, c), 6(a, b)

- Common Core Standards:

    Math: Kindergarten to Grade 3

    - K: Counting and Cardinality, Number and Operations in Base Ten, Measurement and Data, Mathematical Practices (1,5,6,7)

    - Gr 1: Number and Operations in Base Ten, Measurement and Data, Mathematical Practices, Mathematical Practices (1,5,6,7)

    - Gr 2: Number and Operations in Base Ten, Measurement and Data, Mathematical Practices,

Mathematical Practices (1,5,6,7)

- o Gr 3: Measurement and Data, Mathematical Practices (1,5,6,7)

English Language Arts: Kindergarten to Grade 3

- o Reading: Informational Text, Kindergarten through Grade 3

- o Reading: Speaking and Listening, Kindergarten through Grade 3

- o Writing, Kindergarten through Grade 3

- o Speaking and Listening, Kindergarten through Grade 3

- o Language, Kindergarten through Grade 3

- ELS: ALT (a, b, c), PHD (b), SED (b, c, d), CL (a, f), M (c, d), CA (d)

- NAEYC Early Childhood Program Standards: #1, 2, 3, 4, & 9

- NAEYC Guidelines for developmentally appropriate practice: #1, 2, 3, 4

- DEC Recommended Practices in Early Intervention/ Early Childhood Special Education: #2 (A3, A4, A5, A8, A9), 3 (E1, E2, E3, E4, E5), 5 (INS1, INS3, INS4, INS6, INS7, INS11, INS12) & 6 (INT1, INT2, INT3, INT4, INT5)

<table>
<tr><td align="center">**Lesson Plan**</td></tr>
<tr><td>**Curricular Areas:** Social Studies/ Pre-Social Studies; Language Arts, Communication, and Literacy/Pre-Literacy; Physical Education; & Expressive Arts (Music, Movement, and Theater)</td></tr>
<tr><td>**Activity:** Differing Abilities Awareness (set up for at least a week)</td></tr>
<tr><td>**Age:** Primary School Age (Kindergarten to 3rd Grade)</td></tr>
<tr><td>**Goals/Objectives:**

The children will:

- increase their awareness of individuals who have "differing abilities" (or special needs).

- experience activities in daily routine while simulating having "differing abilities" (or special needs).

- simulating having "differing abilities" and experiencing assistive technology; children may need to participate in activities of movement, drawing, painting, and writing.

- share any questions, concerns, or thoughts about their experiences.</td></tr>
<tr><td>**Materials:**

- Plenty of space for setting up stations for: dancing to music, writing a story, drawing, painting, and sculpting with clay, obstacle course, and snack.

- Child sized wheelchairs, crutches, wax paper goggles, ear plugs, masking tape for taping fingers

- CD player or other means to play music</td></tr>
</table>

- Writing (paper and pencils), drawing (paper, markers, and colored pencils), painting (paper, easels or table, paints and brushes, aprons) materials

- Snack, with drinks and food to eat with utensils

Instructions or teacher's/adult's role:

- If a child in the class has some special needs, be sure to discuss this project with this child and family prior to starting. Share with them how you would like other children to be aware of some of the challenges their child and others deal with on a daily basis.

- Borrow child-sized wheelchairs and crutches, make wax paper goggles, and use earplugs or cotton for ears. Using masking tape, tape children's thumbs to palm of hands, then tape pointer and middle finger together, and ring finger and little finger together.

- Set up stations for: dancing to music, drawing, painting, writing, sculpting, and snack. Prepare these stations as you would normally for such activities.

- Tell children we are going to try some activities that might show us how it feels to have challenges and different abilities.

- Divide children in groups (about 7 per group). Each group will have one child-sized wheelchair, crutches, one set of wax paper goggles, one set of earplugs, a roll of masking tape to tape fingers, and an adult to assist. This would be a great opportunity for family member volunteers. Adult will assign simulated equipment (just as individuals cannot "choose" a disability) to each child. With a group of 7, you will have at least 2–3 "peers without similar challenges."

- The purpose is to give a more realistic view, rather than a novelty experience for a few minutes. Adults are strongly encouraged to participate, as they are the strongest models for children. Volunteers or a buddy system would be helpful to serve as aides for children needing assistance or reminding them that one cannot just take off a disability because it is uncomfortable or if having difficulty doing a desired activity.

Linking to IEP or IFSP goals or outcomes:

- Developmental areas of IEP Goals that could be linked to this activity:

    o   Fine motor, Communication, Cognitive

- Examples of IEP goals that could be linked to this activity:

    Fine motor:

    o   _____ (child's name) will participate _____ will increase ability to manipulate classroom objects, grasp pencil and hold scissors and pencil _____ % of time as measured by _____ (evaluation tool)

    Communication:

    o   _____ (child's name) will demonstrate appropriate communication/social skills with peers _____ out of ___ opportunities as measured by _____ (evaluation tool)

    o   _____ (child's name) will seek/respond to information/questions at _____ level _____ out of _____ opportunities as measured by _____

    Cognitive:

    o   _____ (child's name) will increase organization of written work so that it is legible _____% of time as measured by _____ (evaluation tool)

Assessment:

There are many aspects of this project that could be assessed. The assessment can be done through observation, verbally and recorded. Documentation could be enhanced through photographs and videotaping the process and experiences.

Checklist for "Differing Abilities Awareness"

Child's name: Yes/No - Comments

Increased their awareness of individuals who have "differing abilities" (or special needs)? What did child do or say to indicate this?	
Participated in activities while simulating having "differing abilities" (or special needs)? Wheelchair? Crutches? Wax paper goggles (simulate vision loss)? Ear plugs (simulate hearing loss)? Taped fingers (simulate fine motor challenges)?	Yes/No How long? What activities? Yes/No How long? What activities? Yes/No How long? What activities? Yes/No How long? What activities? Yes/No How long? What activities? Yes/No How long? What activities?
Shared questions, concerns, or thoughts about their experiences?	

Linking activity to Standards and Best Practices:

- NEA: 1(a, b, c, d), 2 (a, b, c), 5(a, c), 6(a, b)

- Common Core Standards:

  English Language Arts: Kindergarten to Grade 3:

  o Writing, Kindergarten through Grade 3

  o Speaking and Listening, Kindergarten through Grade 3

- ELS: ALT (a, b, c), PHD (a, b, c, d, f), SED (a, b, c, d), CL (a, b, e, f, g), SS, CA (a, b, d)

- NAEYC Early Childhood Program Standards: #1, 2, 3, 4, & 9

- NAEYC Guidelines for developmentally appropriate practice: #1, 2, 3, 4

- DEC Recommended Practices in Early Intervention/ Early Childhood Special Education: #2 (A6, A7, A9), 3 (E1, E2, E3, E4, E5, E6), 4 (F3), 5 (INS1, INS2, INS3, INS4, INS6, INS7, INS8, INS9, INS11, INS12, INS13) & 6 (INT1, INT2, INT3, INT4, INT5), 7 (TC1, TC2)

Lesson Plan
Curricular Areas: Expressive Arts (Music, Movement, and Theater) & Language Arts, Communication and Literacy/Pre-Literacy
Activity: My Creature Project (long range project)
Age: Primary School Age (Kindergarten to 3rd Grade)

Goals/Objectives:
 	
Over several days, children will:
 	
    • explore words and ideas to formulate their creature.
 	
    • use markers to draw creatures for the project, selecting one of their designs for their creature
 	
    • look over their ideas, thoughts, drawings, and words to draft a story about their creature.
 	
    • complete a final draft on lined paper.
 	
    • using colored clay, transition their 2D creatures into 3D form.
 	
    • observe seeing their creation in another 3D form with a 3D printer
 	
    • with adult assistance, arrange an art show displaying all aspects of this project.

Materials: • Markers, primary and secondary colors, same colors as polymer clay

- Pads of paper (or journal)

- Polymer clay, same colors as markers

- Plastic plates on which to form 3D creatures

- Music in background while children work

- Access to specialist in technology and 3D printer

Instructions or teacher's/adult's role:

- Introduce the overall purpose of the project: e.g. "We get to design really cool creatures, make them into clay, and write stories about them. We will then see your creatures come to life with a 3D printer. Then we will have an art show to share your artwork and designs."

- Encourage children to use their imaginations to come up with words, ideas, and thoughts to design a creature of their choice. Of course, guns or violence in the content will not be allowed.

- Give each child a journal, and markers (with limited palate).

- They can start with the words or the drawing—or both at once.

- Encourage children to elaborate by adding details and color.

- Encourage children to start thinking about:

    o What their creature does?

    o Where does it live?

    o How does it move?

- How does it see?

- How does it hear?

- How and what does it eat?

- What is important to the creature?

- What are other important details about the creature?

They can start writing these ideas in their journal, or dictate to an adult who will help write. If children are dictating to adults, adults must write on a separate page, not the page with the drawing.

- Facilitate children to transition their design of 2D creatures into 3D form.

- Encourage children to reference their 2D design for details and color.

Linking to IEP or IFSP goals or outcomes:

- Developmental areas of IEP Goals that could be linked to this activity:

  - Fine motor, Communication, Cognitive

- Examples of IEP goals that could be linked to this activity:

  Fine motor:

  - _____ (child's name) will participate _____ will increase ability to manipulate classroom objects, grasp pencil and hold scissors and pencil _____ % of time as measured by _____ (evaluation tool)

  Communication:

  - _____ (child's name) will demonstrate appropriate communication/social skills with peers _____ out of ___ opportunities as measured by _____ (evaluation tool)

o _____ (child's name) will seek/respond to information/questions at _____ level _____ out of _____ opportunities as measured by _____

Cognitive:

o organization of written work so that it is legible _____% of time as measured by _____ (evaluation tool)

o _____ (child's name) will increase the ability to reason about geometric figures and properties to solve problems as measured by completion of 2D and 3D artwork.

Adaptations:

- Provide extra time, as needed.

- Larger or thick-handed markers could be offered if needed.

- Marker could have a Velcro strap or taped to a glove for children who cannot grasp.

- Use larger sheet of paper if child has fine motor challenges.

- Tape paper to table to prevent movement if needed.

- Use Sign Language or child's native language when labeling features, colors, and other words.

- Have child dictate part or all of story to adult if handwriting is difficult.

Assessment:

The assessment of "My Creature Project" is multifaceted. Recording how the goals were met can be done verbally, recorded on chart, and through documentation of photos, videos, and child's writings. This can also be part of the several areas of individual child's IEP progress.

Checklist for "My Creature Project"

Child's name: Yes/No Comments

Explored words and ideas to formulate their creature?	
Used markers to draw creatures for the project, selecting one of their designs for their creature?	
Looked over their ideas, thoughts, drawings and words to draft a story about their creature?	
Completed a final draft on lined paper or with assistance by dictating all or part of story to adult?	
Used colored clay to transition 2D creature into 3D form?	
Observed their creation in another 3D form (3D printer version)?	
Participated in aspects of arranging an art show, displaying all aspects of this project, with adult assistance?	

In addition, the project will be documented over the days of production, with the following:

- Photos of each child's design

- Photo of each child's story draft

- Photo of each child's 3D design

- Photos of children's projects and meeting the adults who will assist with the 3D printer version.

- Videos of children drawing, drafting story, sculpting design in clay, and watching 3D printer version

- Videos and photos of children prepping for art show (scheduling day and time, location and arrangement of art work, invitations, refreshments), and photos and videos of art show.

Linking activity to Standards and Best Practices:

- NEA: 1(a, b, c, d), 2 (a, b, c), 3 (a, b), 5(a, b, c), 6(a, b)

- Common Core Standards:

  Math: Kindergarten to Grade 3

  - K: Measurement and Data, Geometry, Mathematical Practices (1,2,3,5,6,7)

  - Gr 1: Measurement and Data, Geometry, Mathematical Practices (1,2,3,5,6,7)

  - Gr 2: Measurement and Data, Geometry, Mathematical Practices (1,2,3,5,6,7)

  - Gr 3: Measurement and Data, Mathematical Practices (1,2,3,5,6,7)

  English Language Arts: Kindergarten to Grade 3

  - Reading: Informational Text, Kindergarten through Grade 3

  - Reading: Speaking and Listening, Kindergarten through Grade 3

  - Writing, Kindergarten through Grade 3

  - Speaking and Listening, Kindergarten through Grade 3

  - Language, Kindergarten through Grade 3

- ELS: ALT (a, b, c), PHD (a, b), SED (a, b, c, d), CL (a, c, d, e, f, g), M (c, d), S (a), CA (d)

- NAEYC Early Childhood Program Standards: #1, 2, 3,

4, & 9

- NAEYC Guidelines for developmentally appropriate practice: #1, 2, 3, 4

- DEC Recommended Practices in Early Intervention/ Early Childhood Special Education: #2 (A3, A3, A4, A5, A7, A8, A9, A10, A11), 3 (E1, E2, E3, E4, E5), 4(F2, F3) 5 (INS1, INS2, INS3, INS4, INS6, INS7, INS11, INS12) & 6 (INT1, INT2, INT3, INT4, INT5), 7(TC2)

THEMATIC PLANS INTEGRATING AUTHENTIC CREATIVITY THROUGHOUT CURRICULUM: AUTHENTIC CREATIVE ART EXPERIENCES FOR VARIOUS DEVELOPMENTAL LEVELS: STANDARDS NOTED; EXAMPLE ACCOMMODATIONS; AND EXAMPLE IEP/IFSP GOALS/OUTCOMES ADDRESSED

Thematic Unit on Oceans

Thematic Lesson Plan
Curricular Area: Math/Pre-Math
Activity: Counting the Ocean
Age: Preschool, 3-5 years
Goals/Objectives: • The children will count dice to create an ocean scene.
Materials: Dice (regular and large), crayons, markers, paper, glue, scissors, pictures of ocean scenes, watercolors (blue)
Instructions or teacher's/adult's role: Ask the children to select something that lives in the ocean (e.g. jelly fish, sea turtles, nautilus, sting ray, shrimp). Have a child roll the large dice. Facilitate the children to count the dots on the dice. After counting the dice suggest to the children to make that number of the sea creature they selected. Then have the children select another item for our picture (treasure chest) and roll the dice again, and draw that many treasure chests in our picture. Children will do this until their picture is complete. When they are finished adding items to the picture, they will paint over the picture with blue watercolors to complete the ocean scene.

Linking to IEP or IFSP goals or outcomes:

- Developmental areas of IEP Goals that could be linked to this activity:

    o Fine motor, Communication, Cognitive, Social-emotional

- Examples of IEP Goals that could be linked to this activity:

    Fine motor:

    o _____ (child's name) will pick up, position and use writing and art tools.

    Cognitive:

    o _____ (child's name) will increase the ability to reason about numbers and counting to solve problems as measured by completion of 2D artwork.

    o _____ (child's name) will increase use of educational materials to _____ (grade or ability level) to complete classroom art projects as measured by _____ (evaluation tool).

Adaptations:

- Children needing extra support will work in a smaller group setting. They will use a modified dice (paper covering numbers past their ability level (only up to 3, etc.)

- Also use the writing support and paper holder, as needed

- The ocean scenes will also be there to help with visualizing the images.

Assessment:

Children will be assessed based on their accuracy counting the dots on the dice, and their accuracy placing that number of items in the picture. They will only be assessed on their counting.

Linking activity to Standards and Best Practices:

- ELS: ALT (a, c), PHD (b), SED (a, b, c, d), CL (a, e, f, g), M (a, d), CA (d)

- NAEYC Early Childhood Program Standards: #1, 2, 3, 4, & 9

- NAEYC Guidelines for developmentally appropriate practice: #1, 2, 3, 4

- DEC Recommended Practices in Early Intervention/ Early Childhood Special Education: #2 (A3, A4, A5, A8, A9), 3 (E1, E2, E3, E4, E5), 5 (INS1, INS3, INS4, INS6, INS7, INS11, INS12) & 6 (INT1, INT2, INT3, INT4, INT5)

Thematic Lesson Plan
Curricular Area: Science/Sensory
Activity: Categorize the Ocean Creatures
Age: Preschool, 3-5 years
Goals/Objectives: • Children will be able to categorize animals that live in the ocean and the jungle.
Materials: pages of jungle animals, pages of ocean animals, blank books (for drawing animals), crayons, t-chart, dry erase marker.
Instructions or teacher's/adult's role: • The children will then help the teacher complete a t-chart of ocean animals and jungle animals. Teacher will read books identifying ocean animals and jungle animals. The children will then help the teacher check the T-chart to see if they matched the book and add any other ideas they saw in the books. • After checking the t-chart the children will be released to their tables to draw a jungle scene and an ocean scene in their blank books. • After their drawings are complete they will be given the pages of animals to cut out and place in the appropriate scene.

Linking to IEP or IFSP goals or outcomes:

- Developmental areas of IEP Goals that could be linked to this activity:

  o Fine motor, Communication, Cognitive, Social-emotional

- Examples of IEP Goals that could be linked to this activity:

  Fine motor:

  o _____ (child's name) will pick up, position and use writing and art tools.

  Cognitive:

  o _____ (child's name) will increase use of educational materials to _____ (grade or ability level) to complete classroom art projects as measured by _____ (evaluation tool).

  o _____ (child's name) will increase the ability to reason categorize to solve problems as measured by completion of 2D artwork.

Adaptations:

- Children who need extra support will be given pages of animals that require less cutting (only cutting across one line between pictures instead of cutting out squares).

- Children will be provided the supports needed due to various physical disabilities (grasp supports and paper holder support).

- Children will be provided a page to help with sorting the animals (they will have to match instead)

Assessment:

You will know the children have succeeded in the task when they have completed their jungle and ocean scenes with correct animal sorting. List any notes you have below.

Linking activity to Standards and Best Practices:

- ELS: ALT (a, c), PHD (b), SED (b, d), CL (a, e, f), S (b, d), CA (d)

- NAEYC Early Childhood Program Standards: #1, 2, 3, 4, & 9

- NAEYC Guidelines for developmentally appropriate practice: #1, 2, 3, 4

- DEC Recommended Practices in Early Intervention/ Early Childhood Special Education: #2 (A3, A4, A5, A8, A9), 3 (E1, E3), 5 (INS1, INS3, INS4, INS6, INS7, INS11, INS12) & 6 (INT1, INT2, INT3, INT4, INT5)

Thematic Lesson Plan

Curricular Area: Language Arts, Communication, and Literacy/Pre-Literacy

Activity: Who Helped the Pout-Pout Fish? by Debora Diesen

Age: Preschool, 3-5 years

Goals/Objectives:

The child will:

- recall sequence of events of the book, The Pout-Pout Fish.

- demonstrate understanding of sequence by putting sequence sheets in order

- illustrated a character through their painting

Materials:

The Pout-Pout Fish by Debora Diesen, sequencing sheets (pre-cut), blank paper, finger paint, finger paint paper

Instructions or teacher's/adult's role:

- Read the book, The Pout-Pout Fish (2013), having the children help read the repetitive sections. After reading the adult will sequence the story with input from the children. "Who was the first one to come up to the "Pout-Pout fish?"

- After the book has been completely sequenced, the adult will demonstrate the sequencing of the book on a large piece of paper with the help of the children.

- The children will then go to their table to sequence their own papers (pre-cut) and glue them to their paper.

- When they have completed their sequencing, children will paint or draw a character of their choosing from the story. Children will continue to illustrate their version of other characters or aspects of the story if they wish. If they wish to continue the story with other characters and happenings, facilitate their writing. This could be a good addition to their journal.

Linking to IEP or IFSP goals or outcomes:

- Developmental areas of IEP Goals that could be linked to this activity:

  o Fine motor, Communication, Cognitive

- Examples of IEP goals that could be linked to this activity:

Fine motor:

  o _____ (child's name) will participate _____ will increase ability to manipulate classroom objects, grasp pencil and hold scissors and pencil _____ % of time as measured by _____ (evaluation tool)

Communication:

  o _____ (child's name) will demonstrate appropriate communication/social skills with peers _____ out of ___ opportunities as measured by _____ (evaluation tool)

  o _____ (child's name) will seek/respond to information/questions at _____ level _____ out of _____ opportunities as measured by _____

Cognitive:

     ○   _____ (child's name) will increase organization of written work so that it is legible _____% of time as measured by _____ (evaluation tool)

Adaptations:

- Provide extra time, as needed.

- Children needing the extra support for sequencing will be provided a sheet to match the sequencing slips to.

- Children with an aversion to finger-painting will be provided a paintbrush to create their character.

- Use larger sheet of paper if child has fine motor challenges.

- Tape paper to table to prevent movement if needed.

- Use Sign Language or child's native language when labeling characters, sequence, and other words.

- If a child chooses not to participate, try partnering her or him with another child to observe and discover, and perhaps motivate the child to participate.

Assessment:

Children will be assessed using their sequencing papers. This can be done through observations, verbal response, and recorded.

Checklist for "Who Helped the Pout-Pout Fish?"

Child's name: Yes/No - Comments

Recalled sequence of book as demonstrated by order of sequence sheets? All or part?	
Illustrated a character through their painting?	
Painted additional characters or part of the story?	

Linking activity to Standards and Best Practices:

- ELS: ALT (a, b, c), PHD (a, b), SED (a, b, c, d), CL (a, c, d, e, f, g), M (c, d), S (a), CA (d)

- NAEYC Early Childhood Program Standards: #1, 2, 3, 4, & 9

- NAEYC Guidelines for developmentally appropriate practice: #1, 2, 3, 4

- DEC Recommended Practices in Early Intervention/ Early Childhood Special Education: #2 (A3, A3, A4, A5, A7, A8, A9, A10, A11), 3 (E1, E2, E3, E4, E5), 4(F2, F3) 5 (INS1, INS2, INS3, INS4, INS6, INS7, INS11, INS12) & 6 (INT1, INT2, INT3, INT4, INT5), 7(TC2)

Thematic Lesson Plan

Curricular Area: Social Studies/Pre-Social Studies

Activity: Ocean Mural

Age: Preschool, 3-5 years

Goals/Objectives:

Children will recall information they have learned about oceans and collaborate to create a class mural based on these facts.

Materials:

Large canvas (8x6) or thick roll of paper, acrylic paint, markers, paper, glue, CD (or smartphone) with ocean sounds.

Instructions or teacher's/adult's role:

- Show the children examples of famous murals. Explain how murals are large paintings or reliefs that show a certain subject or theme. If possible, locate one in the community and visit prior to this activity. Discuss different subjects of the murals that are viewed.

- Explain how they are going to create a class mural of the ocean to hang on the wall. Present the large canvas and discuss how this will be a very special mural that they will be able to look at every day after it is created. Also discuss how we respect each other by not marking over other children's creations.

- Start CD (or smartphone) with ocean sounds.

- Have materials displayed for easy access,

replenishing paints as needed.

Linking to IEP or IFSP goals or outcomes:

- Developmental areas of IEP Goals that could be linked to this activity:

  o Fine motor, Communication, Cognitive, Social-emotional

- Examples of IEP goals that could be linked to this activity:

  Fine motor:

  o _____ (child's name) will participate _____ will increase ability to manipulate classroom objects, grasp pencil and hold scissors and pencil _____ % of time as measured by _____ (evaluation tool)

  Communication & Social-emotional:

  o _____ (child's name) will demonstrate appropriate communication/social skills with peers _____ out of ___ opportunities as measured by _____ (evaluation tool)

  o _____ (child's name) will seek/respond to information/questions at _____ level _____ out of _____ opportunities as measured by _____

  Cognitive:

  o _____ (child's name) will recall facts learned about a topic, as demonstrate through art and verbal response _____ % of time as measured by _____ (evaluation

tool)

Adaptations:

- Provide extra time, as needed.

- Assist child if needing assistance recalling facts about the ocean.

- Larger or thick-handed paint brushes or markers could be offered if needed.

- Marker or paintbrush could have a Velcro strap or taped to a glove for children who cannot grasp.

- Use Sign Language or child's native language when creatures, facts about the ocean, and other words.

Assessment:

Children will be assessed on recalling ocean facts and participation in the mural creation. The checklist below can assist with recording observations, verbal response, and creation process. Documentation of photos and videotaping can enhance the assessment possibilities.

Checklist for "Ocean Mural"

Child's name: Yes/No - Comments

Verbally recalled information learned about oceans? What specifics?	
Illustrated facts recalled through her or his painting? What facts?	
Discussed creations with peers?	
Painted additional characters or part of the story?	

Linking activity to Standards and Best Practices:

- ELS: ALT (a, b, c), PHD (a, b), SED (b, c, d), CL (a, c, f, g), M (a, c, d), S (c, d), CA (b, d)

- NAEYC Early Childhood Program Standards: #1, 2, 3, 4, & 9

- NAEYC Guidelines for developmentally appropriate practice: #1, 2, 3, 4

- DEC Recommended Practices in Early Intervention/ Early Childhood Special Education: #2 (A3, A5, A7, A8, A9, A10, A11), 3 (E1, E2, E3, E4, E5), 5 (INS1, INS2, INS3, INS4, INS6, INS7, INS11, INS12) & 6 (INT1, INT2, INT3, INT4, INT5)

Thematic Lesson Plan

Curricular Area: Expressive Arts (Music, Movement, and Theater) & Visual Arts

Activity: Ocean Song

Age: Preschool, 3-5 years

Goals/Objectives:

Children will:

- demonstrate an understanding of rhythm and volume by creating an ocean song with drums and bells.

- listen to (or view and listen to) ocean song "composition" the class created.

- create a 2D or 3D art project while listening to ocean song "composition" the class created.

Materials:

Drums, ocean sounds on the computer, CD, or smartphone, classical music based on oceans

Instructions or teacher's/adult's role:

- Play a classical song that is based on or inspired by the ocean and help the children discuss. Ask how the sound makes them feel. Have children dictate a list of the sounds that they heard in the song or events that happened while writing them on large paper or easel for easy viewing.

- Assist children in recreating a similar sound or feeling using the drums and bells. If there is a sound they think of but was not in the song, use the ocean sounds on the computer or smartphone to help.

- Help the children "write an ocean song." To help scribe the song use images and write the order on large paper or easel. To show volume, make the images large or small.

- Ask children to play their own song using the rhythms and volumes.

- Record or videotape the children's composition.

- Play the recording or videotape while children are in the free art area, encouraging them to create 2D or 3D artwork as they listen to their composition.

Linking to IEP or IFSP goals or outcomes:

- Developmental areas of IEP goals that could be linked to this activity:

    o Fine motor, Communication, Cognitive, Social-emotional

- Examples of IEP goals that could be linked to this activity:

    Social-emotional & Communication:

    o _____ (child's name) will express feelings through words and creative arts.

    Cognitive:

    o _____ (child's name) will increase use of educational materials to _____ (grade or ability level) to complete classroom art projects as measured by

_____ (evaluation tool).

o _____ (child's name) will increase ability to produce rhythms and various tempos based on sensory input, as measured by _____.

Adaptations:

- Provide extra time as needed.

- Accommodations with art materials as needed.

- Use Sign Language or child's native language as needed.

- If child has a hearing impairment, have him or her close to the CD player and if needed place their hand on it. Make sure that the bass is turned up and allow the child to feel the vibrations that the music is making. Then allow more time and arrangements produce music with instruments with other hand.

- Children who have difficulty with grasping will use the iPad to create their sounds for the song. They will be able to push the drum or bell button to create the sound.

Assessment:

The assessment of "Ocean Song" is multifaceted. Recording how goals were met can be done verbally, recorded on chart, and through documentation of photos, videos, and child's artwork.

Checklist for "Ocean Song"

Child's name: Yes/No - Comments

Demonstrated an understanding of rhythm and volume by creating an ocean song with drums and bells?	
Listened to (or viewed and listened to) ocean song "composition" class created?	
Created a 2D or 3D art project while listening to ocean song "composition" class created?	

Linking activity to Standards and Best Practices:

- ELS: ALT (a, c), PHD (a, b), SED (b, c, d), CL (a, f), M (5), S (c, d), CA (a, b, d)

- NAEYC Early Childhood Program Standards: #1, 2, 3, 4, & 9

- NAEYC Guidelines for developmentally appropriate practice: #1, 2, 3, 4

- DEC Recommended Practices in Early Intervention/ Early Childhood Special Education: #2 (A8, A9, A10), 3 (E1, E3), 5 (INS3, INS4, INS5, INS6, INS7, INS11, INS12) & 6 (INT1, INT2, INT3, INT4, INT5)

Chapter Summary and Looking Ahead

This chapter emphasized the importance of authentic creative art experiences for children by sharing examples of full lesson plans that the early childhood educator can use in the classroom. These lesson plans are specifically designed to meet early learning standards and to integrate IFSP and IEP goals for children with special needs. Sample wording for goals has been included so that the educator will have a template for creating such goals based on the IFSP and IEP of her or his students. In addition, the ideas outlined have included examples of both 2D and 3D art activities. They have been specifically designed to inspire a child's sense of exploration. Some of the plans that have been introduced are thematic in nature and offer opportunities for integrating creativity throughout the early childhood curriculum.

Chapter 6 will demonstrate how authentic creative art can be partnered with and can enhance the early childhood curriculum. This chapter will offer examples of integrating the arts and freedom of creative expression throughout the early childhood curriculum. These examples will include experiences in: (a) Math/Pre-Math; (b)

Science/Sensory; (c) Language Arts, Communication, and Literacy/Pre-Literacy; (d) Social Studies/ Pre- Social Studies; and (e) Expressive Arts (Music, Movement, and Theater).

Suggestions for Additional Reflection and Review

The reader is strongly encourage to view and reflect upon The Dancing, Singing Easel, shared by family child care provider Emily Plank in January/February 2013 Child Care Exchange issue. It is a delightful illustration of authentic, spontaneous creativity in action, which could never have been planned.

See: http://www.childcareexchange.com/eed/news_print.php?news_id=3260

CREATIVITY JOURNAL FOR ALL AGES

Adult Journal Activity #5

Recognizing Authentic Artistic Creativity: Take a look at the following website and PowerPoint:

> http://prekandksharing.blogspot.com/2012/02/childrens-art-process-versus-product.html

> http://www.fairfaxcounty.gov/ofc/docs/webinarhandout-process-oriented-art.pdf

> Explore difference between process (open-ended, exploratory, unique, and individual expression) and product (closed-ended, teacher directed, structured, model to follow) art. Observe artwork at various schools, preschools, and other areas you see children's art displayed. Determine if it is process or product art. If it is product oriented, consider sharing material about, and advocating for process art.

Child's Personal Creativity Journal Activity #5

Activity #5 for Infants (Birth to walking, or 16 months)

Edible finger painting: Using materials of yogurt, Kool Aid, large sheets of paper or washable surface, mix the yogurt with different flavors and colors of Kool Aid. Put a dollop of each color on the paper in front of the infant. Encourage infant to explore, talk about colors, textures, lines, smells, and tastes. For infants who might be tactilely defensive, the paints and paper could be put in a clear plastic bag. Then the infant could touch the outside of the bag to move the paint around.

Continuing to remember that infants take in everything through their senses, and the infant's journal becomes a documentation of the infant's sensory experiences. Again, please attempt to approach this as a journal, and not a scrapbook. It should include only the infant's work or photos of the sensory experiences.

Activity #5 for Toddlers (walking or 16 months to 3-years-old)

Multiple scribbles: Have child choose 3-4 colors of washable markers. Using masking tape, bundle the markers so the toddler can grasp with one hand. Using large roll of paper on the floor or large utility box, encourage the toddler to make marks using all of the space. Give the child the time, the space, the materials, and the positive feedback and reinforcement to create! Take photos of the process. Attach photos of the process and the completed box art in the journal.

Activity #5 for Preschoolers (ages 3 – 5)

Glue/cornstarch dough: Have child assist with measuring and mixing together 1-cup flour, 1-cup cornstarch, and ½ cup white glue. Add water and knead until workable. Encourage child to explore and create. Add food coloring if desired with adding the water. Give the child the time, the space, the materials, and the positive feedback and reinforcement to create! Take photos of the process to include in the journal. If child wants to write a story about her/his creation, add it to the journal.

Activity #5 for Young School-age Children

Painting and drawing to music: Materials needed include a variety of music, paint, paintbrushes, crayons, and paper or canvas. While listening to a variety of types of music, encourage children to paint and draw based on what the music makes them think or feel. Give the child the time, the space, the materials, and the positive feedback and reinforcement to create! Take photos of the process. Attach photos of the process and encourage children to reflect on the experience by writing about it in their journals.

CHAPTER 6

Integrating the Arts across the Early Childhood Curriculum

Carol L. Russell and Heather Caswell

> "Lend your ears to music, open your eyes to painting, and stop thinking! Just ask yourself whether the work has enabled you to 'walk about' into a hitherto unknown world. If the answer is yes, what more do you want?"
>
> - Wassily Kandinsky

CHAPTER OVERVIEW

The arts can enhance the early childhood curriculum. Art can be integrated into the curriculum; and the curriculum can also be effectively incorporated into the arts. It can be either, and worthy of attaining a balance. This chapter's focus is on embedding the arts throughout the curriculum and building pre-academic skills though the arts. Examples of integrating the arts to enhance the early childhood curriculum are illustrated, including experiences in: (a) Math/Pre-Math; (b) Science/Sensory; (c) Language Arts, Communication, and Literacy/Pre-Literacy; (d) Social Studies/ Pre-Social Studies; and (e) Expressive Arts (Music, Movement, and Theater). Numerous examples of how art can be used as a medium for concept development in various curricular areas will be provided. These examples can also be linked with Early Learning Standards, Best Practices from National Association of Education of Young Children (NAEYC) and Division of Early Childhood (DEC). In addition, examples will include integrating the arts and concept development through the arts to implement at home, in various therapies, and in community settings.

Developmental Benefits and Importance of Art in the Curriculum

There is little question in educational circles about how art enhances creativity, imagination, self-expression, and self-esteem. According to art therapist, Ann Rener (2007), "Much has been written about how art enhances creativity, imagination, and self-esteem, but far less is said about how art encourages cognition, critical thinking, and learning" (p. 1). Rener justified the importance of the arts in our current educational system, which now places most emphasis on academic development with little time or value for art. She asserts that the arts are often seen as unnecessary frill, resulting in reduction or elimination of art programs. On the contrary, Rener states that the arts are basic to education. "With the many challenges our public education system faces today, combining art with academic subjects in the classroom becomes increasingly important" (Rener, 2007, p. 1).

Yet, developmental benefits of quality art experiences for young children had been documented for many years. The positive impact in all domains were noted by Caplan (1978), "Experts agree that the kind and quality of art experiences you give your preschool child will have a deep and lasting effect on his abilities, perceptions, and personality. They affect his powers of observation, his emotional health, his confidence, and his ability to express himself" (Caplan, 1978, p. 535). These valuable experiences should be available to all children of all ages. Early quality art experiences can last a lifetime and have the potential to build skills and a strong developmental foundation in all domains.

The developmental benefits of quality art experiences can easily be partnered with all areas of the early childhood curriculum. The arts can also be embedded within therapies for children who have additional challenges or varying abilities. Embedding the arts throughout the curriculum and building pre-academic skills through the arts is not a new approach, however, the possibilities have not been fully explored and often given little value. The data to back this in the public schools is limited, but growing. Robelen (2010) notes that integrating the arts into the overall curriculum is not new, yet seems to be increasing in public schools, although national data is unavailable. Advocates of arts education (visual arts, music, theater, dance) attempt to provide adequate time, "amid the financial straits facing many districts and other challenges, such as pressure to boost test scores in core subjects like reading and math." (Robelen, 2010). In the illustration below, one can easily see the integrations of multiple areas of the curriculum and developmental benefits to the child. The child had been to Kansas City's Sea Life Aquarium and did the follow up drawing of "Tally-Allie" who was a green sea turtle with one flipper missing. The sea turtle had some special needs due to a fishing line being wrapped around her flipper, resulting in one flipper being removed in order to save its life. The original sea turtle's name was Gertrude, but the child named the creature in her drawing after a friend who had some special needs. Figure 6.1 is a photograph of Gertrude at the Sea Life Aquarium in Kansas City, Missouri.

Figure 6.1: Gertrude the Sea Turtle at Sea Life Aquarium in Kansas City, Missouri.

By observing this child's drawing of the sea turtle in Figure 6.2, we notice:

- Math & Art/ Physical & Cognitive Domains Geometry, spatial relationships, balance, planning and sequencing can all be observed through the child's use of lines, colors, shapes, balance, use of space, subject, form, and content in her drawing.

- Literacy/Cognitive & Emotional Domains The child's writing of the words "energetic, graceful, fast, protective, smart, curious" by the drawing expressed the characteristics of the sea turtle. These words transitioned directly into her story (which is to the right of the drawing).

- Science/Cognitive Domain Observation of details of the sea turtle (missing one flipper, words to describe actions based on observing the sea turtle, placement of features and appendages, etc.) were noted expressed from the child's experience at the aquarium.

- Problem solving/Cognitive & Physical Domains Determining how to fit in all of the colors on the sea turtle's back, labeling each color illustrates the child's problem solving and physical skills. In addition, this demonstrated the child's eye-hand coordination and perceptual motor skills.

- Social & Emotional Domains Pride, sense of accomplishment, enjoying her own creation, and sharing with others were evident in the child's discussions with others about "Tally-Allie."

- Emotional Domain Inspiration, motivation, and compassion were evident with the child's drawing, clay creation, and story. Sense of strength and inspiration of survival were expressed by her depiction her drawing and story. Although the sea turtle lost a flipper, she was a survivor, and in this child's eyes was "energetic, graceful, fast, protective, smart curious."

Figure 6.3 shows the child's depiction of Tally-Allie, the Turtle/Shark/Bird in her drawing and clay sculpture. Note the labeling of colors on the turtles back.

Figure 6.2: Tally-Allie, the Turtle/Shark/Bird drawing by Anya, 9 years.

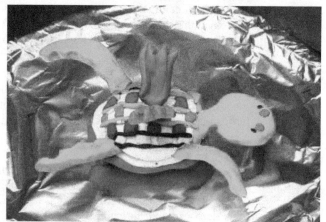

Figure 6.3: Tally-Allie, the Turtle/Shark/Bird designed by Anya, 9 years, in polymer clay

Below is the story Anya wrote about Tally-Allie, the Turtle/Shark/Bird to accompany her drawing and clay sculpture.

Tally-Allie, the Turtle/Shark/Bird

Tally-Allie was a mix of a turtle, shark, and bird. She can fly in the sky over the sea so that she is able to dive down and swim in the water. When she is done swimming, she will go on land and sleep in her small shack by the water. She lived on a world called Green Sea. She loved her home. At night she would open up the roof of her house. The stars would twinkle and the waves rolling in lulled her to sleep. During the day, she would help animals and people in need of help. She ate seaweed and drank coconut juice from the coconuts. She was a vegetarian, because her mom was eaten by a humpback whale named Buddie, he was a bully to everyone. She has a sad story behind her lost fin.

One-day Tally was flying when she saw a boat. She had never seen a fishing boat before, so she dove into the water and swam up to it. The fisherman had just thrown a net in the water because it was tangled up. The net fell on Tally and it strangled her. It cut the blood circulation off completely, and cut a little bit off the other fin. When she was found, she went to an animal hospital. Her fin was amputated because there no blood was running through it. (This story is based on a true story.)

Tally had two friends who did not live in water or the sky. One was named Ice-cream Woman, and the other was named Evil cream. They lived on opposite sides of the island. When Tally had them over, they had ice cream and threw sprinkles in the sky. Ice-cream Woman and Evil cream were sisters, but they had to pretend they were enemies so that they could keep their place in the world. Tally's only relative was another turtle who she called Grandma Sea. Grandma Sea was old, in fact she was 159! Grandma Sea's birthday was in 2 days' time!

An overall philosophy of embedding the arts throughout the curriculum would developmentally benefit young children. Partnering and linking the arts throughout the curriculum is the foundation and focus of such a philosophy. The words we use to describe the method are secondary to the attitude and philosophy of embedding arts throughout the curriculum for all children.

Role of the Educator when Partnering Art and the Curriculum

An essential part of the integrating and linking the arts across the early childhood curriculum is the role and response of adults. Educators who share an overall philosophy of embedding the arts throughout the curriculum work to extend, support, and enhance the experience for the child. Noting various aspects and fostering the child's reflection on the process, as well as the product, promotes extended learning and discovery. Deiner (2005) noted,

> As children feel the impact of the environment, the response they get to their creative efforts plays a large part in their creative development. Educators have an important role in the development of creativity. They can actively support creativity or squelch it by concentrating only on the product that emerges. And they can enhance the experience by having children think more about the process, as it will impact the product" (Deiner, 2005, p. R-130).

As children develop, the experience can be enhanced for both the child and facilitating adult when noting the importance of the process, while balancing both the process and product. Discovery and learning can be richly extended by the role of the adult.

Benefits of Integrating Art into the Curriculum

Dever and Jared (1996) stated that integrating art into the curriculum benefited children in two major ways.

1. Art can give children opportunities to think about what they are learning while they create a representation that reflects their understanding or new knowledge about what they are reflecting in their art.

2. While the children manipulate the art materials, they learn about the characteristics and features of the materials and what they can do with them.

An example of Dever and Jared's first noted benefit is illustrated with the following example. The following curriculum unit about animals in winter demonstrates how integrating art provides opportunities for children to reflect on what they are learning, while completing a representation. (Note: This example would need to take place in a snowy region of the country for the full experience.) Through an integrated art approach, children explored books about animals in snow, went snow sledding outside; made snow angels, and made footprints and other imprints in the snow. The children also recorded their observations through dictations, words, and drawings of various viewings of animals in snow, such as animals outside their classroom windows or while outside, while in their backyards, or when in transit to and from preschool, etc. They also observed animals in the snow at the zoo and recorded their observations with words, dictation, drawings and sculptures. The children noted how their pets grew thicker fur in the winter and shed in the summer. Through journaling, drawings and sculpture, children recorded their experiences and new knowledge about animals in winter. Other areas of the curriculum included dramatic play experiences with winter props, making animal puppets and acting out their behavior in the winter, making bird feeders, painting a large mural about snow activities and animals in the winter, and exploring many books on the topic provided in the library area. Photographs of the experiences documented additional reflection, along with the children's entries in journals or portfolios.

Regarding the second major benefit, learning about characteristics of the materials and possibilities, Dever and Jared (1996) explained,

> As the children actively engaged with the art materials, they made discoveries about what they could do with the materials. For example, during the mural activity the children enjoyed creating unique shades as they mixed various colors of paint. In doing this, they discovered that colors created with crayons do not mix in the same way, as do colors created with paint and that markers mix differently than either crayon or paint. They also discovered that paint bubbles when applied over crayon and that fabric and paper come in a variety of textures and thicknesses and do not feel the same when they are being cut. (Dever & Jared, 1996, p. 5).

Children benefitted in all domains with this manipulation of art materials, which resulted in discovery of features and possibilities of materials. In addition, the potential knowledge and skills gained related to all curricular areas. The sensory experiences benefitted the child's cognitive, physical, and emotional domains. Experimentation with the materials integrated the areas of science, physics, cause/effect, trial and error, invention, discovery, and other areas of the cognitive domain. The aspects of spatial relations benefitted the physical and cognitive developmental domains. Description of spatial relations built language skills, as well. The planning and sequencing that occurred from manipulation of the materials included math skills development and problem solving within the cognitive domain. And finally, manipulation of materials involved motor skills, eye-hand coordination and perceptual motor skills.

These benefits of authentically creative experiences integrated throughout the curriculum are possible for all children. With some advanced planning, observation of the child's skills and consultation with therapists and families, children who have special needs can participate, enjoy, and benefit from these same activities. Educators must step back to note any accommodations or modifications needed to individualize the experience for young children and to ensure successful participation. Adjustments needed could include goal adaptations for the child's individual needs or culture or determining how these objectives might align with any IEP or IFSP goals/objectives/benchmarks if the child is on an Individual Education Plan (IEP) or Individualized Family Service Plan (IFSP).

Window into a Classroom: Best Practices for Inclusion

Any accommodations of materials or instructions should be noted, including need for any assistive technology, communication assistance, additional or accommodations of space, or special materials for the child to be successful such as: adaptive or loop scissors, Velcro for grasp assistance, or larger paintbrushes for children with physical challenges; bright colored materials, large pictures, and large print for children with visual challenges; non-latex gloves to accommodate children with sensory challenges or latex allergies; or pictures and visual cues to give directions and use for communication for children who need assistance with processing or memory. Objectives and accommodations from the individual child's IEP or IFSP can be embedded into creative activities. And finally, any adaptations or modifications in the assessment process that are needed to accommodate children with special needs should be noted. Documentation of progress is essential and particularly needed for evidence of a child on an IEP or IFSP.

More specifics of methods and examples to include all children were incorporated in Chapters 4 and 5, with additional examples provided later in this chapter.

ARTS IN SCHOOLS

To successfully integrate the arts, there must be the arts in schools or resourceful teachers who are well prepared to integrate the arts into the program's environment and curriculum. Both would be ideal. Additionally, the arts must be made accessible to all children regardless of culture or special needs. This is more conveniently implemented in Pre-Kindergarten programs that tend to have more control over the entire day's schedule and curriculum. In the public schools this has been more challenging, as funding for the arts has been questioned and the arts are often the first to be cut. In a speech at the Arts Education Partnership National Forum 2010, U.S. Secretary of Education Arne Duncan agreed with this statement, when he said, "For decades, arts education has been treated as though it was the novice teacher at school—the last hired and first fired when times get tough. The arts can no longer be treated as a frill. The arts are not just a nice thing to have or do if there is free time or if one can afford it. Paintings and poetry, music and design they all define who we are as a people" (Duncan, 2010). The arts should be available to all children. Creative activities need not be just a part of a gifted program. The arts should it be made available and accommodated for children with varying abilities. Duncan went on to relay the words of President and Mrs. Obama, "As the First Lady sums up, she and the president both believe 'strongly that arts education is essential for building innovative thinkers who will be our nation's leaders for tomorrow" (Duncan, 2010).

Several recent studies have supported how visual arts instruction positively impacted reading readiness; how learning to play piano has improved math skills, and how the understanding of symbols needed for reading, math, and writing are similar skills to putting together shapes and colors in creating a painting or sculpture. Arts education has had a major impact on student achievement of individuals with special needs or lower economic levels. As noted by Duncan, students who came from low-income families who played in the orchestra or band were more than twice as likely to perform at the highest levels in math as peers who did not play music. Duncan cited a renowned longitudinal study, Doing Well and Doing Good by Doing Art, James Catterall noted that low-income students at arts-rich high schools were more than twice as likely to earn a B.A. than low-income students at arts-poor high schools. He also found that English language learners at arts-rich high schools were far more likely than peers at arts-poor high schools to go on to college. Although more educational research is needed to see this replicated, Duncan stated,

> "Fortunately, numerous schools are beginning to take these lessons to scale. Last year, I had the privilege of visiting an early learning facility, the Educare Center in Oklahoma City, which is home to one of the 60 schools in Oklahoma's A+ Schools network. Oklahoma's A+ school-network nurtures creativity in every student and a recent evaluation shows not just that the program increases student achievement but boosts attendance and decreases discipline problems as well" (Duncan, 2010).

Duncan cited another success story in Chicago in 2001. Data showed that 1 in 7 elementary schools in the city had no art classes, which included fifteen elementary schools and 7,300 children. Duncan stated, "Through CAPE, the Chicago Arts Partnerships in Education, we brought local artists and teachers into the schools to partner up on integrating arts curriculum with academic subjects. Follow-up studies indicated that students at the CAPE schools performed better on standardized assessment than students who attended schools that did not integrate arts and academics" (Duncan, 2010). Erik W. Robelen, assistant editor and reporter for Education Week, also stated how art education benefits children in other subjects, as well.

> Arts education proponents suggest that studying the arts provides a variety of academic and social benefits to young people and can enhance students' ability to learn other subjects, including the development of skills in reading, language development, and math. It's seen as a powerful way to promote creativity and critical thinking, among other skills" (Robelen, 2014).

Although more research is needed, the academic benefits of the arts and art education have been and continue to be demonstrated.

Validating and Integrating the Arts

The key to validating and integrating the arts in today's society appears to be best accomplished and illustrated through linking the developmentally appropriate creative activities to standards. We live in a culture of standards and evidence of meeting those standards. Although accountability is important, "art for art's sake" seems to be a thing of the past that is lost within systems. Art advocates have demonstrated some accountability, yet as noted earlier, Robelen articulates the current status of the struggle to provide time and support for art in schools, "amid the financial straits facing many districts and other challenges, such as pressure to boost test scores in core subjects like reading and math." (Robelen, 2014).

Art welcomes children to open-ended play that benefits all domains. Integration of the arts through academic and pre-academics is an effective way to give children direct, hands-on experiences that illustrates their understanding concepts and knowledge. Reyner (2007) states, "When children study any given concept, they learn it better and retain it longer if they do an art activity that reinforces that learning" (p.1). The process of the developing child is sequential and individual. The sequence of the child's development progresses from simple to complex. With open-ended, authentic creative art experiences, children can master tasks and discover at their own pace and rate of development.

Art Therapist, Anna Reyner (2007) provided an Activity Analysis of 12 Common Art Ideas in Art Influences Learning. Table 6.1 lists some examples adapted from her list, illustrating the array of developmental skill possibilities through art activities.

Art Activities Linked to Developmental Skills

Art Activity	Developmental Skills			
	Cognitive	Social	Emotional	Sensory-Motor
Open ended drawing	planning /adapting	impulse control	individuality	fine motor skills
Easel painting	decision-making	works Independently	self-expression	fine & gross motor skills
Silly putty	cause & effect change of state	cooperation	stress release	tactile stimulation
Crayon resist	cause & effect	focuses	sensory pleasure	special relations
Group murals	large scale planning	group cooperation	adapts to group	gross motor
Clay sculptures	planning, divergent thinking, demonstrates spatial & 3D concepts	shares art & ideas	self-expression no wrong way	fine & gross motor skills
Collage	plans, predicts, adapts actions sequencing	shares materials	makes choices	visual spatial visual discrimination

(adapted from *Activity Analysis of 12 Common Art Ideas* in *Art Influences Learning* Reyner, 2007)

Table 6.1: Art Activities Linked to Developmental Skills

The National Association for the Education of Young Children's (NAEYC) position statement of Developmentally Appropriate Practice in Early Childhood Programs serving Children in programs from Birth to age 8, stated the following: "3-D-1. Teachers plan curriculum experiences that integrate children's learning within and across the domains (physical, social, emotional, cognitive) and the disciplines (including language, literacy, mathematics, social studies, science, art, music, physical education, and health)" (2009). This integration of learning experiences can be profoundly important to integrating the arts. If we do not have the time or funding to offer an art education program as a separate area of the curriculum (not to imply that cuts to arts education should ever be justified), why not include stronger arts education and ways to integrate the arts in teacher preparation programs? Additionally, if fortunate enough to have an art program, many school districts have only one art teacher for numerous buildings, sometimes for hundreds of children, or throughout the entire district. How can one art education teacher really meet the needs of hundreds of students within a school district, just to state that there an art program or art in the curriculum exists? Why not make the integration of arts part of our daily routine, just the way we do business, regardless of having arts education in the schools? Even when a district is fortunate enough to have art education, consider the possibilities of collaboration with classroom teachers to reinforce art concepts in various curriculum areas.

For example, collaboration between the art educator and classroom teacher might include various activities focused on colors, sizes, and shapes in curricular areas of math or science as a follow up to experiences the art educator has provided in observing and using various colors and shapes in artwork. If the art curriculum included works of art and artists in history, the classroom teacher could partner by posting prints of artwork by these artists for daily observation and discussion. Reading and writing about the same artists would reinforce the content and promote literacy skills. Regardless of funding or current status of a program's art education, integrating art throughout the curriculum for all children is possible and feasible. The challenge is assuring that these experiences are authentically creative, developmentally appropriate, and available to every child.

IMPORTANCE OF PLAY-BASED PHILOSOPHY AND THE CREATIVE PROCESS

Children learn through play. According to NAEYC's position statement on Developmentally Appropriate Practice in Early Childhood Programs Serving Children from Birth through Age 8, "Play is an important vehicle for developing self-regulation as well as for promoting language, cognition, and social competence" (NAEYC, 2009). In this statement, more discussion followed noting how play helps children make sense of their world, interact with others, problem solve, and express and control emotions. Play is natural and universal. Research supports that play serves important physical, mental, emotional, and social functions for humans and other species. This position statement also noted, "Research shows the links between play and foundational capacities such as memory, self-regulation, oral language abilities, social skills, and success in school" (NAEYC, 2009).

Creative play offers much for young children. The aspects of play in the creative process are essential. Active scaffolding in creative play is needed to build upon and develop more mature understanding and skills. It contributes significantly to children's self-regulation and other cognitive, linguistic, social, and emotional benefits. "Rather than detracting from academic learning, play appears to support the abilities that underlie such learning and thus to promote school success" (NAEYC, 2009, p. 14). Play is how children learn. Play is their work.

The following sections offer examples of integrating authentic creative experiences throughout the curriculum. These play-based experiences will include opportunities in Math/Pre-Math; Science/Sensory; Language Arts, Communication, and Literacy/Pre-Literacy; Social Studies/ Pre-Social Studies; and Expressive Arts (Music, Movement, and Theater). Incorporated are suggestions for the integration of art, along with examples linking the following standards Early Learning Standards, NAEYC (National Association of Education of Young Children) and DEC (Division of Early Childhood), and NAEA (National Arts Education Association).

Math/pre-math

Partnership of math and the arts as modes of creative expression: Children draw what they know. This includes opportunities to draw, create, and demonstrate many math/pre-math skills. Counting, classifying and sorting, comparing and ordering patterns, one-to-one correspondence, shape, and form, are all math concepts that can easily be integrated into authentically creative 2D and 3D art experiences. For example, knowledge of numbers and how much or how many of something a child wants to include in her/his artwork is a typical process within much of children's art. This creative process involves everything from number of appendages to how they choose to use the space. The process also entails many shapes, sizes, patterns, and sequences. Children might self-talk as they create, noting numbers of facial features, counting while creating the legs of an insect, or deciding and rolling out clay eggs to place in their clay nest or basket. Problem solving is constant as the child decides the "what and how" of their creation. Even if the child's work is non-objective and not a "something," the math/pre-math knowledge and skills come into play with shape, form, and space with a non-objective creation.

According to Reyner (2007), "Art can be looked at through the lens of mathematics. Young children can work with simple collage materials and beads to introduce numbers, positive and negative space, classification, and sequencing and pattern recognition. Tangrams can be brought in, and art journals can become creative number or shape books" (Reyner, 2007, p. 1). There is much more to math than numbers, formulas, and logic. According to University of Colorado math professor Carla Farsi, "Math is not just about numbers, formulas and logic, math is also about structure, symmetry, shape and beauty. Conversely, art is not only about emotion, color and aesthetics, but also about rhythm, patterns and problem solving" (Reyner, 2007, p. 1).

Creative expression through math combined with visual arts. Figure 6.4 is an example of a drawing created by a 4-year-old child. She liked to repeat the same drawing, and each time positioned the sun in the same place, placed the same number of pedals on the single flower, and the same number of blades of grass at the bottom. She would count the flower pedals and blades of grass as she drew them.

Figure 6.4: Example of drawing by a 4-year-old, demonstrating how math can be partnered with art.

Greg Tang (2003) offered some early elementary level ideas that integrate art with math, science, and problem solving in Math-terpieces: The Art of Problem-solving. This book included famous paintings, accompanied by a poem offering math concepts and practice in addition and making groups. First the child is encouraged to explore the master paintings of various famous artists, such as Monet, Pollock, Picasso, Cezanne, and Degas. Teachers/parents are encouraged to introduce the book, explaining how each page contains a painting by a famous artist. Questions are posted, such as, "Have you ever seen these paintings or sculptures? Which one is your favorite?" Each activity idea related to the specific masters' works, and expanded with open-ended questions, such as:

- Which painting did you like the most? Why? How?

- Which artist do you think was most creative? Why or how?

- Why do you think the artist decided to paint this picture?

- Did the artist use math in the painting? What would change if one item was added or taken away?

- Why is it important to add?

- Can you think of a time you used addition in real life?

(adapted from Tang, 2003)

Play-based approach for blending math and creative experiences, at home or classroom: Young children best learn math concepts through hands-on play and exploration at home or in the classroom. A play-based approach to math lends itself to many authentic creative art projects and concepts. These experiences can have a positive impact on children's view of math. Mayesky (2002) states,

> We may provide creative, stimulating, hands-on experiences that can initiate long-term positive feelings about mathematics, or we may provide a boring stream of workbook pages and dittos. In such a situation, where children are required to sit down, quiet down, and write down, excitement about math may never have a chance to emerge (Mayesky, 2002, p. 346).

Strategies for integrating math with art can naturally be implemented. For example, problem-solving and use of mathematical and spatial skills can be promoted when children are sculpting or assembling 3D artwork. Spatial relationships, size and shape, or recognizing patterns can be encouraged with painting or drawing projects. Use of the problem-solving skills, planning, logical mathematical skills, sequence and completing a design are evident with collages or multi-step art projects. Facilitation of play-based creative experiences linked with math is our responsibility as early childhood educators. We must also increase awareness of this approach for families and educational systems, noting the impact on long-term attitudes about math.

Science/sensory

Partnership of science and art as modes of creative expression: Young children are naturals at experimentation and discovery. According to Mayesky (2002), science is important to young children in three major ways: 1) When children investigate their world in an active way, they are learning by doing. 2) Skills in using senses and sensory awareness can be developed through science. 3) Science offers another avenue to develop creative abilities. Mayesky (2002) says, "Science allows young children a chance to play with ideas and materials in an open environment where there is freedom to explore without fear of being 'wrong' "(p. 319). Learning through play, and exploration without fear of being wrong is at the heart of the creative process.

As stated earlier, the benefits of integrating art into the curriculum expressed by Dever and Jared (1996), was illustrated through the connection of art and science. Children are naturally curious and yearn for discovery and experimentation. When children are given opportunities to think about what they are learning, while reflecting this in their art, they illustrate a multitude of science knowledge. Additionally, what children learn from manipulating art materials links art to science and sensory experiences. Material manipulations welcome cause-effect and discovery. For example, when children observe how paint colors mix and merge or experiment with changing the thickness of paint by adding water, they are discovering. When children note variations as paint dries or observe changes when clay is smashed on the table or between hands, they are actively experimenting. These occurrences demonstrate cause and effect and discovery, which is at the heart of science. Figures 6.5 and 6.6, for example, show how science is reflected in children's artwork.

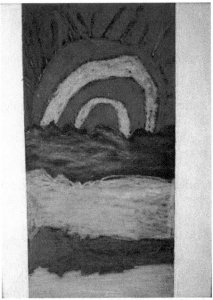

Figure 6.5: The beauty, magic, and mystery of a rainbow are often depicted by young children in their artwork. This bold rainbow is by Ellie, age 7, using colored pastels.

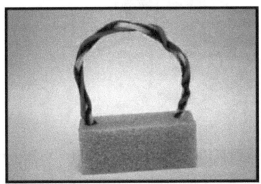

Figure 6.6: Rainbows are also depicted in children's 3D artwork.

Nature can have a profound impact on children's creative experiences, and the creative arts offer many opportunities for children to demonstrate what they know about science. The drawing featured in Figure 6.7, for example, demonstrates the 4-year-old artist's knowledge of the parts of a butterfly. The gift of nature offers many resources from which to base creative experiences and science discoveries, such as:

- Nature offers materials: collage items from nature; water for changing substances; sand, dirt and clay for texture and 3D experiences

- Nature offers subject: animals, plants, pets animals and plants naturally link science and art

- Nature offers process of growth and change: observations can be depicting in creations

- Nature offers aesthetics: observing and depicting beauty of nature

- Nature offers sensory experiences: visions, sounds, smells, tastes, textures

- Nature offers opportunities for environmental activities and study of ecology

Figure 6.7: Example of a drawing by a 4-year-old, demonstrating how her knowledge of nature and parts of a butterfly can easily be partnered with her art.

Play-based approach and repeated experiences to blend science and creative experiences. Creative science activities with a play-based approach offer many possibilities and discoveries. For example, bird feeders, gardening, sounds of nature, cloud images and movements, water play, sand, and soil include many hours of discovery and creative play. Children can observe, discover, and reflect in their artwork the way forces of the environment affect each other. Children's art can also depict how plants affect animals, how animals affect other animals, how climate affects the environment, or ways temperature affects plants, animals, people, or activities.

Even creative movement can help children understand science concepts. Longtime dance education expert, Rima Faber, stated, "We're addressing the science curriculum as required by the county and meeting the standards for dance education in a mutual learning experience. The more we teach through dance integration, the more we realize how dynamically it brings deep and complex learning to children" (in Robelen, 2007, p.1). According to Robelen, "Photosynthesis may be an unlikely topic to inspire an opera or ballet, but in a 2nd grade classroom here recently, the children were asked to use dance to help them learn about that process" (Robelen, 2007, p.1). Robelen went on to describe how small groups of children in a class at Fort Garrison Elementary School collaborated and brainstormed to convey elements of photosynthesis, including water, sunlight, carbon dioxide, and chlorophyll through their dance movements. "They leaned, they reached, they flowed, sometimes with surprising grace" (Robelen, 2007, p. 1). He notes that the goal of integrating arts (including dance) into the curriculum of public schools is gaining strength.

Children need repeated activities to gain concepts and reinforce their understanding. This directly relates to science concepts. Campbell and Jobling (2013) noted how multiple experiences on the same topic are needed for a child to truly comprehend. Having one encounter, doing one experiment, or completing one project will not necessarily result in understanding. Learning occurs best when a topic is repeated in various forms. According to Campbell and Jobling, repeating activities could promote review, deeper understanding, and build confidence. Creative art experiences offer a natural process to repeat activities and reinforce science concepts.

Science and art are easily partnered in the early childhood curriculum. Children naturally draw their environments, including plants, animals, the sky, sun, clouds, and other aspects of weather. Specific and detailed discussion about these aspects with children about their artwork expands their understanding and added details. Other strategies to integrate science in art include: promoting use of objects of nature such as leaves, seeds, sticks, sand, dirt, or rocks in artwork; encouraging children to observe and depict weather and changes in their artwork; or observing animals and insects while encouraging children to draw or sculpt what they observe. Setting up experimentation of color mixing and texture blending, multiple sensory experiences, opportunities for trial and error and problem solving with art materials such as blending various materials to discover how they are affected when mixed or how temperatures impact them.

It is our responsibility, as early childhood educators, to facilitate repeated, developmentally appropriate play-based creative experiences linked with science. Increasing awareness of and advocating for this approach is important to share with families and throughout our educational systems.

Language Arts, Communication, and Literacy/Pre-literacy

Importance of partnership of literacy and the arts as modes of creative expression: Art and literacy play a vital role in the early development of skills and abilities such as self-regulation, cognitive processing, and problem solving all which lead to innovative and creative thinking. The early years are a crucial time to begin exposing children to rich language and awareness and expression of thoughts and feelings, and honoring the innocence of a child's perspective. It is the complexity of literacy that encompasses oral language, reading, writing, listening, speaking, viewing, and visual communication and understanding. All of these are evident attributes in both the creation and interpretation of the arts as well as all pre-academic skills and strategies. Art can be an avenue to further develop, explore, and understand our own literacy development. Just as children begin to understand how scribbles on paper can transform to letters and words with meaning, art can communicate thoughts, perspectives, and emotions in a developmental manner. Literacy is a tool human use to be understood as well as to further understand the context of their lives. Art can also be a tool that can extend, enhance, and further develop this ability to be understood and understand. As literacy develops over a lifespan, humans begin to find ways to better communicate thoughts, understanding, and feelings as well as use literacy to further understand and explore the context of their lives.

Literacy and art allow humans to record, interpret, and document emotions and events, and better understand what it means to be human. Many have memories of how literacy and/or art have impacted their life, assisted in processing feelings, and possibly changed their future. Although individuals might not be able to pin point exactly what strategies and skills were used through an artistic or literary process that allowed them to have this special connection and moment in their life where literacy and art became a tool for movement and momentum in their development. This section will explore literacy partnered with art experiences, strategies, philosophies, and skills that impact the on-going development of humans. Emphasis is placed on why it is important to begin this process in the early years and how working with young children can have an impact on this development over time, providing a foundation for future development.

Integrating pre-literacy and literacy into children's visual art experiences and creative expression through language combined with visual arts. When children see a strong connection between language and the visual world they live in it allows them to use their knowledge and understanding of these connections to further develop emotions, social interactions, and other pre-academic skills. It is this language and experience connection that assists in the continual cognitive, social/emotional, and language development. One means to support a child's natural development process is having extended conversations about the creation and interpretation of visual arts. By asking questions and extending the child's thinking about the "why" behind the "how," we can promote the extension of a child's thought process, inviting the child to think further and with more detail. However, it is essential and necessary to make sure adult opinions and perspectives are not the guide in the conversation. In the act of creative expression, it is the child's voice, opinion, and perspective that should be the guide. Adults need to model mindful listening and engagement. Adults should be prompted by the child's verbal and non-verbal engagement to ask authentic questions pertaining to their creative expression. For children who have not experienced a "visual" world, the sensory of touch and sound become a vital element in their creative process. These types of sensory should be a guide for the interactions and development of creative expression.

Early stages and development of literacy: In the earliest stages of development, the literacy journey begins. This journey involves input and output of understanding and knowing. Literacy can determine the success in this journey and development.

Pre-literacy skills begin in the early stages of language development. Infants and toddlers begin to construct understanding of language as they take in both verbal and nonverbal means of communication from others.

Adult think-aloud provide infants, toddlers, and young children with an understanding of how cognitive processing can be transformed to oral language and the product of this processing. As adults work with infants and toddlers, it is essential to express language that interprets a perspective of the world. Think-aloud allow adults to model this thought process verbally. Think-aloud can take on a familiar feel of a conversation. During a think-aloud, it is important for the adult to allow opportunities for the infant and toddler to engage nonverbally in response to the adult. This is important for a child who has yet to discover her/his ability to verbally communicate in the same oral language. Asking young children questions models cognitive processing and a natural conversation pattern.

In addition to daily conversations, reading stories or poems, and singing songs with infant and toddlers is another way to promote the development of language and pre-literacy skills. It is crucial to remember that listening and viewing are part of literacy development. Rituals and routines of listening to the patterns and rhythm of language through conversation, song, and story impact the future development of speaking, reading, and writing skills. This can result in increased cognitive ability to attend and comprehend, which can support further development in listening and viewing. It is so easy to not pause and allow an infant or toddler to respond because they are not yet producing the verbal communication that adults fully understand. But a simple pause invites a space for response which values the young child's voice, even one that has not yet fully developed the socially expected comprehendible oral language. Pausing, allowing a space of silence, anticipation, allows the infant and toddler to begin to see this is their space and role in the conversation. This is essential for understanding the patterns and rhythms of non-verbal and verbal communication. Additionally, pausing with older children who have cognitive or processing challenges is also essential. It can make the difference between participation and non-participation. Pausing for a response (e.g. counting to self for 6–10 seconds) can clearly define the child's understanding or misunderstanding of the message or concept.

As children develop their oral language, they expand from single words to two-word phrases, and then progress to complete sentences. Modeling this with think-aloud and using purposeful pauses for an anticipated response should continue. However, at this age and stage of development, children will begin contributing and engaging in a more noticeable cognitive and verbal manner.

For many, life is a visual world. Long before speaking, children have seen a world of visuals that have laid the foundation for what they know and understand. Oral language builds upon the visual world as an initial engagement, thus allowing for further communication of thoughts and feelings. Drawing is a child's means of written communication. Hand-in-hand with oral language, children begin to make connections between oral language and written language. Drawing images connects their initial understanding of the visual world and their oral language, which builds a natural pathway to developing a written language. Due to the complexity of this development—as it involves motor, language, and cognitive development—process should be valued over product. Looking at an end product in isolation misses the impact of the process and the critical elements needed to understand a child's literacy.

Assessing the early stages of literacy development: Educators tend to assess the product of writing by looking specifically at letter formation, how an individual holds a writing utensil, and phonological awareness. Although these are elements of literacy, more important elements to assess and further understand are the attitudes, motivations, and cognitive approaches to an individual's reading and writing process. The awareness of meta-cognitive thinking allows young readers and writers to be aware of their strengths and weaknesses, and further develops strategies that support effective writing routines, habits, and skills. It is important to fully understand the interconnected nature of developmental domains and the influence on literacy development. Literacy has the potential to engage an individual through sight, sound, touch, social interactions, and emotional connections. Adults must be aware of how development of one domain of development can influence and impact the development of literacy. For example, physical development vision and hearing can impact the language development, which can be a foundational skill and understanding for further reading and writing skills.

Importance of Family Understanding and Reading Children's Cues of Engagement, and How to Respect and Effectively Respond to those Cues, while Partnering Literacy/Pre-literacy and Creative Artistic Expression. Creating family literacy routines and rituals is an enjoyable way to promote and support literacy development. The key is to promote an ongoing attitude and understanding that literacy is a part of everyday life and how different literacy strategies and skills are used to bring engagement, joy, and understanding to life and the discovering of self. When creating family literacy routines and rituals it is important to listen and observe the child's cues of engagement. Respecting the interests and joys of the child allows the child to discover her/his individualized response and approach to literacy. Each individual has strengths and interests within the literacy spectrum. For example, some children enjoy listening more than speaking and some children feel more confident in the area of reading rather than writing. Some children feel they would much rather write than speak. However, all of the above literacy tasks, skills, and strategies are interrelated. In order to effectively comprehend, one has to apply effective "listening/thinking" skills. To write, a writer must have command of similar strategies of a speaker who orally shares thoughts. However, each task has its unique combination of skills and strategies that allow different literacy tasks to be enjoyable and successful. It is the role of the individual to discover what combination of skills is necessary for personal success. Adults can provide experiences, modeling, and exposure to these skills and strategies, but the child has to determine what feels authentic. By honoring personal preference and respecting a child's growth and development, adults can target the needed areas of growth to support the child's literacy development.

One of the most important factors in the work with young children is to enhance and promote positive attitudes and engagement in pre-academic activities. At a young age, an emotion is associated with a certain task. Therefore, it is critical that pre-academic activities not be a task that is forced or a form of punishment. The activities should instead promote feelings of engagement. Tasks can be challenging and thought provoking, but there is a delicate balance between the moment satisfaction turns into dissatisfaction. If the balance is disturbed dissatisfaction can outweigh the engagement for the child. This can lead to these feelings being associated with the pre-academic task and could result in unnecessary disengagement in the future.

Documenting moments in life is a great place to start in promoting early literacy skills. Reflecting on events and moments that have happened daily, weekly, monthly, and annually promote literacy skills such as retelling, recalling specific details, and articulating details and events in a comprehensive manner. Find times throughout a daily schedule to pause and wonder about a memorable moment in the day or week and have the child describe this moment. Prompt further details as needed to assist the child in describing more details. For example, describe a certain object or place. By doing this orally, it is a type of storytelling that assists in reading comprehension and writing composition as the child further develops those literacy skills.

Set aside a time in which the adult and child can draw memorable events of the moment being told. Remember, depending on the age and development of the child, this could be scribbles, shapes, or actual representations of objects and events. There is neither one right nor wrong way to do this as long as the child knows what the drawing or image represents. As fine motor skills further develop, the adult will see during this ritual that the objects being drawn become more defined and more accurate in the connection between what the child is trying to represent. It is critical to see the process of the conversation and drawing in action, rather than focusing solely on the end product. An adult can model engagement by adding parts to the drawing; however, it is encouraged that the adult be invited to do so. By asking the child first, the child's creative space and process is being honored. The adult can title and date these documents before placing these drawings in a collection, such as a book, folder, or box. This allows the adult and the child to create another ritual of returning to the drawings and storytelling in the future. Consider having the child retrieve the collection at bedtime and then looking through the drawings and retellings of moments becomes a literacy ritual. By doing so, a literacy ritual is being developed and will later impact a child's understanding for writing strategies and reading comprehension, such as pre-writing, revision, or recalling story elements and events. Another ritual to consider is keeping a family writers' notebook, in which the family collectively record, collect, and recall moments of enjoyment and memories.

Responding respectfully to a child's process is essential. Noticing, observing, and asking engaging questions allows the child to continue and prompts further development. Simply acknowledging the actions of a child, without praise or criticism, provides a verbal support that can increase further experimentation and exposure. Children will naturally continue.

The activities and rituals provided above engage adults and children in activities that value the voice of a young child and honor the thoughts and development at that moment in a child's life. When the adult supports, models, and honors the voice of the child, the child will continue to grow in a positive and engaged manner.

Literacy in the early childhood classroom: A workshop is an effective instructional strategy that stands the test of time. It is adaptable to meeting the individual developmental needs of the children within an inclusive learning environment is that of a workshop. A workshop approach works because it honors both the art and the science of literacy development. As with any craft, the space, routines, and rituals developed depend on a working environment that supplies the tools, energy, and materials necessary for successful production. Reading, writing, and creating within a workshop approach allows an individual to gain knowledge from more experienced readers and writers and provides an extensive time to craft and explore, collaborate, and share strategies and individual writing processes.

Window into a Classroom: Best Practices for Inclusion

Within an early learning environment, children should have choice time to explore various areas of interest. During this time, allow children to join the teacher at a writing center/experience. Children at this age have already explored many books through read-aloud and a reading center, so allow children to share their understanding of what makes a good book. Be sure to include all children in this discussion, using alternative means of communication with children who may require this (e.g. Sign Language, Communication Boards, and other technologically supported communication). As children share, the teacher can make connections between what makes a good book and a book most recently read aloud. A child shares that books have pictures. As the child shares this understanding, the teacher opens the book and points to the pictures within the book, asking, "Like this?" The conversation continues with the children sharing what they know about a book. Again, be sure to include all children and allow additional time for those who need it. Working in smaller groups can facilitate full participation.

Similar to the work of Ray (2008), children are then given a blank book to write their own book. The book may have about six pages, allowing the children to explore the cover/title page, beginning, middle, and end of their own story. The teacher should not feel they must lead children through the writing experience, however, accommodations and needed assistive technology supports should be in place. The children's motivation and engagement should be what drives the activity. This allows young children to craft their writing with drawings, returning to drawings on previous pages to make revisions as they want, sharing and talking about their story, and reading their story to their peers. These are some interactions that typically occur when children are left to guide their own interactions with their writing. The teacher's role is to observe, listen, and ask questions in response to the children's individual stories. Questions such as "What happens next?" "What does that look like?" "Are you going to draw those details or write words to share that thinking?" For further exploration and understanding of writing with young children you may want to explore Katie Wood Ray, specifically Already Ready: Nurturing Writers in Preschool and Kindergarten.

A workshop approach to teaching allows educators to meet multiple learning styles in a developmentally appropriate manner. A workshop approach allows young readers and writers to focus on individual strategies while seeing and understanding the big picture of how reading and writing work in the context of life work (Figure 6.8).

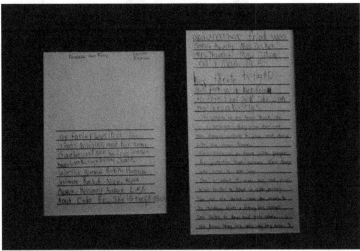

Figure 6.8: Child's handwritten story (with some dictation) from Children Inspire Glass Project.

Social Studies/ Pre- Social Studies, and Partnership with the Arts as Modes of Creative Expression

Social Studies is the study of human beings within their culture and environment. It includes views, values, beliefs, opinions, attitudes, and skills that are needed to become social individuals and can define our culture. Art is an element of culture. Art can help children reflect upon and understand themselves and others. There is a natural connection between social studies and the arts. For example, when children create an "All about Me" book or poster, illustrating themselves, their family, pets, teachers, friends, their house, their community, and likes and dislikes, they are defining who they are, what is important to them, and awareness of their surroundings. They reflect what they know about themselves, others, and their environments. Figure 6.9 is an example of an "All About Me" poster completed by Tyler, age 6.

Figure 6.9: Example of an "All About Me" poster completed by Tyler, age 6.

Another example occurs when children are exposed to different kinds of music, naturally move to music, or follow role models in dance moves. In doing so, they are expressing themselves, defining who they are and their likes and dislikes. Their preferences will most likely reflect that of their family or culture. Dramatic play is a key area for children to learn and demonstrate how to get along with others and appropriate interactions. Also, dramatic play might include discovering how not to get along with others or natural consequences of non-appropriate interactions.

Window into a Classroom: Best Practices for Inclusion

Learning about personal and cultural celebrations, as well as respecting diversity and other cultures and could be easily approached through the arts. Awareness of and respect for those who may have differing abilities, different colored skin, different habits, and general respect for diversity could be accomplished through the arts as well. Including activities to related to how we are alike and different, such as body tracing with each child, facilitating their completion of individual features (such as eye color, skin color, hair color) clothing, even any assistive technology used (e.g. wheelchair, walker, service animal). Have children note similarities (eye color, skin color, hair color, gender). Then have children name differences. Focus on how we have more similarities than differences. Some may need glasses to see better, a hearing aid to hear better, or a communication devise to speak. We may not all walk, but we move; we many not all see or hear, but we all sense something; we may not all speak, but we communicate.

Another activity might include children drawing and writing about their favorite family and cultural traditions and celebrations. Having the children share their stories and drawings while modeling respect for each child, family, traditions, and cultures promotes awareness and acceptance. Again, focus on the similarities. We may all have special family times, foods, and celebrations, we just have a variety of ways we do this.

Diversity awareness could also be accomplished by having children complete a group mural or small group sculpture, while having some children simulate having differing abilities. One child might wear wax paper goggles to simulate a visual impairment, another might have several fingers taped together to simulate fine motor challenges, or another might have ear plugs to simulate deafness or hard of hearing. As children complete the project they can make or suggest various accommodations. The adult working with the children can also suggest accommodations or alternative ways of doing things. In addition, partnering a child who is simulating having a disability with the child to assist, facilitates awareness of the type of assistance one may need with various challenges.

Having children reflect on these experiences by creating drawings, sculptures, and/or writings can extend this experience and offer additional opportunities for creative expression.

In 1994, the National Council for the Social Studies (NCSS) identified ten thematic strands of social studies in which all children K–12 should have experiences. These themes draw fundamental knowledge from social sciences, specifically anthropology, archaeology, economics, geography, history, law, philosophy, political science, psychology religion and sociology. These ten strands of social studies include:

1. Culture

2. Time, continuity, and change

3. People, places, and environments

4. Individual development and identity

5. Individuals, groups, and institutions

6. Power, authority and governance

7. Production, distribution, and consumption

8. Science, technology, and society

9. Global connections

10. Civic ideals and practices

Although the standards lend themselves to school age and older, we can interpret these standards into developmentally appropriate early childhood concepts and activities. For example, as children move from stages of solo play, to parallel play, and then to cooperative play, we can clearly see more awareness of individual development and identity, in addition to developing more consciousness of people, places, and environments. This is evident through children's drawings, sculptures, writings/dictations in journals, and particularly in dramatic play. Many preschoolers take great pleasure in dramatic play and awareness of roles. Family roles and cultures are evident in the dramatic play area.

Window into a Classroom: Best Practices for Inclusion

The following example illustrates the awareness of diversity of family roles and an opportunity to resolve differences.

Eve and Renaldo were playing in the dramatic play area. They were quite cooperative in their play, setting the table, getting the baby dolls in high chairs, and putting dinner on the table. They had just finished dinner and were cleaning up. Eve told Renaldo to vacuum the floor. Renaldo exclaimed, "Men don't' vacuum!" Eve quickly replied, "They do too! My dad does all the vacuuming at our house." Eve and Renaldo went back and forth with their disagreement. Eve refused to take over the vacuuming job and Renaldo did not follow through either. Another child, Cindy, entered the dramatic play area and took over the vacuum. Later in the art area, Eve drew a picture of her family, consisting of her mom, dad, and two sisters. Her dad had a vacuum in his hand!

This example, although amusing to adults observing, illustrated that the role of "dad" vacuuming had not entered Renaldo's mind, nor had he experienced this in his household. Eve, sticking with her view that all dads can vacuum, demonstrated her understanding of a dad's role, which was more flexible and less stereotyped than Renaldo's experience. She reinforced her view and opinion demonstrated by the drawing of her family, with dad holding the vacuum. Even children who tend to be "onlookers" in dramatic play are observing and learning from the play of others. Cindy decided to step in and do the task herself, perhaps as a mediator to calm the play and stop the disagreement. Young children role-play what they know and understand from their own families, cultures, and experiences. Exposure to what other children understand from their own families, cultures, and experiences could bring about more discussion, perhaps disagreement, and potential conflict resolution.

Holiday Arts and Crafts in Relation to Culture

In early childhood programs, holidays and children's ethnic and cultural backgrounds should be respected and approached with sensitivity. However, many traditional holidays in the U.S. have been over emphasized with a host of advertisements, decorations, activities, and crafts that focus on the product. The holiday "art," such as hand turkeys, pre-made or molded ornaments to paint, Xeroxed worksheets or coloring sheets with a holiday theme, cut-and-paste holiday projects, holiday coloring books, or other holiday craft kits, all masquerade as creative art.

Challenge yourself to use the same theme or value of a holiday, while providing authentic creative art experiences that offer free, not prescribed, self-expression. For example, rather than the traditional hand turkey, try offering collage materials such as turkey feathers and fall leaves, ask children to cut out pictures of favorite foods for collaging, or draw or paint the people and things in life for which they are thankful. Instead of pre-cut holiday ornaments or projects with specific step-by-step directions (that often require an adult guide every step, or even complete it for the child), offer various materials (e.g. Styrofoam in various shapes, colored tissue paper, sequence, glitter, colored salt, glue) to make their own original decorations for any time of year, not just winter holiday season. Traditional holidays are typically focused on family and celebration, no matter what one's culture. Focusing open ended art projects on family togetherness and celebrations fits all cultures and backgrounds.

Expressive Arts: Music, Movement, and Theater

Children are unique and have individual methods of expressing themselves. Individual expression depends upon their developmental level, style of learning, abilities, culture, and experiences. Deiner (2005) stated:

> Each has her own special way of being in the world. Creativity is dependent upon the developmental of the child and the child's past experience with the media. What is creative for infants is not creative for toddlers, and what is creative for children who have never experience a particular medium is not creative for children who have much experience with it" (p. 216).

For infants and toddlers, visual art is a sensory experience with random marks that evolve into children discovering the connection between their movements and their marks. Music is soothing for infants, and as they grow into toddlerhood they soon learn the cause-and-effect of their own production of sound with musical instruments. They naturally move to music. Developmentally, toddlers are gaining more control of their bodies and as they gain more skill they try to experiment. Role models with movement and dance can be powerful. As toddlers, they naturally enjoy music and dancing, even if limited use of their physical body requires use of assistive technology (e.g. wheelchair or walkers) for movement and expression. Children can even dance with their eyes! Toddlers enjoy learning songs and want to sing them over and over. Repetition is important for learning.

According to Deiner (2005), creative arts, such as visual arts, music, creative movement, and dramatic play, "provides an opportunity to practice skills in a safe place before using them elsewhere and to learn more about the world. Children with learning disabilities may find the visual arts an emotional release, an opportunity to integrate the visual and tactile senses, and to make a creation that will not be judged by others as right or wrong" (p. 238). Through creative arts children can experiment, practice, and make discoveries at various developmental levels. Sensory-motor integration can be enhanced through music and adding creative movement allows expression of emotions and body awareness. "Dramatic play can be used to help children build successful peer relations and work out fears about specific issues" (Deiner, 2005, p. 282). In particular, using creative arts is a safe way of expressing strong feelings or working through a process. For example, expressing anger through pounding of a drum or smashing a ball of clay or depicting grieving through a detailed or abstract drawing or scribbles or creative movement to express this emotion, are safe ways of expressing difficult emotions. Music, movement, and visual arts are also effective methods of relaxation. Music, dance, and art therapies have demonstrated much success for children and adults with varying abilities, conditions, and life challenges.

Music: There are countless benefits of music in the early childhood classroom or the child's natural setting. In the Role of Music in Your Classroom, Jennifer Jones (2010) stated the importance of music in a child's development, with the following reasons:

- Songs can be used to teach new concepts, vocabulary, and other language and communication skills.

- Songs give children the opportunity to explore adult roles. Children playing with dolls in a dramatic play area will sing lullabies to their dolls or hum while cleaning, emulating what they have seen their parents do.

- Music enhances social development with opportunities to interact with adult and peers, cooperate, and take turns.

- Music assists emotional expression and development by allowing child to express feelings, sooth hurt feelings, and increase self-worth.

- Opportunities for increasing cognitive development through music includes: develop listening skills in songs requiring specific actions at specific times, creativity and imagination by inventing their own song lyrics or dance moves, and increasing attention span.

- Movement to music develops children's awareness of their bodies and what they can do. Benefits include improved balance and coordination. It can also help to develop feelings of self-confidence and fine motor skills.

- Listening to music can help teach children about the basic proper ties of music: loud, soft, fast tempo, slow tempo, and pitch. It can also lead to further creative expression. (Jones, 2010, pp. 90-92)

Regarding music and language, Schiller (2010), who wrote Early Brain Development Research Review and Update, noted how music and language are partners in the brain. She stated the following:

> Linguists, psychologists, and neuro-scientists have recently changed their long-held opinion about the relationship between speaking and singing. The latest data show that music and language are so intertwined that an awareness of music is critical to a baby's language development. As children grow, music fosters their communication skills. Our sense of song helps us learn to talk, read, and even make friends. Brain areas governing music and language overlap. Music and language have much in common. Both are governed by rules and basic elements (word and notes). In language, words make phrases, which combine to make larger phrases and eventually sentences. In music, notes combine and grow to form a melody. (Schiller 2010, pp. 26–30).

How music affects us: Music begins in infancy. Infants naturally respond to music. It is important to provide a variety of musical experiences beginning in infancy (or even prenatally). Throughout development, music can play a major role in our lives. Research supports the power of music. Music can impact our mood and even enhance concentration. Some music can help us focus or relieve stress. Studies have shown how listening to a song can affect different part of the brain with memory and vision areas of the brain lighting up in response to music.

Creative potential of music: Learning the words and melodic tunes to songs have great developmental value. Music, singing, and responding to music are naturally enjoyable to most children. Music offers excellent tools to use for teaching and reinforcing skills in all domains, such as:

- Cognitive: Using songs to teach concepts of letters and numbers, or loud and soft, fast, and slow

- Emotional: How songs can make us feel and move through the melody or words

- Social: Music and musical games welcome children to join in with their peers, at various levels of participation

- Physical: swaying to music, stomping feet, clapping hands, and creative movement to music

Yet, there is major difference between singing songs that already exist and making up your own. Although learning the words and melodies to songs that already exist have developmental value, the creative possibilities of making up your own should be fostered and encouraged. Susan Striker stated, "If music is always presented with complete songs to learn and be sung in only one correct way, creative musical activity is inhibited. Teaching children songs doesn't teach them how to make music" (Striker, 1986, p.195). Just as teaching children to draw or sculpt using only the adult's drawing as a model does not promote authentic creative in their artwork; so, does teaching children songs only one correct way, stifle their creative musical possibilities.

Creative Movement and Music

Most young children are naturally moving and dancing to music and songs. When young children hear music, it is like an invitation to creatively express feelings in response to the music. Researchers identified creative movement as an artistic medium could expand a child's physical, psychological, and social horizons. Research also supported that "dance can enhance creativity, provide an outlet to inner feelings, and encourage freedom of expression" (Jay, 1991, p.305). Creative movement has been noted as the vehicle for children to "learn to make connections within themselves and with others, and to develop the ability to conceptualize about objects and ideas" (Fauman, 1987, p. 56). Through creative movement children can expand knowledge of language, arts, develop social relationships, and be at ease with their own bodies. Successful creative movement experiences for young children (Figure 6.10) can provide the foundation for continued participation and enjoyment of movement activities later in life.

Creative movement opportunities need to be available to all children, whatever their ability level, national origin, or socioeconomic level. Creative movement experiences can offer a model of creative expression through integrated experiences where all children (and adults) learn creatively and grow together, while appreciating the uniqueness and diversity of themselves and others. A quality creative movement program should be designed for motivation of creative expression, physical gain, conceptual, and self-concept enhancement of children and adults who work with them.

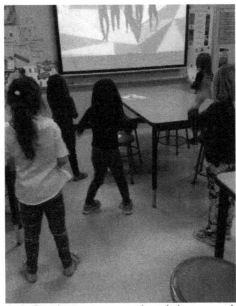

Figure 6.10: Creative movement and music have many benefits.

Success in creative movement or other creative experiences should not measure by comparing children to each other or through competition. The overall focus of abilities (rather than disabilities), an atmosphere that encompasses differing abilities, and an acceptance of creative/divergent thinking should be fostered. Creative movement activities with an attitude of embracing diversity can add to the potential of building a positive self-concept and social competence and increase participation of all children. Creative movement can increase the awareness of one's feelings and acceptance of those feelings, which can also strengthen self-esteem.

Russell (1996) investigated effects of a creative movement program (inclusive versus non-inclusive settings) on young children, ages 4 to 8, with and without disabilities. Measures of participation (individual and/or interactive), self-concept and social competence were compared. Results indicated that children with special needs participated significantly more when they were in inclusive versus in non-inclusive groups, regarding both individual and interactive activities. The model creative movement program used for treatment in Russell's study was very open-ended and promoted individual and self-expression and there was no competition or threat of an incorrect response. In other words, children who have different abilities than their peers in gross and fine motor skills could still participate successfully. This study demonstrated the positive value of inclusion in terms of participation within the context of a creative movement program for children with and without special needs. Simply having children with and without special needs in one physical setting does not define inclusion. Participation in inclusive settings is what makes inclusion work.

As a result of her research outcomes, Russell (1996) shared the following Recommendations for Components of a Quality Inclusive Creative Movement Program.

Components of a quality inclusive creative movement program: It has often been noted that children with special needs are confronted with many disappointments when they cannot achieve at the same level as their peers who do not have special needs. Barton (1982) emphasizes that children with special needs are more similar than they are different as compared to children who are developing typically. Thus, quality creative movement programs should offer integrated experiences where children (and adults) can learn and grow together while appreciating the uniqueness and diversity of themselves and others. With these concepts as the basis, the following are recommended components of a quality creative movement program:

> Physical fitness components: Components of physical fitness include muscular strength, muscular endurance, cardiorespiratory endurance, and flexibility (Barton, 1982). Although these components are primary to physical fitness, there must be a balance with these and other components within a creative dance program. If there is emphasis only on fitness and regimentation children might not be motivated or interested in continued participation.

Tools for relaxation: Through relaxation techniques children will learn the importance of the balance of exercising and relaxing the body to promote healthier bodies, minds, and spirits. Children today are experiencing more stress due to the fast pace of lifestyles. Children with varying abilities can benefit greatly from learning relaxation tools for stressful situations they could experience due to social, emotional or academic challenges.

Window into a Classroom: Best Practices for Inclusion

Ms. Chin's social skills group for young school-age children practices yoga at the end of their 2-hour Saturday session. This helps the children, especially those in the group who have special needs, to transition from their busy morning of work and play to the car ride home from social group.

Developmentally appropriate: Activities should be presented and implemented at the level of each child. It should include direct experiences and allow interactive learning. Although a guide for learning should be planned, adults must build upon the interests and needs of the child. Educators must be flexible and divert from our plans for incidental learning opportunities. The focus should also be on process rather than product. For children who are more product oriented (which is generally children over 4 or 5 years of age) a balance of process and product should be fostered.

Success oriented: Many children with special needs have experienced repeated failures. Creative movement is an avenue for children to succeed, as there is no one right way to do it. This is important for all children, and especially for children facing extra challenges. Barton (1982) stated that dance is one area where children who have special needs can achieve success, which in turn can enhance their self-concept. Children should be guided to enhance growth and progress; however, this should occur individually for each child. This component focuses on the abilities of each child rather than disabilities. It solidifies and promotes the perspective in children, that "I can," versus "I can't."

No competition: Success should not be measured by comparing children to each other or through competition. Children succeed as they participate, move, and expand their skills and knowledge based on their own progress. Ulrich and Collier (1990) noted that in their study regarding perceived physical competence, children with intellectual disabilities very seldom chose to use social comparison to make a decision about what they felt they did well. They compared their physical skill level to what they had previously experienced. Thus, competition or comparisons were not preferred.

Creative, self-expression: Creative movement provides "an opportunity for self-expression in a non-threatening and fun way" (Fisher, 1984, p. 203). Fisher (1984) added that children should be able to non-verbally and/or verbally create and share ideas in an environment that is accepting, which enables the child in feeling that what he/she is expressing is important and valued. The program should motivate movement through the use of fostering children's novel, unique, and innovative ideas.

Increase positive body image, self-awareness, and self-concept: As children expand their knowledge of body awareness, and the relation of their total body in space, they gain more control over themselves and are more comfortable with and accepting of themselves. "Body image is a part of one's self-concept which affects how one behaves, learns, and relates to the world and others" (Fisher, 1984). Fisher (1984) also stated that through increased awareness and acceptance of one's feelings, self-esteem can be strengthened, and one can be more conscious and understanding of others.

Foster independence: Independence and locus of control is important for all children, particularly for those who have experienced more dependent relationships and situations or are at risk for self-helplessness. Children should be encouraged to do as much for themselves as possible. Adults should celebrate when they attain a new independent skill. Again, an important component of a quality creative movement program is the solidifying the perspective in children that "I can" versus "I can't."

Teach concepts: Concepts in most any area of the curriculum can be taught through movement experiences. Examples of this include anatomy (e.g. body parts, muscle groups, bones), directional concepts (e.g. over, under, around, though, above, below, next to, etc.), demonstrating definitions of words (e.g. bend, twist, stretch, shake, melt, fast, slow, freeze, still, flow, dab, flick, glide, float, press, wring, punch, slash, small, medium, large), and fine and gross motor skills. Other examples include sequence, motor planning, problem solving, idea building, cooperation, memory building, shapes, colors, textures, volume, distance, weight, space (positive and negative and how we use it), time, levels, direction, size, rhythm, tempo, duration, energy, strength, force, motion, and environment. This list is not exhausted and can expand with each experience, child, and teacher or other adult working with the child.

Positive and "mirrored" feedback: Providing direct feedback concerning the effectiveness of the child's progress is an important component according to Bufford (1990). Children also need "mirrored feedback" in which the teacher reflects to the child what they are doing (e.g. "The shape you've made with your body is so low, that you couldn't get any closer to the floor" or "You really remembered the order of the movements that you put together"). These statements are not judgmental, they simply reflect, specifically, and in detail what a child has done (be it process or product). This gives the child an opportunity to review and reflect on their own movement(s), learn concepts relating to their movement experiences, and build upon their knowledge. Mirrored feedback also expresses and notices the value and importance of what the child has done and offers positive feedback and motivation to build upon their experiences.

Fun: Primarily, the creative movement program must be FUN! If it is fun, children will be motivated and participate. Children will learn the enjoyment of body movement through movement experiences, sharing ideas, and social interaction.

Motivating: Role models can be very motivating to children. However, role models and physical "equalness" for children with physical disabilities is at times difficult to access, particularly in rural areas, where, for example, there might be only one child using a wheelchair in an entire school district.

A possible suggestion for motivation of children who use wheelchairs or other equipment for mobility, as well as a potential awareness component is suggested by Brasile (1990). According to the results of this research, the individuals without disabilities participated in wheelchairs alongside their peers whose disability required their participation in wheelchairs. He felt this method of integration could promote better comprehension of true abilities of individuals with disabilities through active participation and developing an atmosphere for social integration based on participation on a more equal basis. In addition, this experience can serve as an excellent awareness tool for children without similar challenges. In general, children without special needs experiencing wheelchairs as an awareness activity is not unique. However, the use of such equipment in a dance class or creative movement program is rare.

INVOLVING PARENTS IN THE PROCESS OF INTEGRATING ARTS

Collaborating with families could enhance in our efforts to integrate art throughout the curriculum. Family members (including parents, grandparents, siblings, aunts, uncles) can be valuable resources for fostering children's creativity and facilitating learning. Early childhood educators must reach out to family members to ensure their understanding and awareness of authentic creative art experiences and benefits. This can be shared via a presentation, during conferences, sending home information, a parent letter, and in general daily interactions. Direct, hands-on experiences with examples of authentic creative art activities for family members to experience could be the most effective illustration. Sharing examples of the Adult Journal Activities at the end of each chapter might be a great place to start. Sharing the following developmental benefits of authentic creative art experiences with families could also illustrate the value and importance of such activities.

Children benefit developmentally from authentic creative art experiences. Even lovely scribbles of toddlers demonstrate pre-writing skills, and art elements of shapes, lines, texture, color, and value.

Benefits include:

- Sensory experiences (cognitive, physical, emotional)

- Opportunities to experiment (e.g. science, physics, cause/effect, invent, discover, cognitive)

- Spatial relations (physical, cognitive)

- Planning, sequencing (math, cognitive)

- Problem solving (cognitive)

- Motor skills (physical)

- Eye-hand coordination, perceptual motor skills (physical)

- Pride, sense of accomplishment (emotional/social)

Additionally, Table 6.1 (see p. 252) could illustrate for families the developmental skill possibilities through art activities.

As early childhood educators, we can assist parents in becoming more aware about the value of their children's art. Reyner (2007) stated:

> Art activities involve processes and products. It is the process of doing art that is so important to learning. While parents tend to focus on the product, educators can call attention to the process. Once parents acknowledge the value of art, they are more likely to keep art supplies at home, designate a household area for 'messy art', and become more involved generally in art. (Reyner, 2007, p 1)

For example, when a parent is discussing a child's artwork with a teacher, stating how much they enjoy the child's drawing or sculpture, a teacher could reply, "I really enjoy Stephanie's drawings too. The drawings this semester have really improved her writing, as well" or "Charlie's sculpture really shows us how much he understands about sea turtles, and how many details he observed on our field trip to the aquarium."

Additional suggestions on how best to respond to children's artistic creativity, in addition to "Guidelines for Interactions" with all children were provided in chapters 3 and 4. These are all important to share with and illustrate for families through quality art programs.

Chapter Summary and Looking Ahead

Art expression is natural for children and it is a means to demonstrate what they know. Reyner (2007) stated, "Children love art because it's fun and provides them with authentic self-expression: The freedom of choice, thought, and feeling. Art teaches important skills for living and develops young minds. The US Department of Labor recently published a report that supports these views by concluding, 'Arts education helps students develop skills needed for most jobs in later life, including creative thinking, problem solving, exercise of individual responsibility, sociability and self-esteem'" (p.1).

This chapter provided the justification and tools to integrate and infuse the arts across all curricular areas. This must be accompanied by adequate time for the creative process, which cannot be over emphasized. Time gives power to the overall creative process and experience. Children can be engaged and focused with an appropriate environment, materials, interactions, and TIME! Slowing down for learning through play, allowing TIME to show us how much children know, for problem solving opportunities, to self-express, and create!

Chapter 7 will begin by posing the questions, "What is art?" and "What is beauty?" Introducing children to the foundations of good art, our artistic heritage, viewing and talking with children about art while integrating art elements and principles and additional art dialogue will be presented. Suggestions for art gallery visits with children at various ages and developmental levels will be offered.

Suggestions for Additional Reflection and Review

Technology: An Adventure in Art

Explore the National Gallery of Art's interactive children's page: www.nga.gov/kids Children can browse through some of the world's most famous paintings and even create their own masterpieces!

CREATIVITY JOURNALS FOR ALL AGES

Adult Journal Activity #6

Reflect, repeat, and integrate art. In your journal, reflect on several activities or lessons you have implemented over the last week of your program, or family activities. List them with space under each. Label them by curricular and developmental areas. Check all for any authentic artistic creative expression. Note the possibilities of infusing authentic art into each activity. Plan to repeat one or more of the activities with your artistic creativity ideas integrated. Implement the plan with the additional creative expression aspects. Reflect again after re-implementation of the plan or activity. Make notes on what went well, what could have been done differently, if anything, to improve the experience.

Child's Personal Creativity Journal Activity #6

Activity #6 for Infants (Birth to walking, or 16 months)

Reflect, repeat, and integrate more art. Look back at the activities in the infant's journal or note another activity recently implemented with the infant. Note the possibilities of infusing integrating and enriching the creative experience. Plan to repeat one or more of the activities with additional or alternative ideas integrated. Implement the plan with the additional creative expression aspects. Be sure to document. Reflect again after re-implementation of the plan or activity. Make notes on what went well, what could have been done differently, if anything, to improve the experience.

Continue to remember that infants take in everything through their senses; therefore, the infant's journal becomes a documentation of the infant's sensory experiences. Again, please attempt to approach this as a journal and not a scrapbook. It should include only the infant's work or photos of the sensory experiences.

Activity #6 for Toddlers (walking or 16 months to 3-years-old)

Reflect, repeat, and integrate more art. Look back with the toddler at the activities in their journal or note another activity recently implemented. Ask them if they would like to try one of the activities again. Note the possibilities of enriching the creative experience. Foster the child's input on variations. Plan to repeat one or more of the activities with additional or alternative ideas integrated. Implement the plan with the additional creative expression aspects and/or variations from the toddler's verbal or nonverbal communications. Be sure to document the experience with photos and/or videos. Reflect again after re-implementation of the plan or activity. Make notes on what went well and what could have been done differently, if anything, to improve the experience. Give the child the time, the space, the materials, and the positive feedback and reinforcement to create! Attach photos of the process and product in the journal.

Activity #6 for Preschoolers (ages 3 – 5)

Reflect, repeat, and integrate more art. With the preschooler, look back at the activities in their journal, or note another activity recently implemented. Ask them if they would like to try one of the activities again. Note the possibilities of enriching the creative experience. Foster the child's input on variations. Plan to repeat one or more of the activities with additional or alternative ideas integrated. Implement the plan with the additional creative expression aspects and/or variations from the preschooler's verbal or nonverbal communications. Be sure to document. Reflect again after re-implementation of the plan or activity. Make notes on what went well, what could have been done differently, if anything, to improve the experience. Remember to give the child the time, the space, the materials, and the positive feedback and reinforcement to create! Attach photos of the process and product in the journal. Make notes of what they thought about repeating this activity, what they liked, what they didn't, etc.

Activity #6 for Young School-agers

Reflect, repeat, and integrate more art. With the young school-ager, look back at the activities in their journal or ask them to think of another activity recently implemented. Ask them if they would like to try one of the activities again. Note the possibilities of enriching the creative experience. Foster the child's input on variations. Plan to repeat one or more of the activities with additional or alternative ideas integrated. Implement the plan with the additional creative expression aspects and/or variations from the preschooler's verbal or nonverbal communications. Be sure to document. Reflect again after re-implementation of the plan or activity. Make notes on what went well, what could have been done differently, if anything, to improve the experience.

Remember to give the child the time, the space, the materials, and the positive feedback and reinforcement to create! Attach photos of the process and product in the journal. Make notes of what the child thought about repeating this activity, what they liked, what they didn't, etc. Attach photos in the child's journal.

CHAPTER 7

Fostering Children's Understanding and Appreciation of Art

"It is the supreme art of the teacher to awaken joy in creative expression and knowledge."

- Albert Einstein

CHAPTER OVERVIEW

This chapter begins with the age-old questions, "What is art?" and "What is beauty?" Suggestions are offered for talking with children about art, while integrating the basics of art elements. Strategies for developmentally appropriate art critique/discussions with children, and introducing children to the foundations of good art and our artistic heritage are provided. Included is the importance of incorporating abstract or non-representational artworks and a balance of 3-D as well as 2-D Art. Suggestions for art gallery visits and art discussions with children at various developmental levels and ages are offered. The conclusion of this chapter will offer suggestions for children exploring and discovering artists within their own families.

What Is Art? What Is Beauty?

The following questions about art might emit different responses:

- What is art?

- What is beauty?

- Is beauty only in the eye of the beholder?

- How do we respect children's art preferences and tastes that are not entirely based our own?

- How do we share what we prefer in art, while respecting and honoring each child's likes and dislikes?

- How do we instill respect for each other's (peers) preferences in art?

- How do we respect children's art tastes, while guiding them to new and different artworks?

- How do we do this for ourselves?

- What about nudity in art? How do we approach or choose to avoid viewing nudity in art with children?

This chapter will approach these questions and more.

Aesthetics is beauty, the study of beauty, and investigating the beauty of art and our surroundings. Beauty is all around us—in nature, in objects, in art. Children soak up the environment and its beauty with their senses. Every day, children who are able use all of their senses to take in the visions, sounds, smells, and tactile features of beauty around them. They learn and discover what beauty is from their families, culture, teachers and other adults, peers, and their surroundings. We enhance children's views of what is beautiful through interaction and the environments we provide and expose them to. How we set up our classroom, provide experiences, invite guests, display arrangements, and organize field trips all contribute to the child's formation of aesthetics and what is beautiful.

It is important to talk with children about art, their own and that of the masters and artists in our world and community. We can do this while integrating the basics of art elements and principles with the child's art and artworks done by others, as noted in Chapter 3 Understanding the Elements and Principles of Art and the Importance of Art Appreciation for Effective Teaching. In chapter 8 Children's Art as Communication, "Art Dialogue" is presented in more depth and in relation to communicating with children about their own art, as well. A brief discussion of art critique and discussion is provided below.

Art Critique and Art Discussions with Young Children

Art critique and art discussions with children should be at their developmental level, and begin with self-talk with infants. As children grow older we can guide their exploration while respecting their preferences and tastes for beauty. When we look at artworks with children, we can start the dialogue with questions like:

- What type of artwork is it?

- How is it made?

- What do you see when you look at this artwork?

- What do you think the artist is trying to say?

- How does it make you feel?

- Do you like it? Why or why not?

The following are responses from children in pre-kindergarten to early elementary level taken from the art classroom bulletin board of Kalli Lemka, an elementary art education teacher in Kansas City. Children responded to "What is Art?" with the following statements (featuring their original spellings):

- "It's a painting."

- "Sometimes it shows your feelings."

- "Art is created by the paint brush and the creator and art is a master piece some people are famous from their paintings."

- "Art to me is being creative in any way you want. Also using many colors."

- "It tells a story."

- "Life"

- "Art is anything."

- "Art is everything."

- "Art to me means ALL."

What a delightful variety of responses from these children! These responses demonstrate at a very young age, children have individual definitions of art and what it means to them. The children also shared messages in drawings as depicted in Figures 7.1 and 7.2 which feature photos of the bulletin board.

Figure 7.1: Kalli's elementary art student responses to "What is Art?"

Figure 7.2: Close up of Kalli's classroom responses to "What is Art?"

INTRODUCING YOUNG CHILDREN TO THE FOUNDATIONS OF GOOD ART AND OUR ARTISTIC HERITAGE

Introducing children to the foundations of good art and our artistic heritage is important and should be presented to children at their level. Children are drawn to artworks that include recognizable representations, such as people, animals, houses, and outdoor views of flowers or sunsets. Starting with images of familiarity, such as Renoir's Mother and Child or Van Gogh's Bedroom, is recommended. It is also valuable to introduce abstract or non-representational artworks, such as the work of Pablo Picasso or Jackson Pollock, as well as balance of 3D and 2D art. Sculptures by Henry Moore or Deborah Butterfield's horses offer recognizable 3D figures to which children could easily relate. Doing this also requires self-reflection and education about our own tastes and experiences with art, particularly abstract or non-representational. We tend to stick with the familiar and our own comfort level versus venturing out to learn more about the less familiar art, artists, and styles.

To become more comfortable and familiar with a variety of art and artists, select a location that has original artwork displayed. Examples include art centers, university galleries, junior colleges galleries, art galleries, and art museums in larger cities. Several banks or libraries have original artwork. The key word here is "original artwork" that is available for the public to view. Many locations have websites from which to choose current art shows and displays. Using the guide sheets for Art Gallery Visits for Adults (Figures 7.3 and 7.4), with suggestions for reflection of 2-D and 3-D artwork, try exploring various artworks. This can help inform and prepare one to include these artworks in discussions and explorations with children.

Art Gallery Visit for Adults

Name of Gallery _____

Location _____

Date of Visit _____

Reflections of 2-Dimensional Artwork:

Artist _____

Title _____

Date _____ Dimensions _____

Location in Gallery _____

Medium:

____ oil ____ acrylic ____ tempera ____ fresco ____ watercolor
____ mixed media ____ electronic media ____ pencil
____ charcoal ____ pastel ____ ink
____ woodcut ____ engraving ____ etching ____ lithograph
____ silkscreen other:_____ (no photography, please)

On what is the artwork completed:

____ canvas ____ wood ____ paper ____ wall other:_____

What is the subject matter of the work?

____ religious ____ mythological ____ portrait ____ still life
____ landscape ____ history ____ daily life (genre)
____ nonrepresentational

Describe the use of the Elements in the artwork:
- Line
- Shape
- Color
- Texture
- Value (contrasts, highlights, shading)

Consider the work's title:

Does the title help you interpret what you see?

If the work is nonrepresentational, what feelings does it evoke?

Why did you choose this work, and what does the work mean to you?

How might you introduce this artwork to children? Be specific about art elements and principles you would include in your dialogue.

Figure 7.3: Art Gallery Visit for Adults' Reflections of 2D Artwork

Art Gallery Visit for Adults

Name of Gallery _____

Location _____

Date of Visit _____

Reflections of 3-Dimensional Artwork - Sculpture

Artist _____

Title _____

Date _____ Dimensions _____

Location in Gallery _____

Process:
___ carving ___ □modeling ___ casting ___ assemblage

Material:
___ stone ___ metal ___ clay ___ wood ___ plaster
___ mixed media ___ electronic media other: _____

What is the subject matter of the work?
___ religious ___ mythological ___ portrait
___ heroic (statues or monuments) ___ nonrepresentational
other: _____

Describe the use of the Elements in the artwork:
- Line
- Shape
- Color
- Texture

Consider the work's title:

Does the title help you interpret what you see?

If the work is nonrepresentational, what feelings does it evoke?

Why did you choose this work, and what does the work mean to you?

How might you introduce this artwork to children? Be specific about art elements and principles you would include in your dialogue.

Figure 7.4: Art Gallery Visit for Adults' Reflections of 3D Artwork

These observation guides are helpful to familiarize one with the art, artists, and artistic styles. This exercise can be helpful in preparation for taking children to galleries to explore various types of art. When completing these observational guides, try to explore artworks out of your comfort zone by stretching it to view and complete observation sheets on artworks that you may not find as appealing. Children might not be drawn to the same artwork as adults. When taking children to art galleries, one must follow the lead of the child, making it their choice of art to view based on what they find appealing.

When appreciating art with children, an art critique noted by Fox and Schirrmacher (2015) is a great guide. One would need to adapt wording for various developmental levels and ages. The role of facilitator is essential within the art dialogue or art critique process. Fox and Schirrmacher (2015) suggest selecting and focusing on five points when conducting an art critique or art discussion with children. The following is adapted from their list:

- What type of artwork is it? Is it a painting, drawing, weaving, print, sculpture?

- What are the physical properties (e.g. round, square, solid, moving, framed, etc.?)

- How is it made? Did the artist use clay, wood, paper, paint, yarn, metal, or items from nature/outside?

- What do you see when you look at this artwork? Look at the art elements (line, color, shape, form, design, pattern, space, balance, texture).

- What do you think the artist is trying to say? Try to put the picture into words, what is the message? Pretend the artwork is a book with pictures. What words might do with the artwork? Discuss what you see: people, buildings, animals, events, actions, etc.

- How does it make you feel? Do you feel funny, sad, mad, happy, scared? What did the artist do to make you feel this way?

- Do you like it? Why or why not? What about it makes you like or dislike it? If you could, how might you change it?

Practice the "Art Dialogue" using the 2D and 3D examples shown in Figures 7.5 and 7.6.

Figure 7.5: Example of 2D work entitled, "Looking Back,"
oil painting by Tom Russell, Sr.

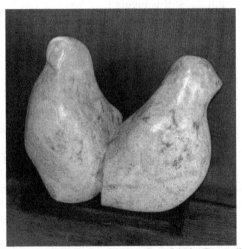

Figure 7.6: Example of 3D work entitled, "Doves,"
alabaster sculpture by Fletch Russell.

It is essential to select and phrase art critique questions and art discussions at the child's developmental level. Keep questions open ended and pause to allow time for a thoughtful response. Avoid rushing or hurrying children during an art gallery visit.

Some regard viewing art and art gallery visits as activities exclusive to adults. Large art galleries and museums have become increasingly child-friendly by including children's programs and activities. Enlightening children to art and artists from infancy on makes art part of their culture. Doing so gives value and importance to art and adds to one's appreciation of art. The following is a list of ideas and suggestions for art gallery/museum visits for various developmental levels, from infancy through school age.

Suggestions to Share with Parents for Art Gallery/Museum Visits with Infants, Toddlers, and Preschoolers

Young minds take in everything. An infant's senses are ready to soak it all in. He or she gazes at the pleasant and distasteful with equal curiosity and attention. Why not share the beauty and diversity of art with infants? It is encouraged, however, to check out the art gallery before bringing the infant. Make sure the infant's basic needs, such as fed, dry, well rested, are met before venturing out.

As you explore an art gallery/museum with an infant consider quality over quantity. Enjoying a few paintings or sculptures with the infant can make the trip worthwhile for both adult and baby. Carefully observe what artwork the infant is viewing and go in that direction. If the baby is in a stroller, take her/him out for closer viewing. Talk slowly and in short sentences about the subjects, color, lines, and shapes. Make comments such as: "Look, there is a baby in this painting, just like you" or "Look at all the green on this painting, just like the green walls in your room" or "Look how big that sculpture is, it is bigger than you and me." Pause for the infant's response (verbal or non-verbal), and note if she/he is looking at another piece. If allowed, take photos to document to review the experience later. When returning to the infant's natural setting, talk about what you saw and relate it back to their environment or activities, sharing photos if possible. Expand, using more words that describe prints of the artwork. These activities build vocabulary and concepts. They can also provide the early foundations of art appreciation.

When introducing toddlers to museums, keep in mind that they are still taking in the world with their senses, but they have increased skill in cognitive, physical motor, emotional, and social areas. Consider the individual child's development when planning your art gallery/museum visit and check out the art gallery prior to the visit.

As toddlers are active and can have limited attention spans, follow the toddler's lead. Engage the child in dialogue noting colors, shapes, lines, and subjects to which they can relate. Make comments such as: "Look, those children are in a boat. Have you ever been in a boat?" or "Look at the yellow in this painting. You just did a pudding painting yesterday that was all yellow too" or "Look at this clay sculpture. We'll have to get out the play dough when we get back home." Pause for the toddler's response (verbal or non-verbal). Try to extend the dialogue with open-ended questions and comments. Use the "Art Dialogue" questions listed earlier, phrasing them at the child's level. For example:

- What kind of artwork is it? Is it a painting, drawing, weaving, print, sculpture?

- Do you see any shapes? Look how this move.

- How did the artist make this? Did she or he use clay, wood, paper, paint, yarn, metal, and items from nature/outside?

If allowed, take photos of the child's favorite pieces, along with a photo of the child standing near the artwork. When returning to preschool or home, talk about what you saw, relating it back to their environment or activities. Be sure to share the experience with families and encourage them to visit the art gallery/museum with their child. If photos were taken, place them in the child's journal or portfolio. Locate prints of some of the artwork you viewed. You can often find them online. Display the photos and prints and review the comments made to build on more details and observations. For example, if the children are painting at the easel or painting rocks outdoors, have them recall or reflect on the colors they observed in the artworks. Or if the child is playing with a baby doll in the dramatic play area, note and reflect upon artwork that was observed that included babies, such as Renoir's Mother and Child. These follow up activities encourage reflection, build vocabulary and concepts, and promote art appreciation at an early age.

Frequent art gallery/museum visits for the preschooler are valuable and can enhance their appreciation for art. Preschoolers are increasingly curious and inquisitive. Their attention span is longer, and they can dialogue about art with a deeper level of understanding. They have more experience with art mediums and can compare their creative artistic techniques and endeavors with that of famous artists. Because of these understandings, more discussion about the art elements and principles, as well as the subject, form, and content can be included. Make the art dialogue a natural conversation and be sure to use accurate terms and encourage the children to do so. Again, this should be at the preschooler's individual level, not be forced, but relaxed and natural. Going into this experience determined to have all children understand certain terms can make this process artificial. Make it fun and natural. To do this, the adult too must feel at ease with the dialogue.

Start with the first three questions from the "Art Dialogue." If interested, expand to the fourth and fifth questions:

- What kind of artwork is it? Is it a painting, drawing, weaving, print, sculpture?

- What are the physical properties (e.g. round, square, solid, moving, framed, etc.?)

- How is it made? Did the artist use clay, wood, paper, paint, yarn, metal, and items from nature/outside?

- What do you see when you look at this artwork? Look at the art elements (line, color, shape, form, design, pattern, space, balance, texture).

- What do you think the artist is trying to say? Try to put the picture into words, what is the message? Pretend the artwork is a book with pictures. What words might do with the artwork? Discuss what you see: people, buildings, animals, events, actions, etc.

- How does it make you feel? Do you feel funny, sad, mad, happy, scared? What did the artist do to make you feel this way?

- Do you like it? Why or why not? What about it makes you like or dislike it? If you could, how might you change it?

This art gallery visit with preschoolers will bring out much discussion and dialogue. Discuss techniques used by artists in artwork they observe and discuss how to try these methods and techniques in their own art projects. Encourage exploration with the technique, but do not imply or encourage copying. Copying discourages children from having their own individual expressive art experience.

As with the suggestions for toddlers, take photos of the preschooler's favorite pieces if the gallery allows, in addition to photos of the child standing near artwork favorites. Share the experience with families. Encourage them to visit the art gallery/museum with their child. Place photos taken in the child's journal or portfolio. Locate prints of some of the artwork viewed. Display them and review the comments made, building on more details and observations in addition to trying new techniques observed in the artwork.

Be sure to follow up with some suggestions from the section later in this chapter for pre-and post-art gallery/museum visits. Preschoolers have advanced to representational play. Role-playing the experiences, they have had is natural and delightful. Enjoy!

Suggestions for Art Gallery/Museum Visits with School-Age Children

The school-age child is sophisticated and skilled in her/his approach to art, both in making art and viewing it. Continued frequent art gallery/museum visits are valuable and will foster their increased knowledge and appreciation of art. School aged children have a longer attention span than preschoolers and their art dialogue can be in depth. Their increased knowledge and involvement with art mediums and techniques allows them to compare what they have experienced with those mediums and techniques used by famous artists. More in depth discussing about the art elements and principles is natural and motivating. Using all questions from the "Art Dialogue" and having children record and/or write and/or draw their reactions and reflections will enrich this process for school-aged children. Figure 7.7 shows a display of famous art pieces and artists that is useful for discussion and follow-up after art gallery visits.

Figure 7.7: A display of famous art and artists can result in more discussion and follow-up after art gallery visits for school-age children.

Again, follow up with some suggestions from the section below for pre-and post-art gallery/museum visits. Compared to preschoolers, school-agers have sophisticated representational play and enjoy role-playing the experiences with more detail and complexity. This could include writing a story, skit, or play on the event, sharing details of their gallery/museum experiences.

School-age children are able to problem solve more complex situations. The children's suggestions for, and creations of, accommodations for individuals with differing abilities could be applied to real situations, as well showing compassion for inclusion of all. This brainstorming and problem solving on the part of the group can make inclusion a natural part of how we do things on a daily basis. This could be naturally applied when preparing for art gallery/museum visits.

Suggestions for Accommodations and Activities for Pre-Post Art Gallery/Museum Visits to Assist Children with Differing Abilities

Some children might need more assistance and adaptations with art gallery/museum excursions. The following activities are appropriate for all children, yet can be particularly helpful for children who need more preparation. Some children have fear and apprehension about new situations. The following activities prior to and following an art gallery visit could have potential to prepare children who have anxiety about unfamiliar places or new experiences. These experiences also offer dramatic play opportunities for all children.

- Have the children assist in creating an Art Gallery in the classroom. Display children's artwork with labels including: child's name, material used, and the title of the artwork if there is one. A different child's artwork could be featured each week as "artist of the week." This could be done in preparation of an art gallery/museum visit and a follow up activity. Facilitate the children adding to the Art Gallery as they observe and experience more from their gallery visit.

- After an art gallery visit, encourage children to discuss, draw and write about this experience. Children who need assistance can dictate words to the adult. Be sure to include all senses, as well as reflections about the experience. This can be both a large group experience, in addition to an entry in each child's individual journal.

- After an art gallery/museum visit, have children create an extended classroom art museum, combining areas of dramatic play, art center, writing center, and other appropriate areas. Bring in boxes and props to set up the areas. Include various people and roles the children have seen in the art gallery or museum (e.g. visitors, tour guides, director of the gallery, security people, gift shop clerk, etc.). The children can include their own artwork for display, in addition to printouts (old calendars of art work well too) of famous artists to display. Be sure to include cardboard stands or places for 3D artwork, as well.

- Increase accessibility awareness with this project by including accommodations in the gallery, such as making the space accessible for visitors in wheelchairs; consider finding a Braille writer or Braille cards to use for labels in addition to the written ones; or having children make a tape recording related to each piece of art, for use by individual with vision challenges to hear about each piece of artwork. Children can explore other ways to make their art gallery accessible for all.

- Coordinating an art show opening with the children and families could extend this project. Children could make up invitations to parents, grandparents, siblings, and friends to visit their art gallery; making snacks for the art gallery visitors; dressing up for the occasion, and showcasing and talking about their artwork.

Social stories. Children with ASD (Autism Spectrum Disorder), NLD (Nonverbal Learning Disorder) have difficulty with transitions, social interactions, or the unknown. Creating social stories, or a series of pictures of the process and appropriate social interactions of going to, visiting, and returning from the art gallery/museum visit can assist children who might have anxiety about going somewhere new or have difficulty with transitions.

Window into a Classroom: Best Practices for Inclusion

Mr. Kevin, a paraeducator who supports children with special needs in Mrs. Tamayo's kindergarten classroom, knows that his student Joontae experiences a great deal of anxiety when the class takes field trips. Kevin decides to write a social story for Joontae to help prepare him for an upcoming museum trip. Kevin researches the Walter's Art Gallery online and incorporates photos of the gallery as well as the specific Matisse exhibit the class will be visiting. He also includes photos of a school bus as the class will be traveling via bus. He then reads this story with Joontae prior to the trip and takes it along with them to read as they progress through the visit. Mr. Kevin's preparations work well; Joontae enjoys the museum visit because he has been shown what to expect.

According to Scattone, Wilczynski, Edwards, and Rabian (2002) "A Social Story is an individualized short story that describes social relevant cues in any given situation. It breaks down a challenging social situation into understandable steps by omitting irrelevant information and by being highly descriptive to help an individual with an ASD understand the entirety of a situation. It includes answers to questions such as who, what, when, where, and why in social situations through the use of visuals and written text" (p. 535–43). The Paraeducator could assist the child by reminding him/her of the social story and referring to the photos. This could ease transitions and assist the child in processing new situations.

What about Nudity in Art? How to Approach or Avoid it with Children?

On the topic of nudity in art, some educators and parents feel we just "should not go there" and avoiding this topic is the safest approach with children. Some adults make a common practice of avoiding "that room" or artworks that include nudity during an art gallery/museum visit with children. Others have gone so far as to cover up art that depicts nudity when children may be in a gallery. Artists have been sculpting and painting nude human figures throughout history. Many people equate nudity with sex; however, nudity and sex are not the same thing. When children observe our nonverbal negative reactions to nudity (e.g. gasps or startling reactions) it conveys the message that nude works of art are a bad thing. Keeping with personal and philosophical program practices, and religious beliefs and preferences, are important to live by. However, consider the implications that overreaction and gasps might convey. Discussion with staff or others involved prior to art gallery visits prepares the adult on how to handle this. Avoidance is not always the answer. As Brian Yoder stated in Nudity in Art: A Virtue or Vice? "Would we really be better off if all of that great art, such a Michelangelo's David, was hidden away? Destroyed? Never made in the first place? Covered with fig leaves? I don't think so" (Yoder, n. d.).

CHILDREN'S AESTHETIC AWARENESS

Researchers support the importance of aesthetic awareness and development in young children. According to Isbell and Raines (2003), "Aesthetics is an area of art concerned with feelings and responses to color, form, and design. There is a basic need to make sense and appreciate the world in which we live. When children have opportunities to view and explore beautiful things in their classroom, they begin to appreciate their environment the classroom should be an aesthetically pleasing and sensory rich environment" (p. 117). Environments for young children can have a major impact on this development. Authors and researchers have shared the importance by carefully designing and setting up how things are arranged and displayed in early childhood environments.

Hillman (2012), author of The Intangibles in the Early Childhood Classroom suggested that children's development of aesthetic awareness begins with how the teacher chose to set up the classroom, and how materials are presented and displayed. For example, when children see how things are in order in the classroom, such as the paints put out fresh every day, separate spaces for various projects, or clutter free areas, it creates an inviting, welcoming, and pleasing environment. A welcoming and inclusive environment should accessible to all, with adequate spaces for movement and seating for children or adults who use assistive technology (e.g. wheelchair, walker, standing frame, etc.). One must be also cautious about an overwhelming environment, particularly for children who are susceptible to sensory overload. Hillman (2012) notes that aesthetics also includes simplicity, such as leaving walls with blank spaces to rest eyes and promote relaxation, particularly for children who may feel sensory overload and need less busy environments. Hillman adds that nature and growth of plant and flowers allows children to observe and discover beauty, color, and smells each day. "Keeping an aesthetic sense alive calls for a great deal of thought and planning that is woven into the very fabric of who you are, how you think, and how you choose your actions. It is like an artist who mixes the colors from her palette, overlaying the colors, one atop another until the blending creates just the right shade of color she sought" (Hillman, 2012, p. 13-14).

In another source from Hillman, noted in Childcare Exchange: The Early Childhood Leaders' Magazine (2012) she noted the importance of children creating artwork and having creative experiences on a daily basis. Hillman stated, "I want the children's eyes to seek out what is beautiful. I want the children to use their hands to please their eyes. I want art to be part of their every day. The most important thing to remember about art projects in early childhood is that children should have opportunities every day to create artistically pleasing projects" (p. 1). She poses these important questions for early childhood educators:

- Are you selective about the materials provided to children for their creative art projects? Are they pleasing to you, to them? Are they safe for use?

- Do you plan art projects well in advance in order to have the necessary materials available?

- Do you pause to sit beside children, observe them work and dialogue with them about their art projects? (adapted from Hillman 2012)

This author would add the following question:

- Do you offer children enough time to complete their creative process; and if not, how do we solve this?

As adults, we tend to rush children though experiences with an urgency to stay on schedule, which could result in robbing children of the full creative experience and possibilities. We might also miss the opportunity to listen and observe to realize what they understand, who they are, what is important to them, and what is happening in their lives. Early childhood educators, parents, therapists, and all adults who work with young children need to ask the above questions of themselves regarding art programs/experiences they provided young children.

An amazing tool for assessing and determining a classroom's level of aesthetic beauty and offering a guide for an inspiring learning environment for young children is offered by DeViney, Duncan, Harris, Rody, and Rosenberry (2010) entitled the Rating Observation Scale for Inspiring Environments (ROSIE).
See:

http://www.childcareexchange.com/catalog/product/rating-observation-scale-for-inspiring-environments-rosie/4100572/

According to Childcare Exchange (2012), "The Rating Observation Scale for Inspiring Environments challenges teachers to examine classrooms in a totally new way with an eye for what is aesthetically beautiful and inspiring. Educators will learn to determine a classroom's level of aesthetic beauty by looking through a lens of nature, color, furnishings, textures, displays, lighting, and focal points. ROSIE then provides images and examples to assist in turning learning spaces into inspirational environments in which children can grow and learn. This groundbreaking tool assesses classrooms in a whole new way!" You can view entire scale at:

https://prezi.com/0w3iryd2ejbo/copy-of-rosie-rating-observation-scale-for-inspiring-environments/

According to the ROSIE, there are three stages of developing inspiring environments for children:

1. Sprouting: This is the beginner stage, where you start to understand the basic principles of making an environment attractive.

2. Budding: In this stage you are becoming more aware and skilled and the environment continues to grow.

3. Blooming: This is the higher level where you have reached your fullest potential (there are 7 principles).

(DeViney, Duncan, Rody, Harris & Rosenberry, 2010)

In this observation scale, these authors note the 7 Principles of Design:

1. Nature Inspires Beauty Nature instills a sense of wonder because it's beautiful.

2. Color Generates Interest Color can be an obstacle to learning; create natural, neutral background, using brighter colors and illustrations to create interest.

3. Furnishings Define Space Décor and furniture defines space in some way.

4. Texture Adds Depth Children learn through their senses; they need the texture to explore and investigate.

5. Displays Enhance Environment Use children's work to enhance the environment; respect their work by displaying in attractive, aesthetic ways.

6. Elements Heighten Ambiance The lighting, olfactory, smells, sounds, etc. all create an ambiance in the classroom. Choose these carefully, while being sensitive to individual sensory sensitivity and preference.

7. Focal Points Attract Attention Children are drawn to focal points, which cause excitement and interest. This can assist with transitions

during arrival, particularly with children who may have difficulty separating from their parents/caregivers.

(adapted from DeViney, Duncan, Rody, Harris & Rosenberry, 2010)

First determining what stage, you and your classroom environment reflect. Then with use of this tool you could move forward, setting priorities and finding ways to inspire children's positive learning and creativity. This tool offers steps to implement ideas to incorporate nature, children's artwork, and everyday classroom materials, along with promoting creativity, learning, and aesthetics. As with all methods or strategies, there are pros and cons. Pros include a new scale to measure quality in an area is absent in most environmental rating scales. The majority of quality rating scales identify essential elements for the early childhood classrooms, but do not address the aesthetic concepts of the environment such as color, focal point, texture, exhibits, lighting, displays, and the use of space. The cons are that this scale only focuses on the indoor environment, resulting in potential bias (as it relies on self-report), and it does not measure interactions in the environment. (DeViney, Duncan, Rody, Harris & Rosenberry, 2010).

The process is easy to follow and can transform an ordinary classroom into creative and beautiful learning spaces to promote creativity and aesthetic appreciation. The ROSIE Scale will guide the educator in assessing and making improvements in the classroom environment and inclusion of nature (plants, animals, and other nature treasures for children to explore), aspect of furnishing (e.g. child-sized, arrangement, how it defines the space), textures (inviting exploration), how color is used throughout the room, displays (incorporating children's work), lighting/smells/sounds, and focal points of the environment (e.g. exciting and inviting attractions).

ARTIST IN THE FAMILY: AN OPPORTUNITY FOR CHILDREN TO EXPLORE AND DISCOVER ARTISTS WITHIN THEIR OWN FAMILY

Most families have an artist or a close friend who is an artist. This person may not be a painter, a sculptor, glassblower, or architect designing buildings. However, this individual started with an idea and creatively gave it form, making this person a visual artist of some kind. It may be Aunt Dorothy who sits for hours designing and hand sewing quilts from her original pattern; or it may be brother Chuck who does wood craft, inlaid exotic wood floors or laminated cutting boards. It might even be a long-lost cousin who is a graphic design body illustrator (tattoo artist). Taking an original idea (no kits) and giving it, visual form makes this person an artist. In other words, someone who is quilting from a pre-made pattern, latch hooking from a pre-made design, or painting by number would not meet this definition.

Assist children and their families to identify someone in their family who might fit this definition. Send instructions for the child and parent (or another adult), to interview this person. The questions below will assist the child and parent in gaining an understanding of what the artist is doing. Try to keep the level of questions and interactions matching the child's developmental level for better understanding and meaningful interactions. Younger children would need more adult guidance. Both child and parent will learn about this person, what motivates him or her, and why this artist has a passion for the creative process. Having the child assist with the interview or integrating her/him in the process with materials can have a profound impact and extraordinary memory for both the child and parent (or other family member).

Ask the artist to demonstrate the process and offer the child a hands-on experience with the materials. The goals of this experience are to facilitate and model a comfortable conversation between the child and artist, and to directly observe the creative process. Documenting this experience with photographs and audio or videotaping will allow review and reflection. Encourage the child to write or dictate a summary and reflection of the experience. If the artist is a member of the family, it can be an immensely gratifying and bonding experience for all.

The following questions are suggested to benefit from this precious opportunity. Integrate as many of the art elements and principles that apply at the child's level.

1. What type of visual artwork does this artist in the family do? Be specific (e.g. painting, drawing, quilter, etc.).

2. Why do they do it? What motivates them? Be specific, ask for particulars.

3. How do they do it? Be specific, ask for details.

4. How long have they done this and why did they start?

5. What is the history about this artist and her/his work?

6. What kind of training did this person have? Was it formal or informal? Was the learning process/technique passed from former generations?

7. Have this individual ever shown their work publicly? If so, where? Have they sold any pieces? Do they give artwork as gifts?

8. If this artist is a family member, do you (the adult interviewer) have a piece of her/his artwork that you treasure? Would you hand this down to your children someday?

9. When did you (the adult interviewer) become aware of this artist's talent? Reflect on this. How old were you, where were you, and did you appreciate what they were doing at the time? Share this with the child.

10. Include a photo of the artist, their artwork, and the child. If the artist involves the child with the materials, photograph this, as it is a central part of this experience.

11. In concluding this interview, how does this artist's work make you (the adult and child interviewers) feel now? Do you understand the idea and the process of what is being created? Do you clearly understand what the artist is expressing through her/his work? What did the child do or say to demonstrate their understanding of the process? Include any other reflections.

If you use this as a family experience for children in your classroom, have the children (or child and parent or family member) share the experience through photos, stories, reflections, and perhaps their own attempts at the medium used by the family artist. A delightful follow up opportunity would be for the child to invite this artist family member to visit the class and demonstrate their talents.

As always, showing gratefulness to those who take the time to share talents with children is encouraged. By doing so, the importance of gratitude is modeled for children. Having the child or children write or draw thank you notes is a wonderful way to demonstrate their appreciation. It also offers a creative opportunity.

Chapter Summary and Looking Ahead

This chapter began with posing the questions, "What is art?" and "What is beauty?" Included was a wide range of definitions for both child and adult. Introducing children to the foundations of good art and our artistic heritage is important, and keeping developmental levels of individual children as the focus while approaching this is essential. Viewing and talking with children about art, while integrating art elements and principles and additional art dialogue were presented for various developmental levels. Incorporating abstract or non-representational artworks, in addition to a balance of 2D as well as 3D art was emphasized. Suggestions for art gallery visits with children at various developmental levels and ages were offered. Discussion regarding the question of how to handle nudity in art was addressed. Recommendations for children exploring and discovering artists within their own family were noted, including an outline for this enriching and bonding opportunity.

Looking ahead to Chapter 8, ways that children express and communicate through their art will be examined. Illustrations of how children draw what they know, who they are, what is important to them, and what is happening in their lives will be presented. Included will be discussion of how pre-writing skills occur through the development of children's drawings and scribbles. Other developmental benefits of creative art process and expression will be noted, including self-confidence, problem solving skills, determination, concentration skills, and self-expression. The role of art therapy will be discussed, specifically how art helps children communicate during difficult times in life.

Suggestions for Additional Reflection and Review

- For more on aesthetics and artistic expression and young children, see: http://kneedeepingrace.com/2012/05/5days-artistic-expression-001/

- Rating Observation Scale for Inspiring Environments (ROSIE) by Jessica DeViney, Sandra Duncan, Sara Harris, Mary Ann Rody, Lois Rosenberry:

  http://www.childcareexchange.com/catalog/product/rating-observation-scale-for-inspiring-environments-rosie/4100572/

- Georgia O'Keeffe Books for Children:

  o Turner, R. M. (1993). Georgia O'Keeffe: Portraits of women artist for children. New York" Little, Brown & Company.

  o Venezia, M. (1994). Georgia O'Keeffe. Danbury, CT: Grolier Publishing.

  o Winter, J. (1998). My name is Georgia: A portrait. New York: Harcourt.

CREATIVITY JOURNALS FOR ALL AGES

Adult Journal Activity #7

Artist in the family: Complete the Artist in the Family activity noted in this chapter. Record all of this in your journal, including photographs. You will learn about this person and why they have a passion for the creative process. If you include a child in this experience, follow up with noting the child's comments and reflections, as well.

Child's Personal Creativity Journal Activity #7

Activity #7 for Infants (Birth to walking, or 16 months)

Art gallery/museum visit: See Suggestions to Share with Parents for Art Gallery/Museum Visits with Infants, Toddlers, and Preschoolers noted earlier in this chapter. Ask the family to share their impressions (including any of the infant's verbal or nonverbal reactions) and any photos that they took so that you may record the visit in the infant's journal. Be sure to note any follow up activities you might provide (e.g. board books about art and artists, talking about colors, shapes, other elements, as well as subject matter). Continuing to remember that infants take in everything through their senses, and the infant's journal becomes a documentation of the infant's sensory experiences. Again, please attempt to approach this as a journal, and not a scrapbook. It should include only the infant's work or photos of the sensory experiences.

Activity #7 for Toddlers (walking or 16 months to 3-years-old)

Art gallery/museum visit: See Suggestions to Share with Parents for Art Gallery/Museum Visits with Infants, Toddlers, and Preschoolers noted earlier in this chapter. Ask the family to share their impressions (including any of the toddler's verbal or nonverbal reactions) and any photos that they took so that you may record the visit in the toddler's journal. Be sure to note any follow up activities you might provide (e.g. board books about art and artists, talking about colors, shapes, other elements, as well as subject matter). Give the child the time, the space, the materials, and the positive feedback and reinforcement the experience.

Activity #7 for Preschoolers (ages 3 – 5)

Art gallery/museum visit: See Suggestions to Share with Parents for Art Gallery/Museum Visits with Infants, Toddlers, and Preschoolers noted earlier in this chapter. Ask the family to share their impressions (including any verbal interactions, dialogue, as well as nonverbal reactions) and any photos that they took so that you may record the visit in the preschooler's journal. Be sure to note any follow up activities you might provide (e.g. books about art and artists, talking about art elements and subject matter). Try the suggested follow up activities in this chapter. Give the child the time, the space, the materials, and the positive feedback and reinforcement the experience.

Activity #7 for Young School-agers

Art gallery/museum visit: See Art Gallery/Museum Visits with School-aged Children noted earlier in this chapter. Record the visit in the school aged child's journal, including photographs, child's notes or photos taken, verbal interactions, dialogue, as well as nonverbal reactions. Be sure to note any follow up activities you might provide (e.g. books about art and artists, talking about art elements and subject matter, any follow up artwork). Try the suggested follow up activities in this chapter. Give the child the time, the space, the materials, and the positive feedback and reinforcement the experience.

CHAPTER 8

Children's Art as Communication

"A child is a dynamic being; art becomes for him (or her) a language of thought."

- Lowenfeld & Brittain

CHAPTER OVERVIEW

Children draw what they know, and in doing so, they communicate who they are, what is important to them, and what is happening in their lives. Children's drawings and scribbles have long been considered to demonstrate pre-writing skills. Yet even before a child develops speech, drawing has offered very young children self-expression of ideas and feelings. This chapter will illustrate how children's art (both 2D and 3D) communicates and demonstrates: their creative spirit, self-confidence, problem solving skills, determination, focus and concentration skills, knowledge, and details they may not be able to put into words. Children's art can also depict a range of emotions and challenges. Art can help children cope with these feelings. The role and benefits of art therapy will also be discussed. In conclusion, a section this author entitles, Children's Art for the Greater Good will include ideas and resources for children to communicate through their art about important topics such as peace, nonviolence, anti-bullying, and sustainability.

Children Draw What They Know

Children interpret their world and their understanding of the world through their art. They tell us what they understand, who they are, what is important to them, how they feel, and what is happening in their lives through their drawings. In observing children within their creative art process, we learn what they understand about their family, culture, fears, joys, and challenges. Children also communicate their hopes and dreams and how they would like their world to be through their art. A child whose parents are divorced, for example, might picture this separation in a family portrait drawing. This child might instead picture how she may want things to be by sketching her parents together in a drawing of the family. Fox and Schirrmacher (2015) state that "Just as photographs of children tell us much about what children look like on the outside, their artwork reveals what they look like on the inside. Children use art to tell us many things about themselves. Learn to read their pictures. Observing children engaged in art and collecting samples of their artwork over time provides a wealth of information" (p. 310).

It is beneficial to have strong partnerships with children and their families as we learn to read children's art. Educators and parents need to look closely and listen carefully to children's communication through their creations. The images alone can tell us a great deal; however, the art dialogue can enhance our understanding. According to Artz.org, "Art can be a good indicator of what a child is actually feeling in their life as well. If they choose to make paintings and drawings of scary events and images, it is often a way to express fears that they have and feel. It is a way for them to explore this scary event in a safe way. By the same pattern, drawing images of happy images that they like can help to indicate some of the safe emotions and areas of their life which they might feel comfort with. This art can be a great indicator of not only what the child is feeling, but of things which the child might want to express but not know how" (Retrieved from http://www.artsz.org/art-therapy-for-children/). As educators and parents reflect with children about their artwork and images, their thoughts and feelings can be more clearly understood.

Children's Art Demonstrates Their Individual Development and Growth

The growth of the child across developmental domains can also be illustrated through his creations. Developmentally, the young child's world is all about himself. Therefore, it seems logical that the focus of most children's art begins with themselves. Their self-portrait emerges with a large, enclosed circle, and appendages of legs, and then arms extending out directly from the circle (See Figure 8.1 below). Children with typically developing artistic skills later add fingers and features of the face, such as elaborating on the eyes, nose, mouth, and hair. Recall Kellogg's (1969) table depicting stages of drawing a person in Chapter 2. It clearly illustrated how the details of neck or trunk emerge later as the child progresses in visual-motor and cognitive skills. These stages of art growth demonstrate the child's advancement across all developmental domains.

Figure 8.1: Example of self-portrait of a 3-year-old (larger figure on right), also depicting her teacher who wore dangling earrings (figure on left). Note the enclosed O, and appendages of legs extending out directly from the O.

Children's Art Communicates What Is Important and What Is Happening in Their Lives

Children draw what is important to them in their lives. Children draw their family members, pets, their house, family activities and holidays, as well as various aspects of their culture. A child with differing abilities might draw her or his wheelchair, glasses, or a hearing aid by the ear. These examples of assistive technology are a central part of that child's world. The child usually remains the center or focus of the artwork and might be a larger figure than the rest.

Children draw what is happening in their lives and how they feel. Through art children communicate events and changes in their lives and feelings about those changes. This could be in relation to positive or negative change. The following examples illustrate how children's art depicts changes in their lives. Grandma might show up in artwork, because Grandma came to visit or to live with the family. A large abdomen on Mommy could indicate the child's understanding that a baby on the way. Mom or Dad could be out of picture when separation or divorce suddenly occurs. A child who has a sibling who is born with special needs might incorporate their thoughts, understanding, and feelings into their art. Figure 8.2 is a 6-year-old girl's drawing of herself and her younger sister, who uses a wheelchair, dancing together.

Figure 8.2: Drawing by a 6-year-old of herself and her younger sister, who uses a wheelchair, dancing together.

Children's Art Communicates Their Emotions

Self-esteem and other emotions and feelings can be communicated through children's art. Children use size, shape, color, and placement in portraying how they feel about themselves or others. A wide range of emotions might be communicated through a child's artwork, such as love, hate, caring, fears, anger, or frustration. For example, if the child represented her/himself as a small figure in the corner, separated, or even missing from the rest of the family in a family portrait, among other feelings, this could communicate they are feeling ignored or insignificant. A child whose painting is covered over in black, whose drawing included repeated markings, scratches, or holes in the paper, might be communicating anger, frustration, anxiety, or other feelings. Therefore, art should offer a safe place to express any of these emotions. Although the child should not be allowed to hurt themselves, others, or materials in the process, freedom to express should be the goal. The goal is not a "pretty picture" or sculpture, it is an individual expression. Their expression should not be judged.

It is important to observe children's artwork and behavior. Looking beyond the artwork to what is happening in the child's life is essential in order to better understand the child and her art communication. Rather than overreacting to a potentially upsetting subject or depiction in a child's drawings, educators need to step back and note issues, challenges, or life complications the child might be facing. For some children with challenges due to differing abilities or those who are in an at-risk environment, this could be the ONE area a child has control over in life. Educators need to share children's drawings with their families and assist them in understanding children's art growth and development. Illustrating how a child is communicating through his art is important for parents to recognize. This would assist families in better understanding their child and her life joys, challenges, and fears, as well as appreciating the child's creative art process and product.

Children's Art Demonstrates Prewriting and Preliteracy Skills

Children's drawings and scribbles have long been considered to demonstrate prewriting and preliteracy skills. Yet even before a child develops speech or forms a letter, drawing has offered very young children self-expression of ideas and feelings. When children's art is partnered with prewriting and preliteracy, children develop verbal and nonverbal communication skills. Children can connect words with actions or concepts when adults talk with children about their art. For example, labeling children's actions and process of art, noting the marks they make, or progression of their 3-D work contributes to their vocabulary and concept development. Listening, modeling balance in conversations, songs, and stories all impact language development skills and comprehension. In addition, the importance of pausing for response is essential when conversing with infants and toddlers through school age when talking with children about their art. Pausing to listen to ideas, planning processes, experimentation, problem solving, frustrations, trial, and error, allows the child time to fully share thoughts or questions. It can also validate their opinions and ideas. Taking time to pause is difficult for some, but an essential piece of fostering the creative process.

Pausing to listen is a matter of respect for the child and validates his voice. Hesitating in action to wait for a nonverbal response from the child is also a matter of respect.

As children mature to a representational level of their artwork, they draw what they know, what is important, what is happening in their lives, or how they want life to be. Children are empowered when drawing how they would like things to be. It offers the freedom of fantasy. With this comes words, stories, and verbal expressions. Telling and writing stories about creations is a natural event for children. Even before children can write, they dictate their stories about their art to an adult to put them in print. Through art, children gain more fine motor strength and dexterity. Benefits include increased eye-hand coordination. All of these are pre-writing skills. Children's art and literacy can easily be integrated. Figure 8.3, for example, shows how drawing and writing skills come together in a 6-year-old girl's birthday card that she made for her dad. Many have wondered, what comes first, the story or the illustration through 2D or 3D form? It is based on individual preference, creative process, and learning style and could change with various moods or projects. Therefore, an integrated process welcomes flexibility, meaning story before art depiction, art depiction before the story, or both at the same time. This opens the door to many possibilities and creative preferences and processes.

Figure 8.3: Drawing and writing skills come together naturally in this 6-year-old's birthday card she made for her dad. She said her dad is blowing out a candle, and she likes to go fishing with him.

Children's Art Communicates through Interdisciplinary Projects

Russell & Russell (2012) at Emporia State University (ESU) illustrated this process with an interdisciplinary project entitled, "Children Inspire Glass Project." Several ESU faculty members from Early Childhood Education and Art explored the educational possibilities of a program modeled after the KIDS DESIGN GLASS program at the Museum of Glass in Tacoma, WA, stretching it further to incorporate university students from educational disciplines. Students from Early Childhood, Elementary Education, Children's Literacy, Art Glass Concentration, Art Therapy collaborated with faculty on this this project. The Children Inspire Glass Pilot Project was successful as the children from the Emporia, Kansas community, ages 5–10, produced a "creature" through drawings, transitioned their creature from 2D to 3D as they created a clay image of their creature design. Throughout the process, the children composed stories about their creation, via journaling. Some children drew first, some wrote or dictated the story first, and some did both at the same time. To facilitate this, children were provided a journal and were encouraged to think of and write words that characterized their creatures while they made their drawings.

Following this, the ESU Glass students reproduced the children's designs in glass, first in clear glass, and then in color. Each child had his or her day at the ESU Hot Shop. Every child examined the clear model of their design, and gave input regarding changes or modifications for the colored version based on her or his design. This empowered the children because they gave feedback to the university students to perfect their designs. The children also shared their story about their creature with the glass students, which gave the glass students more insight into the characteristics and personality of each designed creature. The glass students observed the children's enthusiasm and self-esteem as their designs took on 3D colored glass forms. The children were in awe spending "their day" of production of their creature, closely observing it coming to life in glass form.

The following are examples of the one child's drawings, sculptures, stories, and her designs in glass sculptures created by ESU University Glass instructor, Roberta Eichenberg, and glass students. Figure 8.4 shows the literacy portion of the Children Inspire Glass Project. A professor encourages a child to write words that characterize her creature (Arabella the Fairy) while she draws.

Figure 8.4: Literacy portion of the Children Inspire Glass Project, the drawing and story come together. Assistant Professor, Dr. Heather Caswell encourages child to write words that characterized her creature, while drawing it. Arabella the Fairy comes to life.

Dr. Caswell, as literacy consultant for this pilot project, directed the writing portion of the project. Through a writing workshop approach, children were encouraged to develop stories about their created creature. Prewriting took place through drawing their creature in great detail while discussing with adults and other children the details of their creature. Following this prewriting and creative process, children independently and/or with adult support drafted a story in writing. One-on-one conferencing took place during this writing process. Adults carefully crafted questions and conversation that would honor the individual child's creative process and story development. Through this workshop approach, children became storytellers, weaving their artistic approach of drawing and 3-D creation into their writing process.

Below is the original writing (Figure 8.5) and completed story, authored by the 6-year-old creator of Arabella the Fairy. Note that in the original writing during the workshop, Lauren completed the beginning of her story in her own handwriting and chose to have assistance by dictating the second portion to the adult assisting her. This continuum and flexibility is an important aspect of the writing workshop approach.

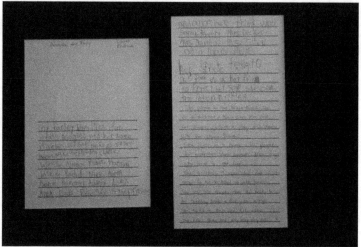

Figure 8.5: Arabella the Fairy, written by Lauren.

Arabella the Fairy
by Lauren Erickson

My fairy lives in a fan. It eats magic and her name is Arabella. She has friends and their names are Kelsey Divinity, Charlie Weslie, Norma Robin, Hannah Jasmine, Rachel Nikki, Aspen Aaron, Heromny, Audrey, Lucy, Anna Coda, Eli. She is the princess and another friend were Sarah Abvery, Mrs. Decker, Mrs. Thumu, Ms. Tilten and many more. Her favorite thing to do is dance with her friends to protect herself. She can turn into a necklace.

The people in the house think she is a necklace they wear her, and she escapes outside to play and dance with her many friends. She lives in a house with people for protection from animals, like frogs, who wish to eat her.

She is about 4 inches tall and it is easier for her to blend in with jewelry. She can also shrink when she needs to, by shedding beads and folding her wings. She talks to boys and girls when she knows they are very, very, very nice.

Figure 8.6: Transitioning Arabella the Fairy from 2D to 3D form.

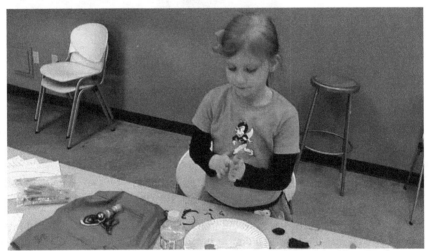

Figure 8.7: Continued Work Transitioning Arabella the Fairy from 2D to 3D form.

Figure 8.8: Arabella the Fairy completed in 3D form.

Figures 8.6 and 8.7 show the work of transitioning Arabella the Fairy from 2D to 3D form. Figure 8.8 features Arabella the Fairy in completed 3D form while Figure 8.9 shows her in clear glass form. In Figure 8.10 Arabella the Fairy's creator observes the fairy's transformation as ESU glass students complete the process. The child gave feedback to the university glass students using this model regarding any changes needed in the final design. Lauren's suggestions were to spread Arabella's wings out wider and make the hair flow more to the front (which you can see was altered in the following photos in colored glass, due to her decisions and feedback). Figure 8.11 shows Arabella the Fairy flying away in the final colored glass form. It was empowering for a 6-year-old to communicate her suggestions of her design to university students and faculty and to see her 2D artwork transformed into several 3D products (Figure 8.12).

Figure 8.9: Arabella the Fairy in clear glass form.

Figure 8.10: Arabella the Fairy comes to life in glass form. The creator, age 6, observes the transformation, as ESU glass students complete the process.

Figure 8.11: Arabella the Fairy flying away in the final colored glass form.

Figure 8.12: Arabella the Fairy in 2D, 3D (colored polymer clay), and final colored glass form, along with her proud 6-year-old creator, Lauren.

Documentation of the creative process and product was a major feature of Emporia State University's Children Inspire Glass Project. Influenced by the Reggio approach, documentation using various types of media (photographs, videos, iPads, etc.), and children's artistic words and creations were consciously used to illustrate and reflect the creative process. According to the Reggio approach, doing so can inspire children to learn from and reflect on the documentation of their endeavors. The Children Inspire Glass Project provided documentation of the children's words, drawings, sculptures, and designs through photographs and videos of these experiences. This offered insight into what was understood and important to the children. This documentation also provided feedback and an illustration of the creative process for families in addition to archiving the project. The outcome from the work of skilled photographers and videographers from this project, the documentation (photos and DVD) illustrating the process of this educational program have been used for display in art shows. This documentation has also been utilized for the children to review. It also provided a teaching tool for various university courses (Art-Glass, Art Education, Art Therapy, Elementary Education, Early Literacy, and Early Childhood Education), and national presentations, and illustrations to accompany grants for future funding of the project.

This project offered a learning process for all disciplines and parties involved, including the children, their families, faculty, students, and others who observed. The finished products were exquisite, yet the journey getting to the end result of the children's art works was equally as important. Both products and process were well documented throughout the project. It is this journey that made this project unique, and it has been and continues to be shared from regional to national and international levels. Faculty members from each discipline involved have shared this project professionally through presentations, displays, and professional writing. The Children Inspire Glass Project was also awarded the 2014 Ervay Family Applied Scholarship Award.

Russell (2012), co-coordinator of the Children Inspire Glass Project, shared a personal reflection about the project:

> Personally, this project has presented an abundant amount of effort and coordination, yet has been one of the most joyful, inspiring, and collaborative projects of my career. It has demonstrated the power of authentically creative experiences for children, and importance of their genuine ownership in that process. This experience has clearly defined for me, as an Early Childhood Educator, the importance of what we do and HOW we do it! It is amazing how children can be engaged and focused when you foster creativity with an appropriate environment, materials, interactions, and TIME! We tend to structure so much of their young lives and hurry them through processes; rather than slowing down for learning through play, giving them TIME to show us how much they know, allowing TIME for problem solving opportunities, and TIME to create.

Children's Perspectives and Perceptions

As adults work with young children, it is essential to express language that interprets their perspective and perception of the world. As noted in Chapter 6, the method of think-aloud or self-talk allows adults to model thought process verbally with very young children, taking on a conversation pattern even if only a few words are used. The adult notes the child's perspective while asking them questions. In doing so, the adult models a natural conversation pattern, which promotes cognitive processing and respects the child's perspective and perception.

Valuing and acknowledging the child's perspective and perception is illustrated in the following example. A teacher was observing a 3-year-old child drawing two figures with markers on a large piece of paper. One was a medium sized circle with legs and arms coming off the circle and facial features with a big smile. The second figure was a very small circle at the top, with a larger circle below it almost filling the page. Then what appeared to be legs and arms were coming off the very large circle. Additionally, long dangling objects were coming off the small circle. One assumption could have been that the child was drawing a snow person. Another interpretation might have been that the child was progressing in art growth and including a trunk in the second figure. The teacher used think-aloud or self-talk, saying, "Oh, I see you have drawn this figure with a larger circle in the middle." The child quickly replied, "Oh that's you with a baby in your tummy and these are your long earrings." This was a delightful reminder for the teacher (who was pregnant) that from a child's perspective, most of what she sees is the protruding abdomen when looking at a woman who is pregnant. The earrings caught the child's eye, as well, and she chose to include them in her drawing. By giving positive feedback, the child's perspective is reinforced. This motivates the child to continue the creative expression, illustrating her perspective and perception.

Photography and videography can be a powerful tool to demonstrate children's perspectives. An example shared by Cruikshank (2011) in Empowering Images:

Using Photography as a Medium to Develop Visual Literacy illustrated the power of communicating a child's perspective. Cruikshank described how children could be encouraged to be photographers as one method of documenting their work and communicating their perspective. She shared the following incident:

> A first step in guiding the children in our class towards intentional photography was to suggest frames for the children's investigations. On one occasion, we took a walk around the school, asking the children to take pictures of interesting points on the walk. As we walked, we passed another teacher. The group paused momentarily while the two teachers spoke. Upon reviewing the photographs, I found a picture of our feet during this pause. This gave me a view from the child's perspective. What for me had been an inconsequential pause during our walk, for the child it had been an important moment. She had not photographed our faces, which makes me think it was not our conversation that had interested her; rather it was the positioning of our feet that caught her attention. Was she looking at the language of our bodies? Did she feel this was an important moment because the feet had stopped? (Cruikshank, 2011, p.1).

Photography offers an ideal medium to remind us of the view from the child's perspective. It gives children the power to record images of importance to them, to document their creations, and to track their individual art growth and progress. Temporary creations, such as block structures or sculptures in material (e.g. snow that will melt), or structures created in a non-secure material (e.g. sand), could be documented through photographs taken by children with adult supervision. Figure 8.13 shows a temporary creation of a sculpture made out of snow. These are wonderful examples to place in the child's portfolio and share with families. Children learn the importance of documentation and the joy of recording their own progress. Encouraging families to do the same at home can create a comprehensive portfolio of the child's creations and perceptions from both home and school.

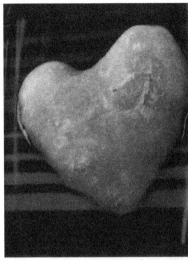

Figure 8.13: A heart-shaped sculpture out of snow and food coloring.

ART AS COMMUNICATION IN DEALING WITH FEARS, TRAUMA, LIFE CHANGES, LOSS, ILLNESS, AND DIFFERING NEEDS

The death of a grandparent, parent, sibling, or even a pet can be traumatic for anyone, particularly a child. When a child tries to make sense of life and how death fits in the picture, it can be confusing and frightening. Conflict or divorce of parents, or being a victim of mental and/or physical abuse can cause intense fear and trauma for young children. Expressing grief, confusion, or fear can be difficult. Young children lack life experiences, coping skills and cognitive understanding needed for expressing emotions in a way for adults to understand. As a result, young children might verbally and emotionally shut down or exhibit inappropriate behavior.

In an article, Art Therapy for Children, from Art Explained and Made Simple (n. d.), "Art can be a good indicator of what a child is actually feeling in their life as well. If they choose to make paintings and drawings of scary events and images, it is often a way to express fears that they have and feel. It is a way for them to explore this scary event in a safe way. By the same pattern, drawing images of happy images that they like can help to indicate some of the safe emotions and areas of their life which they might feel comfort with." Through their art, children can express feelings and things they want to express but are not sure how to communicate. Art has been an effective method for communication, as well as therapy. The role of art therapy is one of healing and assisting individuals in communicating feelings and emotions, especially during difficult times in life. According to Artz.org (n. d.),

Children often do not have the words to be able to define some of the feelings and even trauma that they might be going through. They do not have the vocabulary to articulate feelings that they might be having. Yet, this does not stop those children from feeling those emotions. Not being able to express these emotions can lead to various problems for the children as they grow and the need to express these feelings can manifest themselves in potentially harmful ways. Teaching these children to express themselves through art could end up being a great way for them to not only explore their creative individuality, but to express these potentially traumatic emotions as well" (Artz.org, n. d.).

For children, this therapy method has great potential because children naturally communicate through their art. Children facing or who have faced a serious illness, surgery, homelessness, hunger and starvation, loss of a family member, or abuse have trauma due to these experiences. Figure 8.14 was drawn by an 8-year-old who had just recuperated from emergency shunt replacement surgery due to Hydrocephalus. Hydrocephalus occurs when fluid accumulates in the brain. If not treated, it can cause serious brain damage. She was able to go outside in her wheelchair with her sister for the first time since her surgery. It started to rain, but her joy and freedom to be alive and outside with her sister is clearly depicted in her drawing.

Figure 8.14: Drawing done by an 8-year-old who had just recuperated from emergency shunt replacement surgery

Art and art therapy have been used after disasters, such as 9/11, in homeless shelters, in emergency shelters, in pediatric hospitals for children with various illnesses and special needs, and for children dealing with various losses. Art has also been used to address children's responses to various traumas that some children face regularly, such as domestic violence or drug-related shootings.

"The Day Our World Changed: Children's Art of 9/11" was a joint project of New York University's Child Study Center and the Museum of the City of New York. Bogle (2002) notes how the children's art was a testimony to their intense feelings of fear, courage, anger, and resilience after witnessing violence. Expressing feelings in situations like these is difficult for everyone, particularly for children, who have had less life experience with tragedy. "Encouraging children to draw, and then gently asking them questions about their art, sometimes brings out feelings they have been unable or reluctant to put into words" (Bogle, 2002). Suzanne Silverstein, an art therapist and president and co-founder of the Psychological Trauma Center at Cedars-Sinai stated, "What we find is that children tend to draw the part of the trauma they don't understand—the part they're 'stuck' on Like adults, sometimes what they're saying is not what they're feeling. When they draw, they put it all out on paper" (Bogle, 2002).

The goal for children's art is to put it all out there on paper. Free expression should be the primary purpose and objective of children's art. Many of us, as adults, find a bit of brain relief in writing down the tasks or making the "to do list." Some adults write thoughts and feelings in poems, stories, or journals, which allows feelings and emotions to be put on paper rather than only in our minds. Some adults do this through their artwork, as well. This is parallel to the message (be it positive or negative) that children put in their art. They are better at expressing feelings in artwork than in words on paper. Drawing is a child's means of written communication. It comes naturally for children. The full article and drawings from "The Day Our World Changed: Children's Art of 9/11" can be seen on the National Geographic website:

http://news.nationalgeographic.com/news/2002/09/0910_kidsart.html

CAUTION: AVOID ASSUMPTIONS OR MISINTERPRETING THE CHILD'S PURPOSE OR PRODUCT

The importance of dialogue in assisting children to understand their own art and professional artists' work is paramount to understanding the full meaning and intent of the child's art and their communication through their artwork. By using the art dialogue, we can learn much more about the finished product than simply looking at what the child created. Caution should be taken to not assume an interpretation or purpose of a child's art. One example is a child's depiction of a dinosaur (Figure 8.15). This child's favorite color was purple. She had some special needs and used a wheelchair. When the child's end product had no back legs and one of the front legs shorter, the classroom Para educator responded, "Oh, you made a purple dinosaur, and it has special needs, just like you!" The child replied, "No, you only gave us this much clay and told me I couldn't have more, so I didn't have enough to make all the legs!" Although the adult was present throughout the creation time, she did not realize that the lack of material was the reason behind the final project rather than purposefully missing limbs. Adults must be careful when communicating with children about their artwork, to avoid assumptions. Carefully worded comments and open-ended questions allow the child to share the intent, process, and interpretation of her work. Respect for this is essential to the creative process.

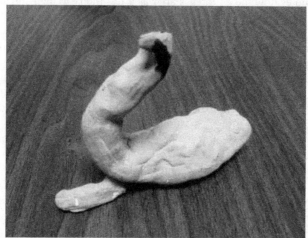

Figure 8.15: Example of child depicting a dinosaur in clay, and misinterpretation of missing appendages.

Another example is a tempera painting by Ryane, age 5 (Figure 8.16). One might look at this painting and think, this child feels like she is riding on a rainbow, going over the rainbow, or dreaming of flying. The space filled with the colors of the rainbow makes one wonder if the child has seen rainbows recently or if the teacher suggested painting a rainbow. Perhaps the child learned a new song about rainbows, such as "I Can Sing a Rainbow" see: https://www.youtube.com/watch?v=nRTdq0VsLGQ.

This song names the order of the colors this child used in her painting. The large flower and small house fit under the rainbow makes one wonder whose house it is and if she likes flowers or has recently picked flowers. The bottom green line grounds the piece, and the almost symmetrical arch of the rainbow demonstrates the child's mathematical skill in balance, shape, and form. The orders of the colors on the rainbow has the primary colors: red, yellow, and blue; and has two secondary colors of green and purple (no orange).

Figure 8.16: Tempera painting by 5-year-old.

Understanding what this child's artwork is communicating would be enriched if we were able to talk with her about her work, or if it were partnered with a story or comments she would add about her painting. It is encouraged to have a literacy component (either the child writing or dictating, or a combination of both) with art projects. It is important to use a different piece of paper rather than on the artwork itself. Lengthy notes on the back of the child's work (other than lightly writing the child's name to be sure the work is clearly identified) should be avoided. When we write words on the child's work, we are communicating several messages:

1. The child's work is not good enough to recognize what it is.

2. The child's mark is not respected when we mark over it or near it, unless it is a collaborative artwork, and this is understood from the beginning.

3. Marking on the back of the child's artwork sometimes marks through or can make an indentation (depending on your utensil).

4. Let the child put their own signature on their creation. You may have to lightly mark on the back for clarity, but not on the front of the work. Do encourage children to always sign their work, even if it is a 3-D artwork.

CHILDREN'S ART FOR THE GREATER GOOD

Children's Art for the Greater Good, according to this author, includes art that focuses on what benefits the people and the world around you, not only what benefits you. As children mature, they learn empathy and caring for others. We see them innocently and compassionately do something for other children or adults. The purpose and idea of Children's Art for the Greater Good would be children sharing their thoughts, ideas, and messages about making the world a better place. This includes children's communication through their art about topics, such as peace, nonviolence, anti-bullying, and sustainability. We already have programs that teach young children to take care of their environments, work towards peace, and advocate against bullying, etc. Since art is a prime area for children to naturally tell us what they know, who they are, what is important to them, and what is happening in their lives, topics such as world peace, recycling, anti-bullying, etc. can be further reflected upon and advocated for through children's art. An example of a child creating art for the greater good is shown in Figure 8.17.

Figure 8.17: Painting entitled, "A Clean Life" by Mikelle, age 8.

The following examples, activity ideas, and resources are offered for home or school projects as examples of Children's Art for the Greater Good. Be sure to double check to assure what you are choosing is authentic art experiences. If they are not, alter them to be authentic by making it more open-ended and not product-oriented.

The following are recycling art activities and other sustainability experiences:

- Recycling crafts for kids: http://www.kinderart.com/recycle/

- Earth Day Art Activities:

  http://www.favecrafts.com/Earth-Day-Crafts/16-Recycle-Crafts-for-Kids

- The Imagination Factory's Trash Matcher

  http://www.kid-at-art.com/htdoc/matchtmp.html

These are anti-bullying art activities and other anti-bullying experiences:

- PACER a National Bullying Prevention Center offers: Kids Against Bullying Center and activities: create a poster, stick puppets role, and unity dance.

  http://www.pacer.org/bullying/resources/toolkits/activities/

- Anti-Bullying Projects from Art room 104:

  http://artroom104.blogspot.com/2012/10/anti-bullying-projects.html

- Chalk for Change: Project Anti-Bully's very first anti-bullying campaign.

  http://www.projectantibully.com/chalk-for-change.html

- From the Bully Proof Classroom: Great Anti Bullying Activities and Lesson Plans by James H Burns

  http://bullyproofclassroom.com/great-anti-bullying-activities

See the following world peace art activities and experiences:

- Posters by children about world peace:

  http://www.globalartproject.org/about/posters.html

  http://www.globalartproject.org/galleries/gallery.php

- http://www.artprojectsforworldpeace.org/

- http://www.dwij.org/forum/only_hearts/art_project.html

- http://imgarcade.com/1/world-peace-art-projects/

> **_Window into a Classroom: Best Practices for Inclusion_**
>
> As suggested in Chapter 4, Discuss with children the many ways we are the same and different. Just as we each have different hair color, skin color, eye color, etc.; we also have different abilities that make us unique. Although, we are more alike that different, helping children experience a taste of what it is like to move, talk, see, or hear a different way, can help them be more sensitive to difference, and overall contribute to the Greater Good. Consider implementing various disability awareness activities while completing artwork and daily routines. For example, use of a child sized wheelchair in the classroom and playground for awareness of what it might be like to have physical challenges, blindfolds or making wax paper goggles to simulate a visual impairment, or taping several fingers together on each hand to simulate fine motor challenges, can all increase awareness of differing abilities. Following up these simulation experiences by encouraging children to draw/paint/sculpt and write/dictate ideas to make their environments better for all will increase accessibility awareness for the common good. A class mural depicting the children's ideas for better access could also be beneficial, increase awareness, and promote the common good. This accessibility awareness artwork could be displayed in the school and community to promote even more awareness of the importance of accessibility and inclusion.

Art is one way we can teach and model the "greater good" for young children. With a better understanding of this, they could not only grow up to be caring and compassionate adults, but will hopefully benefit the human race as a whole.

Chapter Summary and Looking Ahead

This chapter illustrated how children's art, both 2D and 3D, can communicate and demonstrate their creative spirit, self-confidence, problem solving skills, determination, focus and concentration skills, knowledge, and details they might not be able to (or are afraid to) put into words. Art can assist children with safe expression of their emotions, challenges, grief, fears, and coping with these feelings. For children with language challenges, art offers an effective means for nonverbal expression and an avenue for initiating communication with peers and adults. The art area could offer appropriate interaction opportunities, such as listening to and observing role models (peers and adults), offering materials, or asking and responding to questions. When being a part of a group in a safe physical sense, such as in the art area, children with language or communication needs will be encouraged to speak; children with motor challenges have opportunities to express, excel, and create without barriers; and children with behavioral or emotional challenges can express these feelings in a safe environment, free from judgment or criticism.

It is important for early childhood educators and parents to foster and reinforce children's artful expressions of their world and what they understand to increase their methods of communication. Our response to and communication with the child needs to convey that they can freely express themselves, rather than needing to follow through with adult goals, projects, or expectations of his/her art. This should be the child's expression; he or she should have ownership. This must be communicated to them, and we, as adults, must be role model this freedom, as well.

Looking ahead, Chapter 9 will promote understanding of the components of a complete early childhood inclusive arts program. These can relate to any art program from your family philosophy and practices to preschools/school, from community art centers programs to therapies. Strategies and tools to implement such a quality program will be provided. In addition, Chapter 9 will include an Evaluation of Early Childhood Art Program for suggested use.

Suggestions for Additional Reflection and Review

If you have not already done so (as suggested in Additional Readings in Chapter 3), the reader is strongly encouraged to view and reflect upon "The Dancing, Singing Easel" shared by family child care provider Emily Plank in January/February 2013 Child Care Exchange issue. It is a delightful illustration of authentic, spontaneous creativity in action that could never have been planned.

See: http://www.childcareexchange.com/eed/news_print.php?news_id=326

CREATIVITY JOURNALS FOR ALL AGES

Adult Creativity Journal Activity #8

Creative expression: Using at least four pages of your journal, complete the following (taking as much time as needed):

- Trace your whole hand on one page.

- On the next page take some tempera paint (any color, your choice), paint your hand and make a print of your hand.

- On the following page, draw your non-dominant hand, holding your hand out in any position. Draw your hand, as you see it, using the full space of the page. Study your hand closely, and add details with line, value, contrast, and texture.

- On the fourth page, open your non-dominant hand and touch your nose with the palm of your open hand. Now draw what you see, using the full space of the page. This exercise is not focusing on your hand as much as what you see beyond your hand and fingers, to fill the space. Compose the space using the elements of line, value, contrast, and texture.

This idea also needs to be practiced with children. There is no right or wrong way of doing this, as it is not based on skill. It is meant to demonstrate and reflect upon various techniques, elements, and personal expression.

On as separate page, please reflect on all of the above, noting the elements: lines, shapes, texture, color, space, form, and value (if you add shading).

- Which one did you like doing the most?

- Which one demonstrates the most creative expression?

- Which one is authentic art?

Please relate this to the art opportunities that you offer (or plan to offer) children in your classroom.

Child's Personal Creativity Journal Activity #8

Activity #8 for Infants (Birth to walking, or 16 months)

Reflection on gallery visit (or looking at prints from galleries) in journal: At a non-rushed and well-rested time (for both of you), sit down with the infant on your lap to review the journal entries so far. Take time to look at each page with the infant, making comments like, "Oh look, there we were at the art gallery. Remember when we saw the painting of the mommy and baby?" or "Look how big your smile was when you played with the paint in a bag. Remember how we mixed red and blue to make purple?" Remember that infants take in everything through their senses and that the infant's journal becomes a documentation of the infant's sensory experiences. Recalling these sensory experiences reinforces the learning experiences. Infants hear you repeat words to describe their actions, even the elements of lines, colors, and shapes. Taking the time and not rushing the pace is essential and will make a difference. Some quiet music in the background might be pleasant, if it is not too much sensory input. Even trying this before bedtime or nap might work better for some infants. After the review record in the journal any verbal and nonverbal responses from the infant while reviewing the journal.

Activity #8 for Toddlers (walking or 16 months to 3-years-old)

Reflection on gallery visit (or looking at prints from galleries) in journal: Again, at a non-rushed and well-rested time, sit down with the toddler and review the journal entries so far. Take time to look at each page, making comments like, "Remember when we went to the art gallery? We to the sculpture garden and saw a sculpture of a little boy and a bird? Remember how we talked about how he must have liked birds, just like you?" or "Look how big your smile was when you were drawing on the big box! You drew all over it, from top to bottom. It looks like you were really having fun." Remember, toddlers are building vocabulary at an unbelievable pace, every day. Pause for their responses or repeating your words and reinforce their efforts. Toddlers will repeat words you used to describe their actions, feelings, and even the art elements. Taking the time and not rushing is essential! Try some quiet music in the background, if it is not too much sensory input. If prior to bedtime or nap works better, it might be a pleasant reflection process as a routine. After the review record in the journal any verbal and nonverbal responses from the toddler while reviewing the journal.

Activity #8 for Preschoolers (ages 3 – 5)

Reflection on gallery visit (or looking at prints from galleries) in journal: Sit with the preschooler and review the journal entries so far. Take time to look at each page, interacting and making comments about each page, each experience. Preschoolers, too, are building vocabulary at an unbelievable pace, every day. Pause for their responses or repeating your words, and reinforce their dialogue expansion. Taking the time and not rushing is essential! Prior to bedtime or nap might work better for some, and could be a pleasant reflection process as a routine. After the review record in the journal any verbal and nonverbal responses from the preschooler while reviewing the journal. Encourage the child to draw, write words (if they have started writing), or dictate to you how they felt about looking through and reflecting on their journal. Foster the child's understanding that art is another way of communicating; it does not need to be all in spoken or written words.

Activity #8 for Young School-agers

Reflection on gallery visit in journal: Sit with the school-aged child and review the journal entries so far. Take time to look at each page, interacting and making comments about artwork, writings, and each experience. Foster dialogue. Taking the time and not rushing is essential! After the review, encourage the child to record their reflections about the journal so far. Encourage the child to draw and write how they felt about looking through and reflecting on their journal. Assist the child in understanding that drawing, and artwork are another way of communicating, it does not need to be all in spoken or written words.

CHAPTER 9

Building a Quality Inclusive Early Childhood Arts Program

"The wider the range of possibilities we offer children, the more intense will
be their motivations and the richer their experiences."

Loris Malaguzzi – Reggio Emilia founder

CHAPTER OVERVIEW

This chapter will demonstrate how developing and maintaining a quality inclusive
early childhood arts program involves a commitment to offering authentic, creative,
and developmentally appropriate art experiences embedded throughout the curriculum.
It also includes an understanding of the components of a complete early childhood
inclusive arts program. This chapter will define and illustrate these four components:
(a) Sensing and experiencing; (b) Making art (including feedback); (c) Aesthetics; and
(d) Learning about basic elements of art, artists, and their styles (Fox & Schirrmacher,
2015). Partnering with families as an underlying foundation of all early childhood art
programs will be emphasized. Additionally, tools to evaluate quality art programs for
ALL young children are provided.

Developing and retaining a quality inclusive early childhood arts program
requires a commitment to offering authentic creative and developmentally appropriate
art experiences, as well as integrating the arts throughout the curriculum. To do this,
one must have a clear understanding of the components of a complete and
developmentally appropriate early childhood art program. Along with this
understanding must come methods and strategies to include all aspects of such a
quality inclusive program. Justification and sharing with administrators, programs
directors and/or school boards about the integration of the arts throughout the
curriculum and specifics of a quality inclusive early childhood arts program are
essential to establish, maintain, and fund such a program. Efforts to clearly
communicate the components of a quality inclusive art program will increase the
awareness of its benefits. More detail and specifics about the benefits of the arts and
advocating for support of the arts in schools will be included in Chapter 10,
Advocating for the Arts & Partnering with Families.

Components of a Complete Early Childhood Art Program

According to Schirrmacher (2015), there are four components of any complete early
childhood program in the home or school:

    1.   Sensory experiences

> 2. Time, space, and materials for making art (which includes the environment, interactions, and feedback)
>
> 3. Aesthetic experiences
>
> 4. Learning art and artists, and art forms and styles
>
> (Schirrmacher, 2015, pp. 179–182)

Schirrmacher noted the interrelation of all four components (e.g. making art depends on sensing and experiencing), however, separating and defining each is important for a full understanding of how they blend. The first two components should be emphasized in the early years with the final two being introduced gradually. This author would add an underlying foundation of all Art Program Components, Partnering with Families. These components should be guiding principles when designing a developmentally appropriate inclusive art program. They should also serve as the basis for evaluation of an art program.

Sensory Experiences

An individual child's daily sensory experiences offer a multitude of positive and negative feelings as well as ideas, concepts, and "flavors" which impact their lives. These events offer much rich content for their art. As noted in Chapter 4, not all children have had the same experiences, nor do some have similar access to experiences based on differing abilities, culture, or environmental opportunities. Early childhood programs should offer a variety of sensory experiences with individual accommodations as needed. Additionally, early childhood programs have an opportunity to educate and encourage families to understand the importance of offering these experiences on a daily basis.

To create a well-rounded art program, children need opportunities for a variety of sensory experiences. Using multiple senses helps children learn and retain information, which promotes creative thinking. When art activities involve multiple senses, children can more fully experience their environment. Quality art programs should offer opportunities for children to activate the five senses: visual, auditory, tactile, olfactory, and gustatory or taste. Additionally, Fox and Schirrmacher (2015) noted the importance of including the chromatic, thermic, sterognostic, baric, and kinesthetic senses in a quality early childhood art programs.

The chromatic sense "involves the ability to identify, match, and discriminate among colors" (Fox & Schirrmacher, 2015, p. 166). For example, noting the differences in the shades, tints, tones, intensity, or values of color can be gradually introduced to young children. Color paddles, colored cellophane, or tissue paper can be viewed individually or overlapping to discover new colors or different shades or intensities of color.

How things feel regarding temperature, such as hot, cold, warm, etc., constitutes thermic sense. Safety is essential! Extreme heat is discussed with caution of not touching, yet learning that extreme heat helps us cook our food. Examples include:

the sensory table with warm water and ice or snow, describing each and how the contrast feels; discussing how it feels to be out in the snow or rain, near a fireplace, taking a shower or bath, swimming in a lake or pool; or making snow cones; making Jell-O using warm water and ice cubes. All of these experiences deal with temperature perception.

The sterognostic sense involves being able to recognize objects through touch and feel without seeing the object. For example, using a feeling bag or box allows the child to touch with her or his hands, but not see the object. These activities invite rich descriptions of size, texture, shape, weight, and of what material it is made. Asking the child to justify their answers can enhance discussions and questions. This is also a natural segway to disability awareness activities to simulate what it might be like for individuals who have visual challenges.

Window into a Classroom: Best Practices for Inclusion

Visual disability awareness activities are easily incorporated in the arts and early childhood classroom. These activities should include both a sense of what it is like to have a visual challenge, in addition to reflection activities about the experience. Having children experience art activities or general classroom activities while wearing a blindfold or wax paper goggles can offer a small taste of what it is like to have a visual challenge. If offering art activities while simulating a visual challenge, make the same accommodations as you would for a child with a genuine visual challenge, however, include a brief explanation as to why you are making the adaptation. Accommodations such as:

- Using a surface to bring art materials closer (doing the same activities as others),

- Working on white or black to contrast with materials used

- Marking the boundary of paper or working surface with a thick black line or texture to define work surface

- Assuring good lighting

- Using larger tools and surface

- Verbally describing activity and materials in detail if needed, while keeping in mind there are no visual cues (e.g. the finger paint will be cool, the paint has sand in it)

- Progressing slowly

- Encouraging manipulation of items as you talk

- Focusing on tactile experiences

- Using various textured 2-D and 3-D materials, describing each verbally

- Offering contrasting textures for collages or placing in clay or play dough

- Including other senses besides tactile, such as smell, taste, hearing in art experiences

Follow up these experiences by reflecting with children about accessible environments and awareness. Encourage them to draw/paint/sculpt and write/dictate ideas to make their environments better for all, particularly for children or adults with visual challenges.

The baric sense has to do with recognizing if things are heavy or light, or gradations in between. Setting up activities that include determining and categorizing objects as heavy or light assists children with the baric sense. Children can put items in order from heavy to light, or match those that might be the same. Noting the contrast of heavy or light items within the environment offers teachable moments to assist children in relating this to their daily lives.

The kinesthetic sense requires a whole body sensorimotor response. When children move in response to different types of music or sounds, move with their arms out like wings to imitate a bird, or crawl on all fours to pretend to be a dog; they are using their kinesthetic sense. As children dance with scarves or streamers, make shapes with their bodies, jump on a trampoline, crawl through a tunnel, or walk on a balance beam; they are actively learning through their kinesthetic sense. Children use all their senses to take in information and respond with their bodies, using their kinesthetic sense.

We must be sensitive to individual challenges and needs related to sensory experiences. Not all children have had the same sensory experiences. Some children have not had access to certain experiences based on differing abilities, culture, or environmental opportunities.

Window into a Classroom: Best Practices for Inclusion

The following list offers cautions and best practice suggestions for accommodating challenges associated with sensory art experiences:

- Respect and be aware of children who have challenges with sensory experiences (textures, temperatures, sounds). These experiences have potential to cause neurological or behavioral reactions in which they cannot control.

- Explore alternative ways for child participation with textural activities (e.g. gloves with finger paint or when scooping pumpkin seeds out of pumpkins if textures are an issue).

- Break up activity into small, more approachable parts or steps when a child reaches sensory overload. Take one thing at a time and assist child with desensitization.

- Make accommodations in planning, with materials and refer to child's IEP or IFSP goals/outcomes.

- Understand and respect that some cultures to not allow playing with water or food.

- Some early childhood programs (e.g. Head Start) do not allow playing with food (e.g. art projects or sensory experiences), as many children in their programs do not have enough to eat.

The following example demonstrates offering multiple sensory experiences. Planning around a field trip activity is a great illustration of how to facilitate the stimulation of multiple senses in an art project. Using a field trip experience as a starting point to launch creative art activities will help build a real-life experience for the children where multiple senses can be engaged within that environment. In order for children to further discover their own world they must have first-hand experience in real life. Planning a field trip to the local zoo could set the stage for sensory exploration and engagement.

To prepare the children for the zoo field trip, first conduct a "reverse field trip to the zoo" within the classroom environment. This would consist of several different activities, such as creating a zoo in the dramatic play area with stuffed animals and zoologist costumes. During reading time adults could sing songs and read books about the zoo. A variety of art projects could incorporate different materials to emulate the different coats of the animals. This could be done through painting and drawing or using materials such as straw and fake fur. Carrying out such activities before the children actually visit the zoo will help create a context and promote their ability to experience the real zoo visit at a deeper level. (Goosen, 2015)

Fox and Schirrmacher (2015) stated, "Young children are sensory gluttons. Infants and toddlers are fascinated by pattern and detail. They will follow a bug crawling across the floor or marvel at water dripping from a melted icicle. Unfortunately, adults take these experiences for granted and need to recapture some of this childlike wonder and awareness. Children need practice to keep this alive" (p. 180). It is our responsibility as early childhood educators to provide sensory practice and response to these experiences, and share in the child's enthusiasm. We can extend children's understanding by noting these details and promoting exploration with their senses.

Time, Space, and Materials for Making Art (Including the Environment, Interactions, and Feedback)

A major component of a complete quality early childhood program is providing children opportunities to create art on a daily basis. This means allowing time, adequate space, and a variety of materials for making art. Creating visual art such as paintings, drawings, and sculptures, as well as providing time for activities in other areas of the arts such as singing songs, dancing, or dramatic play are examples of the many ways in which this can be accomplished. We can ensure that the arts are incorporated daily when art is integrated throughout the curriculum. When art is integrated into Math/Pre-Math, Science and Sensory, Language Arts, Communication and Literacy/Pre-Literacy, Social Studies, and Expressive Arts (Music, Movement, and Theater) we not only support creativity, but we also enrich learning in these subject areas. Additionally, we foster growth in all domains: physical-fine and gross motor, social/emotional, cognitive, and adaptive. Having a creative corner or free art area where children have time, space, and access to a variety of materials provides freedom to create without barriers or boundaries.

Feedback: Appropriate feedback is an essential part of art programs and the art experience. Positive feedback can be reassuring, yet more can be done to further a child's knowledge and enhance her/his creative experience. In order for feedback to be valuable the adult working with the child must decide on the appropriate feedback for a given situation. This feedback needs to be specific to the individuality of the child and the process of their creative expression. As noted in chapter 2, educators have an important role in the development of creativity and children making art.

It is important to be aware of nonverbal communication of both child and adult. It is more effective to keep the dialogue going only IF the child wishes. Respect the child's need to work without interruptions. With appropriate timing, using Art Dialogue (noting elements of art such as color, shape, line, texture, and balance; asking questions about their work, such as, "Tell me about; How does it make you feel?"), as well as offering Mirrored Feedback about the child's work can be effective in extending and enhancing the creative process.

Learning About Basic Elements of Art, Artists, and Their Styles

Artists of all ages use different styles. The same person could have different styles at different times throughout her or his life. The individuality of art style illustrates how there is no one right way, just the individual's way of expressing. According to Fox and Schirrmacher (2015), introducing children to different artistic styles serves two purposes, "First, it shows children that there are many possible ways to make art. Second, it shows similarities between their own styles and the styles artists have used in the past and continue to use today" (p. 182).

In general, we can talk about artistic movements in three categories: realistic or naturalistic, abstract, and non-objective. As noted in Chapter 7 Fostering Children's Understanding and Appreciation of Art, children are drawn to artworks that include recognizable representations and people and things in their world. Their family, pet, houses, flowers, trees, and other items in nature are of interest and depicted in their own artwork.

A complete and cohesive art program provides children with multiple opportunities to be exposed to a wide range of artwork, various artists who created them, and multiple chances to observe and learn about art elements and principles. As noted in Chapters 3 and 7, talking with children about art elements while giving them feedback about their own art allows them to be more aware of and view these elements in other works of art. Think-aloud and purposeful comparisons and reminders about specific artworks children have viewed, and discussion about art elements observed, assists children in comparing and noting the elements in their own work, to that of famous artists' works. A developmentally appropriate focus for younger children would be on the particular style, materials used, and art elements and principles, rather than on emphasis of the name or history of the artist.

For example, let's say you take your child or a group of children to an art gallery. Perhaps the children indicated interest in the artists who sculpted with clay and were drawn to their 3D artwork. To promote a better understanding of clay and sculpture, you could discuss how an artist's work represents a specific artistic style. You could include a wide variety of clay or play dough recipes and numerous types of tools with which to sculpt. A great resource is Mud works by Mary Ann Kohl. It has a plethora of recipes for various types of magnificent play doughs and clays with very child-friendly directions. Conveniently, each recipe is labeled for age appropriateness. Numerous opportunities for these 3D creative experiences, such as those offered in Mud works, could be provided throughout the year. The children could choose and plan ahead for what play dough or clay recipe they would like to try each week. Experimentation and exploration of their own recipes and utensils add to the possibilities of discovery.

These repeated experiences with sculpture and clays support children's understanding of this style and the concept of 3D creations. Documenting the process and products through photos, videos, and journaling throughout the year also promotes reflection and comparison of their style to other artists and artwork using clay materials for sculptures.

Be cautious about requesting children to produce a replica of famous artworks. Although they might be motivated to try this on their own, encourage their personalized and unique method of artwork, as inspired by famous artists. Facilitate and promote their personal interpretation, style, medium and materials in the process. For example, observing Van Gough's Sunflower and noting the different elements of line, space, color, and texture can have an impact on a child and her/his art. Most likely the child will be painting and drawing sunflowers for a while. Encourage appreciation of the artwork and observe the style and art elements the artist used through think-aloud or Art Dialogue, but also foster the child in creating her/his own unique image. Noting experiences, the child has had or what they know about sunflowers is a good place to start thinking about and creating on their own.

Aesthetics

As noted in Chapter 7, aesthetics is beauty, the study of beauty, and investigating the beauty of art and our surroundings. Beauty is all around us in nature, in objects, and in art. Children soak up the environment and its beauty with their senses on a daily basis. A child's aesthetic development is significantly influenced by his or her surroundings and environment. Children's families, culture, teachers, peers, and others around them also influence their understanding of beauty. We can enhance children's views of what is beautiful through interactions, experiences we offer, and the environments we provide. Classroom and display set up, implemented activities and field trips, and planned guests all contribute to the child's formation of aesthetics and what is beautiful.

A complete early childhood art program should offer an aesthetically pleasing and inviting environment. Aesthetics and fostering the development of creativity in children is the focus of the Reggio Emilia approach. Reggio Emilia philosophy regards the environment as the third teacher. According to this philosophy the classroom is arranged purposely to encourage children to work together to create art. Materials are easily available, and invite them to create a variety of different projects with limited structure by the teacher. Figure 9.1 offers a diagram and explanation of an inclusive classroom that integrates art throughout the environment.

This description of the areas, noting accommodations of space and access to materials would be beneficial to share with supervisors or administrators. These accommodations can align with the child's IEP as well as the Americans with Disabilities Act (ADA) or Rehab 504. This would be particularly helpful if designing/ redesigning/ renovating space and environments to be more inclusive. There are tax credits and potential funding available if funds are used for making general accommodations in the classroom or building that come under the ADA.

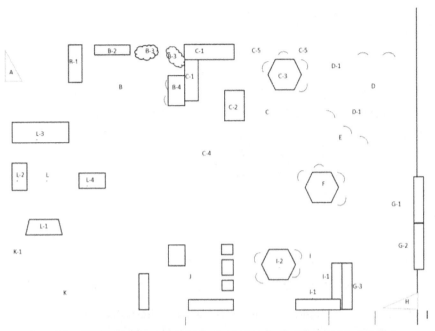

A. Door to hallway/Main Entrance – keep area open and clutter free for easy access for children or adults in wheelchairs or walkers

B. Literacy/Writing Center – space arranged with enough room for children or adults in wheelchairs or walkers
   1. Child sized sofa
   2. Book shelf – book selection includes cultural diversity and individuals with differing abilities
   3. Beanbag chairs
   4. Writing table & chairs – materials to include a journal for each child, various writing materials, paper with: lines, partial lines, no lines for various options. Leave end space open for access for child using wheelchair. . Individual accommodations as needed.
   5. Easy access to all items, and should be labeled in English, Spanish, Braille or other language depending on diversity of group.
   6. On Walls: Posters of Book Illustrations - includes images of cultural diversity and individuals with differing abilities. Include plants in various spaces.

C. Art Center – space arranged for walkers and space arranged with enough room for walkers and wheelchairs; supplies – plenty of space for access, well organized for ease and independence
   1. Free art table - Leave end spaces open for access for child using wheelchair. Individual accommodations as needed.
   2. Planned art table - Leave end spaces open for access for child using wheelchair. Individual accommodations as needed.
   3. Easy access to all items, and should be labeled in English, Spanish, Braille or other language depending on diversity of group.
   4. Double Easel – wheelchair accessible
   5. On Walls: Posters of Master's artwork. Include plants in various spaces.

D. Bathroom – should be accessible (See ADA guidelines and measurements for children's environments)
   1. Posters of Master's artwork for viewing in bathroom

E. Sinks and water fountain – should be accessible (See ADA guidelines and measurements for children's environments)

F. Cultural exploration Center - Leave end spaces open for access for child or adult using wheelchair. Individual accommodations as needed.
   1. Easy access to all items, and should be labeled in English, Spanish, Braille or other language depending on diversity of group.

G. Cubbies 1, 2 & 3

H. Door to Outdoor Play Area – Keep area open and clutter free for easy access for children or adults in wheelchairs or walkers. Access to playground should have no steps, ramped if needed. Playground should be accessible for wheelchairs and walkers.

I. Math Center – Space arranged with enough room for children or adults in wheelchairs or walkers and access to everything in area.

    1. Math shelves – easy access, items labeled in English, Spanish, Braille or other language depending on diversity of group

    2. Math activities table- Leave end spaces open for access for child or adult using wheelchair. Individual accommodations as needed.

J. Dramatic Play Center – Space arranged with enough room for children or adults in wheelchairs or walkers and access to everything in area. Dramatic play area will change with various themes. In contrast to only a "house area", this could be everything from a doctor's office to veterinary office to post office, etc. Materials in area will vary with theme, but always arranged in an accessible manner. Items labeled in English, Spanish, Braille or other language depending on diversity of group

K. Blocks/Carpet Area – Carpet area is utilized as block area during freeplay/choice times, and is also used as a place to gather for group times. If a child is in a wheelchair and able to transfer down to carpet comfortably, then all children will sit on the carpet for group time. If the child cannot comfortably or safely transfer out of chair, then have all other children as well as the teacher in child-sized chairs in a circle so all children will be on the same level.

    1. Block shelves with various sized blocks and other building material. Included on block shelf is large paper so drawings can be a part of labeling or landscape (e.g. lakes, mountain backgrounds, people or animals within block constructions, etc.)

    2. Easy access, with items labeled in English, Spanish, Braille or other language depending on diversity of group

L. Science Center - Space arranged with enough room for children or adults in wheelchairs or walkers and access to everything in area.

    1. Experiment table – include paper and drawing materials to draw ideas, hypothesis, and discoveries

    2. Fish tank

    3. Science discovery shelf – include plants, rocks, shells, etc.

    4. Light table

    5. Easy access to all items, and should be labeled in English, Spanish, Braille or other language depending on diversity of group.

Figure 9.1: Diagram of Inclusive Early Childhood Classroom

Part of the beauty and aesthetics of the environment includes displaying the children's artwork (Figure 9.2). This could be exhibited in various locations. One area should be near the art area and another could be in a hallway or other visible location. Having one area for display near the art center promotes Art Dialogue with opportunities to note art elements and principles just as we do with adult art viewed in art galleries or museums. The art dialogue can inspire the child to create and note these while in the creative process.

Figure 9.2: Even a corner in your home can serve as an art display area.

Artwork displayed should be matted or framed and labeled with the child's name, date created, and materials used. Some children have seen this with professional art in galleries, and doing so, will convey to them that we value their works of art as well. Be certain artwork is displayed at the child's level for comfortable viewing. Children can independently decide what works of their art they would like displayed. However, guide them to include both 2D and 3D art. Inexpensive cases or shelves can be purchased for 3D art such as those shown in the children's art gallery featured in Figure 9.3

Respecting each other's art is a part of the process. Just as we keep "hands off" of famous artwork in museums, we model and foster the same respect when viewing children's art. Thompson (1995) suggested adding the role of docent to the early childhood classroom. This role could include choosing the arrangement of the work, sharing the display with visitors, and perhaps even asking the child artist to talk with someone about their work.

Figure 9.3: Inexpensive glass shelves work well for a children's art gallery, and allows views from various angles to enhance art dialogue with all ages.

Displaying famous artworks, as well as visiting artists who demonstrate and dialogue about their art enhance aesthetic experiences. Visiting an artist's studio such as the one shown in Figures 9.4 allows children to observe not only the artwork of artists, but also the unique opportunity to witness the creative process in action. In doing so, children and adults can note the techniques, materials, art elements and principles while they are being applied. Also, regular excursions to see artwork in the community (art galleries/museums, art in libraries or coffee shops, etc.) can immerse children with aesthetic experiences.

Figure 9.4: Visiting a glass artist's studio offers a child to observe the creative process in action.

As noted in Chapter 7 Fostering Children's Understanding and Appreciation of Art, the Rating Observation Scale for Inspiring Environments (ROSIE) is an amazing tool used to assess and determine a classroom's level of aesthetic beauty. It also offers a guide for an inspiring learning environment for young children (Devine, et. al., 2010).

See: https://www.youtube.com/watch?v=74eRBi_wi40

Partnering with Families: An Underlying Principle

Partnering with families is an underlying principle of each of the above art program components and needs to be embedded in the program's philosophy and guiding principles. All early childhood programs have a philosophy, even if it is not articulated in writing. The program's philosophy can be observed through day-to-day interactions and relations with families. Family communications and partnerships should to be included in a program's written philosophy. A concise family partnership philosophy, understood and practiced by teachers, staff, and families, is the foundation of our work and profession. Early childhood programs need to, "Create environments to entice family engagement" (Stephens, 2005).

The early childhood program's art philosophy and practices provide a great opportunity for "enticing family engagement." Family partnerships are essential for implementing a quality art program and should be at the heart of all components. Stephens (2005) offered Family engagement strategies: Action steps to consider in her article, "Meaningful Engagement: Imagine the Possibilities." The following suggestions from Stephens could be strategies linked to family partnership and the early childhood art program. Her suggestions are related to quality early childhood art programs are summarized below:

1.   Communicate with families in multiple ways.

    a. Share the art philosophy with families and noting process over product, particularly for the youngest in your program.

    b. Invite families to participate in art activities and excursions with a guide for feedback and art dialogue.

2. Distribute surveys to determine parents' hobbies, skills, cultural traditions, or talents.

    a. Are any family members artists or crafts persons? Would they be willing to visit the classroom and share?

3. Organize monthly parent-teacher nights.

    a. Have an art project night. This is also an opportunity to demonstrate the meaning of authentic creative art and process over product.

4. Host special events.

    a. Have an art gallery in the classroom, Children can send invitations and share their work.

5. Seek parent input when trying to understand and guide a child's behavior and work very closely with parents of children with special needs.

    a. Seek family input on accommodations and modification for home and preschool. Parents know their child best.

6. Offer curriculum collaboration opportunities.

    a. Ask families to share ideas and projects with an understanding of authentic creative art. This will also facilitate follow up at home.

7. Find ways to invite and accept parents' technical assistance.

    a. Seek family input and assistance when putting up displays or children's art gallery. This could include helping children with electronic invitations, or even setting up a virtual art gallery.

* See Emporia State University's Children's Art Gallery and Art Gallery Archives at:

https://www.emporia.edu/teach/elecse/early-childhood/virtual-art-gallery/index.html

8. Include families in program governance and oversight.

    a. Invite families for input on program's art philosophy.

9. Create a parent buddy or mentor system.

    a. Encourage families who are active and understand the art philosophy to mentor and share with new families.

10. Offer a parent orientation program for newly enrolled families.

    a. Assist new families in understanding the value of children's art and the programs art philosophy.

11. Distribute an in-house family directory.

    a. This could assist family-to-family communication, as well as coordinating special art activities and excursions.

12. Create opportunities to share or trade family resources.

    a. Art materials and ideas could be shared from family to family.

13. Provide community referrals.

    a. Share information about community art activities and programs from which children could benefit. Be sure to check if authentic creative art experiences are offered. Assist families in understanding the difference between authentic art experiences and those that masquerade as creative activities.

14. Offer parent-teacher conferences.

    a. Conferences are an excellent opportunity to share the child's portfolio and art growth. Encourage a collaborative portfolio, perhaps electronically, so family can add to the art portfolio and have an art growth record when they leave the program.

15. Sponsor an early childhood book or educational materials fair.

    a. Sponsoring appropriate art demonstrations, sharing of art materials, or a book fair with early childhood books focused on art or artists (for infant, toddler, preschooler, and school age levels) will offer another opportunity to experience and understand authentic creative art and the program's art philosophy.

16. Help parents keep children safe at home.

    a. When sharing art activities and materials, be sure to caution regarding items that might be swallowed if child or siblings are under the age of 3, or if a child or sibling likes to put things in her or his mouth.

17. Provide opportunities for community building.

    a. Work with families on community arts projects and advocacy for the arts.

(Adapted from Stephens, K., 2005, pp.20 – 21)

These strategies will be further discussed in Chapter 10 Advocating for the Arts: Partnering with Families, with specific and detailed suggestions for partnership and arts advocacy.

Additional recommendations from other authors include:

1. Provide appropriate and varied experiences provide a variety of materials and tools, encouraging experimentation

2. Balancing process and product, the product becomes more important as children grow and mature

3. Focus on originality foster originality, encourage, value and display original ideas, and model originality of thought and process

4. Note that art belongs to the child respect the personal nature of the child's art, which results in carrying out his or her choices and preferences and makes the process and product authentic ownership of the child

5.   A climate of acceptance nurture artistic expression and support and value creative efforts in a psychologically safe environment

6.   Provide role models invite artists to the classroom, and note when adults (the classroom teacher included) are creative and problem solving in the art process, as well as when using art dialogue.

(Isbell & Raines, 2003, pp. 110 – 114)

Mayesky (2002) also noted that early childhood art program goals should include: (a) process, not product, (b) should consider need of the children, (c) promote originality and independence, (d) foster creative thinking, and (e) respect individualized progress and growth.

All of these suggestions should be considered when developing and maintaining a high-quality inclusive early childhood arts program. Paramount is a commitment to offering authentic creative and developmentally appropriate art experiences while integrating the arts throughout the curriculum. The following Evaluation of Early Childhood Art Program includes recommended questions under each component of a quality art program. This tool was proposed for evaluating your program's art program. Using this process could assure quality of your art program and its developmental appropriateness, inclusiveness, and could evaluate if your program is offering authentic creative art experiences.

Evaluating early childhood art programs: Using the areas noted earlier in this chapter as Components of a Complete Early Childhood Art Program, complete Figure 9.5 a comprehensive evaluation of an early childhood art program. This can be used for your own program, or when evaluating another art program for young children. Determining suggestions for improvement, prioritizing goals, and an action plan to get started are included.

Early Childhood Art Program Evaluation
by Dr. Carol L. Russell
Emporia State University

Using these areas noted as *Components of a Complete Early Childhood Art Program,* pose the following comprehensive list of questions about your own program, or those you observe. Be sure to offer suggestions for growth in areas of challenge. Note what is included and works well, in addition to what is missing. Make suggestions for improvement. The section at the end is to prioritize areas of improvement, with a timeline of what to do, who will do it, and when it will be addressed.

1.) Sensory Experiences

A) Does the program offer opportunities for children to activate the five senses? Note examples of each:
- Visual?
  - Examples:

- Auditory?
  - Examples:

- Tactile?
  - Examples:

- Olfactory?
  - Examples:

- Gustatory or taste
  - Examples:

B) Are there additional experiences that come under the following categories?

- Chromatic senses (involves the ability to identify, match, and discriminate among colors)?
  - Examples:

- Thermic senses (how things feel regarding temperature, hot, cold, warm, etc.)?
  - Examples:

- Sterognostic senses (being able to recognize objects through touch and feel without seeing the object)?
  - Examples:

- Baric senses (recognizing if things are heavy or light, or gradations in between)?
  - o Examples:

- Kinesthetic senses (requires a whole body sensorimotor response)?
  - o Examples

C) Is the program sensitive to individual challenges and needs related to sensory experiences?
- Responds to children who have challenges with sensory experiences (textures, temperatures, sounds)?
  - o Examples of accommodations:

- Modifications for children with other differing abilities (vision, hearing, physical, social, emotional, behavioral or cognitive, language, communication)?
  - o Examples of accommodations:

- Respects and responds to children from cultures who may not allow play with water or food or other practices?
  - o Examples:

Improvement:
* What areas of this component of Sensory Experiences need improvement?

* What are some specific suggestions to better meet this component?

2) Time, space, and materials for making art (which includes the environment, interactions and feedback)

A) Are children provided with multiple daily opportunities to create art?
  - o Examples:

B) Are children allowed enough time, adequate space, and a variety of materials for making art?
  - o Examples:

C) Do children have opportunities and materials for 2-D and 3-D experiences?
  - o Examples:

D) Is music, creative movement, dramatic play offered on a daily basis?
  - o Examples:

E) Is art integrated into other areas of the curriculum?

* Math/Pre-Math
  - o Examples:

* Science and Sensory
    o Examples:

* Language Arts
    o Examples:

* Communication and Literacy/Pre-Literacy
    o Examples:

* Social Studies
    o Examples:

* Expressive Arts (Music, Movement, and Theatre)
    o Examples:

F) Feedback
Is *Art Dialogue* (noting elements of art such as color, shape, line texture and balance; asking questions about their work, such as, "Tell me about...; How does it make you feel?"), being used, as well as *Mirrored Feedback* about the child's work?
    o Examples observed:

Improvement:
* What areas of this component of *Time, space, and materials for making art (including feedback)* need improvement?

* What are some specific suggestions to better meet this component?

3) Learning about basic elements of art, artists and their styles

A) Do teachers talk with children about art elements and principles while giving feedback to them about their own art?
    o Examples:

C) Do artists visit the classroom, or does the class visit artist studios?
    o Examples:

Improvement:
* What areas of this component of *Learning basic elements of art, artists and their styles* need improvement?

* What are some specific suggestions to better meet this component?

4) Aesthetics

A) Does the program provide multiple opportunities to view a wide range of artwork through art gallery visits, prints in classroom, online, and other experiences?
    o Examples:

B) Is children's artwork displayed?
    o Examples:

C) Are Materials are easily available, inviting them to create a variety of different projects with limited structure by the teacher?
    o Examples:

Improvement:

* What areas of this component of *Aesthetics* need improvement?

* What are some specific suggestions to better meet this component?

5) *Partnering with Families ~ Underlying all Art Program Components*

A) Review the items above from Stephens (2005) *Family engagement strategies: Action steps to*

consider in her article, *Meaningful Engagement: Imagine the possibilities* (May/June, 2005).

Brainstorm areas on which to focus and make a program goal.

   o   Examples of areas for growth:

Improvement:

* What areas of this component of *Partnering with families* need improvement?

* List specific suggestions to better meet this component from your examples for areas of

growth above.

APPROACH FOR OVERALL IMPROVEMENT
OF EARLY CHILDHOOD ART PROGRAM

From the "Improvement" section under each component, prioritize component areas of improvement (listing 1 to 5, or noting "no improvement needed"):

_____ *Sensory Experiences*
    Specific improvement needed:

_____ *Time, space, and materials for making art (which includes the*
    environment, interactions and feedback)
    Specific improvement needed:

_____ *Learning about basic elements of art, artists and their styles*
    Specific improvement needed:

_____ *Aesthetics*▯
    Specific improvement needed:

_____ *Partnering with Families ~ Underlying all Art Program Components*
    Specific improvement needed:

Action Plan: Note the following, please be specific:

What will be done to address improvement?

Who must be involved to implement improvement?

When will this occur in the program, the day, or week?

When to assess improvement?

Figure 9.5: Early Childhood Art Program Evaluation

Administrators, programs directors and school boards may need additional information about how integrating the arts throughout the curriculum is beneficial, in addition to the specifics of a quality inclusive early childhood arts program. Establishing, maintaining, and funding such a program may need justification and data. Efforts to clearly communicate the components of a quality inclusive art program will increase the awareness of its benefits. Share the specifics of these components, as well as the program assessment with your colleagues, principles, and other administrators. Invite them into your classroom. Note the benefits, accommodations, and integrations of the arts throughout your curriculum and classroom on a daily basis. Take photos and videos to demonstrate and share. More detail and specifics about the benefits of the arts and advocating for support of the arts in schools will be included in the final chapter, advocating for the Arts & Partnering with Families.

Chapter Summary and Looking Ahead

This chapter described the components of a quality inclusive early childhood arts program, which included: Sensory Experiences; Time, space, and materials for making art (which includes the environment, interactions, and feedback); Learning about basic elements of art, artists and their styles; Aesthetics; and Partnering with Families Underlying all Art Program Components. A comprehensive tool to evaluate these components in effort to provide quality art programs for ALL young children was presented. Additionally, the evaluation tool (Figure 9.5) featured development of and suggestions for implementing a plan of action for improvement.

Chapter 10 will conclude the book, focusing on the importance of partnering with families for quality early childhood art programs (and early childhood programs, in general), as well as advocating for the arts in schools. In doing so we can share awareness and advocate for the benefits, joy, and power of art for all children in early childhood education programs.

Suggestions for Additional Reflection and Review

- For more on aesthetics and artistic expression and young children, see:

  http://kneedeepingrace.com/2012/05/5days-artistic-expression-001/

- Rating Observation Scale for Inspiring Environments (ROSIE) by Jessica DeViney, Sandra Duncan, Sara Harris, Mary Ann Rody, Lois Rosenberry:

  http://www.childcareexchange.com/catalog/product/rating-observation-scale-for-inspiring-environments-rosie/4100572/

CREATIVITY JOURNALS FOR ALL AGES

Adult Journal Activity #9

Evaluation of Early Childhood Art Program Using this tool (Figure 9.5), submit evaluation content and reflections in your journal. Review the components of a quality inclusive early childhood art program. Observe and evaluate a children's art program and then record your evaluation. Note what seems to be included and working well, in addition to what is missing. If appropriate, include suggestions for improvement. Making use of the last portion of the evaluation tool, develop specific goals and plans to work towards the improvement of the children's art program.

Child's Personal Creativity Journal Activity #9

Activity #9 for Infants (Birth to walking, or 16 months)

Infant stimulation cards: Research has shown that the secret to infant visual stimulation lies in high-contrast colors. The development of a newborn's eyes and the structures of the retina that perceive color haven't matured enough to perceive the values and intensities of red, blue, pink, yellow, purple, and green. Black and white are the easiest for babies to perceive and interest in these starkly contrasting colors will pave the way for your baby's brain development. These infant stimulation flash cards will help calm and soothe your baby and increase concentration skills, enhance natural curiosity, and stimulate the creation of brain cell connections. See examples from the following websites:

http://www.brillkids.com/free-download/infant-stimulation-cards.php

or

http://www.attentionworksheets.com/black-white-infant-visual-stimulation-card/

See examples below:

Figures 9.6, 9.7 & 9.8 Examples A, B, & C

Continue to remember that infants take in everything through their senses. The infant's journal becomes a documentation of the infant's sensory experiences. Take photographs of the infant's attention and reactions to the images. Note which ones the baby prefers by recording the number of seconds the infant pays attention to each image. Gradually introduce others.

Activity #9 for Toddlers (walking or 16 months to 3-years-old)

A rubbing from the environment: To facilitate the toddler's creation of a rubbing, gather large crayons, art paper, and masking tape. Locate items (have the child assist) that have interesting textures, such as leaves, shoe soles, bricks, rough stones, embossed cards, etc. and tape paper on or over the items of texture. Give the child the time, the space, the materials, and the positive feedback and reinforcement to create! Take photos of the process. Attach photos of the process and product in the child's journal.

Activity #9 for Preschoolers (ages 3 – 5)

Artist in the family: Share with families the Artist in the Family activity noted in this chapter. Encourage families to complete the activity with their children. Convey the importance of documenting and recording all of the information, interactions, and photographs. When completed, assist preschooler to place all of this documentation in their journal, including photographs. This offers a wonderful potential for a bonding experience with that family member. In addition, the awareness of potential hidden talents might come to view, and the child will learn more about arts, crafts, and art style. This can be particularly meaningful when the artist is a grandparent, because it becomes a multi-generational project. It could have an enormous and positive impact on all involved. Both parent and child will learn about this person and why they have a passion for their own creative process. If they are willing, promote the parent and child to invite the artist in their family to visit and share their passion and talents with the class.

Activity #9 for Young School-agers

Artist in the family: Share with families the Artist in the Family activity noted earlier in this chapter. Encourage them to complete the activity with their child. Convey to them the importance of documenting and recording all of the information, interactions, and photographs. When completed, assist the school-aged child in placing all of this documentation material in their journal, including photographs. As with the preschooler, hidden talents might come to view, and the child will learn more about arts, crafts, and art style. Both parent and child will learn about this person and their creative process. Encouraging the parent and child to invite the artist in their family to visit and share their passion and talents with the class can extend this activity and have a positive impact on all involved.

CHAPTER 10

Advocating for the Arts and Partnering with Families

"The arts' position in the school curriculum symbolizes to the young
what adults believe is important."

- Elliot W. Eisner

CHAPTER OVERVIEW

As discussed in Chapter 1, the list of developmental and academic/pre-academic benefits of authentic creative art experiences for young children is extensive. Extended suggestions for partnering with families for a quality art program will be provided. In addition, methods to advocate for the arts with families to extend advocacy efforts and build stronger partnerships will be offered. Research findings that support art education will be presented. We must partner with families to share this information and collaborate with them on awareness efforts in order to share the joy and power of art in early childhood education.

Partnering with Families to Enhance Artistic Creativity for All Young Children

Partnering with families is an excellent strategy to enhance the artistic creativity of ALL young children. Helping families to be aware of the value of scribbles and art creations, to recognize authentic creative art experiences, and to recognize the need for appropriate feedback are all good starting points. Sharing Rhoda Kellogg's 20 basic scribbles (1970) in Chapter 2 with families will illustrate how scribbles by infants and toddlers demonstrate pre-writing skills. Noting the art elements of shapes, lines, texture, color, and value in their children's artwork will assist families in art dialogue with their children. Suggest parents determine the stages within their children's artwork. Share the art growth stages from both Kellogg and Lowenfeld (Kellogg, 1970, Lowenfeld, 1957) as noted in Chapter 2. Note the developmental benefits of their children's authentic creative art experiences, including:

- Sensory experiences (cognitive, physical, emotional)

- Opportunities to experiment (e.g. science, physics, cause/effect, invent, discover, cognitive)

- Spatial relations (physical, cognitive)

- Planning, sequencing (math, cognitive)

- Problem solving (cognitive)

- Creative expression (cognitive, emotional, social)

- Non-verbal communication (cognitive, language, emotional, social)

- Perseverance, determination, focus, dedication (emotional, social, cognitive)

- Motor skills (physical fine and gross motor)

- Eye-hand coordination, perceptual motor skills (physical)

- Collaboration (social, emotional)

- Pride, sense of accomplishment, confidence (emotional, social)

The Museum of Children's Art (MOCHA) in Oakland, CA has been committed to connecting art education with children throughout Oakland for over 24 years. They have committed to offering spaces where children and their families, "create, share, and connect through art" (MOCHA.org). This site noted the benefits of art to children's learning with the following 20 points:

- Art stimulates both sides of the brain.

- 33% of children are visual learners.

- There are studies that show that children, who make art, read better and get better grades in science and mathematics.

- Children learn by using their senses and art is ideal in this process.

- Children need a place to express themselves at school.

- Art promotes self-esteem.

- Art encourages kids to give more attention to the physical space that surround them.

- Art develops hand and eye coordination.

- Art stimulates perception.

- Art teaches them to think openly. It represents a culture of questioners more than a culture of responders.

- Art teaches that there is more than one solution for a problem.

- Art teaches children to think creatively to solve problems.

- Children can share and reflect on their work of art and learn something about the world they live in.

- When art is integrated with the other subjects in the curriculum, children commit more to the learning process.

- In the process of doing art, the child is exposed to different possibilities, to discover and to freedom, this way they avoid falling into the control and the predictability of the conventional education in the United States of today.

- Art nourishes the human soul. One feels good doing it.

- Art brings the cultural resources of the community into the class.

- Art involves parents and tutors in the school, inviting them to participate as volunteers in diverse activities.

- Art provides a common ground across racial stereotypes, barriers and prejudices.

- Art is valuable all by itself.

(Adapted from: http://www.artsz.org/20-reasons-why-art-is-important-for-children/ Via Museum of Children's Arts in Oakland MOCHA)

The following detailed illustration might help families understand the benefits of art. This example will demonstrate how art helps children develop fine motor coordination and dexterity, eye-hand coordination, trial and error practice, problem solving skills, concentration, determination, satisfaction of project completion, and pure joy.

When children use crayons, markers, pencils, or a paintbrush, they are perfecting the use of their hands. They are carefully refining the control of their dexterity and fine motor skills to create the outcome of their artwork. They are concentrating on their drawing or painting until they are pleased with the outcome. As children create an art piece they may learn from trials and errors. For example, as they fill in the space of their own produced lines, they learn from making strokes too broad, or mixing of colors over their lines, or how best to fill in gaps if they choose.

> By learning to color within the lines (their own lines), children learn the ability to work more slowly, taking their time to ensure that a good job is completed. They learn to finish a project by filling in all of the space and to be careful while doing it, ensuring that nothing outside of the lines is errantly colored. The skill of judging with their eyes on the work their hands are doing is important and painting is one of the easiest ways to get children to master this skill in a way that they find entertaining. They will be learning without ever realizing the fact. (Art Explained and Made Simple, Retrieved from: http://www.artsz.org/kids-art-coordination/).

It is important to demonstrate for families how you are integrating and infusing the arts throughout the curriculum. Let them know and illustrate how you are even meeting learning standards in the process. When you share activities for the week, point out specific developmental benefits and curricular or pre-curricular areas that are integrated specific to the art activity. When artwork is sent home, add a note about these developmental benefits and curricular or pre-curricular areas, as well. Be sure your note is on a separate piece of paper so that it does not disturb any of the child's work.

Note the importance of helping children satisfy their curiosity and foster discovery. Give families specific suggestions for doing this on a daily basis. Suggest ways to value children's efforts and accomplishments despite messes or inconveniences. Offer them a variety of suggestions for open ended, authentic, and creative experiences at home, in the community, at grandma's or grandpa's or any other space. Encourage families to frame 2D artwork and display their children's 3D artwork in a prominent area at home.

Share with families the importance of Mirrored Feedback and Art Dialogue. The following examples are questions and comments that can be shared with families to encourage creativity and the discovery process when talking with their child about his work:

- Can you tell me about your painting/sculpture?

- What part did you like best?

- You've used many colors.

- Did you enjoy making this?

- How did the paint feel?

- The yellow looks so bright next to purple!

- How did you make such a big design?

We can also say, "I noticed the way you…

- are working so hard."

- are coming up with your very own idea."

- trying new ways."

Encourage parents to ask children to talk about their work. Rather than "What is it?", simply "Would you tell me about your picture" offers the opportunity to share if they wish. Impress upon parents that it should be the child's choice. Also, increase parental awareness that the child's art might not represent something, but it could be just a design. Help families understand that expecting children to label her/his products convey it is not created well enough to represent something specific. Sending a letter similar to the sample in Chapter 1 includes this and the benefits listed above.

Implementing a Quality Art Program by Engaging Families and Building Partnerships

As noted in Chapter 9, early childhood art programs need to create environments that invite and entice family engagement. Family partnerships are essential for implementing a quality art program. If we are going to have an impact on the child's attitude about art, and keep her/his creative spirit growing, partnering with families must be at the heart of our work.

The suggestions offered by Stephens (2005) Family engagement strategies: Action steps to consider, noted in Chapter 9, were organized, and extended below for even more ways to assure understanding of the philosophy of art for ALL children.

1. Communicate about art with families in multiple ways:

    - Share the art philosophy with families, noting process over product, particularly for the youngest in your program.

    - Send regular art updates with information about authentic art, art shows, or visiting artists. Include these in your newsletters.

    - Invite families to participate in art activities and excursions, with a guide for feedback and art dialogue.

    - Distribute an in-house family directory to assist with family-to-family communication, and coordinate special art activities and excursions. Be certain to first get permission from families to share their contact information before distributing.

- Help parents be aware of safety with art activities and materials. Be sure to caution regarding choking hazards if child or siblings are under the age of 3, or tends to put things in her/his mouth. Send out information about using non-toxic materials with art projects.

- Use newsletters, technology (email, websites, chat rooms) to share announcements and information with parents about authentic art and the artwork their children are creating.

2. Distribute surveys to determine parents' hobbies, skills, artistic talents, or cultural traditions:

- Are any family members artists or crafts persons? Would they visit the classroom and share?

- Find creative ways for families to share their expertise and arts with your program.

3. Organize and host special events, such as monthly parent-teacher nights, as well as family events.

- Have an art project night. This is also an opportunity to share what is authentic creative art and process over product. Be sure to allow enough time for them to truly understand and experience authentic art. Quality over quantity: have fewer illustrations to demonstrate process over product and ways to value and foster creativity in their children. Remember, many have not themselves experienced truly authentic art, and this may take time and multiple experiences to convey.

- Have an art gallery in the classroom, children can send invitations and share their work.

- Create opportunities to share or trade family resources. Art materials and ideas could be shared from family to family.

- Sponsor an early childhood art books or art educational materials fair. Sponsoring appropriate art demonstrations, sharing of art materials, or a book fair with early childhood books focused on art or artists (for infant, toddler, preschooler, and school age levels) offers families the tools to carry over projects and creative arts at home.

- Organize family trips to art museums, zoos, parks, and aquariums. Be sure to follow up with creative and reflective experiences. Use journals and encourage families to do the same.

4. Find creative ways for parents' and grandparents' assistance with the arts program ways to invite their technical assistance.

- When putting up displays or children's art gallery, seek family input and assistance. This could include assisting children with electronic invitations, or a virtual art gallery.

  * See Emporia State University's Children's Art Gallery and Art Gallery Archives at:

  https://www.emporia.edu/teach/elecse/early-childhood/virtual-art-gallery/index.html

5. Seek parent/family input when trying to understand and guide a child's behavior, and work very closely with parents of children with special needs.

- Seek family input on accommodations and modification for home and preschool. Parents and grandparents know their child/grandchild best!

- Even children who may be left-handed need accommodations. Check with families for their suggestions and share with them how you accommodate (ambidextrous scissors, utensils, rulers, pencil sharpeners, journals, etc.)

- Have families assist directly or through referrals for training in assistive technology and equipment a child may have, in addition to methods and accommodations needed. States have assistive technology projects that are federally funded, and can also be supportive in locating and funding needed assistive technology. Families may have private program therapists who can assist. Additionally, the local school district has therapists and specialists and the child's IEP or IFSP team for consult and collaboration for children who qualify for special education (e.g. vision specialist, occupational therapist, physical therapist, speech language pathologist, and psychologist). Be sure to work together with the family when consulting with other professionals.

6. Include families in various aspects of the program, program governance and oversight; and offer curriculum collaboration opportunities.

- Invite families for input on program's art philosophy and art program.

- Have families with an understanding of authentic creative art share ideas and projects.

- Creatively include families and their talents into program routines. A family member who might play guitar could play during group time and music times; or one who plays the violin or piano could play lullabies for younger children during transition to naptime.

- There are endless possibilities for creative ways parents, siblings, grandparents, and other extended family can offer talents and meaningful assistance.

7. Offer a parent orientation program for newly enrolled families and create a parent buddy or mentor system.

- Encourage families who are active and understand the art philosophy to mentor and share with new families.

- Assist new families in understanding the value of children's art and the programs art philosophy.

8. Offer regular parent-teacher conferences.

- Offer conferences at least twice a year, and more often for infants' families.

- Conferences are an excellent opportunity to share the child's portfolio and art growth. Encourage a collaborative portfolio, perhaps electronically, so family can add to the art portfolio and have an art growth record when the leave the program.

9. Provide community referrals and opportunities for community building and arts advocacy.

- Share community art activities and programs from which children could benefit. Be sure to check if authentic creative art experiences are offered. Assist families in understanding the difference.

- Work with families on community arts projects and advocacy for the arts.

- Organize an art show to share the children's creations with families and the community.

(Adapted from Stephens, K. 2005, pp.20 – 21)

ARTS ADVOCACY

The following statistics regarding visual arts and artists in the United States might be surprising:

- 1.25 million Americans work in the visual arts.

- One in 111 jobs is in art and design.

- The economic impact of art and design exceeds that of sports worldwide.

- The creative industries are an estimated $30 billion export annually.

- Jobs in design have increased 43% in the past ten years.

- By 2016, jobs for artists and designers are predicted to increase by 42% (from the year 2007).

- More people are employed in the visual arts than in all of the performing arts and sports industries combined.

These along with other interesting facts about visual arts are presented by Americans for the Arts, the National Endowment for the Arts, the U.S. Department of Labor, the U.S. Bureau of Labor Statistics, and the Entertainment Software Association (retrieved on March 20, 2015, http://www.incredibleart.org/links/artedu.html).

These facts can be shared and used for art advocacy efforts. According to Arts Education Partnership, Duncan (2010) states that studies have shown that arts education can: assist in closing the achievement gap, help with college and career preparation, improve low performing schools, and increase teacher retention. These findings are also fuel for advocating for the arts for all children.

Advocating for the arts means making it a part of how we, as professionals, live and share each day. To effectively make change we must also come together in an organized fashion. The National Assembly of State Arts Agencies (NASAA) is an organization that "unites, represents and serves the nation's state and jurisdictional arts agencies" (retrieved from: http://www.nasaa-arts.org/About/About-NASAA.php). They offer advocacy tools with specific suggestions for making change and supporting the arts, including areas of: Making your case; Assessing your strength; Mobilizing Your Support; and Expanding Your Influence. These are noted below, and can be found in detail at:

http://www.nasaa-arts.org/Advocacy/Advocacy-Tools/index.php

Making Your Case

Why should Government Support the Arts? Return on Investment: The Federal Government, States and the Arts Fallacies of the Kansas Veto What Do I Say? Tips for Advocacy Meetings

Advocacy and Lobbying: Speaking Up for the Arts

The Arts in Public Policy: An Advocacy Agenda Learning from Legislators Points National

Assessing Your Strength

Arts Advocacy Checklist: A Self-Evaluation Tool for State Arts Agencies

Arts Advocacy Checklist: A Self-Evaluation Tool for Arts Organizations and Advocates

Mobilizing Your Support

Campaigning for Public Arts Support E-Advocacy: On-Line Strategies for Arts Advocacy Strategies in an Economic Downturn

Advocacy for Public Support of the Arts: A Civic Responsibility

Advocacy by Arts Organizations: Tax Laws and Lobbying

Access to Power: Building Political Clout for the Arts

Expanding Your Influence

Forty Action Strategies Advocacy and Term Limits: Developing Arts Support in the Legislature Early

Arts Advocates in the Legislature: A Legislative Caucus on the Arts Ten Ways to Convert Legislators into Arts Advocates

Facing Controversy: Arts Issues and Crisis Communications

(Retrieved on March 12, 2015 from: http://www.nasaa-arts.org/Advocacy/Advocacy-Tools/index.php)

It was suggested to note the comprehensive Arts Advocacy Checklist for Arts Organizations and Advocates as Self-evaluation Arts Advocacy Effectiveness Tool Checklists. The Arts Advocacy Checklist: A Self-Evaluation Tool for Arts Organizations and Advocates is designed "to help arts organizations and advocates evaluate the level of their advocacy involvement against a broad range of activities aimed at enhancing the political environment for the arts in public policy" (retrieved from: http://www.nasaa-arts.org/Advocacy/Advocacy-Tools/Arts-Advocacy-Checklist-for-Arts-Organizations-and-Advocates.php). Section one, titled "Advocacy and Your Arts Organization" contained checklist items that could easily be transformed into advocacy goals. Included are: (a) Establishing an Advocacy Board; (b) Cultivating Political Relationships; (c) Developing Alliances and Grassroots Advocacy; and (d) Building an Audience of Advocates. Under section two, titled Advocacy and the Political Environment for the Arts, the checklist included items that indicate the following: Arts Advocates Work Together; Arts Advocates Are Visible Politically; The Public Is Supportive; Politicians Are Involved. All checklists by the NASAA can be viewed at:

http://www.nasaa-arts.org/Advocacy/Advocacy-Tools/Arts-Advocacy-Checklist-for-Arts-Organizations-and-Advocates.php

Additional resources for advocacy and funding grants can be found at:

- The American Society for Aesthetics, news, links, and ideas to promote art. See more at: http://www.incredibleart.org/links/artedu.html#sthash.0asU0STe.dp uf

- Americans for the Arts: http://www.americansforthearts.org/

- Arts and Smarts: Test Scores and Cognitive Development http://sharpbrains.com/blog/2009/04/16/arts-and-smarts-test-scores-and-cognitive-development/

- ArtsUSA See: http://www.americansforthearts.org/

- International Child Art Foundation See: http://www.icaf.org/

- 10 Lessons the Arts Teach A nice advocacy page by the National Art Education Association. See more at: http://www.art educators.org/advocacy/10-lessons-the-arts-teach

- The National Assembly of State Arts Agencies Strategies for Building Arts Support. See: http://www.nasaa-arts.org/Advocacy/ Advocacy-Tools/E-Advocacy-FINAL.pdf

- National Endowment for the Arts - See: www.arts.gov

- National Art Education Association- See: http://www.arteducators. org/

Accessible Arts:

- National Arts & Disability See: http://www.semel.ucla.edu/nadc

- In Kansas, the Accessible Arts, whose mission is, "to foster creativity and provide educational opportunities for people with disabilities, while hosting an inclusive environment to ENGAGE, EXPLORE and ENJOY the ARTS." See more at: http://accessiblearts.org/

The Incredible Art Department website (www.incredibleart.org) is an amazing resource for art educators and others interested in the arts. This site includes information about activities, advocacy, galleries and museum, children's art galleries, art associations, publications, podcasts, and more.

How Can We Advocate for the Arts for ALL Children?

We must partner with families and communities to enhance the artistic creativity of ALL young children by creating environments and interactions for children to satisfy their curiosity. The responsibility rests with educators to assure that accommodations are made for children who need them, in addition to accessible environments in which all adults and children can take part. The example of the community–university project described below shows how educators can advocate for and develop a quality art experience for their students.

A Community–University Partnership Project

The Children Inspire Glass Project at Emporia State University in Emporia, Kansas provided authentic creative experiences for young children, while partnering with families and advocating for the arts. This pilot project increased family, community, and educational awareness of the importance of creative experiences for young children. The project also honored the authentic design of children, while expanding their design into a unique and exciting process of producing it in glass form. A description of the project is provided below.

CHILDREN INSPIRE GLASS PROJECT AT EMPORIA STATE UNIVERSITY, EMPORIA, KS

In the spring of 2013, a pilot project called, Children Inspire Glass took place, modeled after Museum of Glass' KIDS DESIGN GLASS program. Under the co-direction of Dr. Carol L. Russell (Professor of Early Childhood Unified) and Fletch Russell (sculptor and Adjunct Professor of Art), in collaboration with Art Faculty, Patrick Martin and Roberta Eichenberg, and Dr. Heather Caswell (Early Childhood Unified & Early Literacy Consultant), an extraordinary opportunity for six Emporia area children, ages 5–10 was provided. This opportunity allowed children to create stories and design creatures to be transformed into glass sculpture and celebrated children and their imaginations in collaboration with instructors and students of various educational disciplines who share this enthusiasm.

The program consisted of five sessions. The first four were held at the Emporia Art Center. During this time the children were presented with materials for designing a creature in 2D and 3D form and for composing a story to accompany their creation. When designing their creatures, the color palate of markers and clay were limited to specific colors (primary and secondary, and black and white) to match the color of the glass we ordered, so that we could be as authentic as possible with the children's designs.

Students from ESU's Elementary Education Children's Literature course facilitated the children's stories written about their design, under the direction of Dr. Heather Caswell. Through a writing workshop approach, children were encouraged to develop stories about their created creature. Prewriting took place through drawing their creature in great detail while discussing with adults and other children the details of their creature. Following this prewriting and creative process, children then drafted a story independently or with help from an adult. One-on-one conferencing took place during this writing process. Adults carefully crafted questions and conversation that would honor the individual child's creative process and story development. Through this workshop approach, children became storytellers weaving their artistic approach of drawing and 3-D creation into their writing process.

Showcasing and documentation was an essential component of this project. Several art shows showcased the children's creations, stories, and glassworks produced by ESU glass students at several locations on campus, the community, and in the region. In addition, detailed documentation is featured on ESU's Virtual Children's Art Gallery at: http://www.emporia.edu/elecse/ecart/children-inspire-glass-2013.html

DVDs were produced for documentation, for the children's reflection and keepsake, and for use with art advocacy and grant applications for funding to continue the project in future years. This pilot project was made possible by the efforts of the Early Childhood and Art faculty, the Emporia Arts Council, a grant from the Kathrine K. White Faculty Incentive Grant, and generous support from The C. F. Marshall Trust. The project was recently awarded the 2014 Ervay Family Applied Scholarship Award.

The benefits of displaying the project were multifaceted. The artwork and process has been displayed in art shows at ESU's Children's Art Gallery, ESU's Art Department's Eppink Gallery, the Emporia Arts Center, Baker University's Parmenter Hall Art Gallery, and the ESU Virtual Children's Art Gallery. Students in Glass and Art Education, Art Therapy students, Elementary Education and Early Childhood Unified students were encouraged to view the artwork and also use it as a resource for analyzing children's art growth stages (Kellogg, 1969 & Lowenfeld, 1987), art elements, creative writing, and other class discussions. University students in online classes also benefitted from the display, as photos/videos of the children's drawings, stories, and glass creations are also utilized as a teaching tool.

Benefitting the most from the project were the children, their families, the faculty, and the students who worked directly with them. Children from the project attended, talked with others about their artwork, and autographed the art programs and brochures at each art show (Figure 10.1). One child had moved away from the area, but she was able to participate via Skype.

Figure 10.1: One young artist from the ESU Children Inspire Glass Project autographing an art brochure for a university student from an Art Appreciation Class.

The following photos of the project (see Figures 10.2-10.4), along with stories authored by the children, illustrate the power of creativity in young children.

Figure 10.2: Flying Cheeta designed by Charlie, age 7

Flying Cheeta

Once upon a time there was a dragon (Figure 10.2). He loves to play. His name is Flying. He is from Emporia. He lives in a cave. He is the oldest in the family. He is kind.

At home he enjoys the fireplace with his family. He helps around the house. At 8:30 AM he goes to school. He goes to his classroom to unload. He greets his teacher. Her name is Miss Iilles. He loves everything about school. He has 22 friends. His favorite snack is apple dipped in peanut butter. He is fast.

He loves to play basketball. His mother picks him up. He goes outside with his brother and sister. In the big back yard, they play everyone is it tag. They play outside for a long time with their neighbor. When it is dark outside they go inside and each dinner. He is going to eat pizza. He eats 2 pizzas.

His favorite show is Max and Roobie. He watches his parents tell him to go wash his tongue. He has a toothbrush. It is the size of Ironman. He has Ironman on it. He stores it in the bathroom. He sleeps in the tree house. He is brave. He sleeps good at night.

Figure 10.3: Bella the Horsey Queen designed by Weslie, age 5

Bella the Horsey Queen

The horsey is flying with the turkey and cat. She is the Queen Horsey (Figure 10.3). She has red spikes and takes them off when people come because they are just fake spikes. She has blue wings and purple stripes on her body with six legs.

The Queen Horsey is flying to her castle in Disney Jr. She needs to sit in her queen chair. Her chair is pink with sparkles. The Queen Horsey calls for the princess to do chores. The princess needs to clean her room and the Horsey Queen's room and do all the dishes. She washes the dishes in the sink and dries them all. Then the Horsey Queen says to the princess to take a nap because she is tired. She sleeps until it is time to go to her friend's house.

When the princess leaves, the Horsey Queen takes a nap. She dreams she meets a boyfriend and marries him. Then she woke up from her nap. She flies out of the castle and goes into the woods to find her best friend.

The Horsey Queen's name is Bella. Her friend's name is Pinto. They get married. Then the princess comes home and sees Bella and Pinto. They leave to get the Queen glasses. She can't see really well. Now with the glasses she can read. Then the princess gets glasses.

The Horsey Queen has the power to kill monsters. Then she goes back to her castle to eat a little snack. She likes carrots. Then she finds the princess to take a nap in her bed. When princess sleeps, Horsey Queen just flies, flies, flies!

Figure 10.4: Spike the Dragon designed by Eliot, 9 years

The Story of Spike

Once upon a time there was a dragon named Spike (Figure 10.4). He lived in a cave in the middle of a kingdom. He also helps people and keeps the kingdom safe from attackers. During his free time, he likes to collect treasures like gold, silver and gems. Then one day a house caught on fire. A lot of people blamed it on Spike. But some people didn't think it was Spike. The people made a riot about what had happened. The dragon got locked up.

The next day the fuss continued. Then the dragon was released. Then another fire started, but the dragon didn't do anything because the man who had been starting the fires was caught while he was starting the next fire. After that the man was thrown in jail. The next day everything returned to normal and everyone was happy. Spike had even gained a few friends during this little adventure. The End

Ellie's work is featured with more detail to give a better view of the details of the project for each child. Ellie (5 years old), independently crafted her creature, Flying Seahorse, in 2D and 3D form after her class spent the day at the Sea Life Kansas City Aquarium. The seahorses were her favorite, which was depicted in her artwork (Figure 10.5).

Figure 10.5: Ellie shares the drawing of her creature, Flying Seahorse, after a trip to the Sea Life Kansas City Aquarium.

While participating in the ESU's Children Inspire Glass Project, Ellie was encouraged to develop a story about her created creature. Utilizing a writing workshop approach, prewriting took place while Ellie drew the details of her creature. During this time an adult facilitated discussing details as Ellie was creating. Discussion included:

- Encouraging Ellie to elaborate by adding details and color.

- Suggesting Ellie think about:

    o What her creature does?

    o Where does it live?

    o How does it move?

    o How does it see?

    o How does it hear?

    o How and what does it eat?

    o What is important to the creature?

    o What are other important details about her creature?

Ellie started writing these ideas in her journal, as well as dictating parts to an adult to help her write. During this prewriting and creative process, Ellie drafted her story with adult support. The adult working with Ellie carefully crafted questions and conversation that would honor Ellie's individual and unique creative process and story development. Figures 10.6-10.8 are the pages of Ellie's writing, integrated with parts that she dictated to an adult to write.

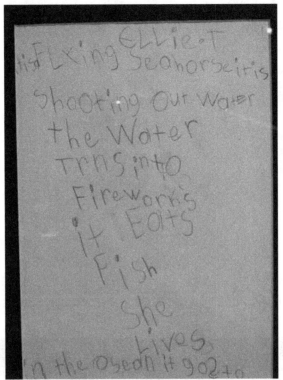

Figure 10.6: Ellie's page 1 of story draft about her creature, Flying Seahorse, in her print.

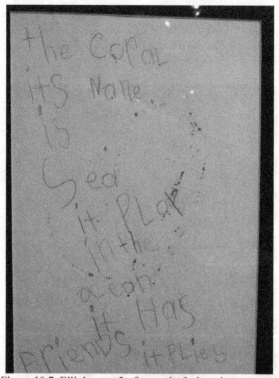

Figure 10.7: Ellie's page 2 of story draft about her creature,
Flying Seahorse in her print

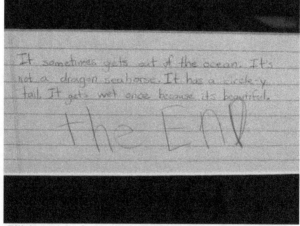

Figure 10.8: Ellie's page 3 of story draft about her creature, Flying Seahorse, with adult
assistance by dictating the final portion of her story

Through this workshop approach, Ellie became a storyteller, weaving her artistic approach of drawing and 3D creation into her writing process. Below is the full printed version of Ellie's story about her Flying Seahorse.

Flying Seahorse

It is Flying Seahorse (Figures 10.9-10.14). It is shooting out water. The water turns into fireworks. It eats fish. She lives in the ocean. It goes to the coral. Its name is Sea It Play in the ocean. It has friends. It flies when it wants. It sometimes gets out of the ocean. It's not a dragon seahorse. It has a circle-y tail. It gets wet once because it's beautiful.

The End

Figure 10.9: Ellie transforms her creature, Flying Seahorse, from 2D to 3D form.

Figure 10.10: Ellie's Flying Seahorse completed in 3D form of polymer clay.

Figure 10.11: The Emporia State University glass students form Ellie's Flying Seahorse design into clear glass form. Ellie was able to give the ESU glass students feedback on what might have needed tweaking from the clear glass model, in planning for the final colored glass sculpture.

Figure 10.12: Emporia State University glass students torching the colored glass to form Ellie's Flying Seahorse design.

Figure 10.13: Proud Ellie, showing off Flying Seahorse design in clear glass form.

Figure 10.14: Ellie enjoying Flying Seahorse creation in her 2D and 3D form, and in colored glass form.

Chapter Summary and Conclusion

We must partner with families in building and advocating for quality art programs for ALL children. Awareness and validation of children's authentic and creative art is the foundation of quality art programs. Advocating for authentic art with families extends our efforts and builds stronger partnerships. Partnering with families to share this information and collaborating with them on art awareness efforts will result in sharing the joy and power of young children's artistic creativity and expression.

CREATIVITY JOURNALS FOR ALL AGES

Adult Journal Activity #10

Create an art gallery, sharing art growth stages. Work with the children and families in your program to formulate an art show in a local arts center, a local gallery, coffee shop, restaurant, bank, library, or other appropriate location. Work together, having the children choose their best artwork (both 2-D and 3-D), write stories about their creations if they wish, make labels for artwork, and set up the art show (making sure artwork is low enough for child level view). Arrange a date and time for an art show opening. Have children help make and deliver mail or email invitations, make snacks, and prepare for the occasion. If they are comfortable with this idea by the time of the event, encourage the children to stay near their artwork to talk with viewers about their work. Record your reflections on the planning and outcome of this activity in your journal.

Child's Personal Creativity Journal Activity #10

Activity #10 for Infants (Birth to walking, or 16 months)

Infant art gallery: Using ideas from the Create an Art Gallery, Sharing Art growth Stages, have a corner or wall set aside to display the infant's art and documentation of the creative process. Be sure to include information about children's art grow stages from Kellogg or Lowenfeld offered earlier in Chapter 2. Use other photos from the infant's creativity journal, enlarging them for display. Nice wooden or plastic frames can be purchased at an economical price. You can keep these to rotate art, or place them in other locations after the art show. Murals are also an effective way to display the process and product of one infant or a group of infants. Figure 10.15 is a mural completed by a group of 1 to 2-year-olds on 4 feet by 6 feet canvas.

Figure 10.15: Mural by 1 to 2-year-olds from Center for Early Childhood Education displayed at ESU Children's Art Gallery

Activity #10 for Toddlers (walking or 16 months to 3-years-old)

Using ideas from the Create an Art Gallery, Sharing Art growth Stages, have a corner or wall set aside to display the toddler's art and documentation of the creative process, with room for both 2D and 3D artwork. Be sure to include information about children's art grow stages from Kellogg or Lowenfeld offered earlier in Chapter 2. Use other photos from the toddler's creativity journal, enlarging them for display. Make sure to display them at a level that works for both children and adults. Nice wooden or plastic frames can be purchased at an economical price. You can keep these to rotate art, or place them in other locations after the art show. Figure 10.16 shows the painting by Cassie, age 2, was on a 4 foot by 5-foot canvas. This was a weeklong process, turning the canvas so the child could access all of the space. Completed in the summer time, a wading pool was conveniently placed nearby for play and rinsing between painting time.

Figure 10.16: Painting on canvas by Cassie, age 2

Activity #10 for Preschoolers (ages 3 – 5)

Using ideas from the Create an Art Gallery, Sharing Art growth Stages, have a corner or wall set aside to display the preschooler's art and documentation of the creative process, with room for both 2D and 3D artwork. Be sure to include information about children's art grow stages from Kellogg or Lowenfeld offered earlier in Chapter 2. Use other photos from the preschooler's creativity journal, enlarging them for display. Make sure to display them at a level that works for both children and adults. Nice wooden or plastic frames can be purchased at an economical price for 2D artwork. You can keep these to rotate art, or place them in other locations after the art show. Figure 10.17 is a mural completed by a group of 4–5 years old on 4 feet by 6 feet canvas.

Figure 10.17: Mural by 4–5-year olds from Center for Early Childhood Education displayed at ESU Children's Art Gallery

Activity #10 for Young School-Age Children

Using ideas from the Create an Art Gallery, Sharing Art growth Stages, have a corner or wall set aside to display the school aged child's art and documentation of the creative process, with room for both 2D and 3D artwork. Be sure to include information about children's art grow stages from Kellogg or Lowenfeld offered earlier in Chapter 2. Use other photos from the school-aged child's creativity journal, enlarging them for display. Make sure to display them at a level that works for both children and adults. Nice wooden or plastic frames can be purchased at an economical price. You can keep these to rotate art, or place them in other locations after the art show. Figure 10.18 is an example of displayed 3D artwork by school-aged children.

Figure 10.18: School-aged child's artwork displayed at eye level of children for easy viewing

Appendices

APPENDIX A
STANDARDS
DEC (Division of Early Childhood) Recommended Practices in Early Intervention / Early Childhood Special Education

Early Learning Standards (ELS)

NAEYC (National Association of Education of Young Children)
Guidelines for developmentally appropriate practice

NEA (National Education Association) Standards

APPENDIX B
ENJOYABLE JUNK & TERRIFIC TRASH SUITABLE FOR ART

APPENDIX C
CHILDREN'S BOOKS ABOUT ART AND CREATIVITY
Books about Art, Music, Movement, and Creativity for children

Appendix A: Standards

<u>Standards and Best Practice Guidelines for Birth to Kindergarten:</u>

DEC Recommended Practices in Early Intervention/
Early Childhood Special Education 2014

The following areas are included in the DEC Recommended Practices. The areas most closely related to the topic of this text (inclusive arts) are in **bold** below, with recommended practices for those areas listed below. The complete list of DEC's recommended practices can be viewed at: http://www.dec-sped.org/recommendedpractices.

1) Leadership
2) Assessment
3) Environment
4) Family
5) Instruction
6) Interaction
7) Teaming and Collaboration
8) Transition

2) Assessment

We recommend the following **assessment practices** to guide practitioners:

A1. Practitioners work with the family to identify family preferences for assessment processes.

A2. Practitioners work as a team with the family and other professionals to gather assessment information.

A3. Practitioners use assessment materials and strategies that are appropriate for the child's age and level of development and accommodate the child's sensory, physical, communication, cultural, linguistic, social, and emotional characteristics.

A4. Practitioners conduct assessments that include all areas of development and behavior to learn about the child's strengths, needs, preferences, and interests.

A5. Practitioners conduct assessments in the child's dominant language and in additional languages if the child is learning more than one language.

A6. Practitioners use a variety of methods, including observation and interviews, to gather assessment information from multiple sources, including the child's family and other significant individuals in the child's life.

A7. Practitioners obtain information about the child's skills in daily activities, routines, and environments such as home, center, and community.

A8. Practitioners use clinical reasoning in addition to assessment results to identify the child's current levels of functioning and to determine the child's eligibility and plan for instruction.

A9. Practitioners implement systematic ongoing assessment to identify learning targets, plan activities, and monitor the child's progress to revise instruction as needed.

A10. Practitioners use assessment tools with sufficient sensitivity to detect child progress, especially for the child with significant support needs.

A11. Practitioners report assessment results so that they are understandable and useful to families.

3) Environment

We recommend the following practices associated with the **child's environment**:

E1. Practitioners provide services and supports in natural and inclusive environments during daily routines and activities to promote the child's access to and participation in learning experiences.

E2. Practitioners consider Universal Design for Learning principles to create accessible environments.

E3. Practitioners work with the family and other adults to modify and adapt the physical, social, and temporal environments to promote each child's access to and participation in learning experiences.

E4. Practitioners work with families and other adults to identify each child's needs for assistive technology to promote access to and participation in learning experiences.

E5. Practitioners work with families and other adults to acquire or create appropriate assistive technology to promote each child's access to and participation in learning experiences.

E6. Practitioners create environments that provide opportunities for movement and regular physical activity to maintain or improve fitness, wellness, and development across domains.

4) Family

Family practices encompass three themes:

1. Family-centered practices: Practices that treat families with dignity and respect; are individualized, flexible, and responsive to each family's unique circumstances; provide family members complete and unbiased information to make informed decisions; and involve family members in acting on choices to strengthen child, parent, and family functioning.

2. Family capacity-building practices: Practices that include the participatory opportunities and experiences afforded to families to strengthen existing parenting knowledge and skills and promote the development of new parenting abilities that enhance parenting self-efficacy beliefs and practices.

3. Family and professional collaboration: Practices that build relationships between families and professionals who work together to achieve mutually agreed upon

outcomes and goals that promote family competencies and support the development of the child.

5) Instruction
We recommend the following practices to support **instruction**:

INS1. Practitioners, with the family, identify each child's strengths, preferences, and interests to engage the child in active learning.

INS2. Practitioners, with the family, identify skills to target for instruction that help a child become adaptive, competent, socially connected, and engaged and that promote learning in natural and inclusive environments.

INS3. Practitioners gather and use data to inform decisions about individualized instruction.

INS4. Practitioners plan for and provide the level of support, accommodations, and adaptations needed for the child to access, participate, and learn within and across activities and routines.

INS5. Practitioners embed instruction within and across routines, activities, and environments to provide contextually relevant learning opportunities.

INS6. Practitioners use systematic instructional strategies with fidelity to teach skills and to promote child engagement and learning.

INS7. Practitioners use explicit feedback and consequences to increase child engagement, play, and skills.

INS8. Practitioners use peer-mediated intervention to teach skills and to promote child engagement and learning.

INS9. Practitioners use functional assessment and related prevention, promotion, and intervention strategies across environments to prevent and address challenging behavior.

INS10. Practitioners implement the frequency, intensity, and duration of instruction needed to address the child's phase and pace of learning or the level of support needed by the family to achieve the child's outcomes or goals.

INS11. Practitioners provide instructional support for young children with disabilities who are dual language learners to assist them in learning English and in continuing to develop skills through the use of their home language.

INS12. Practitioners use and adapt specific instructional strategies that are effective for dual language learners when teaching English to children with disabilities.

INS13. Practitioners use coaching or consultation strategies with primary caregivers or other adults to facilitate positive adult-child interactions and instruction intentionally designed to promote child learning and development.

6) Interaction
We recommend the following practices to **support interaction**:

INT1. Practitioners promote the child's social-emotional development by observing, interpreting, and responding contingently to the range of the child's emotional expressions.

INT2. Practitioners promote the child's social development by encouraging the child to initiate or sustain positive interactions with other children and adults during routines and activities through modeling, teaching, feedback, or other types of guided support.

INT3. Practitioners promote the child's communication development by observing, interpreting, responding contingently, and providing natural consequences for the child's verbal and non-verbal communication and by using language to label and expand on the child's requests, needs, preferences, or interests.

INT4. Practitioners promote the child's cognitive development by observing, interpreting, and responding intentionally to the child's exploration, play, and social activity by joining in and expanding on the child's focus, actions, and intent.

INT5. Practitioners promote the child's problem-solving behavior by observing, interpreting, and scaffolding in response to the child's growing level of autonomy and self-regulation.

7) Teaming and Collaboration

We recommend the following practices to support **teaming and collaboration**:

TC1. Practitioners representing multiple disciplines and families work together as a team to plan and implement supports and services to meet the unique needs of each child and family.

TC2. Practitioners and families work together as a team to systematically and regularly exchange expertise, knowledge, and information to build team capacity and jointly solve problems, plan, and implement interventions.

TC3. Practitioners use communication and group facilitation strategies to enhance team functioning and interpersonal relationships with and among team members.

TC4. Team members assist each other to discover and access community-based services and other informal and formal resources to meet family-identified child or family needs.

TC5. Practitioners and families may collaborate with each other to identify one practitioner from the team who serves as the primary liaison between the family and other team members based on child and family priorities and needs.

Joint Position Statement on Inclusion from Division for Early Childhood (DEC) and the National Association for the Education of Young Children (NAEYC)

Definition of Early Childhood Inclusion

Early childhood inclusion embodies the values, policies, and practices that support the right of every infant and young child and his or her family, regardless of ability, to participate in a broad range of activities and contexts as full members of families, communities, and society. The desired results of inclusive experiences for children with and without disabilities and their families include a sense of belonging and membership, positive social relationships and friendships, and development and learning to reach their full potential. The defining features of inclusion that can be used to identify high quality early childhood programs and services are access, participation, and supports.

Recommendations for Using this Position Statement to Improve Early Childhood Services:
1) Create high expectations for every child to reach his or her full potential.
2) Develop a program philosophy on inclusion.
3) Establish a system of services and supports.
4) Revise program and professional standards.
5) Achieve an integrated professional development system.
6) Influence federal and state accountability systems.

Retrieved from: http://www.naeyc.org/files/naeyc/file/positions/DEC_
NAEYC_EC_updatedKS.pdf

Early Learning Standards

The Early Childhood Education Assessment Consortium of the Council of Chief State School Officers (CSSO) defines early learning standards as:

> "Statements that describe expectations for the learning and development of young children across the domains of: health and physical well being; social and emotional well-being; approaches to learning; language development and symbol systems; and general knowledge about the world around them."

(Retrieved from: http://www.kskits.org/ta/virtualKits/earlyLearningStandards.shtml)

Early childhood professionals must keep in mind that standards for children birth to kindergarten differ greatly from standards created for the K-12 world. Early childhood educators strive to build foundational skills that will help young children learn the content and information in the later grades The Early Learning Standards are a guideline for tracking a child's progress, while accommodating for individuality in gaining these foundational skills (Gronlund, 2006).

Early Learning Standards (ELS) vary from state to state, yet contain the same general domains or developmental content areas. The standards listed below are from Kansas Early Learning Standards. Acronyms for each will be used (e.g. ALT for Approaches to Learning) to note the ELS content areas that fit under various learning activities. This will make variations of ELS easier to translate from state to state.

1) Approaches to Learning (ATL)
   a. Persistence and Engagement in Learning
   b. Initiative
   c. Creativity

2) Physical Development (PHD)
   a. Large Motor Skills

    b.   Fine Motor Skills
    c.   Physical Fitness
    d.   Nutrition/Healthy Eating
    e.   Personal Hygiene
    f.   Safety

3) Social and Emotional Development (SED)
    a.   Character Development
    b.   Responsible Decision Making and Problem Solving
    c.   Personal Development
    d.   Social Development

4) Communication and Literacy (CL)
    a.   Dual Language Learners
    b.   Literature
    c.   Informational Text (non-fiction)
    d.   Foundational Skills
    e.   Writing
    f.   Speaking and Listening
    g.   Language Standards

5) Mathematics (M)
    a.   Counting and Cardinality
    b.   Operations and Algebraic Thinking
    c.   Measurement and Data
    d.   Geometry

6) Science (S)
    a.   Motion and Stability:
        i.   Forces and Interactions
        ii.   Energy
    b.   From Molecules to Organisms:
        i.   Structures and Processes
    c.   Earth's Systems
    d.   Earth and Human Activity

7) Social Studies (SS)
    a.   Government
    b.   Economics
    c.   Geography
    d.   State, United States and World History

8) Creative Arts (CA)
    a.   Dance
    b.   Music

   c. Acting/Theater

   d. Visual Arts

NAEYC (National Association of Education of Young Children) Guidelines for developmentally appropriate practice

1) Creating a caring community of learners
   a. Each member of the community is valued by the others.
   b. Relationships are an important context through which children develop and learn.
   c. Each member of the community respects and is accountable to the others to behave in a way that is conducive to the learning and well-being of all.
   d. Practitioners design and maintain the physical environment to protect the health and safety of the learning community members, specifically in support of young children's physiological needs for activity, sensory stimulation, fresh air, rest, and nourishment.
   e. Practitioners ensure members of the community feel psychologically safe. The overall social and emotional climate is positive.

2) Teaching to enhance development and learning
   a. Teachers are responsible for fostering the caring learning community through their teaching.
   b. Teachers make it a priority to know each child well, and also the people most significant in the child's life.
   c. Teachers take responsibility for knowing what the desired goals for the program are and how the program's curriculum is intended to achieve those goals.
   d. Teachers plan for learning experiences that effectively implement a comprehensive curriculum so that children attain key goals across the domains (physical, social, emotional, cognitive) and across the disciplines (language literacy, including English acquisition, mathematics, social studies, science, art, music, physical education, and health).
   e. Teachers plan the environment, schedule, and daily activities to promote each child's learning and development.
   f. Teachers possess an extensive repertoire of skills and strategies they are able to draw on, and they know how and when to choose among them, to effectively promote each child's learning and development at that moment.
   g. Teachers know how and when to *scaffold* children's learning—that is, providing just enough assistance to enable each child to perform at a skill level just beyond what the child can do on his or her own,

then gradually reducing the support as the child begins to master the skill, and setting the stage for the next challenge.

h. Teachers know how and when to use the various learning formats/contexts most strategically.

i. When children have missed some of the learning opportunities necessary for school success (most often children from low- income households), programs and teachers provide them with even more extended, enriched, and intensive learning experiences than are provided to their peers.

j. Teachers make experiences in their classrooms accessible and responsive to *all* children and their needs—including children who are English language learners, have special needs or disabilities, live in poverty or other challenging circumstances, or are from different cultures.

3) Planning curriculum to achieve important goals
   a. Desired goals that are important in young children's learning and development have been identified and clearly articulated.
   b. The program has a comprehensive, effective curriculum that targets the identified goals, including all those foundational for later learning and school success.
   c. Teachers use the curriculum framework in their planning to ensure there is ample attention to important learning goals and to enhance the coherence of the classroom experience for children.
   d. Teachers make meaningful connections a priority in the learning experiences they provide children, to reflect that all learners, and certainly young children, learn best when the concepts, language, and skills they encounter are related to something they know and care about, and when the new learnings are themselves intercon- nected in meaningful, coherent ways.
   e. Teachers collaborate with those teaching in the preceding and subsequent grade levels, sharing information about children and working to increase the continuity and coherence across ages/grades, while protecting the integrity and appropriateness of practices at each level.

4) Assessing children's development and learning
   The following describe sound assessment that is developmentally appropriate for children from birth through the primary grades.

   a. Assessment of young children's progress and achievements is ongoing, strategic, and purposeful. The results of assessment are used to inform the planning and implementing of experiences, to communicate with the child's family, and to evaluate and improve teachers' and the program's effectiveness.

   b. Assessment focuses on children's progress toward goals that are developmentally and educationally significant.

    c.   There is a system in place to collect, make sense of, and use the assessment information to guide what goes on in the classroom (formative assessment). Teachers use this information in planning curriculum and learning experiences and in moment-to-moment interactions with children—that is, teachers continually engage in assessment for the purpose of improving teaching and learning.

    d.   The methods of assessment are appropriate to the developmental status and experiences of young children, and they recognize individual variation in learners and allow children to demonstrate their competence in different ways. Methods appropriate to the classroom assessment of young children, therefore, include results of teachers' observations of children, clinical interviews, collections of children's work samples, and their performance on authentic activities.

    e.   Assessment looks not only at what children can do independently but also at what they can do with assistance from other children or adults. Therefore, teachers assess children as they participate in groups and other situations that are providing scaffolding.

    f.   In addition to this assessment by teachers, input from families as well as children's own evaluations of their work are part of the program's overall assessment strategy.

    g.   Assessments are tailored to a specific purpose and used only for the purpose for which they have been demonstrated to produce reliable, valid information.

    h.   Decisions that have a major impact on children, such as enrollment or placement, are never made on the basis of results from a single developmental assessment or screening instrument/device but are based on multiple sources of relevant information, including that obtained from observations of and interactions with children by teachers and parents (and specialists, as needed).

    i.   When a screening or other assessment identifies children who may have special learning or developmental needs, there is appropriate follow-up, evaluation, and, if indicated, referral. Diagnosis or labeling is never the result of a brief screening or one-time assessment. Families should be involved as important sources of information.

5)   Establishing reciprocal relationships with families

    a.   In reciprocal relationships between practitioners and families, there is mutual respect, cooperation, shared responsibility, and negotiation of conflicts toward achievement of shared goals.

    b.   Practitioners work in collaborative partnerships with families, establishing and maintaining regular, frequent two-way communication with them (with families who do not speak English, teachers should use the language of the home if they are able or try to enlist the help of bilingual volunteers).

c. Family members are welcome in the setting, and there are multiple opportunities for family participation. Families participate in program decisions about their children's care and education.

d. Teachers acknowledge a family's choices and goals for the child and respond with sensitivity and respect to those preferences and concerns, but without abdicating the responsibility that early childhood practitioners have to support children's learning and development through developmentally appropriate practices.

e. Teachers and the family share with each other their knowledge of the particular child and understanding of child development and learning as part of day-to-day communication and in planned conferences. Teachers support families in ways that maximally promote family decision-making capabilities and competence.

f. Practitioners involve families as a source of information about the child (before program entry and on an ongoing basis) and engage them in the planning for their child.

g. The program links families with a range of services, based on identified resources, priorities, and concerns.

Retrieved from: http://www.naeyc.org/files/naeyc/file/positions/PSDAP.pdf

NAEYC Early Childhood Program Standards

1. Relationships
The program promotes positive relationships among all children and adults to encourage each child's sense of individual worth and belonging as part of a community and to foster each child's ability to contribute as a responsible community member.

2. Curriculum
The program implements a curriculum that is consistent with its goals for children and promotes learning and development in each of the following areas: social, emotional, physical, language, and cognitive.

3. Teaching
The program uses developmentally, culturally, and linguistically appropriate and effective teaching approaches that enhance each child's learning and development in the context of the program's curriculum goals.

4. Assessment of Child Progress
The program is informed by ongoing systematic, formal, and informal assessment approaches to provide information on children's learning and development. These assessments occur within the context of reciprocal communications with families and

with sensitivity to the cultural contexts in which children develop. Assessment results are used to benefit children by informing sound decisions about children, teaching, and program improvement.

5. Health
The program promotes the nutrition and health of children and protects children and staff from illness and injury.

6. Teachers
The program employs and supports a teaching staff that has the educational qualifications, knowledge, and professional commitment necessary to promote children's learning and development and to support families' diverse needs and interests.

7. Families
Program Standard: The program establishes and maintains collaborative relationships with each child's family to foster children's development in all settings. These relationships are sensitive to family composition, language, and culture.

8. Community Relationships
Program Standard: The program establishes relationships with and uses the resources of the children's communities to support the achievement of program goals.

9. Physical Environment
Program Standard: The program has a safe and healthful environment that provides appropriate and well-maintained indoor and outdoor physical environments. The environment includes facilities, equipment, and materials to facilitate child and staff learning and development.

10. Leadership and Management
The program effectively implements policies, procedures, and systems that support stable staff and strong personnel, fiscal, and program management so all children, families, and staff have high quality experiences.

Retrieved from: www.naeyc.org/academy

Standards and Best Practice Guidelines for Kindergarten to 4th grade:

National Education Association (NEA) K – 4th Grade

Standards in Visual Arts

Grade K-4 Visual Arts Standard 1

1) Understanding and applying media, techniques, and processes

- Students know the differences between materials, techniques, and processes
- Students describe how different materials, techniques, and processes cause different responses
- Students use different media, techniques, and processes to communicate ideas, experiences, and stories
- Students use art materials and tools in a safe and responsible manner

2) Using knowledge of structures and functions

- Students know the differences among visual characteristics and purposes of art in order to convey ideas
- Students describe how different expressive features and organizational principles cause different responses
- Students use visual structures and functions of art to communicate ideas.

3) Choosing and evaluating a range of subject matter, symbols, and ideas

- Students explore and understand prospective content for works of art
- Students select and use subject matter, symbols, and ideas to communicate meaning

4) Understanding the visual arts in relation to history and cultures

- Students know that the visual arts have both a history and specific relationships to various cultures
- Students identify specific works of art as belonging to particular cultures, times, and places
- Students demonstrate how history, culture, and the visual arts can influence each other in making and studying works of art

5) Reflecting upon and assessing the characteristics and merits of their work and the work of others

- Students understand there are various purposes for creating works of visual art
- Students describe how people's experiences influence the development of specific artworks
- Students understand there are different responses to specific artworks

6) Making connections between visual arts and other disciplines

- Students understand and use similarities and differences between characteristics of the visual arts and other arts disciplines
- Students identify connections between the visual arts and other disciplines in the curriculum

Retrieved from: http://artsedge.kennedy-center.org/educators/standards/full-text/K-4-standards.aspx

Appendix B: Enjoyable Junk and Terrific Trash Suitable for Art

The following list offers items that could be used for creative art activities. <u>Be certain to keep smaller items that could be swallowed away from children under the age of 3 years, or from children who might tend to put things in their mouths.</u> Several manufacturers offer choke tubes as a guide for measuring items that might be a choke risk. A toilet paper roll could also work for this purpose.

Acorns
Aluminum Foil
Beads (pony, wood, glass, plastic, etc.)
Bells
Book Pages
Brads
Bubble Wrap
Burlap
Buttons
Cardboard Boxes (including flattened food boxes)
Chalk
Charcoal
Christmas Lights
Coffee Filters
Coins
Confetti
Contact Paper
Corks
Cotton Balls
Craft (Popsicle) Sticks
Embroidery Floss
Fabric Scraps
Feathers
Felt
Flowers
Foam Paint
Foam Stickers
Food Coloring
Gems
Glitter
Glitter Paint
Googley Eyes
Keys
Lace

Leather
Leaves
Magazines
Markers
Matches
Mirrors
Newspaper
Packing Peanuts
Pastels (chalk, oil, metallic, etc.)
Pebbles
Pinecones
Pipe Cleaners
Playdough
Pom-poms
Printed Tapes
Q-Tips
Rhinestones
Ribbon
Sand
Sandpaper
Seeds
Sequins
Shells
Small Stones
Sponges
Stamps
Sticks
Stickers
Straws
Thread
Thumb Tacks
Tissue Paper
Toothpicks
Wallpaper
Watercolors
Wood Scraps
Wrapping Paper
Yarn

Appendix C: Children's Books about Art and Creativity

Adelman, B. (1999). *Henry Lichtenstein's ABC*. Boston: Bulfinch Press. ISBN: 0-8212-2591-X
The paintings of Roy Lichtenstein are used to teach children the ABCs through art.

Aigner-Clark, J. (2002). *Baby Einstein: The ABC's of Art*. New York: Hyperion Books for Children. ISBN: 078680882-9
Every letter of the alphabet has a masterpiece to provide an example of its sound.

Aigner-Clark, J. (2001). *Baby Einstein: Van Gogh's World of Color*. New York: Hyperion Books for Children. ISBN: 078680805-5
Children are shown color through the famous paintings of masterpiece artist Vincent Van Gogh.

Alcorn, J. (1991). *Rembrandt's Beret*. New York: Tambourine Books.
ISBN: 0-688-10206-9   Reading Level: Kindergarten +
An old artist reminisces about being trapped in a museum as a boy and conversing with the Old Masters whose self-portraits had come to life. The Old Masters cast lots to see who can paint the boy in one final portrait. Rembrandt, the winner, not only painted the portrait, but presented the boy with his own paintbrushes and beret.

Anholt, L. (1994). *Camille and the Sunflowers*. Hauppage, NY: Barron's Educational Series. ISBN: 0-8120-6409-7
When a stranger moves into Camille's village, he welcomes the man with a bunch of sunflowers. Little did Camille know that the stranger was Vincent Van Gogh! The book tells the story of how Camille and the artist became friends and includes many reproductions of Van Gogh's paintings.

Anholt, L. (2003). *The Magical Garden of Claude Monet*. Hauppauge, NY: Barron's Educational Series. ISBN: 0-7641-5574-1
A curious little girl follows her dog through a gate into a magic garden. There she meets Claude Monet, and he takes her through his garden and studio.

Auch, M. J. (1996). *Eggs Mark the Spot*. New York: Holiday House.
ISBN: 0-8234-1305-5   Reading Level: PreSchool-Grade 2
A chicken named Pauline can lay magical eggs. She can copy anything she sees. Her eggs will help solve a mystery at the art gallery.

Bjork, C., and Anderson, L. (1985). *Linnea in Monet's Garden*. Stockholm: Raben & Sjogren. ISBN: 91-29-58314-4   Reading Level: Grades 4-7
Linnea and her friend, Mr. Bloom, visit Paris and Giverny to study the life and work of French impressionist, Claude Monet.

Black, H. (2000). *A Magic Color Book*. New York: Sterling Publishing.
ISBN: 0-8069-0600-6
Alice likes to paint, but when she discovers colors, everything takes on a new life. This book includes pull tabs to change the colors on Alice's paintings.

Blizzard, G. S. (1993). *Come Look with Me: Animals in Art*. Charlottesville, VA: Thomasson-Grant. ISBN: 0-56566-013-7   Reading Level: Preschool – Grade 3
Masterpiece art is used to identify different animals that children should know. Every painting has a story that goes along with it, plus questions for the children to figure out.

Blizzard, G. S. (1993). *Come Look with Me: Enjoying Art with Children*. Charlottesville, VA: Thomasson-Grant. ISBN: 0-934738-76-9   Reading Level: 5-8 years
The author presents 12 paintings representing various cultures and historical periods. With each painting, she provides several questions to encourage children to pay attention to detail, to look at the artist's intent, and to bridge the past and present. The introduction also includes a useful section for adults on how to use the book with children.

Blizzard, G. S. (1993). *Come Look with Me: World of Play*. Charlottesville, VA: Thomasson-Grant. ISBN: 1-56566-031-5   Reading Level: 5-8 years
Children learn different ways of play through masterpiece paintings and other art creations. The introduction provides adults with ways to use this book with children. Every painting has a paragraph or two that tells a story about what is going on in that painting, along with questions for the children to figure out.

Bornstein, R. L. (1997). *That's How It Is When We Draw*. New York: Clarion Books.
ISBN: 0-395-85029-1   Reading Level: 5-8 years
Poetry is used to show how a little boy draws and paints his artwork.

Brown, L. K., and Brown, M. (1986). *Visiting the Art Museum*. London: Puffin.
ISBN: 0-14-054820-3   Reading Level: 4 years and up
A cartoon family with reluctant children visits an art museum. The parents help the children make connections between art and their studies at school and everyday lives.

Carle, E. (1992). *Let's Paint a Rainbow*. New York: Scholastic.
ISBN: 0-590-32844-1   Reading Level: Birth -7 years
This board book teaches children about the colors of the rainbow, as well as the order of these colors.

Carmack, L. J. (1998). *Phillipe in Monet's Garden*. Boston: Museum of Fine Arts.
ISBN: 0-87846-456-5   Reading Level 3-8 years

Phillipe is a frog in France where the special of the day at a nearby restaurant is frog legs. He escapes the restaurant's grasp and runs into a garden, which ends up being the garden in which Monet found inspiration for his paintings. Phillipe becomes the centerpiece for many of Monet's paintings.

Carroll, C. (1999). *How Artists See Families: Mother, Father, Sister, and Brother.* New York: Abbeville Kids. ISBN: 0-7892-0671-4 Reading Level: 7-10 years
Children are given paintings that correspond with family categories. Then they are given background information on the painting and also an explanation about what the people in the painting are doing or who they were.

Carroll, C. (1999). *How Artists See Play: Sports, Games, Toys, and Imagination.* New York: Abbeville Kids. ISBN: 0-7892-0393-6 Reading Level: 8-10 years
Paintings are presented that go along with the categories. Children are given background information on the paintings and then on the activity.

Carroll, C. (1999). *How Artists See the Weather: Sun, Wind, Snow, and Rain.* New York: Abbeville Kids. ISBN: 0-7892-0031-7 Reading Level: 8-10 years
Paintings depicting weather conditions are shown. Children are given background information on the painting, as well as how the weather affects the world in the painting.

Catalanotto, P. (1995). *The Painter.* New York: Orchard Paperbacks. ISBN: 0-531-07116-2 Reading Level: 4 years & up
This is the story of a little boy and a day with his parents. His father is a painter.

Clayton, E. (1996). *Ella's Trip to the Museum.* New York: Crown Publishers. ISBN: 0-517-70081-6 Reading Level: 4 years & up
On a class trip to the museum, the paintings come alive for Ella. She is taken into each painting she sees. Her teacher cannot see that the paintings are alive and thinks that Ella is just dawdling.

Delafosse, C., and Jeunesse, G. (1993). *A First Discovery Art Book: Animals.* New York: Scholastic. ISBN: 0-590-5502-3 Reading Level: 5 years & up
A factual look at animals in paintings and the media artists may use in creating them. Overlays create interesting presentations of information and add depth to the examples included.

Delafosse, C., and Jeunesse, G. (1993). *A First Discovery Art Book: Paintings.* New York: Scholastic. ISBN: 0-590-55201-5 Reading Level: 5 years & up
A factual look at paintings and the media artists may use in creating them. Overlays create interesting presentations of information and add depth to the examples included.

Delafosse, C., and Jeunesse, G. (1995). *A First Discovery Art Book: Portraits.* New York: Scholastic. ISBN: 0-590-55200-7 Reading Level: 5 years & up

A factual look at portraits and the media artists may use in creating them. Overlays create interesting presentations of information and add depth to the examples included.

Dionetti, M. (1996). *Painting the Wind*. New York: Little, Brown.
ISBN: 0-316-18602-3   Reading Level: 2 – 6 years
A little girl named Claudine is Vincent Van Gogh's only friend in the village where they live in France. After being forced to leave by the townspeople who were afraid of him, Van Gogh gives Claudine a painting of a sunflower, because she was brave enough to stand taller than the rest and become his friend.

Dunrea, O. (1995). *The Painter Who Loved Chickens*. New York: Farrar, Straus & Giroux. ISBN: 0-374-35729-3   Reading Level: 5 years & up
A city artist longs to live and paint in the country. Unable to find buyers for the paintings of chickens that he loves to do, he remains in the city, painting portraits and trying to save money to buy a farm. His goal looks hopeless until he chances to meet an art connoisseur with similar tastes.

Edwards, M. (1991). *A Baker's Portrait*. New York: Lothrop, Lee & Shepard.
ISBN: 0-688-099712-X   Reading Level: 7 years & up
Michelin, a young portrait painter, is in trouble because she always paints exactly what she sees in her portraits, including warts and missing teeth. Now she has been asked to paint her exceedingly plump aunt and uncle. As Michelin searches for a way to be kind and honest, she learns that sometimes you have to look below the surface to see people as they really are.

Everett, G. (1991). *Li'l Sis and Uncle Willie*. New York: Hyperion Paperbacks for Children. ISBN: 1-56282-593-3   Reading Level: 7 – 12 years
Based on the life of painter William H. Johnson, this book tells the story of the summer he returned to the farm where he had grown up and the lifelong impact of his visit on his young niece.

Fox, D., and Marks, C. (1987). *Go In and Out the Window: An Illustrated Songbook for Young People*. New York: Metropolitan Museum of Art.
ISBN: 0-8050-0628-1   Reading Level: 5 years & up
Pieces of masterpiece art are used to illustrate 61 classic children's songs. Brief commentaries are given to provide background information on the artwork.

Galli, L. (1996). *Mona Lisa: The Secret of the Smile*. New York: Delacore Press.
ISBN: 0-385-32108-2   Reading Level: 6 years & up
This is a fictional story of how Leonardo Da Vinci painted the Mona Lisa and gave her that enchanted smile.

Garland, M. (1995). *Dinner at Magritte's*. New York: Dutton Children's Books.
ISBN: 0-525-45336-9   Reading Level: 6 years & up

Bored by vacation at his parents' summer cottage, a young boy looks for entertainment at the home of his neighbors. There he finds two artists, Monsieur Magritte and Monsieur Dali, whose unique perspectives on the world around them make dinner an exciting adventure.

Gibbons, G. (1998). *The Art Box*. New York: Holiday House.
ISBN: 0-8234-1386-1   Reading Level: 4 years & up
This book shows everything that could possibly come out of an art box to create.

Goodman, M. J. S., and Lieberman, N. K. (1999). *Learning through Art*. New York: Guggenheim Museum Publications. ISBN: 0-8109-6910-6   Reading Level: 8 years & up
A painting is shown, and then questions are asked about it, along with a story about the painting. Each painting is followed by activities for the children that pertain to themes in the painting.

Gorbachev, V. (2000). *Peter's Picture*. New York: North-South Books.
ISBN: 1-55858-965-1   Reading Level: 3 years & up
Peter paints his best picture ever, one of an orange flower. On his way home from school, he shows it to every person he passes. They all give him advice about what to do with it, and he becomes confused. He is happy when he goes home and his parents know exactly what he should do with it—put it on the refrigerator.

Green, D. (1999). *My Little Artist*. Marshfield, MA: Vermilion.
ISBN: 0-7651-1742-8   Reading Level: Grades 2 - 6
A little girl visits her grandmother, who used to be a painter. Together, they realize the beauty and life in the garden. The little girl dreams of being a painter just like her grandmother.

Greenberg, J., and Jordan, S. (1998). *Chuck Close: Up Close*. New York: Dorling Kindersley.
ISBN: 0-7894-2658-7   Reading Level: 8 years & up
This book is a look at the work of Chuck Close.

H. Byron Masterson School first graders. (2002). *September 12th: We Knew Everything Would Be All Right*. New York: Scholastic.
ISBN: 0-439-44249-x   Reading Level: 4 years & up

Harwayne, S. (2002). *Messages to Ground Zero: Children Respond to September 11th*. Portsmouth, NH: Heinemann.
ISBN: 0-325-00514-1

Hartfield, C. (2002). *Me and Uncle Rommie*. New York: Dial Books for Young Readers.
ISBN: 0-8037-2520-5   Reading Level: 4 – 8 years

This is the story of a young boy who is sent to Harlem for the summer to stay with his uncle, Romare Bearden (Rommie). He learns many things from his Uncle Rommie.

Heller, R. (1995). *Color*. New York: Puffin Books.
ISBN: 0-689-11858-8   Reading Level: 5 years & up
Children learn about the colors in a set of paints and how they can change if you mix them.

Hest, A. (1996). *Jamaica Louise James*. Cambridge, MA: Candlewick Press.
ISBN: 1-56402-348-6   Reading Level: 4 years & up
Jamaica Louise James tells the story of how the paintings got on the wall of the subway station at 86th and Main.

Hoban, T. (1978). *Is It Red? Is It Yellow? Is It Blue?* New York: Greenwillow Books.
ISBN: 0-68884-171-6   Reading Level: 4 years & up

Hoban, T. (1986). *Red, Blue, Yellow Shoe*. New York: Greenwillow Books.
ISBN: 0-68806-563-5   Reading Level: 4 years & up

Hoban, T. (1993). *Black on White*. New York: Greenwillow Books.
ISBN: 0-68811-918-2   Board Book - Reading Level: Birth -7 years

Hoban, T. (1993). *White on Black*. New York: Greenwillow Books.
ISBN: 0-68811-919-0   Board Book - Reading Level: Birth -7 years

Hoban, T. (1995). *Colors Everywhere*. New York: Greenwillow Books.
ISBN: 0-68812-762-2   Reading Level: 4 – 8 years

Hoban, T. (1996). *Of Colors and Things*. New York: HarperTrophy.
ISBN: 0-68804-585-5   Reading Level: 4 – 8 years

Hoban, T. (1996). *Shapes, Shapes, Shapes*. New York: HarperTrophy.
ISBN: 0-68814-740-2   Reading Level: 4 – 8 years

Hoban, T. (1998). *So Many Circles, So Many Squares*. New York: Greenwillow Books.
ISBN: 0-68815-165-5   Reading Level: 4 – 8 years

Holwitz, P. (2003). *The Big Blue Spot*. New York: Philomel Books.
ISBN: 0-399-23786-0   Reading Level: 3 – 8 years
This is a story about what happens when a plain blue spot of paint starts to drip off the page.

Hubbard, P. (1996). *My Crayons Talk*. New York: Henry Holt.
ISBN: 0-8050-3529-X   Reading Level: 3 – 8 years

This book shows how each color says something when it is drawn.

Hurd, E. T., and Hurd, C. (1971). *Wilson's World.* New York: Harper Collins.
ISBN: 0-06-443359-5   Reading Level: 3 – 8 years
This is a story about what happens when a little boy with a lot of imagination starts to paint.

Hurd, T. (1996). *Art Dog.* New York: Harper Collins.
ISBN: 0-06-024424-0   Reading Level: 3 – 8 years
Art Dog is a guard dog at the art museum. At night, however, he becomes an artist. He puts on a mask and goes into the museum and paints beautiful paintings. The people in the museum wonder who the painter is.

J. Paul Getty Museum. (1997). *A is for Artist.* Los Angeles: J. Paul Getty Museum.
ISBN: 0-89236-377-0   Reading Level: 2 years and up
This alphabet book uses paintings to teach children the letters of the alphabet. At the beginning and end of the book, the words and the letters are all listed for the children to read through.

J. Paul Getty Museum. (1999). *1 to 10 and Back Again.* Los Angeles: J. Paul Getty Museum.
ISBN: 0-89236-525-0   Reading Level: 5 – 8 years
Children are taught to count from 1 to 10 in French. They are given pictures of French furniture for each number. They count forward and backward. At the beginning and the end, the French word for the numbers is given.

Johnson, C. (1955). *Harold and the Purple Crayon.* New York: Harper Collins.
ISBN: 0-06-022935-7   Reading Level: 3 – 8 years
This is the story of a boy named Harold who uses his imagination and his purple crayon to go on an adventure before his bedtime.

Johnson, J. (1994). *The Princess and the Painter.* New York: Farrar, Straus & Giroux.
ISBN: 0-374-36118-5   Reading Level 6 years and up
This book tells the story of what could have happened the day the Infanta Margarita, a princess of Spain, first saw the painting *Las Meninas,* a portrait of her painted by Diego Velazquez.

Keats, E. J. (1996). *The Snowy Day.* New York: Scholastic.
ISBN: 0-590-03031-0   Board Book and Paperback
A little boy named Peter goes out into the snow and experiments with his surroundings.

Kesselman, W. (1980). *Emma.* New York: Dell.
ISBN: 0-440-40847-4   Reading Level: 4 years and up

Emma is a lonely old lady who enjoys remembering the village in which she grew up. She is disappointed that the painting of the village given to her for her birthday does not depict it as she remembers it. Emma decides to paint her own painting of the village and finds she has a talent and a love for art that will keep her from feeling lonely.

Kidd, R. (1997). *Almost Famous Daisy!* London: Frances Lincoln.
ISBN: 0-7112-1070-5   Reading Level: 4 years and up
Daisy decides to enter a painting contest. She dreams about what she wants to paint while examining the work of famous artists from around the world. She writes a note to her parents telling them she has gone to discover what to paint.

King, M. L. (1997). *I Have a Dream*. New York: Scholastic.
ISBN: 0-590-20516-1   Reading Level: 4 years and up
This book takes children on an illustrated journey through Dr. Martin Luther King Jr.'s "I Have a Dream" speech. The illustrations were done by Coretta Scott King award winners and honorary nominees.

Koda-Callan, E. (1998). *The Artist's Palette*. New York: Workman.
ISBN: 0-7611-1360-6   Reading Level: 4 years and up
After her classmates make fun of her drawing, a little girl is afraid to enter it into an art contest and decides to give up drawing forever. When her teacher gives her an artist's palette pendant necklace, the girl changes her mind and decides that she likes her drawing enough to enter it in the contest.

Krull, K. (1995). *Lives of the Artists: Masterpieces, Messes, and What the Neighbors Thought*. San Diego: Harcourt Brace.
ISBN: 0-15-2001-34   Reading Level: 9 -12 years
Written in language appropriate for elementary school children, the author shares the condensed life histories of 16 well-known artists.

Lasky, K. (2000). *First Painter*. New York: Dorling Kindersley.
ISBN: 0-7894-2578-5   Reading Level: 7 years and up
This book tells the story of a prehistoric village and their people. A little girl must go to a cave to ask the spirits to send them water. While there, she starts to draw animals on the cave walls with a stick, thus creating some of the first drawings.

Lawrence, J. (1993). *Harriet and the Promised Land*. New York: Simon & Schuster Books for Young Readers.
ISBN: 0-671-86673-7   Reading Level: 4 years and up
Jacob Lawrence wrote and illustrated the life of Harriet Tubman from birth until her heroism with the Underground Railroad.

Le Tord, B. (1995). *A Blue Butterfly*. New York: Doubleday.
ISBN: 0-385-31102-8   Reading Level: 4 years and up

Le Tord uses Claude Monet's own palette of only eight colors to illustrate her poetic words beautifully. The book celebrates the extraordinary vision of the beloved impressionist.

Leuck, L. (1998). *Teeny, Tiny Mouse: A Book about Colors*. New York: Bridgewater Paperbacks.
ISBN: 0-8167-4898-5   Reading Level: 3 years and up
A mother and child mouse spend a day together pointing out all the colors they see.

Linch, T. (2000). *My Duck*. New York: Scholastic.
ISBN: 0-439-20670-7   Reading Level: 4 years and up
A little girl tries to draw pictures to go with her story, but her teacher criticizes her harshly for her unrealistic drawings. Her drawings come to life, and the girl realizes that they are still good drawings, as long as she likes them.

Lionni, L. (1991). *Matthew's Dream*. New York: Alfred A. Knopf.
ISBN: 0-679-87318-X   Reading Level: 3 - 7 years
A visit to the museum helps Matthew, a little mouse who lives in a dreary attic, discover beauty in the shapes and colors around him. Matthew decides to become an artist so that he can share that beauty with others.

Littlesugar, A. (1995). *Josiah True and the Art Maker*. New York: Simon & Schuster.
ISBN: 0-671-88354-2   Reading Level: 5 - 8 years and up
Young Josiah is fascinated by the Art Maker who comes to paint his family's portrait. As he watches the Art Maker, he learns that true artists are those who can see beyond the surface and into the soul. Josiah vows that one day, he will be an Art Maker, too.

Locker, T. (1989). *The Young Artist*. New York: Dial Books.
ISBN: 0-14-054923-4   Reading Level: Grades 2 - 8
Adrian, a gifted apprentice, refuses to paint a lie in his portraits. He decides to focus on painting landscapes, where he can paint the world as he really sees it. Then one day the king asks Adrian to paint portraits of the royal court. Adrian must decide between painting to please the members of the court and being punished for his honesty.

Logan, C. (1996). *Scruffy's Museum Adventure*. Boston: Museum of Fine Arts, Boston.
ISBN: 0-87846-432-8
Scruffy the dog decides to go into the Museum of Fine Arts, Boston. He discovers that he loves art when he sees all the dog statues and Egyptian artifacts. However, he must hurry through the museum because there is a guard on his tail. Dogs are not allowed in the art museum! When Scruffy gets home, his family promises him his own postcard art gallery.

Mayer, M., and McDermott, G. (1987). *The Brambleberry's Animal Book of Colors*. Stamford, CT: Riverbank Press.

ISBN: 0-681-40163-X
The Panda brothers see color wherever they go. Each page has a picture that is all in that particular color. The color's word is also written on the page.

Mayhew, J. (1997). *Katie Meets the Impressionists*. New York: Orchard Books.
ISBN: 0-531-30151-6   Reading Level: 4 years and up
Katie wanders into all the impressionist paintings she sees on her trip to the museum. She plays with friends and has tea with Monet.

Mayhew, J. (1998). *Katie and the Mona Lisa*. New York: Orchard Books.
ISBN: 0-531-30177-X   Reading Level: 4 years and up
Katie tours many famous paintings at the art museum, with Mona Lisa as her guide. She also discovers how Mona Lisa got her smile.

Mayhew, J. (2000). *Katie and the Sunflowers*. New York: Orchard Books.
ISBN: 0-531-30325-X   Reading Level: 9-12 years
Katie follows all the paintings that have sunflowers and tries to pick the best ones for her grandmother.

McPhail, M. (2000). *Drawing Lessons from a Bear*. New York: Little, Brown.
ISBN: 0-316-56345-5   Reading Level: 4 – 8 years
A little bear realizes that he would rather be an artist than go to "How to Be a Bear" lessons. Children are taken through his life, into adulthood where he teaches a few kids the lessons he learned while growing up.

Merberg, J., and Bober, S. (2002). *A Magical Day with Matisse*. San Francisco: Chronicle Books.
ISBN: 0-8118-3414-X   Board Book - Reading Level: Birth -7 years
Matisse's paintings are used to show children a day around the house with Matisse.

Merberg, J., and Bober, S. (2003). *A Picnic with Monet*. San Francisco: Chronicle Books.
ISBN: 0-8118-4046-8   Board Book - Reading Level: Birth -7 years
Monet's paintings are used to teach children about the outdoors.

Merberg, J., and Bober, S. (2003). *Dancing with Degas*. San Francisco: Chronicle Books.
ISBN: 0-8118-4047-6   Board Book - Reading Level: Birth -7 years
Degas's paintings are used to show the life of a dancer.

Merrill, L., and Ridley, S. (1993). *The Princess and the Peacocks*. Washington, DC: Smithsonian Institution.
ISBN: 1-56282-327-2   Reading Level: 4 -9 years
Told from the point of view of the princess in the painting above the fireplace, this is the story of the controversy between American artist James McNeill Whistler and British businessman Frederick R. Leyland when Whistler redecorated Leyland's dining room

with a peacock motif. The restored dining room is installed in the Freer Gallery of Art at the Smithsonian Institution.

Micklethwait, L. (1992). *I Spy*. New York: Greenwillow Books.
ISBN: 0-688-11679-5   Reading Level: 4 -9 years
A painting is presented for each letter of the alphabet, along with a verbal hint on something the reader is to "spy" within the painting.

Micklethwait, L. (1992). *I Spy: An Alphabet in Art*. New York: Greenwillow Books.
ISBN: 0-68811-679-5   Reading Level: 4 -9 years

Micklethwait, L. (1993). *A Child's Book of Art: Great Pictures, First Words*. London: Dorling Kindersley.
ISBN: 1-56458-203-5   Reading Level: 7 - 17 years
Masterpiece paintings are used to illustrate basic concepts such as family, opposites, the five senses, colors, and seasons for young children.

Micklethwait, L. (1993). *I Spy with Two Eyes*. New York: Greenwillow Books.
ISBN: 0-688-12640-5   Reading Level: 3 years and up
Masterpiece art provides the reader with objects for cognitive counting from 1 to 20.

Micklethwait, L. (1994). *I Spy a Lion: Animals in Art*. New York: Greenwillow Books.
ISBN: 0-68813-230-8   Reading Level: 3 years and up

Micklethwait, L. (1995). *Spot a Cat*. London: Dorling Kindersley.
ISBN: 0-7894-0144-4   Reading Level: 3 years and up
Paintings are presented, and children are asked to find different types of cats.

Micklethwait, L. (1995). *Spot a Dog*. London: Dorling Kindersley.
ISBN: 0-7894-0145-2   Reading Level: 5 years and up
Simple text invites children to search for a challenging-to-find dog hidden in each masterpiece painting.

Micklethwait, L. (1996). *A Child's Book of Play in Art: Great Pictures, Great Fun*. London: Dorling Kindersley.
ISBN: 0-7894-1003-6   Reading Level: 3 years and up
Children learn different ways of play through masterpiece art.

Micklethwait, L. (1996). *I Spy a Freight Train: Transportation in Art*. New York: Greenwillow Books.
ISBN: 0-68814-701-1   Reading Level: 3 years and up

Micklethwait, L. (1999). *A Child's Book of Art: Discover Great Paintings*. London: Dorling Kindersley.

ISBN: 0-78944-283-3   Reading Level: 4 years and up

Micklethwait, L. (2004). *Animals: A First Art Book.* London: Francis Lincoln.
ISBN: 1-84507-027-5   Reading Level: 3 – 6 years
This book provides early experiences with visual art for very young children by introducing them to paintings featuring different animals.

Micklethwait, L. (2004). *I Spy Shapes in Art.* New York: Greenwillow Books.
ISBN: 0-06-073193-1   Reading Level: 4 - 8 years and up
Children have to "spy" shapes in art. Masterpiece art is used for shapes such as squares and triangles.

Micklethwait, L. (2005). *Colors: A First Art Book.* London: Francis Lincoln.
ISBN: 1-84507-285-5
Children are guided to look at masterpiece paintings featuring each of the eight basic colors.

Minnerly, D. B. (1993). *Molly Meets Mona and Friends: A Magical Day at the Museum.* New York: Greene Bark Press.
ISBN: 1-880851-25-3
As Molly tours the art museum, she is pulled into every painting she sees. The illustrations are of masterpiece art.

Moon, N. (1994). *Lucy's Pictures.* New York: Dial Books for Young Readers.
ISBN: 0-8037-1833-0   Reading Level: 3 years and up
Lucy spends all day at school making the perfect collage for her grandfather, who will be visiting her after school. She even spends her recess collecting things to add to her picture. She finishes and shows it to her grandfather, who happens to be blind.

Morrison, T. (1997) *The Neptune Fountain: The Apprenticeship of a Renaissance Sculptor.* New York: Holiday House.
ISBN: 0-8234-1293-8   Reading Level: 6 years and up
A boy named Marco Baicchi in fifteenth-century Rome has very few choices. However, one day he begs Luigi Borghini, a sculptor, to allow Marco to become his apprentice. The work in the studio is not quite what Marco had in mind. He sweeps the floors, melts the hot wax, and does other messy jobs. However, Marco realizes how, little by little, the sculpture for the Piazza Corsanini fountain is taking shape.

Moss, M. (1990). *Regina's Big Mistake.* Boston: Houghton Mifflin.
ISBN: 0-395-70093-0   Reading Level: 5 - 8 years and up
Regina is afraid that she will make a mistake if she tries to draw a picture. With her teacher's encouragement, Regina learns that making the most of mistakes is part of creativity.

Munsch, R. (1992). *Purple, Green, and Yellow.* New York: Annick Press.

ISBN: 1-55037-256-4   Reading Level: 4 - 7 years and up
This is the story of what happens when a girl named Brigid gets markers.

Nikola-Lisa, W. (2000). *The Year with Grandma Moses*. New York: Henry Holt.
ISBN: 0-8050-6243-2   Reading Level: 4 - 10 years and up
This book tells the true story of Grandma Moses' childhood and how she became a painter. The illustrations are paintings done by Grandma Moses.

Ortolja-Baird, L. (2000). *The Body in Art: Hands*. Naperville, IL: Sourcebooks.
ISBN: 1-57071-596-3   Board Book - Reading Level: Birth -7 years
Masterpiece paintings are presented in a board book. Children must look at each painting to find where the hand(s) is/are.

Pinkwater, D. M. (1977). *The Big Orange Splot*. New York: Scholastic.
ISBN: 0-590-44510-3   Reading Level: 4 - 8 years and up
Mr. Plumbean's house looks like all the other houses on his street. Then one day a seagull drops a bucket of orange paint on his roof. Mr. Plumbean decides that his house should reflect his true personality and begins to decorate. His neighbors, however, must be convinced that being different is okay.

Priceman, M. (2001). *It's Me, Marva! A Story about Color and Optical Illusions*. New York: Alfred A. Knopf.
ISBN: 0-679-88993-0   Reading Level: 5 - 8 years and up
Marva is an inventor down on her luck. Her latest invention blows up and spews ketchup everywhere, which causes a whole string of mishaps throughout the day.

Raimondo, J. (2000). *Imagine That! Activities and Adventures in Surrealism*. New York: Watson-Guptill.
ISBN: 0-8230-2502-0   Reading Level: 8 - 9 years and up
This book shows children how to make surrealist art, just like the famous artists.

Reid, K. (2000). *Magical Mondays at the Art Museum*. Richmond, VA: Cockadoodledoo Creations.
ISBN: 0-9702653-0-1
On a magical trip to the art museum on a Monday, a rooster and a hen come alive and give children a tour of the art museum.

Reiner, A. (1990). *A Visit to the Art Galaxy*. New York: Green Tiger.
ISBN: 0-671-74957-9   Reading Level: 6 years and up
When two children reluctantly join their mother on a tour of the art museum, they are drawn into an abstract painting to visit the Land of Modern Art. There, they meet master painters Matisse, Da Vinci, Picasso, and Kline and learn that modern art uses many different media and provides artists with "room to dream."

Reynolds, P. H. (2003) *The Dot*. Cambridge, MA: Candlewick Press.

ISBN: 0-7636-1961-2   Reading Level: 5 - 12 years and up
This is a story of Yashti and how drawing a simple dot on a piece of paper can develop a person into an artist.

Richmond, R. (1992). *Children in Art*. Nashville, TN: Ideals Children's Books.
ISBN: 0-8249-8588-5   Reading Level: 12 years and up
The author presents a collection of children's portraits by well-known artists throughout history. Each painting is accompanied by commentary, providing background information on the artist and subject and comparing similar works.

Ringold, F. (1992). *Aunt Harriet's Underground Railroad in the Sky*. New York: Crown Publishers.
ISBN: 0-517-88543-3   Reading Level: 3 - 7 years and up
This story is a version of Harriet Tubman's adventures in the Underground Railroad.

Roth, S. L. (2001) *It's Still a Dog's New York: A Book of Healing*. Washington, DC: National Geographic Society.
ISBN: 0-7922-7050-9   Reading Level: 5 - 9 years and up

Rozek, K. (2002). *Rudy and the Magical Twin Balloons*. Brookline, MA: Brookline Merrimac.
ISBN: 0-9720871-0-9   Reading Level: 7 years and up

Rylant, C. (1998). *All I See*. New York: Orchard Books.
ISBN: 0-531-07048-4   Reading Level: 5 years and up
This is the story of a little boy named Charlie who befriended a painter named George.

Seuss, Dr. (1996). *My Many Colored Days*. New York: Random House.
ISBN: 0-679-89344-X   Reading Level: 2 - 6 years and up
Dr. Seuss uses catchy rhymes to teach children about colors, but also about the world around them.

Spanyol, J. (2003). *Carlo Likes Colors*. Cambridge, MA: Candlewick Press.
ISBN: 0-7636-2023-8   Reading Level: 2 - 6 years
Carlo the giraffe sees beautiful colors wherever he goes.

Stanley, D. (1994). *The Gentleman and the Kitchen Maid*. New York: Dial Books for Young Readers.
ISBN: 0-8037-1320-7   Reading Level: 7 years and up
In the art museum, the gentleman was facing the kitchen maid, and they liked each other. A young art student named Rusty came in to paint a copy of the gentleman. The kitchen maid was moved to another wing, so while Rusty painted the gentleman, she also painted the kitchen maid on the same canvas so that they could now be together.

Sullivan, C. (Ed.) (1989). *Imaginary Gardens: American Poetry and Art for Young People*. New York: Harry N. Abrams.
ISBN: 0-8109-1130-2   Reading Level: 3 years and up
Sullivan brings two art forms together by presenting visual art with classical poetry.

Sullivan, C. (1991). *Alphabet Animals*. New York: Rizzoli.
ISBN: 0-8478-1377-0   Reading Level: 6 years and up
Photographs, sculpture, and paintings are used to illustrate a humorous poem about each letter of the alphabet.

Sullivan, C. (1992). *Numbers at Play: A Counting Book*. New York: Rizzoli.
ISBN: 0-8478-1501-3   Reading Level: 5 years and up
Photographs, sculpture, and paintings are used to provide opportunities in cognitive counting and number recognition from 1 to 10.

Sweeney, J. (1995). *Once upon a Lily Pad*. San Francisco: Chronicle Books.
ISBN: 0-8118-0868-8   Reading Level: 3 - 8 years and up
During their courtship and marriage, two little frogs wonder about the old man who comes to the lily pond to paint their portrait every summer.

Sweeney, J. (1998). *Bijou, Bonbon, and Beau: The Kittens Who Danced for Degas*. San Francisco: Chronicle Books.
ISBN: 0-8118-1975-2   Reading Level: 3 - 8 years and up
This book tells the story of three kittens who lived with the dancers in a Parisian theater where Edward Degas painted his ballerina paintings. The kittens manage to get on stage during a dress rehearsal and cause confusion.

Tang, G. (2003). *Math-terpieces: The Art of Problem-Solving*. New York: Scholastic.
ISBN: 0-439-44388-1   Reading Level: 6 - 12 years and up
Children learn math concepts through masterpiece art. Every left-hand page not only has a work of art with the artist and the year, but also with information about the painting and how it could be connected to a math concept and a little about the painting. It also tells the children which era it came from, such as Impressionist, Post-Impressionist, and Cubist.

Thomas, A. (1994). *Pearl Paints*. New York: Henry Holt.
ISBN: 0-8050-2976-1   Reading Level: 3 years and up
When she receives a set of paints for her birthday, Pearl becomes so engrossed in painting that she cannot think of anything else. She even dreams of things to paint in the style of the great masters. Pearl uses up all her birthday paints, but her masterpiece mural so impresses her family and friends that they bring her more paint to paint pictures just for them.

Tinus, A. W. (1994). *Young Goat's Discovery*. Santa Fe, NM: Red Crane Books.
ISBN: 1-878610-38-4   Reading Level: 3 years and up

This is a story about a little boy's goat who notices a picture of himself carved onto a mountain wall. He goes to the library and learns all about the Hopi Indian tribe and how they drew on the mountain.

Walsh, E. S. (1991). *Mouse Paint*. San Diego: Red Wagon Books.
ISBN: 0-15-200265-0   Board Book - Reading Level: Birth -7 years
Three mice find jars filled with yellow, blue, and red paint. They paint everything they see, and children see how colors can be mixed to make other colors.

Warhola, J. (2003). *Uncle Andy's*. New York: G. P. Putnam's Sons.
ISBN: 0-399-23869-7   Reading Level: 4 - 8 years and up
This book is a fictional account, written by Andy Warhol's nephew, of actual events that took place when a little boy went to stay with his Uncle Andy during the summer.

Watson, A. (1992). *The Folk Art Counting Book*. New York: Harry N. Abrams.
ISBN: 0-8109-3306-3   Reading Level: 3 years and up
Pieces of American folk art are used to provide experiences in cognitive counting for the numerals 1 to 20.

Weitzman, J. P., and Glasser, R. P. (1998). *You Can't Take a Balloon into the Metropolitan Museum*. New York: Dial Books for Young Readers.
ISBN: 0-8037-2301-6   Reading Level: 4 years and up
A little girl carrying a balloon goes into the Metropolitan Museum of Art. She discovers that her balloon cannot come with her, and a museum guard promises to look after it. Birds come and cut the balloon loose, and it sails over New York. As the little girl is viewing paintings, the illustrations show the balloon seeing the same things in real life.

Winter, J. *September Roses*. New York: Farrar, Straus & Giroux.
ISBN: 0-374-36736-1   Reading Level: 7 years and up

Wolkstein, D. (1992). *Little Mouse's Painting*. New York: Sea Star Books.
ISBN: 1-58717-125-2   Reading Level: 4 years and up
Little Mouse decides to paint a picture instead of visiting her friends one evening, but her friends do not see in her painting what she sees. This book teaches children that there can be different points of view about the same thing.

Yenawine, P. (1991). *Shapes*. New York: Doubleday.
ISBN: 0-385-30315-7
Children are told how different artists use shapes in their paintings.

Yenawine, P. (1993). *Colors*. New York: Museum of Modern Art.
ISBN: 0-7607-1886-5
Children are told how different artists use different colors in their paintings.

Yenawine, P. (1993). *Lines*. New York: Museum of Modern Art.
ISBN: 0-7607-1883-0
Paintings featuring different lines and angles are presented. Children are asked to identify different elements of the paintings.

Yenawine, P. (1993). *People*. New York: Museum of Modern Art.
ISBN: 0-7607-1884-9
Famous paintings of people are shown, and questions are posed that children can answer based on the paintings.

Yenawine, P. (1993). *Stories*. New York: Museum of Modern Art.
ISBN: 0-385-30256-8   Reading Level: 7 years and up
Paintings in which a story is being told are presented to children in a question-and-answer format.

Young, J. (1999). *The Art of Science: A Pop-Up Adventure in Art*. Cambridge, MA: Candlewick Press.
ISBN: 0-7637-0754-1   Reading Level: 9 years and up
Science is taught through art in an interesting pop-up format.

Zadrzynska, E. (1990). *The Girl with a Watering Can*. New York: Chameleon Books.
ISBN: 0-915829-64-9   Reading Level: 8years and up
The little girl from Renoir's *The Girl with the Watering Can* comes to life and makes mischief among the masterpieces in the National Gallery of Art in Washington, DC. A serious conversation with St. Jerome in Bellini's *St. Jerome Reading* convinces the little girl to put everything back the way she had found it.

Zadrzynska, E. (1993). *The Peaceable Kingdom*. New York: M. M. Art Books.
ISBN: 0-9638904-0-9   Reading Level: 6 years and up
The animals from the *Peaceable Kingdom,* painted by Edward Hicks, escape and run around New York. The painted children have to run after them and get all the animals back into the painting in the museum.

Ziefert, H., and Rader, L. (1994). *Pete's Chicken*. New York: Tambourine Books.
ISBN: 0-688-13256-1   Reading Level: 3 years and up
Pete's feelings are hurt when his classmates make fun of the rainbow-colored chicken he drew in art class. After some thought, Pete comes to the conclusion that his artwork should be as individual as he is.

Integrating Art into the Inclusive Early Childhood Curriculum

Glossary

A

ability level – refers to what a child is developmentally able to do, taking into account any challenges the child may have, physically, cognitively, or socio-emotionally.

Abstract art – an artistic style that uses shape, form, color, and line, and does not attempt to represent external reality.

activities – learning activities for children based on their developmental level, while making accommodations for individual needs.

adaptations – the process of accommodating or modifying activities for all children to participate, regardless of any challenges or ability level.

advanced cognitive development – refers to children with unique gifts and talents with advanced intellectual abilities. Keep in mind that children with advanced cognitive abilities could have motor skills and socio-emotional development closer to their chronological age.

Advocating for the Arts for all Children – increasing family, community, and educational awareness of the importance of creative experiences for young children, and honoring their authentic creative expressions.

aesthetics – is beauty, the study of beauty, and investigating the beauty of art, and our surroundings.

aesthetics in art programs – four areas of aesthetics regarding children's art programs: sensory experiences, beautiful and creative experiences, times space and materials for making art, and introduction to art world.

Americans with Disabilities Act (ADA) - The *Americans with Disabilities Act (ADA)* became law in 1990. This civil rights law prohibits discrimination against individuals with *disabilities* in all areas of public life, including jobs, schools, transportation, and all public and private places that are open to the general public.

anti-bias – a belief of equality, without exclusion, prejudice, bias, or discrimination

anti-bias curriculum – according to NAEYC, this is an approach to early childhood education, with values-based principles and methodology in support of **respecting and embracing differences and acting against bias and unfairness**.

Art

authentic creative art – process oriented, creative, true and free expressive art experiences; without presubscribed directions or molds or models to follow for The Greater Good…includes ideas and resources for children to communicate through their art about important topics such as peace, nonviolence, anti-bullying, and sustainability.

    masquerading art – product oriented art activities, with only one right way of completing. Experiences that include molds of figures, cookie cutters, coloring sheets, coloring books, patterns to follow, step-by-step instructions are all examples of activities that masquerade as art.

the arts, validating and integrating the arts – art welcomes children to open-ended play that benefits all domains. Integration of the arts through academic and pre-academics is an effective way to give children direct, hands-on experiences that illustrates their understanding concepts and knowledge. The key to validating and integrating the arts in today's society appears to be best accomplished and illustrated through linking the developmentally appropriate creative activities to standards.

what is art? – art happens when someone takes any type of material and transforms it into a purposeful statement. Art is taking an idea or feeling and giving it form. Art can be two-dimensional (2D), developed on a flat plane or surface, such as drawing, painting, printmaking, or photography. Art can also be in three-dimensional (3D) form, with spatial depth as well as height and weight. Examples of 3D artwork include sculpture, crafts (glass, wood, metal, fiber, clay), and architecture.

2D art – art that is two–dimensional (2D), developed on a flat plane or surface, such as drawing, painting, printmaking, or photography.

3D art – art that is three–dimensional (3D) form, with spatial depth as well as height and weight. Examples of 3D artwork include sculpture, crafts (glass, wood, metal, fiber, clay), and architecture.

art activities

  authentic creative art activities – process oriented, creative, true and free expressive art experiences; without presubscribed directions or molds or models to follow

  activities masquerading as creative art – product oriented art activities, with only one right way of completing. Experiences that include molds of figures, cookie cutters, coloring sheets, coloring books, patterns to follow, step–by–step instructions are all examples of activities that masquerade as art.

  linked to developmental skills – art that offers children open–ended, creative expression that benefits all developmental domains (physical, cognitive – including language, social, emotional).

art as communication – children draw what they know and communicate who they are, what is important to them, and what is happening in their lives. Even before a child develops speech, drawing can offer very young children self-expression of ideas and feelings. Children's art (both 2D and 3D) communicates and demonstrates: their creative spirit, self–confidence, problem solving skills, determination, focus and concentration skills, knowledge, and details they may not be able to put into words. Avoid assumptions or misinterpreting child's purpose or communication.

art as learning and intervention tool – authentically creative art experiences for children of various ages, developmental, and ability levels can meet early learning standards and meet IFSP/IEP goals for children. The developmental importance of making creative art experiences accessible for all children is essential.

art appreciation – fostering children's understanding and appreciation of art.

art area. *See* art center

art center – an area in the classroom where a teacher guides the child's creative growth by arranging an appropriate learning environment where the child could function with minimum assistance from an adult. This physical setting of a variety of materials should be functional for the individual child. Shelves should be open and easily accessible so that children are able to experience a sense of relaxed boundaries that help to facilitate the creative process.

art critiques – Art critique and art discussions with children should be at their developmental level, and begin with self–talk with infants. As children grow older we can guide their exploration while respecting their preferences and tastes for beauty.

art dialogue. *See also*, art discussion – interactions adults have with children about their art. Art dialogue and art critique with children should be at their developmental level, and begin with self–talk with infants. As children grow older we can guide their exploration while respecting their preferences and tastes for beauty.

art discussion – art critique questions and discussions at the child's developmental level, while viewing artwork with the child. Keep questions open ended, and pause to allow time for a thoughtful response. Avoid rushing or hurrying children during an art discussion.

art display – display of children's artwork, showcasing the children's creations and design.

art education – refers to education of the visual and tangible arts, including visual and performing arts. Components of a complete early childhood art education program include: sensory experiences; time, space, and materials for making art (which includes the environment, interactions, and feedback); aesthetic experiences; learning art and artists, and art forms and styles.

Art Elements and Principles – Elements and principles of art are the observable properties of matter, including: line, color, shape/form, texture, space, value, mass or volume, pattern, balance, and design or composition. These elements can be seen in 2D and 3D works of art of any level of artistic creations. Not every artwork contains all of the elements and principles, however, most have several.

art gallery/museum – places for the display and/or sale of artwork.

art materials – Basic art materials include: tools for mark making (such as crayons, pencils, markers, chalk, pastels, with larger tools or grippers for children with fine motor challenges); paper in a variety of colors, shapes, sizes, thickness, and textures (including magazines, cardboard, newsprint, tissue paper, crepe paper, sand paper, white drawing paper, colored construction paper – both traditional and various skin tones); items for cutting, fastening, and attaching, such as: scissors (some double–handed ambidextrous scissors or with accommodations), glue, glue sticks, paste, tape, hole punches, staplers, string, pipe cleaners; items for painting and making prints, such as: paint, brushes, sponges and other items with textures; collage items: nature items, fabric, old jewelry, wall paper, wrapping paper, yarn; material for sculptures, such as: clay, polymer clay, playdough, recipes for various 3–D doughs, aluminum foil, cardboard boxes, bubble wrap, cotton balls, pipe cleaners, beads, pom–poms.

art program – Components of a complete early childhood art program include: sensory experiences; time, space, and materials for making art (which includes the environment, interactions, and feedback); aesthetic experiences; learning art and artists, and art forms and styles.

art show – display of children's artwork, showcasing the children's creations and design. Art shows in galleries are displays of professional artist's work.

art supplies. *See* art materials

art therapy – the role of art therapy is one of healing and assisting individuals in communicating feelings and emotions, especially during difficult times in life. Through art, children can express feelings and issues they want to express but are not sure how to communicate. Art therapy has been used to address children's responses to various traumas that some children face regularly, such as domestic violence or drug–related shootings.

artist – individuals who produce art.

artist studio – location where the artist produces her/his artworks.

artistic development. *See also* artistic growth – stages of artistic growth and development are universal and have even been linked with the first marks of the human race. Just as children of the same age chronologically would vary in their mental age, so children's drawings vary individually in their rate of artistic growth and development. Individual development and needs of children with differing abilities also impact artistic development and growth.

artistic development. *See* artistic growth and artistic developmental theories

artistic developmental theories – theories that present stages of artistic growth and development. Primary artistic developmental theorists are Rhoda Kellogg and Viktor Lowenfeld.

artistic growth. *See also* artistic development – The stages of artistic growth and development are universal and have even been linked with the first marks of the human race. Just as children of the same age chronologically would vary in their mental age, so children's drawings vary individually in their rate of artistic growth and development. Individual development and needs of children with differing abilities also impact artistic development and growth.

artistic heritage – art that is created and preserved by a culture and nation, including traditional artistic goals of that culture and nationality. Introducing children to the foundations of good art and artistic heritage is an essential component of a quality art program.

arts advocacy. *See* advocating for the Arts for all Children

assessing creativity – assessment process that measures creativity through a series of exercises. The Torrance Tests of Creative Thinking (TTCT) is one of the most common tests used to assess creativity in both children and adults. It measures two areas: Figural (Thinking Creatively with Pictures/Drawings) and Verbal (Thinking Creatively with Words). Through these exercises, children or adults demonstrate their creative abilities.

assessment of activity objectives – This section of a lesson plan is about accountability, how well objectives were met/not met. How will you know what the children learned? This relates directly to the objectives, and demonstrates how the data will be record or documented. The documentation or tool for documentation is essential. A chart, checklist or specific manner you will collect this data. Also, evaluation of one's teaching should be included here.

asymmetrical – not evenly or equally balanced.

authentic creative art – process oriented, creative, true and free expressive art experiences; without presubscribed directions or molds or models to follow.

authentic creative art experiences – activities that offer process oriented, creative, true and free expressive art experiences; without presubscribed directions or molds or models to follow.

B

balance – is demonstrated how an artist incorporates positive and negative space. This involves two ways: symmetrical (evenly or equally balanced) and asymmetrical (not evenly or equally balanced).

balance of artistic process and product – focusing on the process of the creative experience and outcome or the art product.

barriers and obstacles to creativity – common ways adults discourage creativity in children, including surveillance, evaluation, rewards, competition, Over–control, restricting choice, and pressure.

benefits of role models in inclusive settings – research demonstrating increased participation of the children with special needs in inclusive, rather than non–inclusive groups, which supports the importance of role models and suggests additional benefits for all children in the inclusive settings.

brain development – the left hemisphere of the brain controls the right side of the body while the right hemisphere governs the left side. Hemispheres are joined by the corpus callosum, which serves as communication between them. Although both hemispheres work together, we refer to "left–brain" as controlling speech, reasoning, math, and factual kinds of activities and "right–brain" as the spatial skills, visual imagery, nonverbal, sensory, and creative side.

brainstorming – solving problems or coming up with ideas through group discussion.

brain research – study of the brain and impact of early childhood experiences.

Building a Quality Inclusive Early Childhood Arts Program – demonstrates how developing and maintaining a quality inclusive early childhood arts program involves a commitment to offering authentic, creative, and developmentally appropriate art experiences embedded throughout the curriculum. Components include: sensing and experiencing; making art (including feedback); aesthetics; and learning about basic elements of art, artists, and their styles

C

centers. *See also* art center – areas within the early childhood classroom, including areas for art, blocks, fine motor, dramatic play, music and movement, science, literacy and writing, and math.

checklist – list of items used for assessing how objectives are met, for self–evaluation, anti–bias curriculum or books, etc.

child–centered approach to art – process oriented art, unstructured, giving options and freedom of expression.

child development – development include the young child's physical, social, emotional, and cognitive development. These domains do not develop in isolation of each other, nor do they develop evenly. Each child has an individual rate and area of growth as influenced by their genetics (nature) and their environment (nurturance, or lack of it).

Children Inspire Glass Project at Emporia State University – an extraordinary opportunity for Emporia, Kansas area children, ages 5–10, fostering children to create stories and design creatures to be transformed into glass sculpture. This ongoing project celebrates children and their imaginations in collaboration with instructors and students of various educational disciplines who share this enthusiasm.

children with differing abilities – also referred to as children with special needs or children with disabilities.

children's art – demonstrates individual development and growth, communicates what is important in their lives, communicates their emotions, and demonstrates pre–writing and pre–literacy skills.

children's art for The Greater Good – includes ideas and resources for children to communicate through their art about important topics such as peace, nonviolence, anti–bullying, and sustainability.

children's art gallery – place for the display of children's artwork display, showcasing the children's creations and design.

classroom environment – should offer developmentally appropriate experiences, with child–sized furnishing, accessible for all children, include nature, textures, color used throughout the room, displays, lighting/smells/sounds, and focal points of the environment (e.g. exciting and inviting attractions). Areas within the early childhood classroom, including areas for art, blocks, fine motor, dramatic play, music and movement, science, literacy and writing, and math.

The Rating Observation Scale for Inspiring Environments – challenges teachers to examine classrooms in a totally new way with an eye for what is aesthetically beautiful and inspiring.

chromatic sense – allows one to identify, match, and discriminate among colors, such as noting shade differences, as well as tints, tones, intensity, or values of color.

clay – a stiff, sticky substance from the earth, that can be molded and sculpted when wet, and dried in a kiln.

cognitive development – the cognitive or intellectual area of child development.

cognitive – intellectual development.

color – is produced when light is on an object and reflects back to the eye.

colors

    mixing primary colors to make secondary – red and yellow make orange; red and blue make purple; yellow and blue make green.

    primary colors – red, yellow, blue.

    secondary colors – orange, green, purple.

coloring books. *See also* anti–coloring book – is a book containing lined art in which to color inside the lines. Coloring books offer practice in fine motor skills, however, no creative expression or process is involved.

cognitive, language, communication considerations in art – demonstrates individual development and growth, communicates what is important in their lives, communicates their emotions, and demonstrates pre–writing and pre–literacy skills. Accommodations are needed for children with cognitive, language, communication challenges to fully participate.

components of a complete early childhood art program – include sensory experiences; time, space, and materials for making art (which includes the environment, interactions, and feedback); aesthetic experiences; and learning about art and artists, and art forms and styles.

components of art – include subject, form, and content.

conformity – a major factor that interferes with the development of creativity.

creativity versus and schools – studies support that conformity, caused by a highly–structured curriculum (e.g. authoritarian treatment with only one correct way, one correct answer), a structured and precise time schedule, time limits, prescribed pattern and copying can stifle creativity.

Constructivism – an artistic style where various mechanical objects are combined into abstract mobile forms. This style and has influenced aspects of modern architecture and design, and originated in Russia in the 1920s.

content – or the Why: The Content offers the essential meaning or significance of work of art. It gives more to the story, the details, and the elaboration of the meaning.

convergent thinking – non–creative thinking, with one right answer.

crafts – product oriented, teacher directed activities, with presubscribed directions, molds, or models to follow.

creative art. *See* authentic creative art

creative artistic abilities, age and individual development. *See* artistic growth stages

creative development – See artistic growth. *See also* artistic development

creative expression – process oriented art, unstructured, giving options and freedom of expression.

creative growth – See artistic growth. *See also* artistic development

creative thinking – the ability to see things in new ways, make something unique or original, thinking unconventionally, or combining unrelated things to make something new.

creative movement – is an artistic medium that develops children's awareness of their bodies and what they can do, explore movement and music, and promote creativity. Benefits include improved motor skills, balance and coordination. It can also help to develop feelings of self–confidence and communicate emotions.

creativity. *See* creative thinking

creativity and child development – are linked to developmental skills. Art that offers children open–ended, creative expression that benefits all developmental domains (physical, cognitive – including language, social, emotional).

creativity and the brain – creativity is an inherent and natural function of the brain that has the capacity to be fostered or stifled. Changes in the central nervous system and various organs underlie many emerging abilities.

creativity and time – children need time to creative, slowing down for learning through play, time to show us how much they know, and time for problem solving opportunities.

creativity theories. *See* developmental stages of artistic growth. *See also* artistic developmental theories

Creativity Journals. *See* Personal Creativity Journal

critical thinking – reasoning that requires making decisions and problem–solving.

cultural diversity – recognizing the existence of a variety of cultural or ethnic groups within society.

curricular areas – include: math/pre–math; science/sensory; language arts, communication, and literacy/pre–literacy; social studies/pre–social studies; expressive arts: music, movement, and theater.

curriculum anti–bias part as integrated in curriculum – according to NAEYC, this is an approach to early childhood education, with values–based principles and methodology in support of **respecting and embracing differences and acting against bias and unfairness**.

curriculum development – the process of planning learning activities for children with short term, long term, and individualized goals and objectives.

D

dance. *See also* creative movement – is an artistic medium that develops children's awareness of their bodies and what they can do, explore movement and music, and promote creativity. Benefits include improved motor skills, balance and coordination. It can also help to develop feelings of self–confidence and communicate emotions.

design or composition – involves the overall success of arrangement and artwork, relating more to the adult artist.

Design stage – The designs stage has two components: combines and aggregates. Two united diagrams form a combine. This is typically demonstrated by three to four–year–old children. Aggregates three or more united diagrams form an aggregate. This is also typically demonstrated by three to four–years–old.

Developmental Benefits of Authentic Creative Art Experiences – Children benefit developmentally from authentic creative art experiences. Even scribbles by toddlers demonstrate pre–writing skills, and art elements of shapes, lines, texture, color, and value. Benefits include: sensory experiences (cognitive, physical, emotional), opportunities to experiment (e.g. science, physics, cause/effect, invent, discover, cognitive), spatial relations (physical, cognitive), planning, sequencing (math, cognitive), problem solving (cognitive), motor skills (physical), eye–hand coordination, perceptual motor skills (physical), and pride, sense of accomplishment (emotional/social).

developmental stages of artistic growth. *See also* artistic developmental theories – stages of artistic growth and development are universal and have even been linked with the first marks of the human race. Just as children of the same age chronologically would vary in their mental age, so children's drawings vary individually in their rate of artistic growth and development. Individual development and needs of children with differing abilities also impact artistic development and growth. Primary artistic developmental theorists that outline the stages of artistic growth are Rhoda Kellogg and Viktor Lowenfeld.

developmental stages of creative art. *See* Developmental stages of artistic growth and artistic developmental theories

Diagram of Inclusive Early Childhood Classroom – plans of a classroom that offers developmentally appropriate experiences, with child–sized furnishing, accessible for all children, including areas for art, blocks, fine motor, dramatic play, music and movement, science, literacy and writing, and math.

diagrams – stage of development in art growth depicting drawn outline of shapes, including: circle (and oval); cross; X, square (and rectangle); triangle, and odd or organic form, typical of three–years–old.

dictation – the action of saying words aloud to be written, typed, or somehow recorded differing abilities – a person first term referring to an individual with challenges with a functional ability. Stating a person with differing abilities puts the person first, and the challenges or disability second.

disabilities – challenges with or loss of a functional ability.

disability awareness – educating people about disabilities.

disability awareness activities and materials – experiences that help children see the many ways we are the same and different. Just as we each have different hair color, skin color, eye color, etc.; we also have different abilities that make us unique. Simulating what it might be like to have differing abilities, such as taping fingers together on each hand to simulate fine motor challenges and then paint or draw; paint or drawing while wearing wax paper goggles to simulate a visual challenge, or create in art area while using a wheelchair for accommodating space and access to materials. Including materials that welcome diversity, such as: dolls with broken limbs should be bandaged, braced, or make a prosthesis for the doll, and anti–bias equipment and materials (books, posters, videos) that depict individuals with special needs, as well as multicultural and non–gender bias materials.

Divergent thinking – characteristics of divergent or creative thinking include: Fluency – many ideas or solutions, emphasis on number of ideas produced; Flexibility – different ideas which cross categories or break boundaries, ability to think in another way or change direction; Originality – unique or original ideas, one–of–a–kind idea; Elaboration – add details to the ideas; expanding to make it more complex.

Diverse. *See* cultural diversity

Division of Early Childhood (DEC) – The Division for Early Childhood (DEC) promotes policies and advances evidence–based practices that support families and enhance the optimal development of young children (0–8) who have or are at risk for developmental delays and disabilities. DEC is an international membership organization for those who work with or on behalf of young children (0–8) with disabilities and other special needs and their families.

dramatic play – a type of play that involves make believe or playing out family roles and cultures. Dramatic play is a key area for children to learn and demonstrate how to get along with others and appropriate interactions.

E

early childhood art programs. *See also* Art education – refers to education of the visual and tangible arts in early childhood, including visual and performing arts. Components of a complete early childhood art education program include: sensory experiences; time, space, and materials for making art (which includes the environment, interactions, and feedback); aesthetic experiences; learning art and artists, and art forms and styles.

early childhood art program evaluation – a tool for evaluating the quality of an early childhood art program.

early childhood education – a term used to describe any type of educational program that serves children in their early years, including birth to age 8.

Early Learning Standards (ELS) – describes expectations for the learning and development of young children.

education and conformity – studies support that conformity, caused by a highly–structured curriculum (e.g. authoritarian treatment with only one correct way, one correct answer), a structured and precise time schedule, time limits, prescribed pattern and copying can stifle creativity.

education crisis – refers to the need for creative freedom, divergent thinking, with opportunities to problem solve and build independence. With increased standards, requirements for more testing and documentation, meeting Individualized Family Service Plans (IFSP) and Individualized Education Program (IEP) goals and outcomes, and less fun and play in education, we have reached a crisis in education of our children.

emotional development – a developmental domain referring to feelings and emotions, understanding how and why they happen, learning about one's own feelings and those of others, and developing effective ways of managing them

Emporia State University's Children Inspire Glass Project. *See* Children Inspire Glass Project at Emporia State University

English Language Learners (ELL) – individuals who are learning English as a second language.

Enjoyable Junk & Terrific Trash Suitable for Art – a list of low or no cost items to use for art projects.

environment. *See* Classroom Environment and The Rating Observation Scale for Inspiring

equal access to the arts for all children – art experiences and programs accessible for all children, with accommodations and modifications to fully participate.

evaluation. *See* assessment of activity objectives

F

families. *See* partnering with families, and invovling parents and families

feedback – is an essential part of art programs. This feedback needs to be specific to the individuality of the child, and the process of their creative expression.

feelings. *See* emotional development

field trips – a trip away from the classroom, giving children a firsthand experience. Field trips to art museums/galleries and artist's studios can enhance an art program and expand children's knowledge of art, artists and their styles.

flexibility – different ideas which cross categories or break boundaries; ability to think in another way or change direction.

fluency – many ideas or solutions; emphasis on number of ideas produced.

food and art – refers to controversy how about using food as a material in art projects. Some programs have guidelines or policies when it comes to using food for art projects (e.g. Head Start) prohibit use of food with art, as many children do not get enough food to eat. For example, using noodles or peanut butter in an art project seems illogical to a child who is hungry every day or does not have the luxury of eating three meals a day.

form – or the How: Form refers to how the artwork is organized or arranged. The Form gives the artwork unity.

G

Gardner's Theory of Multiple Intelligences – Howard Gardner's theory of multiple intelligences had a significant impact on education, proposing "seven kinds of smart" or "multiple intelligences" with the purpose of maximizing the potential of each child. Rather than a single general ability to define intelligence, there are eight intelligences, according to Gardner (1983): Verbal–Linguistic: Excels in words and language (reading, writing, speaking and listening); Logical–Mathematical: Excels in reasoning, logical thinking, problem solving and numbers; Musical: Excels in musical expression, learning through songs, sensitivity to rhythms and beats; Visual–Spatial: Excels in shapes and designs, learning visually, able to organize ideas and represent images visual–spatially; Bodily–Kinesthetic: Excels in sports, learning through physical movement and awareness of body and environment; able use body to convey ideas/emotions and problem solve; Interpersonal: Ability to work effectively with others, organize people, work cooperatively and collaboratively; Intrapersonal: Ability to understand inner feelings, learning through feelings and attitudes, involving self–reflection and metacognition; understanding one's own emotions and goals; Naturalistic: Loves and understands the natural world, plants, animals, nature.

geometric shapes – shapes, including: circle (and oval); cross; X, square (and rectangle); triangle and others.

gifted and talented – refers to children who have advanced cognitive development.

goals – an observable and measurable outcome within a lesson plan or activity, with one or more objectives to be met.

group art activities/projects – can enhance social interactions for all children, and be particularly beneficial for children who have challenges with social relationships, and may need assistance guidance for social experiences

H

holiday art – many traditional holidays in the U.S. have been over emphasized with a host of advertisements, decorations, activities, and crafts that focus on the product. The holiday "art," such as hand turkeys, pre–made or molded ornaments to paint, Xeroxed worksheets or coloring sheets with a holiday theme, cut–and–paste holiday projects, holiday coloring books, or other holiday craft kits, all masquerade as creative art. Holidays and children's ethnic and cultural backgrounds should be respected and approached with sensitivity.

human figure drawings – children prefer to draw humans, as is evident from observing most any child draw. Children often draw themselves and those closes to them. They know their family members and what they do. They may draw how life is, how they would like it to be, what they imagine, or even what they fear. Regardless, humans are a major subject of children's art. Kellogg presents stages of drawing a human within the art growth stages.

I

Impressionism – a painting in style, originated with French painters of the 1870s, illustrating natural appearances of objects with of dabs of primary colors and light.

inclusion – Including all children regardless of abilities. Freedom to explore and create applies to all children, and more thought, understanding, and planning is needed to be truly inclusive. For example, some children may need assistive technology such as an adapted device to fully participate. Others might need their own materials and designated work space to be successful.

inclusive art – equal access and participation in art program and activities, including all children, regardless of abilities or culture.

Inclusive Early Childhood Classroom. *See* also Diagram of Inclusive Early Childhood Classroom – classroom that includes all children, regardless of abilities or culture.

Inclusive Environment. *See* Diagram of Inclusive Early Childhood Classroom – Planning inclusive environments includes both physical and interactive aspects.

inclusive setting. *See* Diagram of Inclusive Early Childhood Classroom

individual differences – respecting individuality, with strategies for valuing individual differences, working with young children from culturally diverse backgrounds, and utilizing guidelines for accommodating young children with various special needs will also be incorporated.

individuality in education – an educational philosophy that respects and makes accommodations for individual abilities and differences.

Individualized Family Service Plans (IFSP) – is a plan for special services for young children with developmental delays which applies to children from birth to three years of age. Teachers need to link activities and lessons plan to IFSP Outcomes.

Individualized Education Program (IEP) – is a plan for special services for a child (ages 3 to 21) who has a disability or requires specialized accommodation, as defined by federal regulations. Teachers need to link activities and lessons plan to IEP Goals.

infants – birth to walking, or 16 months.

　　sensory motor experiences – infants (birth to walking, or 16 months) take in everything through their senses (feeling, tasting, smelling, hearing, and seeing) and motor development (fine and gross motor).

intelligence – cognitive development.

interactions to promote creativity – interactions, art dialogue, and feedback are essential components of art programs. Feedback needs to be specific to the individuality of the child, and the process of their creative expression. Mirrored Feedback reflects back to the child about their work. Feedback statements can easily include the art elements and principles.

K

Kellogg's artistic growth stages – Rhoda Kellogg describes stages of artistic growth and development as universal, and have even been linked with the first marks of the human race. Stages include: Placement Stage, Basic scribble stage, Shapes Stage, Diagrams Stage, and Pictorial stage.

kinesthetic sense – requires a whole body sensorimotor response. When children move in response to different types of music or sounds, move with their arms out like wings to imitate a bird, or crawl on all fours to pretend to be a dog; they are using their kinesthetic sense. As children dance with scarves or streamers, make shapes with their bodies, jump on a trampoline, crawl through a tunnel, or walk on a balance beam; they are actively learning through their kinesthetic sense. Children use all their senses to take in information and respond with their bodies, using their kinesthetic sense.

L

language development – a developmental domain involving language and communication.

language arts – includes language arts, communication, and literacy/pre–literacy, and importance of partnership of literacy and the arts as modes of creative expression. Art and literacy play a vital role in the early development of skills and abilities such as self–regulation, cognitive processing, and problem solving all which lead to innovative and creative thinking.

learning styles. *See* Gardner's Theory of Multiple Intelligences

Least restrictive environment (LRE) – Individuals with Disabilities Education Act (IDEA) requires that children with disabilities be educated in the least restrictive environment (LRE), and have the same opportunities and access to programs as their peers without disabilities.

left hemisphere (brain). *See also* brain development – the left hemisphere of the brain controls the right side of the body while the right hemisphere governs the left side. Hemispheres are joined by the corpus callosum, which serves as communication between them. Although both hemispheres work together, we refer to "left–brain" as controlling speech, reasoning, math, and factual kinds of activities and "right–brain" as the spatial skills, visual imagery, nonverbal, sensory, and creative side.

lesson plan – planned activity for children in various areas of the curriculum.

    lesson plan format – utilized for planning activities, including goals, materials, teacher interactions, adaptations, assessment, and reflections.

letter to families – communication with families about art, art growth, and promoting creativity.

line – is a visible mark between two points, with width, direction, and length in 2D artwork. In 3D, we see outlines of the form.

linking creativity and child development. *See* creativity and child development

literacy. *See also* language arts – the partnership of literacy and the arts are important modes of creative expression. Art and literacy play a vital role in the early development of skills and abilities such as self–regulation, cognitive processing, and problem solving all which lead to innovative and creative thinking.

M

mass or volume – relates to the height, width, and length of 3D artwork.

masquerading art – product oriented art activities, with only one right way of completing. Experiences that include molds of figures, cookie cutters, coloring sheets, coloring books, patterns to follow, step–by–step instructions are all examples of activities that masquerade as art.

materials. *See* art supplies

mirrored feedback – reflects back to the child about their work. Feedback statements can easily include the art elements and principles.

misinterpreting, misinterpretation – avoid assumptions or misinterpreting children's purpose or communication in their art. Children draw what they know and communicate who they are, what is important to them, and what is happening in their lives. Even before a child develops speech, drawing can offer very young children self–expression of ideas and feelings. Children's art (both 2D and 3D) communicates and demonstrates: their creative spirit, self–confidence, problem solving skills, determination, focus and concentration skills, knowledge, and details they may not be able to put into words. Adults must be careful and avoid assumptions of child's purpose or misinterpreting her/his communication.

movement. See music and movement

Multiple Intelligences. *See also* Gardner's Theory of Multiple Intelligences

murals – are large paintings or reliefs that show a certain subject or theme. They can be done as a group or a one person. Show the children examples of famous murals. If possible, locate one in the community and visit. Discuss different subjects of the murals that are viewed. Murals are also an effective way to display the process, product, and developmental level of one age group.

Museum of Children's Art (MOCHA) – the Museum of Children's Art (MOCHA) in Oakland, CA has been committed to connecting art education with children throughout Oakland for over 24 years. They have committed to offering spaces where children and their families, "create, share, and connect through art".

music – begins in infancy. Infants naturally respond to music. It is important to provide a variety of musical experiences beginning in infancy (or even prenatally). Music, singing, and responding to music are naturally enjoyable to most children. Music offers excellent tools to use for teaching and reinforcing skills in all domains, such as: Cognitive: Using songs to teach concepts of letters and numbers, or loud and soft, fast, and slow; Emotional: How songs can make us feel and move through the melody or words; Social: Music and musical games welcome children to join in with their peers, at various levels of participation; Physical: swaying to music, stomping feet, clapping hands, and creative movement to music.

music and movement. *See also* creative movement – is an artistic medium that develops children's awareness of their bodies and what they can do, explore movement and music, and promote creativity. Benefits include improved motor skills, balance and coordination. It can also help to develop feelings of self–confidence and communicate emotions.

N

native language – child's first language, or language they learned in their home. Some children learn more than one language, thus having bi–lingual, and have first languages.

National Assembly of State Arts Agencies (NASAA) – the National Assembly of State Arts Agencies (NASAA) is an organization that "unites, represents and serves the nation's state and jurisdictional arts agencies" (retrieved from: http://www.nasaa–arts.org/About/About–NASAA.php). They offer advocacy tools with specific suggestions for making change and supporting the arts, including areas of: Making your case; Assessing your strength; Mobilizing Your Support; and Expanding Your Influence.

National Association for the Education of Young Children (NAEYC) – The National Association for the Education of Young Children (NAEYC) is a large nonprofit association in the United States representing early childhood education teachers, para–educators, center directors, trainers, college educators, families of young children, policy makers, and advocates.

nonrepresentational art. *See also* Abstract art – an artistic style that uses shape, form, color, and line, and does not attempt to represent external reality.

nudity in art – how to approach or avoid with children – some educators and parents feel we just "should not go there" and avoiding this topic is the safest approach with children. Some avoid "that room" or artworks that include nudity during an art gallery/museum visit with children. Others have gone so far as to cover up art that depicts nudity when children may be in a gallery. Artists have been sculpting and painting nude human figures throughout history. Many people equate nudity with sex; however, nudity and sex are not the same thing. When children observe our nonverbal negative reactions to nudity (e.g. gasps or startling reactions) it conveys the message that nude works of art are a bad thing. Keeping with personal and philosophical program practices, and religious beliefs and preferences, are important to live by. However, consider the implications that overreaction and gasps might convey. Discussion with staff or others involved prior to art gallery visits prepares the adult on how to handle this. Avoidance is not always the answer. As Brian Yoder stated in Nudity in Art: A Virtue or Vice? "Would we really be better off if all of that great art, such a Michelangelo's David, was hidden away? Destroyed? Never made in the first place? Covered with fig leaves? I don't think so" (Yoder, n. d.).

O

objectives – an observable and measurable outcome(s) within a lesson plan or activity. Accountability regarding how well objectives were met/not met, and documentation or data that supports this information. A chart, checklist or specific manner is needed to collect data to demonstrate how objectives are met.

observation. *See also* assessment of activity objectives – informs us about accountability, how well objectives were met/not met or what the children know or have learned. The documentation or tool for documentation of observation is essential. A chart, checklist or specific manner you will collect this data. Many observation tools are available for children's development, early childhood environments, art programs, etc.

olfactory sense – sense of smell

open–ended activities – experiences that allow children to problem solve and discover, and will value and promote creative thinking.

open–ended questions – Questions to allow children to problem solve and discover. Include open–ended questions into the daily routine and curriculum will value and promote creative thinking.

originality – unique or original ideas; one–of–a–kind idea. Adults need to focus on originality, foster originality, encourage, value and display original ideas, and model originality of thought and process.

outdoor activities – most any art activities that are done indoors, can also be implemented outdoors. The lighting outside affects and enhances colors and clarity of art materials. The outdoors also offer many resources for observation and materials from nature.

P

painting – process of applying paint to a surface with various methods, such as paintbrush, hands and fingers, or other utensils and tools.

paper – material used in art area, paper in a variety of colors, shapes, sizes, thickness, and textures (including magazines, cardboard, newsprint, tissue paper, crepe paper, sand paper, white drawing paper, colored construction paper – both traditional and various skin tones).

partnering with families – Partnering with families is an underlying principle in art programs and early childhood, in general. It needs to be embedded in the program's philosophy and guiding principles. A concise family partnership philosophy, understood and practiced by teachers, staff, and families, is the foundation of early childhood work and profession.

partnering with parents. *See* partnering with families

pattern – demonstrates repetition or reoccurring sequence or alternating of shapes, colors, textures, lines, etc.

perception – the ability to see, hear, smell, taste, and become aware of something through these senses.

Person First Philosophy – is the foundation of inclusion and underlies our practices of valuing differences while making environments and experiences accessible for all. Person First is a philosophy of seeing the person first, the disability second. This does not deny the disability; it simply views the person first. The person is not the disability (e.g., don't refer to the person as "the disabled" or "the handicapped"); rather, the person has a disability.

Person First Language – using words and communications that reflect Person First Philosophy, referring to and seeing the person first, the disability second.

Personal Creativity Journals for all ages

For the teacher or pre–teacher, parent/family member or any adult: A Personal Creativity

Journal will help them explore the topics and experiences through drawings and reflections.

For the child: This Personal Creativity Journal will help the teacher or parent motivate children to keep their own journals with entries of drawings and reflections. This could easily be a partnership activity between home and school.

physical considerations – making accommodations and modifications based on a child's individual physical developmental domain referring to a child's motor skills (fine and gross), control over body and movement, visual, hearing, and other aspects of physical development.

physical development – a developmental domain referring to a child's motor skills (fine and gross), control over body and movement, visual, hearing, and other aspects of physical development.

Play–based Philosophy – Children learn through play. According to NAEYC, "Play is an important vehicle for developing self–regulation as well as for promoting language, cognition, and social competence" (NAEYC, 2009). Play helps children make sense of their world, interact with others, problem solve, and express and control emotions. Play is natural and universal. Research supports that play serves important physical, mental, emotional, and social functions for humans and other species. This position statement also noted, "Research shows the links between play and foundational capacities such as memory, self–regulation, oral language abilities, social skills, and success in school" (NAEYC, 2009). A play based philosophy in early childhood is essential to the creative process.

preschoolers – ages 3 to 5 years.

representational drawings and sculptures

primary colors – red, yellow, blue

primary school age – children ages 5 – 8 years or kindergarten to 3rd grade.

printing – as in writing and pre–writing skills emerges from scribbles by toddlers that demonstrate pre–writing skills to more legible letter of the alphabet.

prints – a process in art in which paint is applied to an object or texture, and pressed onto a surface. When the object or texture is lifted, it makes an image or print.

process oriented art – is authentic creative art – process oriented, creative, true and free expressive art experiences; without presubscribed directions or molds or models to follow.

process versus product – process oriented art offers creative, true and free expressive art experiences; without presubscribed directions or molds or models to follow; whereas product oriented art activities, offer only one right way of completing, such as experiences that include molds of figures, cookie cutters, coloring sheets, coloring books, patterns to follow, step–by–step instructions are all examples of activities that masquerade as art. Process oriented offers authentic and creative art experiences.

product oriented art – offer only one right way of completing, such as experiences that include molds of figures, cookie cutters, coloring sheets, coloring books, patterns to follow, step–by–step instructions are all examples of activities that masquerade as art

Project approach – a philosophy and curriculum approach that uniquely and authentically follows the interests of the child or children, fostering exploration and discovery. The Project Approach highly values the child's individuality, self–esteem, builds on natural curiosity, facilitates children's interactions, questions, problem–solving, and reflections.

puppets – a moveable 3D model of a person, animal or object, used for imaginative play, interactions, and social stories.

Q

Quality Inclusive Early Childhood Arts Program – involves a commitment to offering authentic, creative, and developmentally appropriate art experiences embedded throughout the curriculum. Components include: Sensing and experiencing; Making art (including feedback); Aesthetics; and (d) Learning about basic elements of art, artists, and their styles. Partnering with families as an underlying foundation of all early childhood art programs will be emphasized.

questions

close–ended – yes or no questions, one right answer, questions that do not encourage or allow children to problem solve and discover.

open–ended questions – questions to allow children to problem solve and discover. Open–ended questions into the daily routine and curriculum will value and promote creative thinking.

R

rainbows in children's artwork – the beauty, magic, and mystery of a rainbow are often depicted by young children in their artwork.

Reggio Emelia approach – Reggio Emilia schools of northern Italy have been committed to quality early childhood education and support for families for over 60 years. Many theorists including Rousseau, Pestalozzi, Froebel, Dewey, Piaget, and Vygotsky influenced founder of Reggio Emilia schools, Loris Malaguzzi. Aesthetics and fostering the development of creativity in children is the focus of the Reggio Emilia approach. Reggio Emilia philosophy regards the environment as the third teacher. According to this philosophy the classroom is arranged purposely to encourage children to work together to create art. Materials are easily available, and invite them to create a variety of different projects with limited structure by the teacher. Children are actively learning – exploring, questioning, problem solving, and representing their experience in a number of ways.

Rehab 504 – Section 504 of the Rehabilitation Act of 1973 created and extended civil rights to people with disabilities. It has provided opportunities for children and adults with disabilities in education, employment and other settings. It allows for reasonable accommodations based on individual needs, such as a private study area or individual assistance.

relaxation – through relaxation techniques children will learn the importance of the balance of exercising and relaxing the body to promote healthier bodies, minds, and spirits. Children today are experiencing more stress due to the fast pace of lifestyles. Children with varying abilities can benefit greatly from learning relaxation tools for stressful situations they could experience due to social, emotional or academic challenges. Music, movement, and visual arts are also effective methods of relaxation. Music, dance, and art therapies have demonstrated much success for children and adults with varying abilities, conditions, and life challenges.

right hemisphere (brain). *See also* brain development – the left hemisphere of the brain controls the right side of the body while the right hemisphere governs the left side. Hemispheres are joined by the corpus callosum, which serves as communication between them. Although both hemispheres work together, we refer to "left–brain" as controlling speech, reasoning, math, and factual kinds of activities and "right–brain" as the spatial skills, visual imagery, nonverbal, sensory, and creative side.

S

safety issues – must be considered with all art projects, environment, and materials.

scaffolding – a teaching strategy within the child's zone of proximal development, in order to offer assistance and questioning at the appropriate level for each child. Active scaffolding in creative play is needed to build upon and develop more mature understanding and skills.

scribbling – the toddler's Basic scribble stage of artistic growth is described by Rhoda Kellogg. Kellogg (1970) found 20 basic types of scribbles alone, which are also universal.

secondary colors – orange, green, purple; resulting from mixing primary colors to make secondary: red and yellow make orange; red and blue make purple; yellow and blue make green.

self–concept – beliefs one has about one's self.

self–esteem – self–respect, confidence in one's self.

self–talk – with daily interactions, self–talk with infants about lines, colors, and shapes in the various environments, in nature, home, at the grocery store, everywhere.

senses – five senses: visual, auditory, tactile, olfactory, and gustatory or taste

sensory activities. *See* sensory experiences

sensory experiences – children come to know their world through their senses. According to Piaget, infants learn through sensorimotor experiences, or through senses and movement. Art experiences for infants should include experimentation, manipulation, and discussion about what the child is doing. Sensory experiences have cognitive, physical, emotional, and social benefits.

sensory motor experiences for infants – according to Piaget, infants learn through sensorimotor experiences, or through senses and movement. Art experiences for infants should include experimentation, manipulation, and discussion about what the child is doing.

shape/form – shape is use of area in 2D space or outside form; Form is the volume of 3D activities to illustrate shape/form.

singing – Infants naturally respond to singing and music. It is important to provide a variety of musical experiences beginning in infancy (or even prenatally). Music, singing, and responding to music are naturally enjoyable to most children. Music offers excellent tools to use for teaching and reinforcing skills in all domains, such as: Cognitive: Using songs to teach concepts of letters and numbers, or loud and soft, fast, and slow; Emotional: How songs can make us feel and move through the melody or words; Social: Music and musical games welcome children to join in with their peers, at various levels of participation; Physical: swaying to music, stomping feet, clapping hands, and creative movement to music.

social development – how a child learns to interact with others, develops relationships, handles conflicts with others.

social, emotional, and behavioral considerations – children with social, emotional, and behavioral challenges need supports, accommodations, and diagnosis, as needed. Art therapy can be a positive support for children with these challenges.

social interaction – exchange between two or more individuals, how we act and react to those around us.

social stories – a concept devised by Carol Gray in 1991 to improve the social skills of people with autism spectrum disorders (ASD). They are used to model appropriate social interaction, through acting out or describing a social situation, noting appropriate social cues, appropriate responses, and the perspective of others.

space – the area the artist uses, as determined by the size of the paper, canvas, wood, stone, etc. There is positive (space taken up by created things) and negative space (space surrounding or between things).

Standards – expectations for the characteristics or quality of programs, schools, child care centers, and other educational settings. Professional organizations that present standards for various areas of early childhood education include: DEC (Division of Early Childhood) Recommended Practices in Early Intervention / Early Childhood Special Education; Early Learning Standards (ELS); and NAEYC (National Association of Education of Young Children) Guidelines for developmentally appropriate practice.

strategies for using art as learning and intervention tool. *See* art as learning and intervention tool.

strategies for valuing individual differences – respecting individuality by using strategies for valuing individual differences, working with young children from culturally diverse backgrounds, and utilizing guidelines for accommodating young children with various special needs will also be incorporated.

strategies to promote creative thought. *See also*, interactions to promote creativity – Appropriate, meaningful, and individualized interactions can foster and promote creative thinking and processes in young children. These interactions need to be exchanges, with communication in both directions. In order for these meaningful interactions to be successful both listening, and the wait time sometimes required for children to respond (especially for children with special needs) are crucial. Meaningful interactions include appropriate feedback to a child's creative process, which is individualized and accommodated as needed. Being a "mirror" for the child's efforts and reflecting verbally what the child is doing provides opportunity to describe this process using art vocabulary. These interactions also provide reinforcement for children on an individual basis.

SUAVE – stands for Socios Unidos para Artes via Educacion, Or United Community for Arts and Education, a volunteer professional development program in Southern California, developed in 1993 by Meryl Goldberg, in collaboration with local arts educators, art center staff, and elementary teachers and principals. "The Philosophy underlying the program is that teaching *through* the arts (in contrast to more traditional teaching *about* the arts) can be a powerful pedagogical tool for teachers to help students both further their subject– matter understanding and be introduced to the arts themselves" (Goldberg, 2004, p. 14).

subject – or the What of components of art: The Subject is the central focus of the artwork: the person, thing, ideas, intension of the work.

symmetrical – evenly or equally balanced.

T

tactile kinesthetic, *See* kinesthetic sense.

tactilely defensive – hypersensitivity to touch and textures, to the point of one feeling uncomfortable or even pain

teacher–directed approach – product oriented activities, often with presubscribed directions, molds, or one right way of completing. Experiences that include molds of figures, cookie cutters, coloring sheets, coloring books, patterns to follow, step–by–step instructions are all examples of activities that masquerade as art and utilize the teacher–directed approach.

technology –

    general technology – Technology use within the classroom to benefit all children. For example, Children could have access to images of art, Artists, And their styles via images online.

    assistive technology – children may require using technology just to participate, access, or interact with others. Assistive technology needed for participation in art requires adults to learning about the devices, in order to assist the child with participation and interaction.

texture – describes what 3D work actually feels like to the touch; in 2D there can be a visual feel of texture.

thematic approach – an approach to teaching where all subject areas are integrated under one theme, crossing curriculum areas. A thematic approach is often used in early childhood education, since preschool children learn through interactive, integrated activities. Themed units incorporate areas of blocks, fine motor, dramatic play, music and movement, literacy/pre–literacy, math/pre–math, science, social studies, as well as the arts for a well–balanced curriculum.

thematic lesson plans. *See* thematic approach

thematic units. *See* thematic approach

three–dimensional art (3D) – art that is three–dimensional (3D) form, with spatial depth as well as height and weight. Examples of 3D artwork include sculpture, crafts (glass, wood, metal, fiber, clay), and architecture.

tint – the outcome of adding white to any color.

toddlers – walking or 16 months to 3–years–old

tone. *See also* value – is the lightness and darkness used in artwork.

Torrance Tests of Creative Thinking (TTCT)

troubleshooting – Sometimes children get frustrated, doubt their own abilities, and get creatively or artistically blocked or stalled. When children convey these messages, verbally or non–verbally, we need to be ready to respond with guidance and positive supports.

two–dimensional art (2D) – art that is two–dimensional (2D), developed on a flat plane or surface, such as drawing, painting, printmaking, or photography.

types of learning. *See* Gardner's Theory of Multiple Intelligences.

U

Units. *See* thematic approach.

unity – components of art include subject, form, and content, which combine to give the artwork unity. Simply stated, these are the What, the How, and the Why of the artwork, defined as: Subject or the What: The Subject is the central focus of the artwork: the person, thing, ideas, intension of the work; Form or the How: Form refers to how the artwork is organized or arranged. The Form gives the artwork unity; Content or the Why: The Content offers the essential meaning or significance of work of art. It gives more to the story, the details, and the elaboration of the meaning.

V

value. *See also* tone – is the lightness and darkness used in artwork.

visual art elements and principles – elements and principles of art are the observable properties of matter, including: line, color, shape/form, texture, space, value, mass or volume, pattern, balance, and design or composition. These elements can be seen in 2D and 3D works of art of any level of artistic creations. Not every artwork contains all of the elements and matter, principles, however, most have several.

visual sense – involves looking and seeing.

visual–spatial – use of shapes and designs, learning visually, able to organize ideas and represent images visual–spatially.

W

warm – colors that symbolize hit our warmth including red, yellow, and orange.

watercolor – transparent colored paints that mixes with water for use on watercolor paper

weaving – an art form, using fabric to interlace, passing in one direction with others at a right angle to them.

Z

zone of proximal development (ZPD) – the range of what a child can do without help, and what she/he can do with assistance from an adult or peer. The concept was introduced by psychologist Lev Vygotsky (1896–1934) during the last ten years of his life.

Index

A

R

S

REFERENCES

Arnheim, R. (1974). *Art and visual perception: A psychology of the creative eye* (2nd ed.) (pp. 162–215). Los Angeles, CA: University of California Press.

———. (n. d.). *Art explained and made simple.* Retrieved on March 12, 2015, from http://www.artsz.org/kids–art–coordination/

———. (n. d.). *Art therapy for children.* In *Artsz.* Retrieved on March 1, 2015, from http://www.artsz.org/art–therapy–for–children/

———. (n. d.). *Arts advocacy checklist: A self–evaluation tool for arts organizations and advocates.* Retrieved from http://www.nasaa–arts.org/Advocacy/Advocacy–Tools/Arts–Advocacy–Checklist–for–Arts–Organizations–and–Advocates.php

———. (n. d.). Museum of Children's Art (MOCHA). In *Artsz.* Retrieved March 12, 2015, from http://www.artsz.org/20–reasons–why–art–is–important–for–children/

Bogle, L. S. (2002, September 10). "Children and 9/11: Art helping kids heal." *National Geographic News.* Retrieved from http://news.nationalgeographic.com/news/2002/09/0910_kidsart.html

Campbell, C., & Jobling, W. (Eds.). (2013). *Science in Early Childhood.* Cambridge, United Kingdom: Cambridge University Press.

Capacchione, L. (1989). *The creative journal for children: A guide for parents, teachers, and counselors.* Shambhala.

Caplan, F. (Ed.) (1978). *The parenting advisor.* Garden City, NY: Doubleday/Anchor Press.

Chandler, P. A. (1994). *A place for me: Including children with special needs in early care and educational settings.* Washington D.C.: National Association for the Education of Young Children.

Copple, C., & Bredekamp, S. (Eds.). (2009). *Developmentally appropriate practice in early childhood programs serving children from birth through age eight* (3rd ed.). Retrieved from http://www.naeyc.org/files/naeyc/file/positions/position%20statement%20Web.pd

Cruikshank, A. (n.d.). *Empowering images: Using photography as a medium to develop visual literacy. Exchange Every Day (Childcare Exchange).* Retrieved from https://www.childcareexchange.com/catalog/product/empowering–images–using–photography–as–a–medium–to–develop–visual–literacy/5019553/

Deiner, P.L. (2005). *Resources for educating children with diverse abilities: Birth through eight* (4th ed.). Clifton Park, NY: Thompson Delmar Learning.

Depauw, K. P. (1990). "PE and sports for disabled individuals in the United States." *Journal of Physical Education, Recreation, and Dance, 61,* 22–23.

Dever, M. T., & Jared, E. R. (1996). "Remember to include art and crafts in your integrated curriculum." *Young Children, 51*(3), 69–73.

DeViney, J. Duncan, S., Rody, M.A., Harris, S, & Rosenberry, L. (2010). *Inspiring spaces for young children.* Silver Spring, MD: Gryphon House.

———. (2010). *Rating Observation scale for inspiring environments.* Silver Spring, MD: Gryphon House.

———. (2015). Division for Early Childhood (DEC) of the Council for Exceptional Children (CEC). Retrieved from http://www.dec–sped.org/recommendedpractices

Downey, J., & Garzoli, E. (2007). "The effectiveness of a play–based curriculum in early childhood education." *Teach play–based learning.* Retrieved from http://www.teachplaybased learning.com/8.html

Duncan, A. (2010, April 9). *The well–rounded curriculum: Secretary Arne Duncan's remarks at the Arts Education Partnership national forum.* Retrieved from http://www2.ed.gov/news/speeches/2010/04/04092010.html

Elkind, D. (1981). *The hurried child: Growing up too fast too soon.* Reading, MA: Addison–Wesley.

Fox, J. E., & Berry, S. (2008). *Early Childhood News.* Excelligence Learning. Retrieved from http://www.earlychildhoodnews.com/earlychildhood/article_view.aspx?ArticleID=113

Fox, J. E., & Schirrmacher, R. (2009). *Art and creative development for young children* (7th ed.). Stamford, CT: Wadsworth, Centage Learning.

Fox, J. E., & Schirrmacher, R. (2015). *Art and creative development for young children* (8th ed.). Stamford, CT: Centage Learning.

Freud, S. (1964). *An outline of psychoanalysis: Standard edition of the works of Sigmund Freud*. London, England: Hogarth Press.

Froebel, F. (1993). *Frederick Froebel 1782–1852*, in *Prospects: The quarterly review of comparative education. 23(3/4), 1993, 473–491*. Paris, UNESCO: International Bureau of Education. Retrieved from http://www.ibe.unesco.org/publications/ThinkersPdf/frobele.PDF

Gardner, H. (1983). *Frames of mind: The theory of multiple intelligences*. New York, NY: Basic Books.

Gardner, H. (1993). *Creating minds: An anatomy of creativity seen though the lives of Freud, Einstein, Picasso, Stravinsky, Eliot, Graham, and Ghandi*. New York, NY: Basic Books.

Goldberg, M. (Ed) (2004). Teaching English learners through the arts: A SUAVE experience. Pearson Education, Inc.

Goleman, D., Kaufman, P., & Ray, M. (1993). *The creative spirit*. New York, NY: Plume.

Goodale, R. A. (1970). "Methods for encouraging creativity in the classroom." *Journal of Creative Behavior, 4*(2), 91–102.

Goodenough, F. L. (1928). "Studies in the psychology of children's drawings." *Psychological Bulletin, 25,* 272–279.

Goosen, Brittany (2015). Assignment for course shared with permission.

Gronlund, G. (2006). *Making standards come alive: connecting your practices to early childhood curriculum to state standards*. St. Paul, MN.: Red leaf Press.

Harms, T. (1972). "Presenting materials effectively." In H. P. Lewis (Ed.), *Art for the preliminary child* (pp. 92–109). Washington D.C.: National Art Education.

Harris, M. B., & Evans, R. C. (1973). "Models and creativity." *Psychological Reports, 33,* 763–769.

Healy, J. (2004). *Your child's growing mind: Brain development and learning from birth to adolescence* (3rd ed.). New York, NY: Harmony.

Hildebrand, V. (1974). "Adding creativity to the curriculum." *Forecast for Home Economics, 20,* 28–29.

Hillman, C. B. (2012, March/April). *The intangibles in the early childhood classroom. Exchange: The Early Childhood Leaders' Magazine, 204,* 12–14.

Hurlock, E. B. (1972). *Creativity*. Child development (5th ed.). New York, NY: McGraw Hill.

The Incredible Art Department. (2015, March 12). Retrieved from http://www.incredibleart.org/

Isbell, R. T. & Raines, S. C. (2003). *Creativity and the arts with young children*. New York, NY: Thompson Delmar Learning.

Jacobson, L. (2007). "Famed early–childhood philosophy expands horizons." *Education Week, 26*(22), p.10. Retrieved from www.ebscohost.com/ACADEMIC/education–research–complete

Jones, J. (2010, March/April). "The role of music in your classroom." *Exchange: The Early Childhood Leaders' Magazine*. Retrieved from http://www.artseveryday.org/uploadedFiles/What_We_Do/News/News_from_the_Field/2010/The%20Role%20of%20Music%20in%20Your%20Classroom.pdf

Karns, M. (n.d.). *Art for children with special needs*. Retrieved from http://www.scholastic.com/browse/subarticle.jsp?id=4082

Kellogg, R. (1969). *Analyzing children's art*. Palo Alto, CA: Mayfield.

Kim, K. H. (2011). "The creativity crisis: The decrease in creative thinking scores on the Torrance Tests of Creative Thinking." *Creativity Research Journal, 23*(4), 285–295.

Kohl, M.A. (1989). *MUDWORKS: Creative Clay, Dough, and Modeling Experiences*. Beltsville, MD: Gryphon House.

———. (1994). *Preschool art: It's the process, not the product*. Beltsville, MD: Gryphon House.

Kohl, M.A., Ramsey, R., & Bowman, D. (2002). *First art: Art experiences for toddlers and twos*. Beltsville, MD: Gryphon House.

Lark–Horowitz, Lewis, H. P., & Lucas, M. (1967). *Understanding children's art for better teaching.* Columbus, OH: Charles Merrill Books.

Lee, J. M., & Lee, D. M. (1960). *The child and his curriculum* (3rd ed.) (pp. 501–557). New York, NY: Appleton–Century–Crofts.

Lowenfeld, V. (1957). *Creative and mental growth* (3rd ed.). New York, NY: Macmillan.

Lowenfeld, V., & Brittain, W. L. (1987). *Creative and mental growth* (7th ed.). New York, NY: Macmillan.

MacKinnon, D. W. (1962). "The nature and nurture of creative talent." *American Psychologist, 17*(7), 484–495.

Margolin, E. (1968). "Conservation of self–expression and aesthetic sensitivity in young children." *Young Children, 24,* 155–160. Retrieved from: www.naeyc.org/yc/

Martin, N. (2009). *Art as an early intervention tool for children with autism.* London, England: Jessica Kingsley.

Maslow, A. (1970). *Motivation and personality.* New York, NY: Harper & Row.

Mayesky, M. (2002). *Creative activities for young children* (7th ed.). Albany, NY: Delmar Thompson Learning.

Miller, R. (1996). *The developmentally appropriate inclusive classroom in early education.* Albany, NY: Delmar Publishing.

Mitchell, L. C. (2004). "Making the most of creativity in activities for young children with disabilities." *Young Children, 12(2),* 2004, 46 – 49. Retrieved from https://www.naeyc.org/files/tyc/file/MitchellVol2No2NEXT.pdf

Museum of Children's Art (MOCHA). (2015, March 12). Oakland, CA. Retrieved from http://www.artsz.org/20–reasons–why–art–is–important–for–children/

National Assembly of State Arts Agencies (NASAA). (n. d.). "Advocacy Rules." Retrieved on August 31, 2015 from: http://www.nasaa–arts.org/Advocacy/Advocacy–Tools/index.php

Peter, L. J. (1977/1979). Picasso (pp. 25). In L. J. Peter (Ed.), *Peter's Quotations: Ideas for Our Time.* New York NY: Bantam Books.

Piaget, J. (1960). *The child's conception of the world.* Totanna, NJ: Littlefield, Adams, & Co.

Ray, K. & Glover, M. (2008). *Already Ready: Nurturing Writers in Preschool and Kindergarten.* Heinemann.

Reyner, A. (2007). *Art influences learning.* Monterey, CA: Excelligence Learning. Retrieved from http://www.earlychildhoodnews.com/earlychildhood/article_print.aspx?ArticleId=509

Robelen, E. W. (2010, November 16). "The infusion of the arts appears to be gaining a stronger foothold at a time when advocates are struggling to ensure time and support for their disciplines." *Education Week.* Retrieved from http://www.edweek.org/ew/articles/2010/11/17/12dance_ep.h30.html?tkn=QMCCWIRjHC%2F0slNDl4zZ8rXN8uhpy6nMmADy&cmp=clp–sb–ascd

Robinson, K. (2006, February). *How schools kill creativity* [Video file]. Retrieved from http://www.ted.com/talks/ken_robinson_says_schools_kill_creativity

Rogers, C. R. (1962). "Toward a theory of creativity." In S. J. Parnes & H. F. Harding (Eds.), *A sourcebook for creative thinking* (pp. 63–72). New York, NY: Scribner.

Rogers, C. R. (1975). "Towards a theory of creativity." In P.E. Vernon (Ed.), *Creativity* (4th ed.) (pp. 137–152). Baltimore, MD: Penguin Books.

Russell, C. L. (1981). *Environmental control of preschool art and the creative artistic abilities of the young child* (Unpublished master's thesis). University of Arkansas–Fayetteville, Arkansas.

———. (1996). *An exploration of the effects of creative movement in experiences on the participation of young children with and without special needs in inclusionary and non–inclusionary settings* (Unpublished doctoral dissertation). University of South Dakota, Vermillion.

———. (2008). "Art for all children." *The International Journal of the Arts in Society, 2*(5), 89–98.

———. (2012). *Background of the children inspire glass project [Handout]. Department of Elementary Education/Early Childhood/Special Education,* Emporia State University, Emporia, KS.

Samuelsson, I., Sheridan, S., & Williams, P. (2006). "Five preschool curricula: Comparative perspective." *International Journal of Early Childhood, 38*(1), 11–30. Retrieved from www.ebscohost.com/ACADEMIC/education–research–complete

Saracho, O., & Spodek, B. (1995). "Children's play and early childhood education: Insights from history and theory." *Journal of Education, 177*, 129–148.

Scattone, D., Wilczynski S.M., Edwards, R.P., Rabian B. (2002). "Decreasing disruptive behaviors of children with autism using social stories." *Journal of Autism and Developmental Disorders, 32*(6), 535–543.

Schiller, P. (2010, March/April). "Early brain development research review and update." *Exchange: The Early Childhood Leaders' Magazine.* Retrieved from http://www.ecementor.org/articles–on–teaching/Early_Brain_Development_Research_Review.pdf

Schirrmacher, R. (2006). *Art and creative development for young children.* New York, NY: Thomson, Delmar Learning.

Stephens, K. (2005, May/June). "Meaningful family engagement: Just imagine the possibilities." *Exchange: The Early Childhood Leaders' Magazine.* 163, 18–23.

Striker, S. (1986). *Please touch: How to stimulate your child's creative development.* New York, NY: Simon & Schuster.

Tang, G. (2003). *Math–terpieces: The Art of Problem–Solving* (1st ed.). Scholastic Press. Retrieved from http://www.rif.org/documents/us/Mathterpieces_All–Activities.pdf

Thompson, C. M. (1995). "What should I draw today? Sketchbooks in early childhood." *Young Children, 48*(5). 1995, 6–11

Torrance, E. P. (1965). *Rewarding creative behavior: Experiments in classroom creativity.* Englewood Cliffs, NJ: Prentice–Hall.

———. (1969). *Creativity. What research says to the teacher.* Retrieved from http://files.eric.ed.gov/fulltext/ED078435.pdf

———. (1974). *Torrance Test of Creative Thinking.* Lexington, MA: Ginn & Company, Personal Press.

———. (1974). *Torrance Tests of Creative Thinking.* Scholastic Testing Service.

———. "A National Climate for Creativity and Invention." *Gifted Child Today (GCT), 15*(1), 10–14.

———. (1998). *Torrance test of creative thinking norms Technical manual figural Forms A & B.* Bensenville, IL: Scholastic Testing Service.

Turnbull, A. (2008). Keynote at the *2008 Inclusion Institute.* Chapel Hill, NC. Retrieved on June 6, 2016 from https://www.youtube.com/watch?v=jfYBydcLaNo

Turnbull, A. P. & Turbiville, V.P. (1995). "Why must inclusion be such a challenge?" *Journal of Early Intervention, 19*, 200–202.

Wodtke, K. H., & Wallen, N. E. (1965). "Teacher classroom control, pupil creativity, and pupil classroom behavior." *Journal of Experimental Education, 34*, 59–64.

Yoder, B. K. (2015, March 16). *Nudity in art: A virtue or vice?* Retrieved from http://artrenewal.org/articles/2012/Nudity/Nudity_Virtue_or_Vice.php

About the Author

Dr. Carol L. Russell, Professor of Early Childhood Unified at Emporia State University, has taught higher education for over 37 years. She has served on local and national committees, and received numerous grants and awards. She is Co-Director of ESU's *Children Inspire Glass Project* and the ESU's *Children's Art Gallery*. Russell has authored and presented nationally and internationally on various topics, including: artistic creativity, inclusion, children with special needs and their families, ADA and accessibility, curriculum adaptations, and advocacy. Publications include Art for ALL Children in The International Journal of the Arts in Society. *Integrating Art in the Inclusive Early Childhood Curriculum* is culmination of her more than 40 years of interdisciplinary research and teaching experiences in inclusive arts with young children and their families.

CPSIA information can be obtained
at www.ICGtesting.com
Printed in the USA
LVHW060657081019
633411LV00010B/14/P

9 781863 350297